AFRICAN AMERICANS
VOICES
OF
TRIUMPH ™

LEADERSHIP

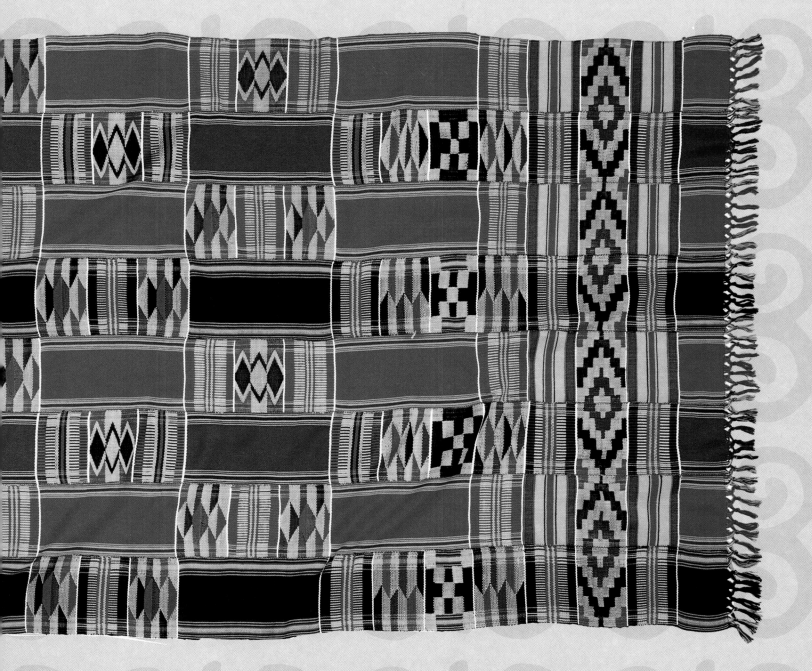

VOICES OF TRIUMPH KENTE CLOTH

Textiles, perhaps more than any other art form, reflect the cultures from which they come. They are at once personal, societal, religious, and political—invaluable vehicles for the spread of ideas from one culture to another. In Africa, woven cloths have served these functions for more than two thousand years, conveying the vibrant essence of an African aesthetic.

Kente, the type of cloth seen on the cover, is the primary woven fabric produced by the people of the old Ashanti Kingdom of Ghana. This particular cloth was specially designed and woven in Ghana to convey the theme "African Americans: Voices of Triumph."

Although the Ashanti tend to favor strips of uniform color, the varying colors in this kente cloth express the many paths taken by all our people—and especially the multiple destinations of black slaves who were removed from the shores of Africa.

The traditional red, gold, and green repeated in the middle of the design is one of the several variations of the "liberation colors" recognized by children of African descent all over the world: red for the blood (shed by millions in captivity), gold for the mineral wealth (prosperity), and green for the vegetation of the land of Africa (home).

The weavers of Ghana and other countries throughout West Africa have long adapted foreign elements to suit their own needs, creating unique motifs to express cultural values. Among the motifs incorporated in the design for this cloth is *abusua foa* (the council of elders) represented by the boxes arranged in an X ("all ideas coming together at one point") to symbolize leadership, consensus, and the voice of the people.

The stepped border motif, which seems to connect all the strips, symbolizes unity, interdependence, and cooperation as prerequisites for the advancement of the people.

The "shield" motif symbolizes defense against the countless assaults and obstacles encountered in the course of our lifetime.

Finally, the diamond, rarest, hardest, and most precious of all the minerals of Africa, represents the many-faceted soul of the children of Africa in America and reflects both their power to endure and their growing triumph in the struggle for freedom and equality.

AFRICAN AMERICANS
VOICES
OF
TRIUMPH™

LEADERSHIP

BY THE EDITORS OF TIME-LIFE BOOKS
ALEXANDRIA, VIRGINIA

WITH A FOREWORD BY DR. HENRY LOUIS GATES, JR.

TIME LIFE

Time-Life Books is a division of
TIME LIFE INC.

PRESIDENT and CEO, TIME LIFE INC.:
John M. Fahey

EDITOR-IN-CHIEF: John L. Papanek

TIME-LIFE BOOKS
MANAGING EDITOR: Roberta Conlan
Executive Art Director:
Ellen Robling
Director of Photography and Research:
John Conrad Weiser

PRESIDENT, TIME-LIFE BOOKS:
John D. Hall
*Vice-President, Marketing,
Time-Life Education*:
Rosalyn McPherson Andrews
Marketing Director, Time-Life Education:
Russell J. Haskins
Project Coordinator, Time-Life Education:
Theresa Mixon

TIME-LIFE CUSTOM PUBLISHING
Production Manager: Prudence G. Harris
Promotions Manager: Gary Stoiber
Financial Manager: Dana Coleman

The Voices of Triumph™ Development
Team gives special thanks to Quincy
Jones, who joined hands with us early
in the project, supported our vision,
and believed in our goal.

**AFRICAN AMERICANS:
VOICES OF TRIUMPH™**
Series Directors: Roxie France-Nuriddin,
Myrna Traylor-Herndon
Series Design Director: Cynthia Richardson

Editorial Staff for **LEADERSHIP**
Administrative Editor: Loretta Y. Britten
Picture Editor: Sally Collins
Text Editors: Esther Ferington,
Paul Mathless
Art Director: Alan Pitts
Associate Editor/Research:
Sharon Virginia Kurtz
Writer: Darcie Conner Johnston
Assistant Editors/Research: Michael Howard,
Dionne Scott, Terrell Smith,
T. Nieta Wigginton
Assistant Art Director: Kathleen D. Mallow
Senior Copy Coordinators: Anne Farr,
Colette Stockum
Picture Coordinator: Jennifer Iker

Editorial Operations
Production: Celia Beattie
Library: Louise D. Forstall
Computer Composition: Deborah G. Tait
(Manager), Monika D. Thayer,
Janet Barnes Syring, Lillian Daniels

Special Contributors: George Daniels,
Glenn McNatt, John Sullivan (editors);
Russell L. Adams, Karen Grigsby Bates,
Elza Boyd, Herb Boyd, Denise Critten-
don, Marfé Ferguson Delano, Betty De
Ramus, Rosalyn Hamlett, Sarah
Labouisse, Frank McCoy,
Allison McLaurin, Clarissa Myrick-Harris,
Diane Patrick, Lisa Respers, Jarelle
Stein, Hollie I. West, Martin Weston
(writers); Chellyn Angebrant, Ellen
Gross, Catherine Hackett, Maurice Hall,
Melva Holloman, Greg S. Johnson, Bar-
bara Levitt, Kate Loving, Schulanda

Manning, Gwen Mullen, Catherine Par-
rott, Patricia Paterno, Sonia Reece, Elizabeth Schleichert, Janet Sims-Wood, Marilyn Terrell, Elizabeth Thompson
(researchers); Mel J. Ingber (indexer)

Educational Consultant: Gladys
Moore Twyman, Social Studies Coordi-
nator, Coordinator of the African Infusion
Project, The Atlanta Public Schools,
Atlanta, Georgia.

Correspondent: Christina Lieberman,
New York. Valuable assistance was also
provided by Elizabeth Brown and Kath-
eryn White, New York.

**Library of Congress
Cataloging in Publication Data**
African Americans : voices of triumph.
Leadership / by the editors of
Time-Life Books.
p. cm.
Includes bibliographical references (p.)
and index.
ISBN 0-7835-2254-1 (trade)
ISBN 0-7835-2255-X (lib. bdg.)
1. Afro-Americans—History. 2. Afro-
American leadership. 3. Afro-
Americans—Biography.
I. Time-Life Books.
E185.A2585 1994
973'.0496073—dc20
93-21147
CIP

AFRICAN AMERICANS: VOICES OF TRIUMPH™
consists of three volumes: *Perseverance*, *Leadership*, and *Creative Fire*.
For more information about the VOICES OF TRIUMPH™ volumes and
accompanying educational materials call or write 1-800-892-0316,
Time-Life Customer Service, P.O. Box C-32068, Richmond, Va. 23261-2068,
or ask for VOICES OF TRIUMPH™ wherever books are sold.

As a young child growing up in the 1950s, the first black leader I can recall was the Reverend Dr. Martin Luther King, Jr., whom my parents and I saw on the television evening news in 1956 during the bus boycott in Montgomery, Alabama. Listening to his eloquent and inspired words, we all knew that this 26-year-old minister, husband, and father faced death threats, harassment, and bombing attacks simply for his role in trying to desegregate the city's buses. Yet Dr. King's vision never faltered, and he and 50,000 other black residents of Montgomery did not stop until their battle was won. As a man of God, a scholar, and someone with experience of the wider world, he gave me a glimpse of my own future possibilities as a black man.

My parents, my teachers, and other adults of the town introduced me to more African American leaders—to Richard Allen, founder of the African Methodist Episcopal church, who insisted black men and women have the full dignity of worship; to the poet Phillis Wheatley, for whom one of our local segregated schools was named; to educators Booker T. Washington, who hoped to lead the race to economic uplift, and Carter G. Woodson, often called the father of black history, both of whom came from my own state of West Virginia; and to biologist George Washington Carver, the first black student to earn a bachelor's or a master's degree from Iowa State University, who turned his advanced education to improving the lot of small southern farmers, black and white alike. They also spoke of other inspirational leaders, from scholar and activist W. E. B. Du Bois to New York's proud congressman Adam Clayton Powell, Jr.; from college president Mary McLeod Bethune to sports legends like Joe Louis, Wilma Randolph, Althea Gibson, and Jackie Robinson, whose achievements soared far beyond the playing field.

The examples of these leaders, some still living during my childhood and some long dead, stirred my heart and helped lift my own eyes to the horizon. Providing an example to follow is, after all, a key function of any leader of any race. But far too many other black achievers in fields as diverse as science, medicine, business, religion, education, and even politics remained buried in obscurity, unnoticed or forgotten by the writers of our nation's history books. Growing up, I did not know—and surely no one else in town knew—about William Shorey, a black San Francisco whaling captain who made 14 trips to the Arctic Ocean, or about Rebecca Lee, the first black woman doctor in America, who brought health care to the former slaves of Richmond in the years after the Civil War. In my elementary school and at home, I never heard about such vanished figures, famous in their own day, as Richmond's Maggie Lena Walker, the first African American woman to found a bank, or Paul Cuffe, a Revolutionary War-era merchant who became the wealthiest black man in America and an avid proponent of a return to Africa. All of these men and women charted a course for black Americans—and all of them can be found in this book, the *Leadership* volume of African Americans: Voices of Triumph.

In bringing to light the little-known black leaders of our American past as well as those whose fame endures to this day, the Voices of Triumph project seeks to reclaim what was once known to all. Moreover, the book pays due tribute to the leaders of today, from the black astronauts and space scientists of the National Air and Space Administration, to the ministers of our nation's great black churches, to black lobbyists who helped shape our country's policies toward the apartheid regime in South Africa. "Without vision, the people perish," says the Bible, and it is perhaps only through leaders that such visions can be grasped. Read on to discover the wealth of black leadership that already forms part of the national tapestry of past and present—and to glimpse the leaders of the days to come.

Henry Louis Gates, Jr.
W .E. B. Du Bois Professor of the Humanities
Harvard University

EDITORIAL ADVISORY BOARD

DR. HENRY LOUIS GATES, JR.
is the W. E. B. Du Bois Professor of
the Humanities, professor of English, and chairman of the Department of Afro-American Studies at
Harvard University. He is the author
of several books and the senior editor for the African Americans: Voices
of Triumph project.

DR. MAYA ANGELOU
is a well-known poet,
author, educator, historian, playwright, and
civil rights activist. She
is the Reynolds Pro-
fessor of American
Studies at Wake Forest
University.

**REVEREND DR.
CALVIN O. BUTTS**
is pastor of New York
City's Abyssinian
Baptist Church. He also
has taught courses in
urban affairs and black
church history at the
university level.

**DR. DOROTHY I.
HEIGHT**
has spent a lifetime as
an activist for civil and
human rights in the
United States and
around the world. She
serves as president of
the National Council of
Negro Women.

DR. RUTH B. LOVE
is a consultant on
education issues at the
city, state, and national
levels. She has served
as superintendent
of schools for several
major urban school
systems across the
country.

BOARD OF CONSULTANTS

DR. BENJAMIN S. CARSON
is Director of Pediatric Neurosurgery at Johns Hopkins Hospital in Baltimore. He is a motivational speaker for young people across the United States.

WILLIAM H. GRAY III
is president and chief executive officer of the United Negro College Fund and a former U. S. congressman from Philadelphia. He has long been an advocate for education.

FOR LEADERSHIP:

Dr. Russell L. Adams is chairman of the Department of Afro-American Studies at Howard University. A political sociologist, he has written extensively in the fields of human relations and history. He also has been a curriculum materials consultant to a variety of governmental agencies in the United States and abroad.

Dr. Molefi K. Asante, chairman of the Department of African American Studies at Temple University, is founder of the Afrocentric philosophical movement. He has authored numerous books and articles on African American and African history and culture. Dr. Asante is also a curriculum consultant for school districts in the United States.

Dr. James Comer, who received the Harold W. McGraw, Jr. Prize in Education in 1990, is the Maurice Falk Professor of Child Psychiatry at the Yale Child Study Center and associate dean of the Yale School of Medicine. His school-improvement model is currently being used in school districts in 25 states.

Dr. Sulayman S. Nyang is professor and former chairman of the Department of African Studies at Howard University. He has served as a member of the board of the African Studies Association and is currently on the editorial board of several international journals. He writes extensively on African, Islamic, and Middle Eastern issues.

Dr. Willie Pearson, Jr., is professor of sociology at Wake Forest University. His research has centered on science education, science policy, and minority participation in higher education. He is the author of three books on black scientists and serves on the editorial boards of two scientific journals.

GORDON PARKS
came to national attention as an award-winning photographer for *Life*. He is a composer, best-selling author, and film director, and has been widely recognized for his contributions to the fine arts.

REVEREND DR. DEFOREST B. SOARIES, JR.
is pastor of First Baptist Church of Lincoln Gardens in Somerset, New Jersey. He is known for economic empowerment programs and for his work with youth.

CONTENTS

LEADERSHIP

OPENING ESSAY

A PROUD HERITAGE OF LEADERSHIP...12

ONE

FRONTIERS OF SCIENCE...24

TWO

THE POWER OF ENTERPRISE...74

A PROUD HERITAGE OF LEADERSHIP

"What is Africa to me?" asked Countee Cullen, a poet of the Harlem Renaissance, the black literary and artistic movement that flourished in the early 20th century. Throughout the centuries since enslaved Africans were first brought to North America, each generation of African Americans has had to fashion its own answer to this question. For some, Africa has represented a lost homeland; for others, a future Zion. Africa has also symbolized an egalitarian vision of humanity, a past and a future in which men and women judged one another by their achievements rather than by the color of their skin. But even during periods when Africa was regarded, sadly, as a badge of shame, it remained critical to the search for a black identity in the New World.

The desire to return to Africa has waxed and waned several times over the centuries. In the 1700s, for example, many blacks viewed themselves as transplanted Africans, temporarily stranded in the New World and destined one day to return to their homeland. Even after large numbers of slaves and free black Americans converted to Christianity during the 1800s, they deliberately gave their churches names like African Methodist Episcopal to distinguish them from white denominations.

By the mid-1800s, however, when a number of prominent white Americans suggested the repatriation of free blacks to colonies in Africa, a skeptical majority of black Americans rejected the scheme outright. To their minds, encouraging free blacks to leave the country was simply a way to consolidate the institution of slavery. Several hundred black Americans did embrace the idea, however, seizing the opportunity to go back to the land of their ancestors, where they established the state of Liberia.

In the years immediately after emancipation, American blacks paid relatively little attention to Africa, instead devoting themselves single-mindedly to securing their full rights as American citizens. By then the European scramble to carve up Africa was well under way, accompanied by a flood of self-serving propaganda that depicted "The Dark Continent" as a land of primitive, pagan peoples and savage practices. Inevitably, the ugly rhetoric had some effect; Africa seemed too backward for many black Americans to seriously consider returning there.

Attitudes changed again after World War I as racial tensions in the United States worsened. The writers and artists of the Harlem Renaissance dreamed of a lost African utopia, and the black American followers of Jamaican activist Marcus Garvey laid ambitious—but never fully realized—plans to emigrate en masse to the motherland.

Even as the pendulum swung first one way and then the other, however, scholars were compiling impressive evidence of Africa's rich history, a history that most African Americans are eager to learn and proud to claim as their own. The vast continent—true cradle of civilization—has produced thousands of extraordinary men and women over the centuries whose leadership in every field of endeavor helped shape their rich and vibrant cultures.

No short survey could hope to do justice to more than a tiny fraction of these outstanding individuals, epitomized here by a portrait of the pharaoh Menes, an ancient African leader who first united the land of Egypt sometime between 3100 and 2600 BC. The profiles of five other historical figures on the pages that follow can only hint at the full variety of African leadership. These men and women are important today not only because they serve as examples of excellence but also because they made significant contributions to Africa and to the world. As American children of slavery seek to reclaim their proud African heritage, the names of these leaders resound ever more clearly across the centuries.

A SHREWD POLITICIAN

Queen Nzingha, a 17th-century ruler of the Ndongo people, who inhabited what is now central Angola, is revered by modern Angolan schoolchildren as a heroic figure whose astute political alliances kept her nation free of European control for more than 30 years. A key element in her maneuverings was, as is depicted here, a treaty made in the 1640s with the Dutch, which held off incursions by the slave-trading Portuguese. Indeed, one of the most famous stories about Queen Nzingha concerns a visit she made to the Portuguese governor in Luanda a few years before becoming queen.

Serving as an emissary for her brother, King Mbandi, Nzingha had been instructed to forge an alliance with the white men, offering Mbandi's assistance in subduing the rival Imbangala people. When Nzingha appeared before the governor, she found him seated on his throne, while she was expected to stand. Unwilling to parlay on such unequal terms, she sat upon one of her servants, whom she ordered to get down on all fours. The Portuguese, impressed as much by her imperious demeanor as by her negotiating skills, soon came to terms.

In 1624 Mbandi died—possibly, it is said, at Nzingha's orders—and Nzingha became queen. Beginning a relentless war on the Portuguese, she took on the ceremonial role of a male—leading her troops in battle, wearing men's garb, and insisting that she be addressed as king. Besides her alliance with the Dutch, she also formed military alliances with neighboring peoples by a canny appeal to their pride as Africans. Her efforts were successful until 1659, when a series of military defeats forced the queen to make peace with her longstanding enemy. In exchange for local self-government and the return of several royal hostages, she reluctantly signed a treaty giving the Portuguese free rein in the slave trade.

PROPHET OF THE ASHANTI NATION

From earliest childhood, according to Ashanti oral tradition, the 17th-century West African priest Okomfo Anokye showed a rare gift for prophecy and for politics. At a relatively young age he became a priest to the royal court of the Denkyiras, a powerful and prosperous coastal people with links to the Atlantic slave trade.

The Denkyiras dominated their neighbors in what is now Ghana, and it was there that Okomfo Anokye met Osei Tutu, a royal hostage from the northern kingdom of Kwaaman. Like Osei Tutu, who chafed at being held against his will, Okomfo Anokye hated the Denkyiras; years earlier, they had killed his mother as a sacrifice to their gods. The shared resentment led to a fast friendship between the two.

When Osei Tutu's uncle, the Kwaaman ruler, died in 1697, the hostage was permitted to return home to succeed him and to take Okomfo Anokye with him as a priest and spiritual mentor. Okomfo Anokye is said to have advised Osei Tutu to make his capital at the town of Kumasi.

But Okomfo Anokye's most important service came when Osei Tutu called a great meeting of all the local Ashanti chiefs, hoping to form a confederation under his rule to defeat the hated Denkyiras. As depicted at left, Okomfo Anokye is said to have summoned a sacred Golden Stool, which he called forth from the sky in a cloud of thunder and smoke. Okomfo Anokye told the assembly that the stool held the spirit of the Ashanti people and marked the beginning of a new Ashanti nation. Awed, the leaders agreed to join forces under Osei Tutu. Their new unity brought victory over the Denkyiras and endured long enough to stave off European encroachments for two decades.

A LEGENDARY MERCHANT QUEEN

As one of humanity's oldest documents, the Bible offers invaluable glimpses of long-ago events. Yet many details remain lost in the mists of time. No scholar can be certain, for example, of the identity of the female ruler that the Bible calls the Queen of Sheba. But there are two strong possibilities: Bilqis, a queen of what is now Yemen—and Makeda, the Ethiopian ruler depicted here.

According to the *Kebra Negast*, or *Glory of Kings*, the earliest record of Ethiopian history, Makeda became queen in 1005 BC, presiding over a huge empire that stretched from Upper Egypt and Ethiopia across parts of Arabia, Syria, and India. The size of her realm assured the queen's interest in trade, and her merchants roamed far and wide across desert and sea.

Among these merchants was one named Tamrin, who gave Makeda a glowing account of his transactions with King Solomon of Judea. The young queen decided to conduct her own trading mission to the Jewish king, and as the *Kebra Negast* relates the story, she traveled to Judea in a caravan of 797 camels laden with "gifts," a euphemism for trading goods.

Makeda and Solomon formed an instant bond, spending many hours discussing trade and religion. Solomon even persuaded Makeda to adopt the God of Israel as her own. After some six months, Makeda left Judea, having exchanged her goods for lavish gifts from Solomon. By then, the two had conceived a son, born during Makeda's homeward journey.

At the age of 22, the prince, ibn al-Hakim—guided by the aged Tamrin—traveled to Judea to meet his father. The doting Solomon sent his son back with a Judean entourage, from whom Ethiopia's Falashas, or black Jews, trace their ancestry. When ibn al-Hakim succeeded his mother, he took the name Menelik. For more than 28 centuries thereafter—with the exception of one 300-year gap—Ethiopian monarchs traced their ancestry through him to Queen Makeda and King Solomon.

A GREAT SCHOLAR
IN EXILE

The Islamic scholar Ahmed Baba grew up in the late 16th century in Timbuktu, the academic center of West Africa's Songhai Empire. There he established himself as an extraordinary intellect, and his future seemed secure. But then, in 1591, the army of the Moroccan caliph al-Mansur overran the city. Three years later, Ahmed Baba and other leading citizens of Timbuktu were carried north in chains to the Moroccan capital of Marrakesh and thrown into prison.

At the behest of local scholars, who begged for Ahmed Baba's release, the prisoner was given an audience with the caliph. Upon his arrival, however, Ahmed Baba found al-Mansur seated behind a curtain. According to another scholar's account, Ahmed Baba spoke boldly: "If it is your wish to speak to me," he declared, "come forth from behind that curtain." Al-Mansur obeyed, and from then on, Ahmed Baba was treated with respect in Marrakesh.

Although living in exile, Ahmed Baba, shown elucidating the Koran in the artist's conception here, became known throughout Africa as a man of wisdom. Magistrates came to him with matters of the gravest import, and because his knowledge of Islamic holy writ was profound, his word was taken as law. "I carefully examined from every point of view the questions asked me," Ahmed Baba later said, "and having little confidence in my own judgment I entreated the assistance of Allah, and Allah graciously enlightened me."

After 12 years, Ahmed Baba was at last allowed to go home. The scholars of Marrakesh honored him with a formal farewell, and one of them offered the customary wish for his return. On hearing this, however, Ahmed Baba exclaimed, "May Allah never bring me back to this meeting, nor make me return to this country." Returning to Timbuktu, Ahmed Baba lived and worked well into old age, producing more than 40 texts on topics as diverse as law, religion, philosophy, mathematics, and rhetoric.

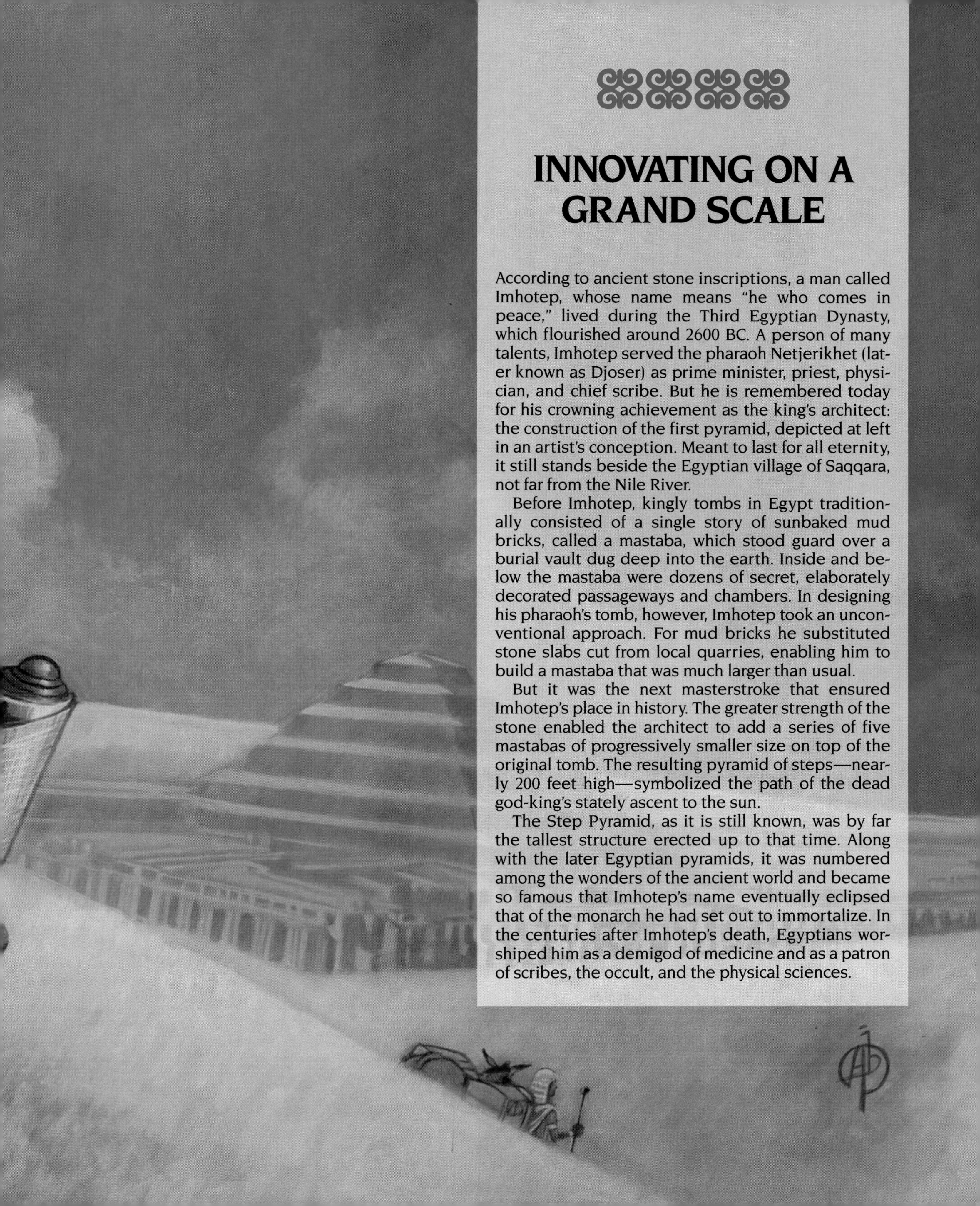

INNOVATING ON A GRAND SCALE

According to ancient stone inscriptions, a man called Imhotep, whose name means "he who comes in peace," lived during the Third Egyptian Dynasty, which flourished around 2600 BC. A person of many talents, Imhotep served the pharaoh Netjerikhet (later known as Djoser) as prime minister, priest, physician, and chief scribe. But he is remembered today for his crowning achievement as the king's architect: the construction of the first pyramid, depicted at left in an artist's conception. Meant to last for all eternity, it still stands beside the Egyptian village of Saqqara, not far from the Nile River.

Before Imhotep, kingly tombs in Egypt traditionally consisted of a single story of sunbaked mud bricks, called a mastaba, which stood guard over a burial vault dug deep into the earth. Inside and below the mastaba were dozens of secret, elaborately decorated passageways and chambers. In designing his pharaoh's tomb, however, Imhotep took an unconventional approach. For mud bricks he substituted stone slabs cut from local quarries, enabling him to build a mastaba that was much larger than usual.

But it was the next masterstroke that ensured Imhotep's place in history. The greater strength of the stone enabled the architect to add a series of five mastabas of progressively smaller size on top of the original tomb. The resulting pyramid of steps—nearly 200 feet high—symbolized the path of the dead god-king's stately ascent to the sun.

The Step Pyramid, as it is still known, was by far the tallest structure erected up to that time. Along with the later Egyptian pyramids, it was numbered among the wonders of the ancient world and became so famous that Imhotep's name eventually eclipsed that of the monarch he had set out to immortalize. In the centuries after Imhotep's death, Egyptians worshiped him as a demigod of medicine and as a patron of scribes, the occult, and the physical sciences.

FRONTIERS OF SCIENCE

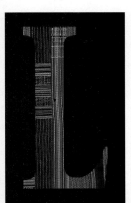

ate on a February night in 1935, the lights were still on in a chemistry lab at Indiana's DePauw University. A 37-year-old African American chemist named Percy Julian was working into the night, caught in the grip of almost unbearable tension. As he held a test tube just out of range of the flame from a Bunsen burner, Julian knew that he stood at a crossroads in his professional life. He was about to see a dream come true . . . or perhaps watch his career go up in smoke.

Before arriving at this dramatic moment, Julian had lived through years of frustration and despair over obstacles placed in his path simply because he was black. But he had always carried with him memories that strengthened his resolve. He could easily conjure up the image of his grandparents, both former slaves, bidding him farewell as he left for college: His grandfather waved a hand with two fingers missing, the penalty he had paid, as a slave, for the crime of learning how to read and write.

Though Julian had gone on to finish first in his class at DePauw in 1920, his faculty adviser was urged to "discourage your bright colored lad" from seeking an advanced degree, because he could never get a job suited to his level of education. But Julian would not be swayed from his course, earning a master's degree from Harvard University in 1923 and a doctorate from the University of Vienna in 1931.

Now, his future was on the line. The head of chemistry at England's Oxford University had challenged Julian's findings, and the American was determined to vindicate himself. If Julian were now proven wrong, his career might end on the spot.

Three years of hard work were contained in Julian's test tube. The crystals it held were meant to be an exact copy of the chemical precursors to a rare and expensive drug known as physostigmine, which was made from an extract of the highly poisonous Calabar bean of west-central Africa. A cheap, synthetic physostigmine might mean help for millions of glaucoma sufferers. But for Julian's synthetic to be worth anything, the precursors had to behave precisely like their natural counterparts. So far, they had. Now they faced a final test, literally a trial by fire—they had to have the same melting point as the natural substance.

Julian's assistant stood before a second burner, holding a test tube containing crystals of the natural Calabar extract. At a signal, both men held their test tubes over the burners and tensely waited for the crystals to melt.

A moment later, the assistant cried, "I'm melting!"

Almost at once, Julian exclaimed, "Me too!"

Each man checked his thermometer: the same temperature. Percy Julian had tri-

umphed. A brilliant career awaited him as one of the nation's leading chemists. Over
the years, he created inexpensive copies of other costly drugs, including synthetic
male and female hormones, which are used in treating cancer and were themselves
the precursors to the development of birth-control pills; and synthetic cortisone, a
powerful painkiller for arthritis and other miseries of muscle and bone.

But although Julian dedicated his life to alleviating suffering, he could do little
to alleviate the racism suffered by African Americans. Throughout most of American
history, highly talented black inventors and scientists like Percy Julian succeeded only
through grim determination in the face of a racism that stalked them every step of the
way. From gifted mechanics working in solitude to brilliant medical students negotiating the discriminatory barriers before them, African Americans overcame. When the
country's industrial and technological growth began to accelerate in the late 19th
century, black genius kept pace with—and sometimes led—the surge. And when corporate and academic laboratories became the focus of research and new product development in the increasingly complex world of the 20th century, African American
savants, by the sheer force of their talent and determination, shouldered their way
onto elite creative teams in many fields. Today, though their numbers in the vanguard
of the nation's scientific efforts are still disproportionately low, black Americans are
playing an ever greater part in the country's struggle to remain the world leader in
scientific and technological innovation.

Before the Civil War, Europe had held that title. Innovation in the United States
was mainly limited to practical inventions by craftsmen and laborers. An exception to

this rough-and-ready creativity, however, was Benjamin Banneker, a free black man who was born in 1731 in Baltimore County, Maryland. The first known African American scientist, he developed an early and lasting interest in mathematics.

At the age of 40, Banneker met a white neighbor named George Ellicott, who sensed that the two had similar interests. Ellicott lent Banneker two astronomy books, a telescope, and drafting instruments. Banneker delved enthusiastically into his new reading material and began scanning the skies with the telescope. Soon, he had worked out a prediction of an eclipse of the sun—a difficult feat at the time.

He decided to compute a set of ephemerides—charts showing the rising and setting times of the moon, sun, and other stars derived from mathematical calculations based on astronomical observations. Often published in almanacs, such charts were used by seamen to calculate their positions at sea and to work out schedules of high and low tides for help in navigating coastal waters. Farmers relied on them for planting times and weather forecasts; others used them to note special events.

Banneker sent his ephemerides to a publisher, but by the time the publisher had satisfied himself that the calculations were accurate, it was too late to get an almanac out for the following year. So Banneker laid the work aside and instead got involved in a project to survey the boundaries of the young American nation's new capital. In February 1791, Banneker joined a surveying team that began laying out the perimeter of a federal district that would straddle the Potomac River around the port of Georgetown, Maryland. During the three months Banneker worked on the project, he gained further know-how in taking astronomical measurements.

After returning to his farm, Banneker continued his observations of the skies. By June 1791 he had completed all the calculations for a 1792 ephemeris. The result, that December, was a best-selling 24-page almanac. Over the next six years, Banneker published 28 known editions.

Though Banneker's fame as a scientist was highly unusual among blacks in his day, his abilities may not have been unique. Of the 60,000 free blacks and 750,000 slaves in America in the late 18th century, some unquestionably contributed to science and medicine and invented new technology, though they received little or no recognition. In 1790 the U.S. Patent Act was passed to encourage innovation and to protect the property rights of inventors. Free blacks had a legal right to obtain patents, but few did. The first black known to have been awarded a patent was Thomas L. Jennings, whose dry-cleaning process was patented in 1821. As for slaves, their rights to the fruits of their ingenuity were not recognized by the Patent Office on the grounds that they were not citizens and thus had no legal rights.

The first black inventor to have an impact on an entire industry was a freeman named Norbert Rillieux, who in 1846 patented a device that revolutionized sugar refining. Rillieux, born in 1806 in New Orleans, was the son of a wealthy French planter and a free black woman whom the Frenchman had owned as a slave. Young Rillieux attended Catholic schools in New Orleans and studied engineering in Paris at L'Ecole Centrale. Graduating at age 24, he was so highly regarded that he was asked to stay and teach applied mechanics.

Benjamin Banneker, America's first African American scientist, wore Quaker garb in this portrait, which appeared on the cover of several editions of his popular almanac, first published in 1791.

While in Paris, Rillieux remembered how, as a boy, he used to watch slaves use long-handled ladles to stir and scoop thick, boiling sugarcane juice from one kettle to the next in a series. The water in the juice boiled away, leaving a thicker mixture of molasses and sugar in each succeeding vat. Finally, in the last and smallest vat, the mixture was heated until it crystallized. The hot, backbreaking process was slow and inefficient, and the sugar it produced was often crude and caramelized.

Rillieux designed an improved system but couldn't get French manufacturers interested in it. In 1840, he returned to New Orleans and after a false start or two persuaded a cane grower to install the new system on his estate. The apparatus, called the multiple-effect vacuum pan evaporator, was a complete success, saving on labor and fuel and producing fine granulated sugar.

Before long, thousands of evaporators had been installed at sugar refineries in Louisiana, Mexico, and Cuba. Norbert Rillieux became wealthy, and sugar, previously a luxury, was now readily available. Rillieux had done away with the relays of sweating slaves and their ladles. A single operator could work the system, simply by opening and closing valves. Ironically, Rillieux's invention had an unforeseen consequence: With sugar production rendered easy and cheap, the market for the product skyrocketed, and the demand for slaves to work the cane fields rose with it.

Rillieux had been able to patent his invention because he was free. Not until the Fourteenth Amendment made them citizens would former slaves get a similar chance. With liberty came a flood of inventions. Several hundred patents were granted to freed slaves in a variety of occupations. Some states displayed the inventions of former slaves in "Emancipation expositions" held on the anniversary of the Emancipation Proclamation. African Americans also organized their own fairs.

Most of these inventors were gifted, self-taught individuals with no formal education. Indeed, about 80 percent of black Americans in the post-Civil War decades were illiterate, and no more than a handful had a university-level science education. Edward Bouchet, a 24-year-old from New Haven, Connecticut, became the first African American to earn a doctorate from an American university. Yale awarded him a PhD in physics in 1876 for his dissertation on geometrical optics.

Even before the Civil War, however, some African Americans had managed to attend northern medical schools and practice as physicians, and 1868 saw the opening of the first black medical school, Howard University's College of Medicine in Washington, D.C. Eight years later, a second medical school for blacks, Meharry Medical College, was founded in Nashville, Tennessee. Facilities at both schools were meager, however, and suitable positions for new graduates were almost nonexistent. Freedmen's Hospital, a black institution in Washington, was virtually alone in taking African American MDs for internships, residencies, and staff appointments.

Howard's medical school would not even have survived but for the intervention, in 1873, of a black physician and Civil War veteran, Dr. Charles Purvis. A worldwide financial panic that year, brought on by fiscal instability in Vienna and overspeculation on railroad stocks in the United States, reached down to Howard. Money for the salaries of medical faculty dried up, and the university requested their resignations. On July 1, Dr. Purvis and two colleagues gathered to confront the threat to the school.

In his first year as surgeon in chief at Freedmen's Hospital in Washington, D.C., Dr. Daniel Hale Williams, shown reading in his study at the hospital, took part in 533 operations. The mortality rate was an amazingly low 1.5 percent.

They agreed to teach without pay, supporting themselves through private practice. The university okayed the plan and kept the doors of the school open.

In 1882 Purvis was appointed surgeon in chief of Freedmen's by President Chester A. Arthur, thus becoming the first African American to head a civilian hospital. (Another black physician, Dr. Alexander T. Augusta, had run a Union army hospital during the Civil War.) Purvis remained chief of Freedmen's until 1894, moving later to Boston, where he set up a private practice.

Replacing Purvis as the new head of Freedmen's was Dr. Daniel Hale Williams. Like many black physicians, Williams had risen to his position from difficult early circumstances. He was born in 1856, in Hollidaysburg, Pennsylvania. When he was 11, his father died, and his mother left him to fend for himself. He moved around frequently and eventually came to Janesville, Wisconsin, where he became apprentice to the town physician.

Williams went on to the Chicago Medical College and, upon graduating in 1883, opened an office in Chicago. Few patients showed up, however, until he got the opportunity to perform surgery on an important woman in the community. The operation, which Williams carried out in the patient's own dining room, was a success, and the grateful woman spread word of "Dr. Dan's" remarkable talent. Soon, his small waiting room was packed.

In 1890 Williams learned of a young black woman, Emma Reynolds, who aspired to be a nurse but had been refused admission by every nursing school in Chicago. Williams's response: "We'll start a hospital of our own, and we'll train dozens and dozens of nurses." His initiative drew an enthusiastic response from the African American community. Just 18 months after he met Emma Reynolds, Provident Hospital, the first in the United States operated by blacks, opened with 12 beds in a building at Dearborn and 29th streets. Reynolds and six others enrolled in the first class of black nurses in America.

Two years later, on a hot July day, Williams made surgical history at Provident when a man named James Cornish was rushed to the hospital after having been stabbed in a bar brawl. Cornish showed signs of a wound in the heart area, which was then regarded as fatal. No one would have blamed Williams if he had prescribed bed rest and opium—and let the man die. Instead, Williams watched Cornish's face, held his wrist, laid his hand down gently, and said, "I'll operate."

With no x-rays to guide him, no breathing apparatus to keep Cornish's lungs inflated, and no blood transfusions—techniques that were all still in the future—the 37-year-old surgeon undertook the daring procedure in the suffocatingly hot converted bedroom that served as an operating room. He opened a small, neat trapdoor in the patient's chest and bent over to assess the extent of the wounds and decide how to mend them. Suturing deftly, he repaired damage to the left internal mammary artery and—most dramatic of all—closed a wound in the quivering sac known as the pericardium, which covered the beating heart itself. Then he closed the incision in the skin, applied dressing, straightened his aching back, and mopped his brow. The historic operation was ended. No one had thought to time it.

Fifty-one days later, Cornish was discharged—whole and healthy again. Suddenly, word spread. Newspaper headlines screamed: "Sewed Up His Heart! Remarkable Surgical operation on a Colored Man" and similar formulations. What lay behind the headlines was the fact that Daniel Hale Williams was becoming a highly creative surgeon, a trailblazer for new medical procedures.

In September 1894, when Williams left Chicago for Washington, D.C., to take over direction of Freedmen's Hospital, he found a run-down institution. But the new chief soon brought order, respectability, and a vital sense of professionalism to the hospital. He reorganized it, established internships, revamped the nurse-training program, and even inaugurated a horse-drawn ambulance service.

Williams's surgical accomplishments were often discussed by the members of the all-white District of Columbia Medical Society. But the society would neither invite him to speak at their gatherings nor admit him or the other black physicians who

Elijah McCoy received prominent coverage in the four-volume 1915 work *The Colored Inventor*, which carried his likeness (*above*). McCoy's automatic lubricator for locomotives (*right*), first patented in 1872, eliminated the risk of collisions between rolling trains and those stopped for oiling. Steam entered the device through the pipe at the top, preventing the oil from congealing and forcing it out in regulated amounts to keep moving parts lubricated. The lubricator shown here is a later model, patented in 1898.

practiced at Freedmen's to membership. Black doctors were also excluded from the American Medical Association (AMA), of which the D.C. Medical Society was an affiliate. Worst of all, African American doctors were denied privileges at most American hospitals and had to refer patients to white physicians for admittance to a hospital.

Within a few months after arriving in town, Williams moved to give local black physicians the benefits of a professional organization. In concert with several colleagues, he founded the Medico-Chirurgical (from the Middle French for "surgical") Society of the District of Columbia, an organization open to whites as well. And that December he helped form the National Medical Association, an African American counterpart to the AMA.

In 1898, Williams resigned from Freedmen's and returned to Chicago. Over the next decade he visited 20 states and helped persuade 40 hospitals to serve blacks. In 1913, he was appointed associate attending surgeon at Chicago's Saint Luke's Hospital, which until then had been an all-white institution. That same year, he became a charter member of the American College of Surgeons, the only black among its 100 founders. He died on August 4, 1931.

While men like Daniel Hale Williams were achieving brilliant careers based on top-drawer professional education, other African Americans were demonstrating a technological inventiveness that in most cases flowered *despite* educational inadequacies. Swept up in the expansion of American industry following the Civil War, these mechanical geniuses often made their mark in one of the most dynamic of the country's businesses—the railroads. The growing network of rails provided jobs, though often hazardous ones, for many African Americans. One of these black railroad men was Elijah McCoy, whose daily flirtation with on-the-job danger proved to be a source of creative inspiration for him.

McCoy was the son of slaves who had fled Kentucky in 1837 via the Underground Railroad and settled in Canada. There the young McCoy developed a fascination with machines. His father, who had become a successful lumberman, encouraged the boy's interest and eventually sent him off to Scotland to further his training. McCoy studied mechanical engineering and completed an apprenticeship in Edinburgh to become a master mechanic and engineer. He returned to North America around 1870, settling in Ypsilanti, Michigan, where, despite his education, the best job he could get was that of locomotive fireman on the Michigan Central Railroad.

Trains in those days had to make frequent stops for oil to prevent their moving parts from wearing out prematurely or seizing up. Whenever the train stopped, McCoy had to climb down and walk around the hot, steaming engine to do the job by hand. He would then climb back on board, and the train would speed onward—until the next oiling stop. The stops were costly in both time lost and manpower needed to keep tight lubrication schedules. In 1872, after two years of experimenting in a machine shop, McCoy invented and patented a lubricating cup that would supply oil, drop by drop, to moving parts while the train was rolling.

McCoy developed many more automatic lubricating devices that were installed in factories and on steamships and ocean liners. At first, white workers belittled his devices as "nigger oil cups," but they listened carefully when the oilers were installed and he gave instructions on their use. His manufacturing standards were so rigorous that competitors' lubricating devices could not match his, and his name, according to legend, was the source of the expression used to describe things that are the genuine best—"the real McCoy."

But it took time and money to develop and market prototypes. And patenting could mean fees for draftsmen, attorneys, and others. To continue his work, McCoy, like many other impecunious black inventors, assigned partial or total rights to patents in return for cash. Some of McCoy's most lucrative inventions were assigned to the Elijah McCoy Manufacturing Firm, a company in which he, ironically, held little stock. He died relatively poor in 1929.

While McCoy's devices kept trains running smoothly, Granville T. Woods's invention kept them running safely. With his "induction telegraphy" system, patented in 1887, moving trains could send and receive messages, keeping abreast of the whereabouts of other trains. Woods was born in 1856 in Columbus, Ohio. Early in life, he developed two loves—railroads and electricity. After jobs in his youth in a machine shop and on a railroad, he opened an electrical engineering shop in Cincinnati to develop and manufacture his own products. His first patent, in 1884, was for a steam-boiler furnace. Other inventions soon followed, and his reputation spread, attracting the interest of some of America's largest companies. He sold the rights to an improved telephone transmitter to the American Bell Telephone Company of Boston.

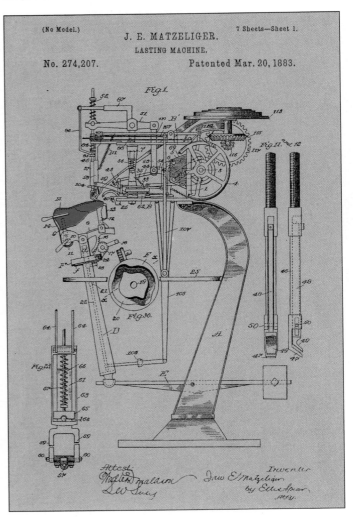

In 1888, Woods invented an overhead electric power supply system for trains and streetcars. His "troller," or grooved wheel, enabled a locomotive or car to draw electric current from overhead power lines without friction. The wheel gave rise to the word *trolley*. Woods then moved to New York City, where he produced 18 more inventions, including an incubator and an automatic electric circuit breaker. He also invented the electrified "third rail," now used by subway systems around the world.

Woods had to go to court to protect his telegraph patent against Thomas Edison and Lucius Phelps, each of whom came out with a system similar to his. Though he eventually won his case, the legal fees outstripped his ability to pay. Despite his many valuable inventions, Woods, too, died in virtual poverty, in 1910.

A contemporary of McCoy and Woods in that prolific period of American invention was Jan Ernst Matzeliger, who was destined to be one of the few American inventors to revolutionize an entire industry. A 25-year-old black man from

Jan Matzeliger's portrait (*left*) hangs in the First Church of Christ, the only congregation in Lynn, Massachusetts, that welcomed him. He bequeathed to the church much of his stock in the company that sold his shoe-lasting machine. So complex was the machine (*left, below*) that the U.S. Patent Office sent an expert to study it close up.

After inventing an inexpensive process for making light-bulb filaments, Lewis Latimer (*below*) joined Thomas Edison's crack research team in 1884, where he distinguished himself in scientific inquiry and as an expert witness in patent lawsuits. Later Latimer helped found Edison Pioneers, an "alumni association" of those who had worked with Edison.

Dutch Guiana, South America, Matzeliger could barely speak English when he settled down in Lynn, Massachusetts, the center of the American shoe industry, in 1877. He led a quiet life in Lynn, painting, reading science books, polishing his English at night school, and working in a shoe factory.

At the time, there was no machine that could connect a shoe's upper to its sole. The job was the domain of well-paid, unionized hand lasters, who pulled, pleated, tucked, tacked, and stitched leather into place around the foot-shaped mold called a last. Shoe manufacturers well knew the advantage to be won with a machine that could mechanize this final step of the process, and they had already invested a quarter of a million dollars in unsuccessful prototypes.

Matzeliger studied the hand lasters at their painstaking work and took on the challenge. Tending to his regular factory job all day, he labored through the night designing and building a machine that could duplicate the hand laster's artful movements. After six months, he demonstrated his first crude model. Refusing an offer of $50 for it, he went back to work on improving the machine. Years went into the effort, and Matzeliger was forced to scrimp, living on a nickel a day for food. But his own money ran out, so he got financial support—in return for a two-thirds interest in the invention—and was finally able to finish a prototype.

When the test day arrived, Matzeliger gathered his backers and turned on his contraption. It worked by moving the last forward while mechanically operated tools punched holes in a leather upper and drew it over the mold, fitting the upper snugly to a sole at the toe and heel and stitching it down. Then the machine fed nails to a driving mechanism that hammered them into place, and the shoe was finished. Elapsed time: one minute. The factory test turned out 75 pairs of women's shoes in a day. Later, with modifications, it produced up to 700 pairs, compared with the 50 pairs a hand laster could do. Matzeliger patented the machine in 1883.

Within a decade, his machine was in demand around the world. Eventually, with money from additional investors, the United Shoe Machinery Corporation was formed, which during its first 25 years earned more than $50 million and captured 98 percent of the shoe-machinery business. Matzeliger, however, did not see much money. He had pushed his frail body so hard working on his machine that, weakened by a cold, he contracted tuberculosis and died in 1889, a month before his 37th birthday.

Whereas Jan Matzeliger's invention was the product of keen observation and technological aptitude, another gifted black inventor, Garrett Morgan, launched his career with an accidental discovery that helped promote a widespread and long-lived fashion among black Americans: He stumbled upon a formula for hair straightener.

The seventh of 11 children, Morgan was born in 1875 on a farm in Paris, Kentucky. At age 14, after just six years of school, he left home, eventually moving to Cleveland, Ohio. His first job there, as a sewing-machine adjuster for a clothing manufacturer, sparked his interest in the machines, and in 1907 he opened a sales and repair shop for sewing machines. He prospered and by 1909 was operating a tailoring shop with 32 employees.

A jack-of-all-trades, Morgan tried to solve a stitching problem that left woolen thread scorched by the friction of fast-flying sewing machine needles. One night he applied to the needle a chemical solution he had mixed, attempting to reduce the friction. Just then his wife called him to dinner, and he wiped the solution off his hands onto a handy piece of cloth, a wiry-fibered swatch of something then in use called pony fur. After supper, he returned to his work to discover an odd thing: The fur had been straightened, apparently by his concoction. Possibilities stirred in his head, and, with his neighbor's permission, he spread some of the solution onto the neighbor's Airedale—a large breed of terrier with a wiry coat. When the dog went home, its owner did not even recognize it. Morgan then spread the stuff on his own head, little by little, and looked in the mirror: Eureka! His hair was straightened. He bottled the solution and established the G. A. Morgan Hair Refining Company, which was still going strong in the 1970s.

In 1912 Morgan invented a "breathing device," an early version of a gas mask. Consisting of a hood that fit snugly over the head and an attached breathing tube that hung to the ground and drew in the relatively clean air found at floor level in places filled with smoke and fumes, Morgan's device was a natural for fire and police departments. He himself gave it a dramatic real-life test. On July 24, 1916, a tunnel explosion five miles out into Lake Erie and 250 feet below the surface trapped 11 workmen. Ten rescuers went down into the hellish atmosphere of toxic fumes, smoke, and dust. All 10 were killed. Then Garrett Morgan, his brother, Frank, and two other volunteers wearing Morgan's hoods with long breathing tubes descended into the deathtrap and managed to bring out two survivors and four bodies. Newspapers around the country reported the rescue, and orders for the hood flooded in. But when buyers learned that Morgan was black, many canceled.

Morgan wasn't through with inventing—or with saving lives. While driving in Cleveland, he saw a car collide with a horse and carriage. The incident inspired him in 1923 to invent a signal for managing traffic at intersections. Morgan sold the patent rights to the device—which ultimately became the pervasive traffic light—to General Electric for $40,000. Thereafter he concentrated on civic affairs, running for mayor of Cleveland in 1931. Although he lost, his campaign focused public attention on the need for relief for the unemployed, improved housing, and better city hospital accommodations. He died at age 88 in 1963.

A far more celebrated benefactor of society was George Washington Carver—perhaps to this day the nation's best-known African American scientist. Carver was born into slavery in 1864 or 1865. As a youth he wandered the Midwest, completing high school in Kansas. In 1894 he became the first black graduate of Iowa State College, specializing in botany and agriculture and finishing at the top of his class.

Carver received a master's degree in 1896 and came to the attention of Booker T. Washington, founder of Tuskegee Institute, who offered

Fearing that fire and police departments in 1914 would be unwilling to accept a black man's invention, Garrett Morgan (*above*) presented himself as Big Chief Mason, a Native American, to demonstrate his breathing hood (*below*). By 1923, however, eager acceptance greeted another of his inventions, a traffic signal (*right*) that added an intermediate "half-mast" position—the equivalent of today's yellow light—to the stop-and-go signals then in use.

him a job as head of the school's Department of Agriculture. At their first meeting, Washington said, "Your department exists only on paper, Carver, and your laboratory will have to be in your head." Undaunted, the new faculty member created a makeshift lab with scraps from around campus. He used a heavy teacup for a mortar. A horseshoe became his classroom bell; a kerosene lamp served as a Bunsen burner.

In 1897, with a small allocation of state funds, Carver set up the Tuskegee Agricultural Experimental Station, where he taught new farming techniques and published informative, easy-to-read bulletins for local farmers. He proved to be an early example of what today would be called an environmentalist, teaching a philosophy of taking nature as a whole, in which ideally nothing is wasted and everything has a use.

On a 20-acre patch of poor land, he had his students put theory into practice planting cowpeas, which acted as a fertilizer and replenished the depleted soil with nitrates. Then he put in sweet potatoes, and finally cotton. When he harvested 500 pounds per acre, far more than had ever been produced elsewhere in the area, farmers were impressed. They began heeding his words on crop rotation to restore soil debilitated by one-crop cotton or tobacco cultivation.

Carver geared his station toward practical farming. His bulletins were how-to publications that showed cause and effect and followed a crop all the way into the kitchen. Bulletin No. 31, for example, was "How to Grow the Peanut and 105 Ways of Preparing It for Human Consumption." He left virtually no subject important to farmers untouched, publishing 44 bulletins between 1898 and 1942 on a wide variety of topics, from raising sweet potatoes to finding uses for native clays.

With peanuts, Carver was almost too successful. As the boll weevil increasingly devastated cotton crops in the period between 1890 and 1910, Carver advised farmers to cultivate peanuts instead. Before long, peanuts had replaced cotton as the number one crop in the farming belt from Alabama to Florida, and farmers using Carver's methods enjoyed bumper harvests. To create a market for the glut of peanuts, he went back to his lab and stayed holed up there for days, emerging with "recipes" for two dozen different products that could be made from peanuts—everything from milk to printer's ink. Eventually, he developed more than 300 different products from the peanut, which became a valuable cash crop. He also devised uses for other botanical products and by-products, creating synthetic marble from sawdust, woven rugs from okra stalks, and 118 products from sweet potatoes—including rubber.

The white-controlled peanut industry, after swallowing its racist inclinations, claimed Carver as its spokesman and sent him to Washington to battle for protective tariffs for American-grown peanuts. In 1921, Carver walked into the U.S. Capitol and sat before a tariff hearing of the House Ways and Means Committee. He had been allotted 10 minutes, but with his flair for the dramatic and his fascinating demonstrations of the versatility of the peanut, he charmed the congressmen into giving him unlimited time. When he was finished, his enthralled audience applauded, and the committee recommended the highest tariff rate the peanut industry had ever had.

Carver died in 1943, a little over a year after a museum dedicated to him was

opened. Honored both in life and in death, he was initiated into the Royal Society of Arts, Manufactures and Commerce of Great Britain in 1916, received the NAACP's Spingarn Medal—awarded annually for outstanding achievement in any field—in 1923, was memorialized on a U.S. postage stamp in 1949, and became a member of the New York University Hall of Fame in 1973. YMCA buildings, scores of public schools, and even a naval vessel were named after him, and the first national monument to an African American was built at his birth site, near Diamond, Missouri.

Despite success stories like Carver's, few African Americans were at the forefront of scientific research in the 20th century. Only 13 science doctorates were conferred on blacks before 1930, and most research laboratories remained closed to them. Medicine was still the field that held the most promise for the scientifically inclined; between 1910 and 1930, while the total number of American physicians stabilized, the

World-famous botanist George Washington Carver oversees students in a turn-of-the-century coeducational science class at Tuskegee Institute. Carver was more than 25 years old before he gave up his cherished idea of becoming an artist and turned to agricultural science as a career.

ranks of black physicians increased by almost a quarter. Even so, by 1940 there were only 4,000 black doctors in the United States, the vast majority of them treating only black—and poor—patients, and nearly all of them locked out of white hospitals.

One of those first 13 black PhDs in science was Ernest Everett Just, who conducted pioneering experiments in biology largely in a secluded laboratory by the sea. When he emerged with his achievements in hand, he, like other black researchers, felt the chill of rejection by the scientific establishment.

Just was born in 1883 in Charleston, South Carolina. At age 17, with five dollars in his pocket, he worked his way north to New York City and then to Kimball Union Academy in Meriden, New Hampshire. He graduated number one in his class in 1903 and entered Dartmouth College, where he also excelled, graduating magna cum laude in 1907. Hired by Howard University to teach English, Just was then persuaded to switch to biology. He settled in as an instructor.

In the summer of 1909 Just began to pursue graduate work as a research assistant studying marine invertebrates and embryology at the Marine Biological Laboratory at Woods Hole, Massachusetts. He published his first paper in 1912, "The Relation of the First Cleavage Plane to the Entrance Point of the Sperm." The paper gained him fame in the scientific community, using a brilliant argument to demonstrate that in the marine worm N*ereis*, the location of the sperm's entry point on the egg determines where cell division will take place within the egg. The work earned him, in 1915, the first Spingarn Medal.

Just spent the 1915-16 academic year on leave from Howard, earning a PhD in zoology at the University of Chicago. As it happened, he was experiencing difficulties at Howard, where his teaching load was extremely heavy, and his research facilities were poor. An $80,000 grant to Just from the Julius Rosenwald Fund, a foundation that aided black educators and organizations, came with a stipulation that the university lighten his teaching load. Meeting that condition left some of Just's courses uncovered and led to strained relations between him and the administration.

In addition, Just felt hemmed in by his racial identity; it stigmatized him among scientists in the United States, and he was offended by the appellation "Negro scientist." Except for Woods Hole, Just was locked out of the best laboratories in the country, and funding for his work was limited. He believed Europeans were more interested in his research than in his race, so in 1929 he accepted the first invitation ever tendered to an American to conduct research at the prestigious Kaiser Wilhelm Institute for Biology in Berlin.

But when Hitler's rise to power in 1933 loosed an aggressive, lethal racism in Germany, Just left. Moving back and forth between France, Italy, and the United States over the next seven years, he was caught in France when the German army overran most of that country in May and June 1940, and he briefly landed in a German prison camp. He managed to win release and fled to Spain, then to Portugal, and finally to America. He died in Washington, D.C., on October 27, 1941.

An entirely different response to racial discrimination was the hallmark of another talented young black scientist, Dr. Louis Wright, who was inclined to face bigotry down whenever and wherever he saw it. In addition to his trailblazing career as a

physician, Wright served as chairman of the board of directors of the NAACP through 17 of its most turbulent years.

Wright was born in 1891 in La Grange, Georgia. His father, a Meharry Medical College graduate, died in 1895, and his mother married another physician, William Fletcher Penn, Yale Medical School's first black graduate. Wright earned a bachelor's degree from Clark College in Atlanta in 1911 and won admission to Harvard Medical School by performing well in an impromptu oral chemistry quiz given him by a skeptical professor. Although he graduated fourth in his class in 1915, no Boston hospital would accept his application for internship, so he went to Freedmen's.

Returning to Atlanta after his internship, Wright practiced for about a year before the United States entered World War I. He enlisted as a first lieutenant in the army medical corps, but his angry, unaccepting reaction to the racism he witnessed in the service provoked his white commanding officer into vowing never to recommend Wright for a promotion. Once in France and tested in battle, however, Wright ended up in charge of the unit's surgical wards, received a Purple Heart as a casualty of a German poison gas attack, and was promoted to captain.

After the war, Wright opened an office in New York City, and in 1919 was appointed the first black physician at Harlem Hospital—or at any New York municipal hospital, for that matter. Starting as the hospital's lowest-ranked physician, he rose to become director of surgery and, eventually, president of the medical board. In 1934 he followed in the footsteps of Daniel Hale Williams to become the second African American admitted to the American College of Surgeons.

An authority on surgery for head injuries and fractures, Wright wrote a chapter in the 1938 edition of Charles Scudder's *Treatment of Fractures*. In 1948 he founded the Harlem Hospital Cancer Research Foundation, where he conducted investigations in chemotherapy with one of his two physician daughters, Dr. Jane Wright. He died in 1952, some six months after being saluted by Eleanor Roosevelt, Ralph Bunche, and others at a function held in his honor.

Another African American physician in a class by himself was Dr. Charles R. Drew, who loomed so large in the history of medicine that his life became the stuff of myth. Drew was born in 1904 in Washington, D.C. He grew up in a middle-class neighborhood and was a four-letter athlete in high school. He went on to Amherst College, where his football coach praised him but his professors were less enthusiastic, as he sometimes neglected his studies.

Drew had been considering medicine as a career but had gone to Amherst on an athletic, not an academic, scholarship and did not have the funds for medical school. Instead, he stuck to sports after graduation, coaching for two years at Morgan College in Baltimore and teaching biology and chemistry. In 1928 he entered McGill University's medical school in Montreal, Canada, where he excelled again at sports, though he was soon performing outstandingly in academics as well. Here he did his first research on blood groupings, his interest in the subject having been piqued by a friend, a British instructor at McGill named John Beattie.

In 1935, thirty-one years old and his internship and residency completed, Drew became a pathology instructor at Howard University and quickly moved up the ranks

Biologist Ernest Just (*above, right*) goes on a specimen-gathering cruise from the Marine Biological Laboratory located at Woods Hole, Massachusetts.

Beginning in 1949 at the research center founded by her father, Dr. Louis Wright, at Harlem Hospital, Dr. Jane Wright, shown at right, made many of the first important advances in cancer chemotherapy. She later continued this work at the New York University Medical Center in Manhattan.

of the medical school faculty. After a few years he was awarded a fellowship at Columbia University's College of Physicians and Surgeons and was appointed to a surgical residency at Presbyterian Hospital, a leading New York research and teaching hospital affiliated with the college.

There, between 1938 and 1940, he honed his surgical and research skills, writing a doctoral dissertation entitled "Banked Blood." Blood transfusion was by then an established procedure, but much remained to be learned about the best ways to preserve and handle donated blood, especially in large quantities. From his own research Drew demonstrated that plasma—blood fluid with the cells and platelets separated out—was easier to preserve than whole blood and was thus safer for blood banks to keep and dispense. In his dissertation, Drew consolidated the results of his research, his experience in establishing a blood bank for the hospital, and virtually everything else that was known on the subject worldwide. The work earned him a doctor of science in medicine degree, the first ever awarded to an African American, in June 1940. He returned to Howard with a promotion.

But World War II had erupted in Europe, and the soaring number of casualties in Britain generated a need for blood transfusions. Drew's old friend John Beattie, now chief of the transfusion service of the Royal Air Force, sent a much-publicized cable to Drew asking for an amount of dried plasma that was more than the total then in existence in the entire world. Beattie sent another cable to Britain's Blood Transfusion Betterment Association recommending Drew—one of the world's leading experts on blood preservation and blood plasma—for the job of supplying it. The association appointed Drew medical supervisor of its Blood for Britain program. Within two weeks he had installed a system for processing all plasma in a central laboratory, thus ensuring quality control, and for collecting blood with refrigerated mobile units. Drew's project met Britain's needs until the government managed to develop its own plasma program.

In January 1941 the association issued a report for which Drew wrote the technical section, outlining the lessons learned from the Blood for Britain program. He became famous overnight—for the wrong reason: He did not develop transfusion as a medical procedure, as myth had it. His contribution, a major one, was to make significant discoveries of his own, synthesize them with sometimes-contradictory findings from American and British laboratories, and apply the knowledge to the creation of practical blood-bank operations when they were most needed, in the heat of World War II.

America took note. The government planned a national blood-collection program for its armed forces, which Drew was asked to help establish. But on orders from the military, black donors were barred; only "white" blood was deemed acceptable, which led to the absurdity that Drew himself was prohibited from donating blood in the program he headed. At some point, the policy changed to the extent that African Americans could now donate blood, but "black" blood would be segregated for use only with black servicemen.

Drew was infuriated, in part because his colleagues

39

in the medical community remained silent about the outrageous insult even though they possessed scientific proof that all human blood was the same—categorizable by type but no different from race to race. Drew resigned from the program and returned to Howard to teach. In 1946 he became medical director of Freedmen's Hospital.

Myth not only obscured his works in life but also surrounded his tragic death. At 2:15 a.m. on April 1, 1950, Drew and three other black physicians left Washington by car for Tuskegee, Alabama, to provide care at a free clinic. He had been through an exhausting day and had had only two hours' sleep. In Petersburg, Virginia, Drew took the wheel. At 7:50 a.m., two miles north of Haw River, North Carolina, he dozed off. The car careened off Route 49 into a plowed field, turning over three times. None of the three passengers suffered life-threatening injuries, but Drew was left hanging out of the car with his right foot caught under the brake pedal. His left leg was nearly severed, he had internal injuries, and he was in shock. The car had rolled over on him.

Drew was rushed to Alamance County General Hospital, in Burlington, North Carolina, where three white physicians worked desperately but unsuccessfully to save his life. Somehow the tale arose that Drew, the "developer of blood transfusion," bled to death on the steps of a white hospital that would not admit him because he was black. Considering his experiences with the military and the nature of life in the South in 1950, the story was certainly plausible. But it simply was not true.

After World War II, the United States finally gained ascendancy over Europe in the achievements of its scientists, dominating the Nobel Prize awards in science. After the war, too, American society opened up somewhat to allow more blacks to enter traditionally white colleges and universities. Career opportunities in science opened up as well, although by as late as 1984, blacks were still underrepresented, making up about 12 percent of the population but only one percent of all scientists with PhDs.

A career in science was not merely rare among black professionals, it was an anomaly. One reason, said Herman R. Branson, who earned a PhD in physics from the University of Cincinnati in 1939, was that sociocultural factors that drew young people to the sciences were not operating in the black community. There was no scientific intellectual tradition to speak of.

Doing his part to begin creating such a tradition was a man who is today one of the most distinguished mathematicians in the world and the only black mathematician to be elected to the National Academy of Sciences. Born in Illinois in 1919, David Blackwell earned bachelor's, master's, and doctoral degrees in mathematics at the University of Illinois by age 22, one of only eight blacks to receive a PhD in pure mathematics between 1875 and 1943. He was nominated to be a Rosenwald Fellow at the Institute for Advanced Study at Princeton University, but his candidacy encountered racist resistance. "Princeton University objected to appointing a black man as an honorary member of the faculty," he remembered later. But, he added, "the Director of the Institute just insisted and threatened," and the objections were withdrawn.

All Blackwell had ever aspired to do was teach elementary school. But after postgraduate work at Princeton, he aimed a little higher—teaching at the college level. "It was the ambition of every black scholar in those days to get a job at Howard Universi-

Dr. Charles Drew, here in his Freedmen's Hospital laboratory in the late 1940s, gained worldwide renown for his blood-bank expertise. But his chief passion was his work as a teacher at Howard University, nurturing the quest for knowledge among young African American medical students.

ty," he said. But if Howard wouldn't have him, he'd go wherever else there were black faculty and black students: "There were 105 black colleges at the time, and I wrote 105 letters of application."

After teaching at Southern University in Baton Rouge, then at Clark College, and then for 10 years at Howard, he moved in 1955 to the University of California at Berkeley, where he became the first tenured black professor in the institution's history. One of the world's leading authorities on statistics and probability, Blackwell now holds the rank of professor emeritus of mathematics and statistics at Berkeley.

A modern-day black scientist who can trace his intellectual lineage back two centuries to Benjamin Banneker is Benjamin Peery. Like Banneker, Peery found his scientific milieu by looking heavenward. "I can remember as a youngster standing in my backyard in the frigid Minnesota air," he says, "gazing up at the stars one night and becoming infuriated at not knowing what it was all about." Not long afterward, the black youth cracked his first astronomy book. "I've never really recovered from it. From that moment I simply followed my own bliss." His bliss has carried him to a status as one of only perhaps a dozen black astronomers in the United States today.

At the University of Minnesota in the 1940s, Peery began his studies in aeronautical engineering, but soon switched to physics. After earning a master's degree from Fisk University and a PhD from the University of Michigan, he joined the astronomy faculty at Indiana University for a time. He then taught for 17 years at the University of Illinois before moving on to a professorship in the astronomy department at Howard University, which he held until his retirement in 1991.

Greatly interested in enticing more schoolchildren into a love of science, Peery applied in 1993 for a grant from the National Science Foundation to assemble a team that will show future teachers how to stimulate the natural scientific curiosity of elementary-school students. Children are excited about science during their formative years, he contends, but get turned off because many teachers can't adequately answer their probing questions. He is committed to helping teachers make a difference in children's receptivity toward science at an early age, when it matters most.

Scientists know that while aspirants in the arts, humanities, or business can propel themselves into a career from as late a starting point as their final college years, science aspirants cannot. Children who aim toward a scientific career must, from the earliest grades onward, feed a growing hunger for knowledge, discipline themselves to hone their minds, become comfortable with mathematics, chemistry, and physics, and amass information about their subject. Like a dancer, whose body must be trained in childhood or never, tomorrow's scientists—African American or otherwise—must begin their science studies today.

Shirley Ann Jackson needed no prodding to start the journey. Rather, she is one of those who show the way. She was the first black woman to earn a PhD from the Massa-

chusetts Institute of Technology, in 1973, as well as the first black woman in the country to receive a doctorate in physics. As a theoretical physicist at AT&T Bell Laboratories, Jackson has performed work in high-energy theory that is recognized internationally.

"Everybody called me 'the brain,'" Jackson said in an article in a Bell Laboratories periodical, "but my family, neighbors, teachers and fellow church members respected me and encouraged me to do well." Born in Washington, D.C., in 1946, Jackson credits her interest in science to her father's help in constructing science projects and to her parents' strong belief in education. She entered school- and city-sponsored science fairs, winning first place in one for a project monitoring environmental influences on the growth of mold and bacteria, creating the project from things she found around the house.

Blacks and women were virtually nonexistent in her discipline when she received her PhD in theoretical particle physics from MIT. "You can imagine the field was not totally ready to have a black woman," she told an interviewer years later. "People wouldn't sit next to me in class; I wasn't invited to study groups."

Jackson has worked at some of the world's premier labs. From 1973 to 1976 she was at the Fermi National Accelerator Laboratory in Batavia, Illinois, with a year's leave during that period to work at the European Center for Nuclear Research in Geneva. Since 1976 she has been with AT&T Bell Laboratories. She is a Fellow of the American Physical Society and of the American Academy of Arts and Sciences, and is currently a professor of physics at Rutgers University in New Jersey.

For all her struggles at MIT, Jackson at least had a handful of African American fellow students to compare notes with. Such a luxury was not afforded another black scientist who succeeded at MIT—as a faculty member. Dr. James H. Williams, Jr., a professor of mechanical engineering who holds a PhD from England's Cambridge University, is the School of Engineering Professor of Teaching Excellence at MIT.

Williams was born and went to school in Newport News, Virginia, and worked in the Apprentice School of the Newport News Shipbuilding and Drydock Company. Customarily, the few blacks in the school were steered toward blue-collar training as electricians, machinists, and welders. Williams, however, became the first African American to be chosen for the company's design track, and performed so well that he was sent on to MIT, where he earned a BA in 1967 and an MA in 1968. Because of his love of teaching, Williams returned to MIT after his stint in England. He has combined his great popularity as a teacher with a lonelier role as a prod to the university's administration. He wants MIT not only to expand its outreach to black students but

Mathematician David Blackwell, shown here around 1990, has blazed new trails in game theory, probability, and half a dozen other fields. "I'm not interested in doing research," he has said. "I'm interested in understanding, which is quite a different thing."

Physicist Shirley Ann Jackson, long a fixture at AT&T Bell Labs, teaches four days a week at Rutgers University. "I wanted to have students and to teach them how to do research," she has said. "It's nice to pass on what you know."

also to add to his solitary presence as the one African American on a faculty of 941.

Despite Jackson's and Williams's individual successes at MIT, the burden of leadership in science education for African Americans has largely fallen on the shoulders of traditionally black colleges and universities. In the early 1990s, though enrolling less than 20 percent of all black college students, these institutions awarded some 40 percent of all bachelor's degrees earned by blacks in the sciences. Still, relatively few black high-school students are aiming at a career in science. Such challenging subjects as mathematics do not get translated into a commitment to science for most black schoolchildren.

But the problem is not intractable. Suggestions proliferate, as is evident from the hundreds of programs initiated to keep minority students on track and to clear obstacles from their path to science, mathematics, engineering, and medicine. In Chicago, Nobel Prize-winning physicist Leon Lederman helped create a teachers' academy that offers intensive 16-week courses for elementary-school teachers. The goal is to help them make science "warm and interesting and illuminating," as Lederman put it.

Since 1975, a mentoring program of the National Action Council for Minorities in Engineering (NACME), with backing from 200 industry donors, has helped more than 4,700 students earn engineering degrees, and these graduates account for 10 percent of all engineers from minority groups entering American industry. The council now aims programs at fourth graders, says NACME president George Campbell, Jr., "before they get channeled out of science."

A black man who rose to the highest administrative post in American science can testify from his own experience to the importance of mentors. Walter Massey, director of the National Science Foundation (NSF) from 1991 to 1993, was helped by sympathetic elders at several key points on his road to a PhD in physics from Washington University in St. Louis. Eager to repay in kind, Massey started an Inner City Teachers of Science program while on the Brown University faculty. And at NSF he created a program to link colleges that train significant numbers of African American science students with other colleges, school systems, and businesses in regional partnerships to help the black students along. Each of 10 regional alliances across the country receives one million dollars a year from the program.

All of these efforts have something in common: They are built on the idea that if more black students can be attracted to a life devoted to science study now, and helped to stay there, more will surely be available in the future to take their place in the ranks of American science.

BREAKING A MEDICAL MONOPOLY

In the world of late-19th- and early-20th-century medicine, women doctors were rare, and black women doctors even rarer. Indeed, as late as the 1920s in the United States, out of the thousands of physicians in the country, only 65 African American women were known to be practicing medicine.

Mostly, these remarkable women were from the upper strata of black society, young ladies whose families could afford medical school tuitions—assuming the would-be physicians could gain admission in the first place.

Even a successful matriculation guaranteed nothing. Pioneering black women quickly learned that they were under a comprehensive burden of discrimination: Established hospitals were both racist and sexist, caring little for either women or blacks as interns and residents. The black hospitals then springing up were heavily biased in favor of male applicants. Finally, the new women's hospitals, which provided openings for women doctors, showed little sympathy for black aspirants.

Yet the indomitable spirit of these African American women prevailed. The physicians profiled below honored their profession in private practice, at community clinics, and on medical missions abroad. A number of them established their own medical facilities, nursing schools, and social-service agencies. Some crusaded effectively for aid to the poor and women's rights. In every sense of the word, they triumphed.

Rebecca Lee

"I early conceived a liking for and sought every opportunity to be in a position to relieve the suffering of others." So said Rebecca Lee, the nation's first African American female physician.

Born a free woman in Richmond, Virginia, in 1833, Lee was raised in Pennsylvania by an aunt whose devotion to medicine as a lay doctor inspired her niece. Young Rebecca began as a nurse and then, in 1859, enrolled in Boston's New England Female Medical College.

But about the time the Civil War broke out, she had to discontinue her schooling, not to resume until several years later. The college readmitted her only because of local abolitionist sentiment and because she possessed a scholarship granted by Senator Benjamin Wade, a powerful abolitionist from Ohio. At that, the institution was reluctant to grant Lee a degree. Sources disagree on whether this reluctance grew out of racism or a concern that her grasp of the material was inadequate. "Some of us have hesitated very seriously in recommending her," read the faculty notes for February 1864, "and we do so only out of deference to the present state of public feeling."

None of that mattered greatly to Rebecca Lee. With her "Doctoress of Medicine," she returned to postwar Richmond, where she brought health care to the newly freed slaves in that shattered Confederate capital. After that, she maintained a successful practice for many years in her hometown, then went north again to Boston. There, in 1883, she published A Book of Medical Discourses, in which she drew on her wide experience to counsel women on how to care for themselves and their children.

Rebecca J. Cole

Rebecca J. Cole

History has offered more details about the life of the nation's second black female physician. Born in Philadelphia on March 16, 1846, Rebecca Cole showed early prowess by graduating from the Institute for Colored Youth (now Cheyney University of Pennsylvania) at the tender age of 17—with a $10 prize for "excellence in classics and mathematics, and for diligence in study, punctuality and good conduct." Four years later, in 1867, she became the first African American to graduate from the Woman's Medical College of Pennsylvania, launching a trailblazing career that spanned half a century.

Dr. Cole's passion was medical social services—health care for the poor and helpless. She was appointed resident physician at the New York Infirmary for Women and Children, founded in 1857 by Elizabeth Blackwell, the first woman of any race to earn a medical degree in America.

Cole's assignment as a "sanitary visitor" took her into the city's most destitute ghettos to provide women with simple and practical instructions on preserving their health and that of their families. Blackwell commended her for carrying on the work with "tact and care." The squalor, poverty, and injustice Cole witnessed on her rounds turned her into a lifelong fighter for public-health education and civil rights.

Moving on to Washington, D.C.,

Cole cared for the unwanted as head of the Government House for Children and Old Women. Later, in Philadelphia, she ran another refuge for the homeless and operated the Woman's Directory, dispensing free legal and medical aid to the needy.

While in Philadelphia, she disputed the stereotype of black neighborhoods as "naturally" unhealthy, unsanitary, and seething with vice, challenging the statistics compiled by white-run social agencies as reflecting the prejudices of men who, as she put it, were "warped" by "colorphobia."

Throughout, Rebecca Cole campaigned tirelessly for legal reforms to combat poverty among her people. "These," she insisted, "are the things that we can do to attack vice, disease, and crime in their strongholds, for they have no complexion and they always yield to such and to no other treatment."

Susan McKinney Steward

Several things may have led Susan McKinney Steward to become the third African American woman physician. She lost both of her brothers during the Civil War. She attended a niece who had

fallen grievously ill. And in 1866, she watched in despair and grief as cholera swept the neighborhoods of her Brooklyn, New York, home, taking hundreds of lives.

Whatever her motivation, in 1867 Steward entered New York Medical College for Women under the tutelage of its founder, Dr. Clemence Sophia Lozier, a wealthy white female physician. Though Steward's family was among Brooklyn's black elite and could afford to pay her tuition, she chose to work her way through school, emerging in three years as the first black woman doctor to hang out a shingle in New York State.

For a specialty, she chose homeopathy, which advocates, among other things, the prescrib-

Susan McKinney Steward

ing of drugs only in minute doses. Steward made a resounding success of her practice, counting men and women, white as well as black, among her many satisfied patients. Before long, she opened a second office in Manhattan and then cofounded the Brooklyn Woman's Homeopathic Hospital and Dispensary.

With boundless energy, she gave of herself as physician at the Brooklyn Home for Aged Colored People, presented numerous scholarly papers before homeopathic societies, and traveled widely. Her second husband, whom she married in 1896, two years after the death of her first, was chaplain of the famed all-black 25th Infantry "Buffalo Soldier" Regiment, and when she joined him at such posts as Fort Missoula, Montana, and Fort Niobrara, Nebraska, she brought her medicines with her.

Too full of vital force to settle simply for being a doctor, Susan Steward was also a devoted missionary, a zealous suffragette, and a supporter of the Women's Christian Temperance movement. Eventually, she and her husband moved to Ohio, where she brought her energy to Wilberforce University as school physician. Little wonder that when she died in 1918, a eulogy for her was delivered by no less a personage than the great black scholar W. E. B. Du Bois.

Halle Tanner Dillon Johnson

Her life was all too brief—she was barely 36 years old when she succumbed to complications during childbirth. Yet in that span Halle Johnson made her mark, through medicine, on one of the nation's great black institutions.

In 1891, Johnson was nearing graduation as the only black student in her class of 36 at the Woman's Medical College of Pennsylvania when a letter arrived from Booker T. Washington. The eminent educator and principal of Tuskegee Institute, in Alabama, wrote that he believed his school should employ a black resident physician and that the black community in the town of Tuskegee should be served by one. For an annual salary of $600, she was being asked not only to teach and to minister to students and faculty but also to compound her own prescriptions, for the school was hard-pressed to meet the cost of medicines otherwise.

The daunting job aside, Alabama law demanded that doctors wishing to practice in the state pass a grueling written examination. Alabama newspapers ridiculed the mere idea of a black woman daring to apply.

But Johnson went courageously ahead. She traveled to the state capital in Montgomery, and for 10 exhausting days underwent the rigors of the examination, taking tests on one subject each day. After three nerve-racking weeks she heard the results: She had passed with an average of 78.81, becoming the first African American woman admitted to medical practice in the state. And she immediately fulfilled Booker T. Washington's hopes, establishing a dispensary and training program for nurses as well as tending the town's black residents.

Alice Woodby McKane

Halle Tanner Dillon Johnson

Alice Woodby McKane

In the early 1890s, the only hospital care regularly available to African Americans in Savannah, Georgia, was at an ancient infirmary founded for blacks by charitably inclined whites. Alice Woodby McKane, yet another distinguished alumna of the Woman's Medical College of Pennsylvania, changed all that. In 1893, the year after she received her medical degree, McKane and her physician husband founded a dispensary, a hospital, and a school for nurses to give Savannah's African American community its first black-run health care facility.

Being medical pioneers for black people became the McKanes' career. Two years later, the couple carried their profession to Monrovia, Liberia, where they opened and operated the first hospital in that young African republic. Then, they returned home and devoted themselves to building their hospital and training school into a first-class institution that operated continuously for the next 71 years.

Justina Ford

When Justina Ford applied for her Colorado medical license in Denver in 1902, the examiner sighed and said, "Ma'am, I'd feel funny taking a fee from you. You've got two strikes against you to begin with. First off, you're a lady. Second, you're colored."

"I know," smiled Ford, newly graduated from medical school in Chicago. "I've thought it all through. This is just the place I want to practice."

And so she did for the next 50 years, as Colorado's only black woman physician and surely its best-known obstetrician. Ford delivered something like 7,000 babies in her time, going to the mother if the mother was not able to come to her.

Remarkably for a doctor, she never owned a horse and buggy or a car, but made all her house calls by streetcar or taxicab— which may have been a sensible thing, considering Denver's rugged winters. "I just pick up the phone and say my name and the cab rushes out," she once said. "All the drivers know me."

Denver's Baby Doctor, as she came to be called, welcomed all comers: black, Hispanic, Native American, Asian, and white. "Whatever color they show up, that's the way I take them," she allowed, and was said to have learned eight languages in the process. She also accepted payment in anything from apples to chickens or whatever goods a family might offer; one mother could not afford to pay anything at all for the delivery of her baby until the child was 13 years old, which was all right with Ford.

Someone once asked her to write a book. "Book?" she exclaimed. "Now where would I find time? I'm getting busier every day." Actually, she may have tapered off a touch in later years, but she was still delivering babies until a few weeks before she died in 1952 at the age of 81.

Justina Ford

WITHOUT KNOWLEDGE OR CONSENT

In an Alabama farm field, Nurse Eunice Rivers hands a sharecropper suffering from syphilis his "medication"—most likely nothing more than aspirin or vitamins

Just before planting season in the spring of 1930, news began to spread among the black tenant farmers of rural Macon County, Alabama, that "government doctors" had arrived in the area to cure "bad blood." Health conditions among local blacks were appalling. Entire families suffered from disease and malnutrition, but—being poor, uneducated, and neglected by white officials—all they could do was resign themselves to a hard fate.

Thus the stage was set for one of the most shameful chapters in American medical history. For the next 40 years, federal and local medical personnel, scientists, and administrators would conspire against hundreds of Macon County's black farmers in the name of science, deliberately denying them treatment for a fearful disease that went by the name of bad blood among the unsuspecting population—even as they began to die from it.

In many cases, "bad blood" meant syphilis. Some 36 percent of the black sharecroppers, who made up more than 80 percent of the county's population, were infected with the syphilis bacterium, *Treponema pallidum*. The result could be crippling arthritis, heart disease, blindness, insanity, and even death. Not knowing what ailed them but desperate for help, they flocked to makeshift clinics set up by the U.S. Public Health Service (PHS), under a program headed by Dr. Taliaferro Clark of the agency's Venereal Disease Division.

In the beginning, the government's intentions were honorable. Although no cure existed then for syphilis, for nearly two years afflicted blacks received a treatment of arsenic compounds and mercury ointment, which could sometimes keep the disease from doing its worst damage and from being passed on to new victims. However, the PHS clinicians, deciding that their patients were too ignorant to understand medical terminology, did not mention the word *syphilis* and adopted instead the local euphemism *bad blood*. They never informed those who tested positive for syphilis that they had a disease that could kill them, or even that they could pass it on to others.

Whatever its faults, the program was living on borrowed time: The Great Depression dried up its funding in early 1932. Disappointed, Clark de-

vised a plan to convert the canceled program into a six-month study of untreated syphilis, seeking to test—and possibly disprove—a widely held racist notion that the disease was less deadly to black victims than to white. More important, though, Clark hoped to show the need for continuing treatment. Tuskegee Institute, a predominantly black college founded by Booker T. Washington, was located in Macon County, and Clark argued that its medical facilities—a well-equipped hospital and outpatient clinic—could be used for x-rays and examinations.

Tuskegee's medical director, Dr. Eugene Dibble, went to the institute's head, Dr. Robert Moton, with Clark's new idea, convinced that the study would bring prestige to the medical department as well as unique training opportunities for its students. "Dr. Clark," wrote Dib-

ble to Moton, "predicts that the results of this study will be sought after the world over. Personally, I think we ought to do it." Moton consented.

In October 1932, then, PHS clinicians returned to Macon County. As before, they did not discuss the name or the nature of the disease—and this time they led their patients to believe they were treating them when they were not. Instead, they were assembling an experimental group of about 400 male subjects in the later stages of the disease and conducting purely diagnostic tests. Except for a few doses of mercury and arsenic in the early days of the experiment, the unwitting men received no help. As

A government doctor draws blood to check the progress of syphilis in a Tuskegee subject during his annual exam in the early 1950s.

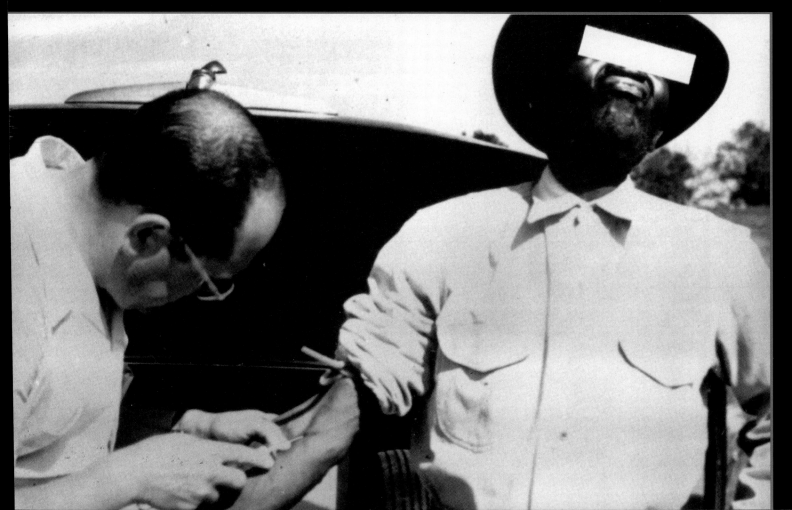

one subject, Charles Pollard, remembered, "They just went to doctoring on us and said they was gonna treat us. And they just said 'bad blood.'" In fact, the PHS's only purpose in what came to be called the Tuskegee Syphilis Study was to observe the disease as it progressed unimpeded through the body.

Clark had intended to end the experiment after all of the men had undergone a few checkups and diagnostic tests. But when he retired in 1933, control of the project fell to Dr. Raymond Vonderlehr. "The proper procedure," Vonderlehr wrote to another PHS official, "is the continuance of the observation of the Negro men used in the study with the idea of eventually bringing them to autopsy." A man apparently blind to the ethical considerations of this scientific inquiry, Vonderlehr sought to extend the study indefinitely to obtain the ultimate piece of research: the men's bodies after death. Incredibly, he secured cooperation not only from state health officials but also from Tuskegee Institute, where the autopsies would be performed, and from local doctors, who agreed to turn away any of the group seeking treatment.

The program ran like clockwork. Vonderlehr sent a team of health officials once a year to examine the subjects. The rest of the time, Eunice Rivers, a local black nurse and graduate of Tuskegee's nursing school, dispensed "pink medicine"—common aspirin—and "spring tonic," a vitamin-and-iron concoction. She also took the men to their annual exams—and made sure they stayed away from any real treatment facility. Nurse Rivers grew fond of them, but she never

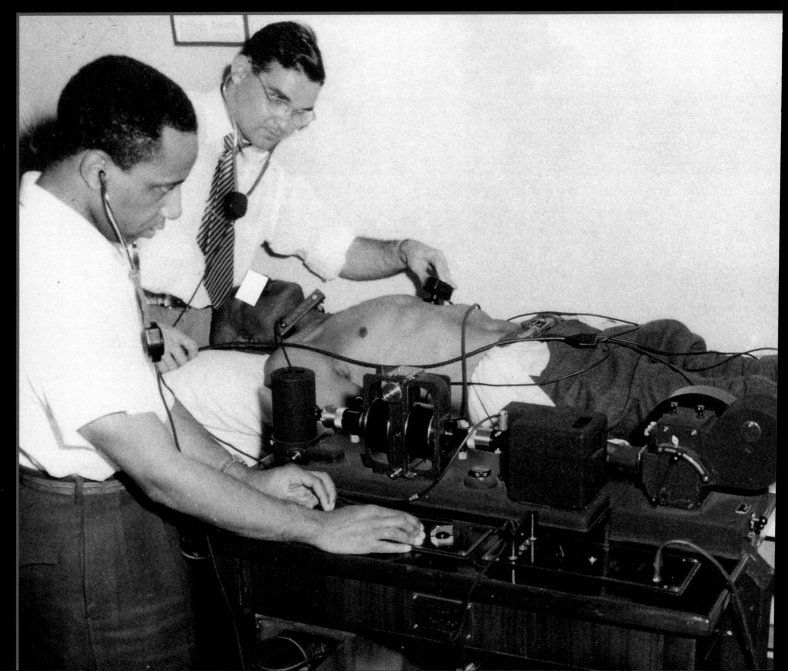

let her personal feelings interfere with the project, even as she watched the men's bodies being taken to Tuskegee after death. "As a nurse being trained when I was being trained," she explained in 1953, "we were taught that we never diagnosed; we never prescribed; we *followed* the doctor's instructions!"

One of the ironies of the situation was that the men felt special. They looked forward to the hot meals they were given on their annual clinic days, and as an inducement to keep them in the program, the PHS offered to pay for a proper burial upon their deaths.

In the late 1930s, when the callous experiment was only a few years old, the PHS ran a national campaign to combat venereal disease—but barred the Tuskegee subjects from mobile treatment units in Macon County. A few years later the wonder drug penicillin was discovered, and it quickly showed itself to be an effective and relatively safe cure for syphilis. By now, though, the program was well entrenched, and no one in the PHS saw fit to offer the drug to the men.

In the same way, the agency ignored the Nuremberg Code for the Protection of Human Subjects that emerged from the 1947 trials of Nazi doctors who had experimented on humans; somehow the PHS justified exempting the hapless sufferers of Macon County from the protections of its doctrine of informed consent.

The web of deception finally began to unravel in the late 1960s. Around that time, Bill Jenkins, a black epidemiologist, discovered the situation and mailed telling documents to the press. Nothing happened. But soon afterward, a venereal disease worker with the PHS named Peter Buxtun also learned of the study, and in 1972 he bundled up the files he had uncovered and handed them over to an Associated Press reporter. On July 25 the story broke in the *Washington Star* newspaper. Within three months, the Tuskegee Syphilis Study was abruptly terminated. By then, at least 28 and perhaps as many as 100 men had died from the disease.

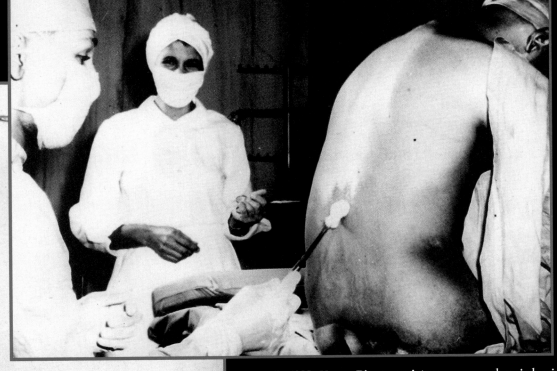

In 1933, Nurse Rivers assists a doctor as he draws fluid from a subject's spinal cord. Used to measure nerve and brain damage, the procedure was extremely painful and sometimes caused excruciating headaches that laid the men up for days.

A PHS physician and his assistant conduct an electrocardiogram to determine the health of a subject's heart. Syphilis often weakens the heart and blood vessels, paving the way for a heart attack—and sudden death.

ORIGINAL MIND BEHIND THE SCENES

On the morning of November 29, 1944, a team of surgeons gathered around an operating table at Johns Hopkins Hospital in Baltimore. They were about to begin a daring new experimental procedure—and the details had been worked out by a black man whose education had gone no farther than high school. Before the surgeons lay a frail infant named Eileen Saxon, one of thousands of "blue babies" born every year—children with hearts that do not pump enough blood into their lungs, leaving them with insufficient oxygen in their tiny bodies.

Eileen's condition, known as congenital cyanotic heart disease, produces a deep blue pallor like that caused by suffocation—and it can be fatal. The Hopkins surgeons planned to open the baby's chest cavity and perform a delicate operation following a protocol developed by the team's lead surgeon, Dr. Alfred Blalock, and his chief research assistant, Vivien Thomas. A man with no formal medical training, Thomas had worked out the details of the procedure in the lab, using canine hearts. Blalock had learned the technique from Thomas during experimental surgeries.

On the morning of Eileen's surgery, Dr. Blalock entered the room where the patient—barely visible under her sterile drapes—lay on the operating table. But Vivien Thomas, whose gifted hands had even cut and sharpened the tiny needle that the doctor would use, was not there. Refusing to begin without him, Blalock called Thomas to the operating floor. As the surgeon applied his scalpel to one of the baby's arteries, he asked Thomas, who stood at his right shoulder,

"Is the incision long enough?" Thomas replied calmly, "Yes, if not too long." Blalock continued to check with Thomas about every detail of the procedure, and finally, almost three hours later, the operation was finished. Over the next several days, the baby turned from blue to pink. "It was almost a miracle," Thomas said later.

The success of the operation gave new hope to parents of blue babies. "They came by automobile, train, and plane," wrote Thomas years later in his autobiography, describing the great influx of young patients at Hopkins. Working closely together, Thomas and Blalock had opened up a new medical specialty, modern cardiac surgery, that would save countless lives.

In the 1940s, however, the sight of Thomas in his white lab coat walking through the dimly lit corridors of Hopkins presented an unusual sight. The medical staff was emphatically all white at the time; other than Thomas, the only black men employed there were janitors.

The unlikely partnership between Thomas and Blalock had been forged in 1930, when the 19-year-old Thomas accepted the doctor's offer to work as a lab assistant at Vanderbilt University, in Nashville. Thomas intended to keep the job only until he saved enough money to

Vivien Thomas's many innovations included a respirator—a forerunner of the one he is observing below—that "breathed" for his animal patients during experimental surgery by inflating their lungs.

52

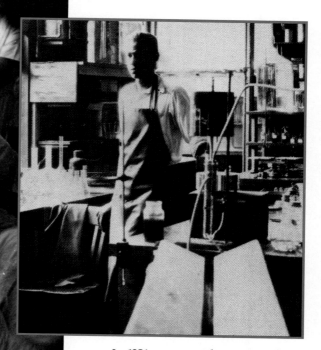

In 1931, a young Thomas stands in the experimental surgery laboratory at Vanderbilt University, where he and Dr. Blalock conducted their first research on shock trauma. Their work would lead to the development of blood and plasma transfusions used to treat soldiers in World War II.

enroll at Tennessee Agricultural and Industrial State College. From there he planned to attend Meharry Medical College, also in Nashville, where he hoped to realize his dream of becoming a doctor. But the Depression wiped out his savings, and he stayed on at Vanderbilt—thus beginning a collaboration that would last for more than three decades.

When Johns Hopkins Hospital offered Blalock the position of surgeon in chief in late 1940, he insisted on bringing Thomas with him. As at Vanderbilt, Thomas conducted experimental research, not only in cardiac surgery but also in traumatic shock and high blood pressure. Thomas's brilliance as a researcher was perhaps exceeded only by his skill in developing and carrying out intricate surgical procedures. Thirty years before Hopkins admitted its first black surgical resident, Thomas was teaching such procedures to the hospital's white surgeons. But in the mid-1940s, Thomas informed Blalock that he planned to leave to take work as a carpenter because he could not support his family as he wished on his Hopkins salary. The hospital offered to nearly double his pay—and he stayed.

By 1964, when Dr. Blalock retired, Thomas had made peace with the fact that he had never attended college, and he continued to supervise the surgical laboratories at Hopkins for another 15 years. In 1976, though, his nearly forgotten dream came true when the university awarded him an honorary doctorate and, in 1977, an appointment to the medical school faculty. "To have an honorary degree conferred upon me was far beyond any hope or expectation I could imagine," Thomas wrote. "The ovation on the awarding of the degree was so great that I felt very small."

SHARING IN A GREAT ADVENTURE

When the National Aeronautics and Space Administration (NASA) launched its moon-landing project in the early 1960s, during the heyday of the civil rights movement, it sparked interest among many newly optimistic African Americans—not only would-be astronauts, but also scientists in a wide variety of specialties whose work touched on space exploration.

The first African American to try for astronaut status was Captain Edward Dwight, a seasoned air force pilot with a degree in aeronautical engineering. In 1961, Dwight received a letter from President Kennedy inviting him to apply to test-pilot school as a step toward becoming an astronaut. Dwight completed the test-pilot training in 1963 and had advanced to spaceflight training when Kennedy was assassinated.

Several months afterward, Dwight was passed over for selection by NASA, a victim, he felt, of racial dis-

Lawrence

crimination. He later left the military and became a successful sculptor.

In June 1967, NASA chose Major Robert H. Lawrence, Jr., an air force pilot with a PhD in nuclear chemistry, to be the first black astronaut. Six months later, he was killed in a crash. More than 10 years would pass before the ranks of U.S. astronauts were cracked by any more African Americans, who began having an impact with the growth of the space shuttle program in the 1980s. By contrast, black scientists working on the ground (*pages 59-61*) have been able to make important contributions to the space program from the start.

NASA ASTRONAUTS

"Guy" Bluford

U.S. Air Force Colonel Guion Bluford was the first African American to fly in space, traveling aboard the shuttle *Challenger* in August 1983. Although he was a decorated fighter pilot who flew 144 combat missions in Vietnam and logged over 1,000 hours as a pilot trainer, NASA tapped "Guy" Bluford to be a mission specialist rather than a shuttle pilot when he became an astronaut in 1979 —an assignment that would give full scope to his expertise in aerospace engineering. Bluford held both an MA and a PhD in that field, despite having been told by high-school guidance counselors that he was "not college material" and should learn a trade. Bluford ignored their advice and ended up in what he feels is exactly the right place. "The job is so fantastic," he says, "I don't need a hobby. My hobby is going to work."

On his first flight, Bluford coor-

dinated scientific and engineering experiments aboard the spacecraft. He also was in charge of deploying a communications satellite for the Indian government and made medical measurements to test the biophysiological effects of space travel.

On his next shuttle flight, a West German-sponsored mission aboard the *Challenger* in 1985, the crew deployed a Global Low Or-

Astronaut Ronald McNair plays his saxophone on a 1984 flight of the shuttle *Challenger*, the same craft in which he and six others lost their lives two years later.

Astronaut candidate "Guy" Bluford (*near left*) experiences zero gravity on a training flight of a KC-135 aircraft in 1979.

biting Message Relay satellite and performed experiments in fluid physics, materials processing, life sciences, and navigation.

Aboard the *Discovery* in 1991, Bluford gathered data on the external shuttle environment and outer space, using, for example, a "horizon ultraviolet program," an instrument that measures characteristics of the earth's horizon and analyzes contamination created by the shuttle. On his fourth space voyage in 1992, the crew of the *Discovery* put a top-secret military satellite into orbit and conducted various experiments.

At the end of that mission, Bluford had logged more than 688 hours outside the earth's atmosphere. In July 1993, he retired from NASA and the air force to take a job in private industry.

Ronald McNair

In 1957, when the Soviets inaugurated the Space Age with their Sputnik satellite, six-year-old Ronald McNair was so excited he could talk of nothing else. The precocious youngster, son of a schoolteacher and an auto-body repairman in Lake City, South Carolina, had started school at the age of four—after his father changed the date on the boy's birth certificate. "He was more than ready," the elder McNair recalled later, "and I didn't see any sense in keeping him at home."

In high school, along with his continued interest in space travel young Ronald excelled at football, basketball, and track, and went on to graduate magna cum laude from North Carolina Agricultural and Technical State University in 1971. After earning a doctorate in physics at the Massachusetts Institute of Technology in 1976, he joined Hughes Research Laboratories in Malibu, California. While there, he realized his boyhood dream when he was one of 35 candidates chosen in 1978 for astronaut training from a pool of 10,000 applicants.

During his first flight, aboard the shuttle *Challenger* in 1984, McNair helped deploy two communications satellites. He also was responsible for testing the shuttle's new 50-foot remote manipulator arm, designed for use on future missions to capture damaged satellites and pull them into the shuttle's cargo bay.

On his return from that mission, Lake City honored him with a Ron McNair Day that featured a parade, fireworks, and speeches. The town's main street was renamed Ronald E. McNair Boulevard and his boot prints were impressed in a cement slab in the town park, a place he had once been barred from entering because he was black.

The explosion that took the lives of McNair and his six *Challenger* crewmates on January 28, 1986, shocked the world. Flags flew at half-mast, and millions turned on their automobile or front-porch lights to show that they shared in the sorrow. In December 1986, when MIT dedicated the Ronald E. McNair Building as a home for its Center for Space Research, the astronaut's four-year-old son, Reginald, unveiled an engraving of McNair's thoughts when he first saw the earth from space: "My wish is that we would allow this planet to be the beautiful oasis that she is, and allow ourselves to live more in the peace that she generates."

Astronaut Charles Bolden mans the pilot's station aboard the shuttle *Columbia* near the end of a six-day, 96-orbit mission in 1986.

Charles Bolden

When NASA first began seeking candidates for the space shuttle program in 1977, Marine Corps flyer Charles Bolden considered applying for astronaut training—but then decided not to. Although he had recently been approved for the navy's rigorous test-pilot school, he figured the odds against meeting the elite standards of the space program were too great.

During his test-pilot training, however, Bolden learned that some of the astronauts were people he knew. They were not superhumans, but men and women, whites and minorities—friends. He applied to NASA and was chosen for the 1980 class.

In 1981, Bolden completed training to qualify as a shuttle pilot—in effect, the copilot to the shuttle commander, who actually lands the spacecraft. His first mission came in 1986 aboard the shuttle *Columbia*, whose crew put a satellite into orbit and conducted experiments in astrophysics and materials processing.

Bolden's next, and most challenging, mission came in 1990 in the *Discovery*, when the crew had the job of deploying the Hubble Space Telescope. One of the arrays of solar panels on the telescope failed to open out into place, and, says Bolden, "We were about five minutes away"

Frederick Gregory

A rarity for a pilot, Frederick Gregory can fly both helicopters and planes. Gregory's interest in flying began in his teens, when he saw a show by the air force's Thunderbirds precision flying team at Andrews Air Force Base, near his home in Washington, D.C. He won admission to the Air Force Academy, and after graduation and helicopter training he spent several years flying air force helicopters—including rescue helicopters in the Vietnam War. He has also logged time as a pilot in more than 50 other types of aircraft and served as a NASA test pilot before being chosen as an astronaut.

At first, Gregory viewed the space program with only mild interest, because early NASA spacecraft were designed to be rocketed up and parachuted down, their pilots only along for the ride. But then came the shuttle, which actually needed a pilot to land. Gregory applied for astronaut status and was selected in 1978. He flew in space for the first time in 1985 as pilot, and achieved command of the shuttle—the first African American to do so—for his next two missions.

from sending two crew members out on a spacewalk to fix it. Just then, ground control managed to solve the problem.

By his third mission, aboard the *Atlantis* in 1992, Bolden had become commander, in charge of a seven-person crew to measure chemical and physical properties of the atmosphere. The mission confirmed ozone depletion in the skies over the South Pole.

For his fourth ascent, scheduled for 1994, Bolden is slated to command the first mission in space to have a mixed crew of Russians and Americans. The astronauts are to conduct experiments in "growing" semiconductor wafers in zero gravity; subsequent testing on earth will determine if the wafers perform faster in computers than those produced in normal gravity.

Gregory has delved into aeronautical innovation, helping to test an automatic aircraft-landing system. He also has designed a revolutionary "sidestick throttle controller" that permits one-hand operation of speed, roll, and pitch functions.

Space exploration, Gregory has said, might be likened to a child's progress in school. Not much should be expected from a kindergartner, but by the time the student finishes graduate school, the investment is ready to pay off. As he puts it, "I think we're just in the first grade right now. The more we do it, the smarter we get."

In a shuttle simulator, Commander Frederick Gregory practices some of the flight-control functions he will perform during mission STS-44, launched in November 1991.

Mae Jemison

In the mid-1980s, NASA's corps of astronauts included African Americans and women, but no African American women. Mae Jemison made it her business to correct that deficiency.

As a young girl growing up on the South Side of Chicago, Jemison knew that space travel was in her future. So determined was she to study space sciences that even in kindergarten she rejected any suggestion that she scale back her ambitions. "My teacher asked me what I wanted to be when I grew up, and I told her a scientist," Jemison recalls. "She said, 'Don't you mean a nurse?' Now there's nothing wrong with being a nurse, but that's not what I wanted to be."

Jemison received encouragement from her father, a maintenance supervisor, and mother, an elementary-school English and math teacher. Both her parents supported her interest in astronomy and spaceflight and understood when she spent her spare time haunting libraries and devouring books in those fields.

In 1973, at age 16, Jemison entered Stanford University on a scholarship. While earning a bachelor's degree in chemical engineering she also completed all the requirements for a degree

Dr. Mae Jemison calmly awaits the explosive ascent she will experience in an ejection-seat simulator, part of her survival training as an astronaut candidate in September 1987.

in African and Afro-American Studies. She then took an MD degree at Cornell University. During medical school, she spent one summer as a volunteer at a refugee camp in Thailand.

From 1983 to 1985, Jemison served as Peace Corps medical officer for Sierra Leone and Liberia. There she managed health care for Peace Corps volunteers and U.S. embassy personnel. She also developed and took part in research projects on hepatitis, rabies, and schistosomiasis, a serious infectious disease caused by a waterborne parasite. Upon returning to the States, she went into private practice in Los Angeles and began taking graduate courses in engineering at UCLA in preparation for her dream of joining the space program. She applied to NASA and was accepted for astronaut training in 1987.

After four years of handling various ground duties for shuttle flights, she made her own ascent into space as a science-mission specialist aboard Spacelab-J, a joint U.S.-Japanese effort in 1992. (Spacelabs are self-contained 60-foot-long work chambers that fit in the cargo bay of a shuttle.) Jemison performed experiments to measure the reactions of living organisms in the zero-gravity environment of space and was a coinvestigator on a human bone cell research experiment.

Despite putting in 12-hour days on their experiments, Jemison and the other crew members had time to relish being in space and seeing the earth from a matchless perspective. "One of the first sights that I saw when I first went into orbit was the city of Chicago," Jemison says. "I went to the window, looked down, and, literally, we passed right over it." After the mission, Chicago organized a citywide tribute to its hometown astronaut.

In 1993, Jemison left NASA to pursue her interests in education and health care and to help give disadvantaged youngsters more opportunities to prepare for careers in science and technology.

Bernard Harris

As Bernard Harris lifted off in the shuttle *Columbia* on April 26, 1993, he was fulfilling a 24-year-old ambition. As a boy growing up in Tohatchi, New Mexico, he would look up at the vast star-studded sky at night and dream of space travel. After watching the television broadcast of the first humans walking on the moon, he knew he wanted to be an astronaut.

Harris earned a bachelor's degree in biology from the University of Houston in 1978 and then applied for the astronaut program without success. After receiving an MD degree from the Texas Tech University School of Medicine, he applied for the astronaut program again and was instead hired by NASA as a life sciences staff member, in 1987.

During his two years on the staff, Harris received training as a flight surgeon and headed up a project to investigate crew members' loss of physical conditioning during missions. Astronauts lose muscle tone and bone mass as their bodies begin adapting to the weightless environment in space; after a week or so aloft they often have difficulty in moving about upon their return to earth. Harris's team devised exercises and equipment that astronauts could use to stay in condition in space.

While working on this project, Harris again applied for astronaut training and this time was accepted. He served as a mission specialist in Spacelab-D2, which nestled in the *Columbia*'s cargo bay on that 1993 ascent. The mission, NASA's 55th shuttle flight, was a 10-day joint effort by a combined seven-person German and American crew. The astronauts conducted more than 90 experiments in materials sciences, medicine, physical science, astronomy, and robotics. As medical officer, Harris followed up on his earlier work by conducting tests on how humans respond to living in space and how they can safely remain in space for extended periods. Now that he is finally an astronaut and has a space mission under his belt, Harris has given voice to a dream—that of practicing medicine in space.

Clad in a training version of the suit used for spacewalks, astronaut Bernard Harris prepares to enter a pool of water where, with the help of attached weights, he will achieve neutral buoyancy to simulate weightlessness.

NASA SCIENTISTS

Katherine Johnson

When aerospace technologist Katherine Johnson joined the space program at its inception in the 1950s, Jim Crow still prevailed in a large part of the country and women were primarily housewives. She needed courage and self-confidence to overcome the many obstacles in her way.

Johnson's long road to NASA began on a farm in West Virginia. During the school year, her father would move the family to town so his children could go to high school. She went on to West Virginia State College, specializing in mathematics and French, and then taught public school for several years following graduation.

In 1953, Johnson signed on with NASA's predecessor, the National Advisory Committee on Aeronautics. Her first assignment was to a racially segregated worker pool, where she was to do routine mathematical calculations. But after once being loaned to the Flight Research Division, she never returned to the pool.

Soon Johnson was interpreting data from secret "pilotless aircraft"—in actuality, prototype spacecraft. In preparation for the Apollo moon-landing project, she calculated the trajectories for putting a spacecraft into a lunar orbit, sending a lunar lander to the moon's surface, returning it to the spacecraft, and returning the mission to earth. She also developed simple emergency navigational methods that astronauts could use on spacecraft that have lost contact with ground control on earth—work that is critical for manned interplanetary travel.

Honored for outstanding work, Johnson retired in 1986 after more than 30 years' service with the space program.

U.S. Air Force flight surgeon Vance Marchbanks did pioneering research on crew safety.

Vance Marchbanks

In 1960, Air Force Colonel Vance Marchbanks capped a distinguished career in military medicine when he was chosen to be a medical monitor for NASA's Project Mercury. From a station in Nigeria, one of a string of posts around the world, Marchbanks monitored astronaut John Glenn's vital signs through sensing devices attached to Glenn's body as he orbited the earth in 1962. Previously, Marchbanks had conducted research showing that adrenal hormone content in blood and tissue has a direct link to physical exhaustion in flight-crew members.

After retiring from the military, Marchbanks served as chief of environmental health services for the Hamilton Standard Division of the United Aircraft Corporation, which developed the space-suit and life-support system for the Apollo project.

In 1980, NASA mathematician Katherine Johnson feeds data on interplanetary trajectories and space navigation through a "card reader" to a central computer.

During zero gravity aboard a KC-135, NASA engineer Robert Shurney monitors a phenomenon called apparent acceleration.

Robert Shurney

Test engineer Robert Shurney has helped come up with solutions to many of the knotty little problems astronauts encounter when, in the zero-gravity environment of space, they attempt simple things that are done almost unconsciously on earth. He thought up the idea, for example, of keeping morsels of food from floating away by mixing them with tapioca pudding—other binding edibles were added later—and packaging the food in containers similar to sardine cans to control the amount released.

Shurney helped design and test other devices necessary to enable astronauts to cope with weightlessness, including toilets for the Apollo program in the 1960s and 1970s as well as for early shuttle missions. He also developed the tires used on the lunar rover; built of aluminum, the tires had an exterior surface of wire mesh to give them traction on the dusty lunar surface.

At the Marshall Space Flight Center in Huntsville, Alabama, from 1968 to 1990, Shurney was in charge of testing these and other devices in weightless conditions on the KC-135 test plane.

"Ozzie" Williams

O. S. "Ozzie" Williams's aerospace career took off when he brashly talked his way into a job at Republic Aviation in Farmingdale, New York, in 1942. He was still one of only a handful of African American technical staff in the industry when he went to work at the Grumman Corporation almost 20 years later.

Under a Grumman contract with NASA, Williams supervised the development of the small rocket engines that would steer the lunar landing module on Project Apollo's moon missions. These maneuvering engines, says Williams, were "overdesigned"— built to handle more than the work they were created for. That extra capacity helped save the lives of the astronauts aboard Apollo 13 in April 1970 after an explosion knocked out the main rocket and forced the moon flight to be aborted in midspace.

With their chief source of propulsion gone and power for their life-support systems dwindling, the crew had to depend on the lunar module's small rockets to get headed back toward earth. Then they had to use Williams's 16 tiny steering rockets to maneuver the craft to reenter earth's atmosphere at a safe angle.

Had the steering rockets not been up to the task, Apollo 13 might have struck the atmosphere at too shallow an angle and caromed off into space to be lost forever, or come in too steeply and been incinerated from the friction of a too-rapid descent. Ozzie Williams's devices proved to be the little engines that could, and the Apollo 13 astronauts splashed down safely in the Pacific.

Standing before a photograph of an actual lunar module on the moon, O. S. Williams holds a scale model of the craft.

George Carruthers

Astrophysicist George Carruthers is a visionary who has had the satisfaction of seeing a long-cherished idea realized. As a child, his two great passions were astronomy and space exploration. Long before the prospect of space travel had moved off the pages of comic books and onto engineers' drawing boards, he was excited about the possibility of making astronomical observations from a platform in space, outside the obscuring mantle of the earth's atmosphere.

At Chicago's Adler Planetarium,

George Carruthers examines the Naval Research Laboratory's far-ultraviolet camera/spectograph he developed for use on the moon.

where the teenage Carruthers was a fixture in the early 1950s, astronomers scoffed at his notion. But the young dreamer went on to earn a PhD in aeronautical and astronautical engineering, and later, at the Naval Research Laboratory in Washington, D.C., he designed the far-ultraviolet camera/spectrograph carried on Apollo 16 in 1972. The device, set up on the surface of the moon, recorded distant objects and phenomena in space, feats that were impossible with cameras using visible light or based on the earth. Photographs brought back from the mission disclosed dense concentrations of interstellar gas and dust, stars in the process of forming, and planet atmospheres—in deep space.

Patricia Cowings

When her NASA colleagues tell her, "You make me sick," Patricia Cowings takes it as a compliment. Part of her job is to induce nausea in people—including astronauts. Her subjects sit strapped in a chair that spins them in a circle at high speed. From their malaise she seeks to learn how human bodies adapt to the environment of zero gravity, as on shuttle missions.

Cowings, director of psychophysiological research at NASA's Ames Research Center in California, is developing ways for astronauts to avoid motion sickness. She stresses "autogenic feedback training"—teaching subjects how to change their physiological responses to improve their well-being. The training includes biofeedback—learning how to alter rates of heartbeat, blood pressure, and other functions—self-hypnosis, and desensitization.

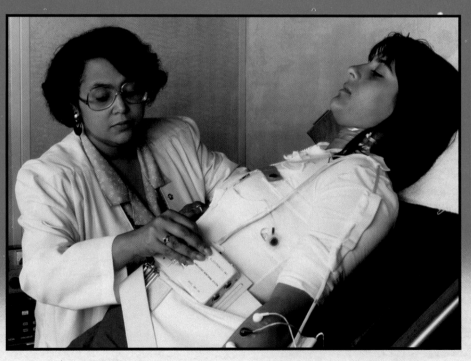

Cowings has worked with astronauts since the late 1970s and had the distinction of being the first American woman to receive astronaut training, although she has never flown in space.

Psychophysiologist Patricia Cowings monitors the responses of a volunteer test subject on a tilt table during a study of the effects of zero gravity on blood pressure.

TREATING SICKLE CELL ANEMIA

On Christmas Day, 1904, twenty-year-old Walter Clement Noel could barely breathe. The wealthy West Indian had been fighting a mysterious respiratory ailment since Thanksgiving, two months after he had sailed to the United States to begin studies at the University of Chicago College of Dental Surgery—where he was probably the only black student at the time. On December 26, he managed to walk the short distance from his home to Chicago's Presbyterian Hospital, which often treated the school's students, where his case came to the attention of physicians James Herrick and Ernest Irons. Puzzled by Noel's symptoms, the doctors took a sample of his blood for analysis, little realizing that they were about to uncover an ancient disease that originated in West Africa and has since spread throughout the world.

Adjusting the lens of his microscope to bring the patient's blood cells into clear focus, Dr. Irons—an intern working under Herrick at the time—found himself peering at an extraordinary sight. Red blood cells, or erythrocytes, normally appear round, but most of those on the slide were oddly crescent- or sickle-shaped. Neither he nor Herrick nor any other doctor on the staff had ever seen anything like them.

Herrick and Irons combed through medical books and journals, looking for other cases like Noel's, but they came up empty-handed. All they could do for the young man was treat his symptoms and keep looking for answers. Noel readmitted himself to the hospital several times over the next few years, until he graduated and sailed home in May 1907.

Nine years later, at the age of 32, he died of pneumonia.

Noel's condition seemed unique—until Herrick published a report on their patient's symptoms in November 1910, and, one by one, similar cases began to surface. Over the next 20 years, doctors and scientists documented enough of the syndrome—which they named sickle cell anemia—to learn that it is passed genetically from parents to their children, that it can be fatal, and that most of its victims are black.

Every physical trait in human

Unlike a normal red blood cell (*above, right*), rigid, misshapen sickle cells (*above*) often jam up in the blood vessels of sickle cell anemia victims, causing pain and other problems.

beings—from height to eye color—is determined by pairs of genes, with one copy of the gene for any given trait coming from each parent. Some traits are recessive, meaning that they will not be expressed if the gene carrying that trait is paired with a copy of the gene carrying the dominant, or overriding, trait. Thus, as many as one in 12 African Americans carries the red-blood-cell gene for the sickle cell trait, but because the second, dominant gene in the pair is normal, the sickle cell trait is not expressed, and the people lead entirely normal, productive lives. A child born to parents who are both carriers, however, stands a one-in-four chance of inheriting two copies of the sickle cell gene. One in 500 African Americans has the disease.

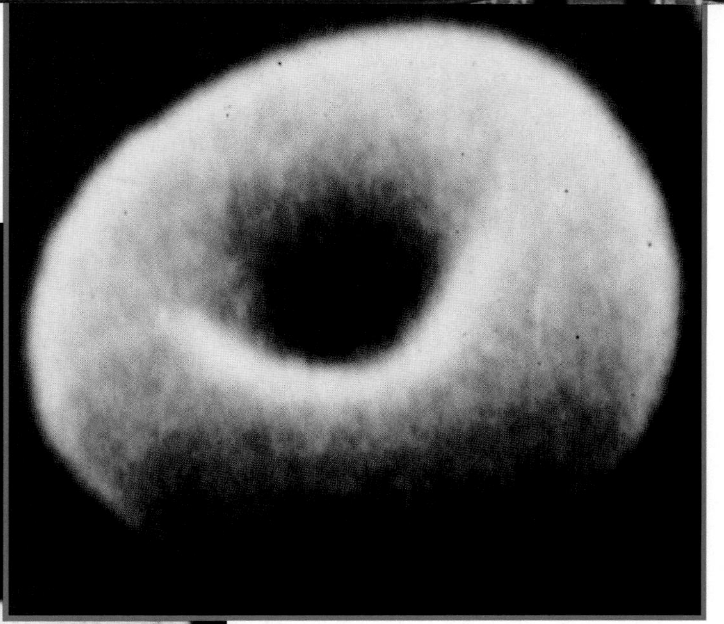

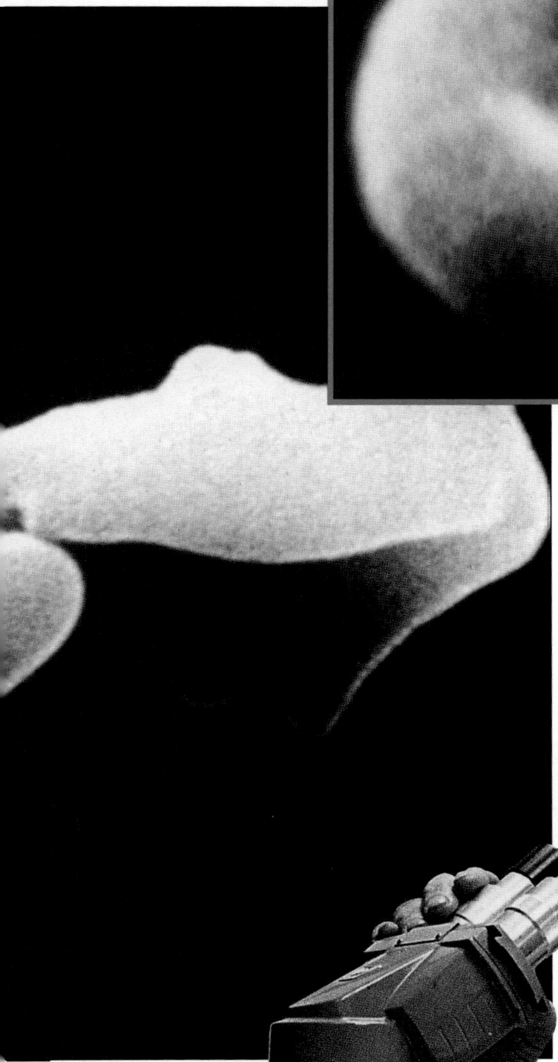

These individuals suffer a variety of symptoms, ranging from swollen hands and feet and delayed puberty to strokes, extensive organ damage, and respiratory infections, including the pneumonia that killed Walter Clement Noel. In addition, because the deformed red blood cells are rigid, they periodically plug up the blood vessels and bring on what are called sickle

A pioneering crusader, Dr. Roland Scott spent some 50 years at Washington's Howard University researching sickle cell anemia and helping its victims before he retired in 1990.

As chief of the Molecular Hematology Unit at the National Institutes of Health in Bethesda, Maryland, Dr. Griffin Rodgers, shown here in 1991, has been working with sickle cell patients in experimental gene therapy.

cell crises: attacks of pain that can immobilize the patient for anywhere from a few hours to a week or longer. Also, the sickled cells are short-lived, breaking down in less than 30 days compared with 120 days for normal cells. The body cannot replace them fast enough, so the victim lives in a chronic state of anemia.

For years, doctors and researchers focused on pinpointing symptoms and making patients more comfortable by administering codeine and other painkillers. The first glimmer of substantive progress appeared in the early 1940s, when Dr. Roland Scott, a young faculty member in the Department of Pediatrics at Howard University's College of Medicine in Washington, D.C., began to document the symptoms he saw in children at Freedmen's, the university's affiliated hospital. Scott soon developed a passionate interest in the mysterious disease. The man who would become known as the "father of sickle cell disease research" published his findings in detail and put on exhibits at both national and international medical meetings, bringing the disorder to the attention of the larger medical community.

In the years that followed, other researchers joined in the effort. They discovered the genetic basis of sickle cell anemia and that sickle cells produce a different kind of oxygen-carrying hemoglobin from that in normal blood cells—a discovery that may prove important in treatment. Yet because sickle cell disease mainly afflicts the black population, the pioneering studies of Scott and others sparked little sense of urgency in a society then accustomed to neglecting the needs of African Americans. The federal government devoted almost no money to sickle cell research, and the public at large remained virtually ignorant of the disease.

It was not until 1972—almost three decades after Scott's first articles on the subject appeared—that Congress enacted the Sickle Cell Anemia Control Act, which commanded the National Institutes of Health to set up 10 national centers to treat and counsel sickle cell victims, educate the public, and work toward a cure. Howard University was chosen as one of the sites, and Dr. Scott directed the program in research, screening, and patient care.

Meanwhile, in Detroit, another black American physician was making tremendous contributions toward alleviating the misery and confusion caused by sickle cell anemia. Charles Whitten, a graduate of Meharry Medical College in Nashville, Tennessee, had felt frustrated during the early years of his practice when young sickle cell patients came to him for help. "We had tests to diagnose the disease, but we were not doing anything for these children except to offer minimal care for the physical complications," he said years later. Whitten vowed to do whatever he could to change the situation.

While others studied the cause and course of the disease, Whitten focused on the problems faced by the people living with it, such as unemployment and depression. In 1971, he founded the National Association for Sickle Cell Disease (NASCD), which has formed chapters in 70 cities. The NASCD reaches out to the black community to provide free testing for the trait, to ensure that afflict-

In the early 1970s, Dr. Charles Whitten (*shown at left in* 1989) founded the National Association for Sickle Cell Disease and the Sickle Cell Detection and Information Program, which sent a mobile testing and counseling unit (*below*) into the black community in and around Detroit.

ed children receive health care, and to offer genetic counseling to prospective parents who carry the trait. The agency also seeks funding for research in the treatment and cure of sickle cell anemia.

In the same year, Whitten also founded the Sickle Cell Detection and Information Program, a community service program operating throughout Michigan. Two years later, the indefatigable organizer started the Comprehensive Sickle Cell Center at Wayne State University in Detroit and directed it until 1993. During its 20-year history, the program received more than $17 million in grants from the National Institutes of Health.

Thousands have benefited from these education and treatment programs, but a cure for sickle cell anemia remains elusive. So far, the most successful approach has involved bone-marrow transplants, in which marrow that produces normal blood cells is extracted from the hips of healthy donors and injected into sickle cell patients. The treatment is far from ideal, however. The chances of finding a donor with the proper

marrow type from outside the patient's immediate family are slim—sometimes as low as one in a million. Many patients suffer when the body's natural defense system attacks the new marrow because it is foreign tissue.

One of the most promising lines of investigation may be the gene-therapy studies conducted by Dr. Griffin Rodgers, a senior researcher at the National Institutes of Health. For the past decade Rodgers has been working with hydroxyurea, an experimental anticancer drug. Hydroxyurea in effect switches on a gene, present in all human beings, that is normally programmed to almost completely stop working at birth; this reactivated gene produces fetal hemoglobin—a kind of hemoglobin that helps prevent sickle-shaped red blood cells from forming. Other researchers have discovered that injections of butyrate, a compound found naturally in the body and also used as a flavor enhancer, stimulate the production of fetal hemoglobin. "We're cautiously optimistic," said Rodgers. "For the first time, we're treating the underlying disease instead of simply the complications."

FREE TEST
& INFORMATION

SiCKLE MOBiLE

THE SICKLE CELL DETECTION AND INFORMATION PROGRAM, INC.

WATCHFUL EYE ON THE ENVIRONMENT

One day in the early 1950s, Warren Washington raised his hand in chemistry class at Jefferson High School in Portland, Oregon, to ask his teacher why egg yolks are yellow. Instead of immediately satisfying the boy's curiosity, she nursed it along. "She wouldn't answer questions in the normal way teachers do," recalled Washington years later. "She'd say, 'Gee, let's see if we can find out.'" Intrigued by her challenge, Washington hunted down the answer and discovered that yolks get their distinctive color from sulfur compounds. But more important, the youth also discovered in himself a passion for scientific research.

"I have a natural curiosity about how things work and about nature," says Washington, who went on to become an atmospheric scientist and a renowned expert on global warming—the gradual heating of the planet caused by increasing concentrations of certain gases, notably carbon dioxide, in the air. Since 1987 he has directed the Climate and Global Dynamics Division of the National Center for Atmospheric Research (NCAR) in Boulder, Colorado. There he helped develop innovative computer models that attempt to predict the effects of natural phenomena and human society's habits on earth's long-term weather patterns, or climate.

Washington—shown at left in front of a satellite view of the earth—credits much of his success to the encouragement and

These NCAR computer images show possible temperature changes in the years 2010 (*above*), 2040 (*right*), and 2070 (*far right*) in the "business as usual" scenario, in which no effort is made to curb the greenhouse gases pumped into the atmosphere. In the red areas, winters will average more than 9 degrees Fahrenheit warmer; in the orange, 7 to 9 degrees; in the yellow, 5 to 7 degrees. On other land (*green*) and sea (*blue*) areas, increases will be less than 5 degrees.

support he received from his parents, both of whom were college educated, and to his own determination to follow his dream. In college, he pursued an education in physics and atmospheric science, or meteorology, and ultimately earned a PhD from Penn State in 1964.

While he was still working on his doctorate in 1963, he accepted a job offer from NCAR to apply his skill with computers to the recently emerged science of forecasting weather by computer. Using numerical values for temperature, pressure, and other simple weather processes, the earliest computers could manage a one-day weather forecast at best. During the next decade, Washington began to work with much more powerful machines—the so-called supercomputers—devising elaborate models that account for such complex aspects as ocean currents and atmospheric chemistry over long spans of time. "Not only are the models mimicking the real atmosphere," says Washington, "but they are also capable of explaining past climates"—and of predicting climate far into the future (*below*).

Since the 1970s, Washington has become a much-sought-after expert on the greenhouse effect. Worldwide pollution from industry and automobiles, combined with unrestricted deforestation, is changing earth's atmospheric balance of carbon dioxide and other greenhouse gases—so named because they behave like greenhouse windows, holding in the heat from sunlight. As the amount of these gases continues to increase, the warming effect may cause potentially calamitous changes in the environment.

Washington, who has advised every president since Jimmy Carter, is an advocate for tougher environmental regulations. "We have a warning sign from the models about possible climate change," he has noted, "and we should start to act prudently." Washington admits that computer predictions are not perfectly accurate, "but what we're talking about is magnitude, not whether greenhouse warming exists."

In 1993, the American Meteorological Society elected Washington to serve the following year as the first black president in its history. Concerned that he is one of only a handful of African Americans in his field, Washington cofounded the Black Environmental Science Trust, a nonprofit foundation that promotes science education for African American students. Says the distinguished scientist and policy adviser, "Blacks are a large untapped resource for the nation's future."

Dr. Carson exhorts Baltimore-area students to "think big," a theme he presents in inspirational speeches to young people around the country.

Garbed in sterile gown, mask, hood, and gloves, Carson performs delicate brain-tumor surgery, viewing his work through a microscope.

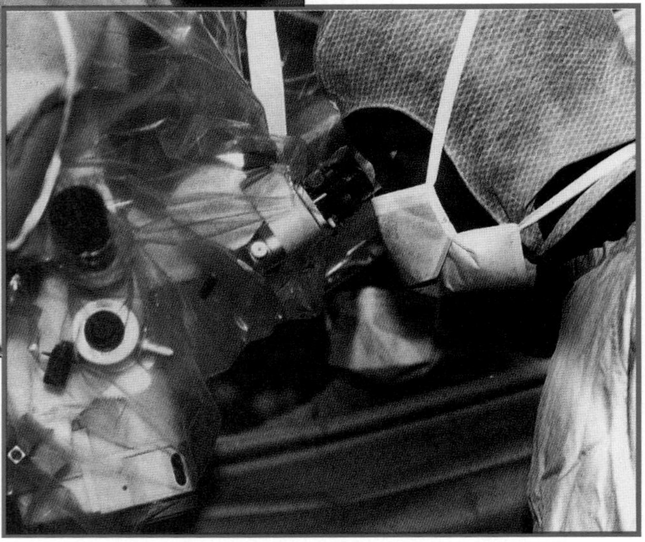

FROM MEAN STREETS TO OPERATING ROOMS

Today, he is a world-famous neurosurgeon who specializes in treating children. But when he was growing up in poor neighborhoods in Boston and Detroit, living in a family abandoned by his father, Benjamin S. Carson often gave vent to a hair-trigger temper and did so badly in school that other students called him dummy.

Finally, when he was 10, his mother laid down the law. He and his older brother, Curtis, could watch no more than three television programs a week, and each had to read two library books a week and write reports on them. Soon after he began the required reading, young Ben discovered

that he had a knack for science. His terrible schoolwork began to improve, and before long he was a top student. But his grades went downhill again in high school, where his temper was increasingly getting the best of him and he placed being "one of the guys" ahead of studying.

Through all the ups and downs of those turbulent years, however, Carson held on to a dream. As an eight-year-old, he had heard the minister at his family's church tell an inspiring story about a missionary doctor. From that day forward, he dreamed of becoming a doctor himself.

In his middle teens, Carson

reached a turning point in his life when an outburst of anger one day made him lunge at a friend with a knife. Tragedy was averted only because the blade struck the other boy's belt buckle and broke.

Horrorstruck at what he had done, Carson ran home and holed up in the bathroom for three hours, praying to God for help in curbing his violent behavior. His temper ceased to be a problem from that day on.

Soon he was getting top grades again, and won a scholarship to Yale. From there it was on to the University of Michigan Medical School and then a residency in neurosurgery at Baltimore's Johns

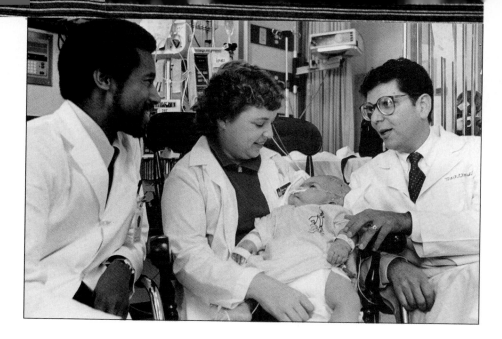

Carson, Nurse Dottie Lappe, and Dr. Mark Rogers check on eight-month-old Benjamin Binder, joined at the back of the head to his brother Patrick until a 70-person surgical team led by Carson successfully separated them in a 22-hour operation in 1987.

Hopkins Hospital, the first ever for a black doctor at Hopkins.

While a resident, Carson became friends with a neurosurgeon from Perth, Western Australia, who urged him to consider practicing there for a year or so. Unwilling at first because of what he had heard about Australia's long-time whites-only immigration policy, he and his wife, Candy, agreed to make the move after learning that the country's racist laws had been abolished in 1968. He applied to and was accepted by the Sir Charles Gardiner Hospital in Perth. Within a few months he was doing two or three operations a day. In 1984 he returned to the States and joined the Johns Hopkins medical school faculty; several months later, at age 33, he was named director of pediatric neurosurgery—the youngest in the country.

Carson was sometimes mistaken for an orderly during his early years in medicine; few nurses or patients had seen a black brain surgeon before. "When I did encounter prejudice," he said later, "I could hear Mother's voice in the back of my head saying things like 'Some people are ignorant and you have to educate them.'"

Since then, Carson has become famous for operating on brain disorders that other doctors consider untreatable. Although "last-resort" surgery is controversial, Carson has scored an impressive success rate and has many grateful parents in his corner.

Not only has he performed intricate surgery to separate Siamese twins attached at the back of the head and sharing major blood vessels (*left*), but he has also revived a procedure called a hemispherectomy, used on children who suffer from certain kinds of drug-resistant epilepsy. The procedure, which removes as much as half of the brain, was abandoned in the 1960s because some patients died and others lost speech and memory abilities. Of Carson's first 20 hemispherectomy patients, 19 survived and 18 were virtually seizure free.

As one colleague has put it, Carson "is more brave than controversial," adding that not everyone has "the guts and talent" to take on the hardest cases.

Shown with his family, Carson enjoys the fruits of a decision he made to stop work at a reasonable hour each day. "There's always just a little more to be done," he says. "I may as well leave work unfinished at 7:00 p.m. instead of 11:00."

FUTUREMAKERS: ON THE CUTTING EDGE

In response to a journalist's query, Dr. Raphael Lee, one of the brilliant African American scientists profiled below, acknowledged that yes, certainly, "there have been times when I have been subjected to clearly racially motivated confrontations and/or attacks." As Lee noted, however, it was impossible to know for sure when various obstacles to his career had been racial in intent: "It is the fundamental nature of biological systems to be competitive. And man is no exception." In any case, he continued, he also believed that opportunities had arisen because of, not in spite of, his background. And he put a firm period to the reporter's question by saying: "I have tried to take advantage of every opportunity."

That is the nub of it. In science as in everything else, the African American men and women who seize the chance, who compete and excel, are among the nation's futuremakers. On the cutting edge of medicine—and of all technology—they are shaping and directing America's drive into the 21st century.

Raphael Lee

At the University of Chicago Medical Center, where he is director of the Electrical Trauma Program, Dr. Raphael Lee's research offers fresh hope for the thousands of people worldwide who suffer high-energy electrical burns each year. Such burns, often from industrial accidents or lightning strikes, are far worse than ordinary thermal burns, which mainly affect surface areas. Electrical burns follow whatever path the current takes through the body. Of those victims who survive the initial shock, three-quarters lose a limb eventually, and almost all are permanently disabled in one way or another.

Yet treatment lagged for years because burn mechanisms were misunderstood. It remained for Dr. Lee and his colleagues to find the answer by applying what he calls a multidisciplinary approach. Lee, who was born in South Carolina in 1949, is one of those rare men who can move with ease between the sciences; he has a doctorate in electrical engineering from the Massachusetts Institute of Technology as well as an MD.

The doctor theorized that electrical field was the greater villain, not, as was assumed, the heat

In his laboratory at the University of Chicago, Dr. Raphael Lee uses a laser-scanning microscope to study a muscle cell damaged by high-voltage electric current.

generated by the body's electrical resistance. In 1986, his team set out to compare the effect on muscle cells of numerous short pulses of current with that of a single long, hot shock. They discovered that short pulses, while generating little heat, were just as lethal to the cells. Examination of cell membranes showed numerous tiny perforations that eventually resulted in collapse.

Could these "electroporated" membranes be resealed and thus salvaged? Dr. Lee thought so, and turned to poloxamer 188, a soaplike substance widely used as an emulsifier in drugs. In 1990, P-188 worked, at least on rat tissue. If electroporated human membranes can be bathed in P-188 and healed in like fashion, there may be applications far beyond electrical trauma.

Christine Darden

Mathematician-engineer Christine Darden may well be the one who determines whether or not there will be widespread supersonic airline travel in the future. Darden is leader of the Sonic Boom Group at NASA's Advanced Vehicles Division in Hampton, Virginia. Her job: to help design a supersonic transport that will carry 300 passengers great distances at twice the speed of sound—and with minimal sonic boom. That is a tall order. "Sonic boom," she says, "is a very, very tough problem."

Darden's path to NASA began in childhood. Her training started at age three when her schoolteacher mother took her along to class in Union County, North Carolina, rather than leave her home with a sitter. Darden fell in love with math, especially geometry,

and pursued it to a magna cum laude from Hampton Institute in 1962, then an MA from Virginia State College in 1967.

That year she started work at NASA—in a dreary job solving equations. "I wanted to know what the equations meant," she recalls, and she persisted until in 1973 she won classification as an aerospace engineer. From then on, it was up, up, and away—to a PhD in 1983 and a rich career dealing with the complexities of sonic booms.

Darden's laboratory today is a four-foot-square supersonic wind tunnel in which 12-inch metallic models are subjected to speeds as high as three times the speed of sound. One promising technique is to redistribute most of the sonic boom horizontally and upward to reduce its effect on the ground.

An expert on sonic booms, NASA engineer Christine Darden plays a major role in future supersonic transport design. The model at left is designed for optimum efficiency by smoothing out airflow over the highly swept wings at supersonic speeds.

Michael Spencer, Gary Harris

Pacesetters in microelectronics, Michael Spencer and Gary Harris work with dazzling new materials and mechanisms to extend the performance of everything from satellite communications systems and supercomputers to lasers and jet engines.

Much of this research is what Harris calls first-line technology: experimenting with the basic materials of electronics, actually growing novel crystals for semiconductors, and examining the properties of such exotic materials as silicon carbide and gallium arsenide. If anything ever was interdisciplinary, this is it, says

Michael Spencer (*standing*) and Gary Harris spearhead Howard University's research into microelectronics. The instrument is an atom accelerator used to modify semiconductor materials.

Spencer, explaining that "in some cases, the research encompasses chemistry, materials science, solid-state physics, and electrical engineering."

Home base for the two pioneers is Howard University's Materials Science Research Center of Excellence, where they have been funded to the tune of $9 million since 1983 by the National Science Foundation, NASA, and a number of private companies. Cornell graduates themselves—in 1980, they were the first African Americans ever to receive electrical engineering doctorates from that university—Spencer and Harris are well aware of their special role at Howard, and of Howard's special role in the black community.

Because of their scientific eminence, they are deluged with lucrative offers from private industry. But they remain at Howard pursuing their research and enhancing the university's reputation for distinction in all things. "If African American schools are going to make a real impact they have to be doing work at the graduate level," says Harris. But the trouble, continues Spencer, is that "most black institutions lack a tradition in scientific research. This is the first time such questions are being grappled with, so in a real way we are pioneers."

As professors, they are of course teachers as well, ardently committed to training a strong cadre of African American engineers. To insure a steady flow of students, the two have recruited master's and doctoral candidates from a number of black colleges. "Howard University," says Spencer, "has a unique opportunity to become a center of excellence in the world because of its geographical location and its financial resources."

Meredith Gourdine

Prolific inventor, pioneering engineer, businessman, medal-winning Olympic athlete, and all-around role model for young African Americans—Meredith Gourdine is a 20th-century Renaissance man.

Like many accomplished blacks, Gourdine, who was born in 1929, came up the hard way. His Brooklyn neighborhood was so tough, he recalls, that "we fought our way to school and back." He was very bright, but he ran with gangs himself and might not have amounted to much— until his ambition was galvanized by the spectacle of his best friend suffering a brain-damaging accident as a result of violence. "It scared me," he says, enough so that he zipped through high school and earned an academic scholarship to Cornell University. There he made advanced physics look easy while captaining the track team and winning a silver medal in the long jump (24 feet, 10.5 inches) at the 1952 Helsinki Olympics; another four centimeters and he would have brought home the gold.

The young man's science was definitely ahead of its time. He earned a doctorate in engineering science from the California Institute of Technology in 1960 and then, in 1962, became chief scientist of the Curtis Wright Corporation's Aero Division. In 1964 he launched his own research-and-development company, Gourdine Systems. Gourdine is best known for his seminal work

Despite the dark glasses that hide his sightless eyes, inventor Meredith Gourdine displays the cool and confident appearance of a man of limitless vision whose most revolutionary innovations still lie in the future.

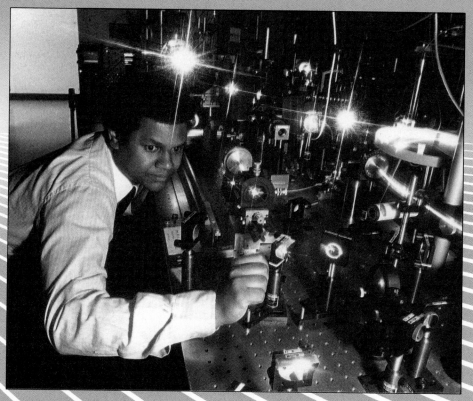

Dr. Anthony Johnson experiments with pulses of laser light to test the optical properties of glass fibers for future communications systems. Optical fibers can transmit billions of bits of data per second.

in three fields: electrogasdynamics, whereby high-voltage electricity is produced from flowing gas; thermovoltaics, which converts chemical and thermal energy into electricity; and vortadynamics, a technology using fluid vortices to transfer heat, mass, and momentum.

In the late 1960s, Gourdine Systems employed 60 people. The boss himself enjoyed a 26-room mansion in West Orange, New Jersey. "On paper, I was a multimillionaire. And I lived like one," says Gourdine. Then he went bust. One invention, a paint-spray system that employed electrogasdynamics to apply uniform coatings to complex objects, cost more to market than it returned. New York City nearly purchased 500 units of another product, an invention to capture the soot-filled emissions from apartment-house incinerators, until incinerators were banned altogether.

Gourdine suffered a further blow in 1973 when he lost his sight from progressive diabetic retinopathy. But he believes that blindness has simply amplified his powers of concentration. He has since founded Energy Innovations, in Houston, Texas, which, among other projects, is producing miniaturized superbatteries for missile electronics and developing ways to cool the chips in ever-tinier computers. The business is going nicely. "The smaller you make these microprocessors, the harder it is to get the heat out," says Gourdine. "But we're doing it very well, thank you."

Anthony Johnson

From fourth grade on, when his parents gave him a chemistry set, physicist Anthony Johnson knew what he wanted to do: He wanted to do science. He soon knew something else: He wanted a PhD. "I didn't quite know what it was," he remembered later, "but I heard that it gave you a license to do interesting science, and that you could get rich and have fun at the same time." Today, Anthony Johnson has his PhD—granted by the City University of New York in 1981—and is a member of the staff of AT&T Bell Laboratories in Holmdel, New Jersey. So far, he considers the highlight of his career the opportunity he had to co-chair the 1992 Conference on Lasers and Electro-Optics—the world's largest laser meeting, with over 7,000 in attendance.

At Bell Labs, Johnson researches lasers and fiber optics, seeking to make quantum jumps in communications technology. A laser produces a narrow, intense beam of light that can be pulsed at very rapid rates. When these pulses are sent along hair-thin glass fibers, the results are astonishing. Only so much information can be sent down a copper wire, but, says Johnson, "by using the nearly limitless capacity of optical fiber, a system can transmit as many as 600,000 phone conversations simultaneously."

And the future, Johnson believes, is wide open. The key to high capacity is the laser's pulse rate. "We have already achieved 350 billion pulses in a single second," he says. His contribution has been to produce extremely short pulses of light and pass them down fibers. As just one example of what that means, Johnson says that "one day people could have access to entire libraries directly from their home telephone/computer/television system."

THE POWER OF ENTERPRISE

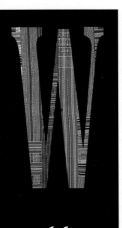

At left, a 1993 discussion show for teenagers typifies the black-oriented programming of Black Entertainment Television—a company founded and led by African American entrepreneur Robert L. Johnson.

hat is the difference between solvency and bankruptcy? In 1899, Charles Clinton Spaulding of the North Carolina Mutual and Provident Association (NCM) might have said it was $40. That was the value of the death claim on a life insurance policy sold by NCM, a black-owned and -managed insurance company based in Durham. Forty dollars was also more than the one-year-old firm had in its cash reserves. Spaulding and the firm's two founders got the money, however, and NCM stayed in business, proving to its customers that the company fulfilled its obligations—no matter what.

Cash flow was a familiar problem for many of the era's new black-owned businesses, propelled into existence by the pressing needs of the black community and scraping by on shoestring budgets. Despite the end of slavery in 1865, African Americans found themselves increasingly marginalized and segregated. In 1896, two years before NCM was founded, the United States Supreme Court had ruled that racial segregation in public facilities was constitutional. The separation of the races, buttressed by later rulings, reinforced the status of black Americans as second-class citizens isolated from the economic and social mainstream.

The men who started NCM did not like this reality. But Aaron McDuffie Moore, Durham's first black physician, and his partner, entrepreneur and former slave John Merrick, were steeped in the economic vision of Booker T. Washington, the era's most prominent black leader. While acknowledging the injustice and absurdity of segregation, Washington urged black men and women to work toward economic uplift and self-reliance for the race. NCM's founders followed that advice.

Hoping to preserve and pass on black assets and perhaps make a profit, Merrick, Moore, and five investors contributed $50 each to start NCM in 1898. Their money laid the financial foundation for the company. But Spaulding—Moore's 25-year-old nephew—was the architect of its success. Hired part-time as an agent in 1899 after managing a local black-owned store, Spaulding was promoted to general manager a year later. NCM's founders, busy in their other enterprises, left their one employee to serve as "manager, agent, clerk, and janitor," as Spaulding later recalled. He was more than up to the task, quickly demonstrating an aptitude for the insurance business.

During the next five decades, Spaulding built the company into a national economic power, steadily expanding NCM's sales territory as he trained a topnotch sales and clerical staff and added accident and accidental death insurance to the firm's product line. By 1920, NCM had gained access to 71 percent of the black American population by establishing offices in nine southern states and Washington, D.C.

In the early years of the Great Depression, the firm's annual income from premiums slid downward from $1.9 million in 1930 to $1.6 million in 1933. But in 1934, premium income rebounded 14 percent—and never flagged again. Spaulding later said that the Depression "taught us how to manage more efficiently." Perhaps it did. In 1939, NCM became the largest black-owned company in the United States, attracting so many other African American enterprises to Durham that the city's business district was called America's Black Wall Street. And Charles Spaulding never stopped selling. He became a pioneer of saturation advertising, making sure that pens, fans, and calendars bearing the firm's name were dispersed liberally by his agents until the NCM name was impossible to miss. When Spaulding died in 1952, after 53 years at the company, he left behind an insurance powerhouse. By the early 1990s, NCM had $220 million in assets and just under $9.5 billion of insurance in force.

The story of Charles Spaulding's rise from one-man work force to executive of a major insurance company is just one chapter in the epic of black American business history. This larger tale is not new, but in the past there were few financial griots to sing it. It is a story stretching from 18th-century New England, where black merchant captain Paul Cuffe owned and sailed his own fleet (*pages* 94-95), to Manhattan in the 1990s, where the late Reginald F. Lewis, succeeded in 1993 by his half brother Jean S. Fugett, Jr., presided over TLC Beatrice, a $1.6 billion international food processing and distribution company (*pages* 110-111). Its protagonists are men and women who not only had to calculate their financial resources before delving into business or seeking work, but also had to gauge their personal resistance to the inevitable forces of racism and economic discrimination both subtle and blatant. Paul Cuffe might not understand some of the businesses run by black Americans today, or the high-tech professions in which some make a living. But he would surely understand the commitment of each new generation, not only to make profits but also to help African Americans become economically self-reliant.

As Cuffe's own example suggests, the history of black Americans in business stretches back centuries, into the slavery era. From the 1600s to the end of the Civil War in 1865, most black Americans were enslaved and thus barred from nearly every economic opportunity. Only a few slaves, usually craftsmen, were hired out for pay and allowed to keep a fraction of their wages, enabling a small number to buy freedom for themselves and family members. Other black Americans escaped or gained freedom under an owner's will. But for most, liberty remained an unreachable goal.

Even for so-called free blacks—perhaps a tenth of the African American population—being free did not mean living freely. State laws in every region restricted the rights of free African Americans, often limiting their ability to earn a living. In North Carolina, free black peddlers had to have special licenses. In Maryland, former slaves had to get licenses to sell corn, wheat, or tobacco. Social customs also raised barriers. In the North, one black Rhode Islander wrote, "to drive carriage, to carry a market basket after the boss, and brush his boots, or saw wood and run errands, was as high as a colored man could rise to."

Throughout the country, most free African Americans labored in low-paying jobs

Soon after North Carolina Mutual's move in 1906 into its own newly constructed office building, the firm's early leaders sat for a side-by-side portrait (*above*) that includes, from left to right, cofounder and medical director Aaron Moore; field manager John Avery; cofounder and president John Merrick; his son Edward Merrick, who worked as an agent; and general manager Charles Clinton Spaulding. At right, Spaulding shows off the company's new finance department.

as carters, laundresses, stevedores, and the like. But in the 1840s those positions began to slip away as new immigrants willing to work for lower wages arrived. Many factory owners replaced skilled blacks with similarly trained Irish and German newcomers. "Whenever the interests of the white man and the Black come into collision in the United States, the Black man goes to the wall," observed J. F. W. Johnson, an English visitor, in the 1850s. "It is certain that wherever labor is scarce, there he is steadily employed, when it becomes plentiful, he is the first to be discharged."

Some black workers also became strikebreakers—a course of action endorsed by prominent abolitionist Frederick Douglass, who had tried vainly to secure technical training for blacks seeking to enter crafts and trades. Douglass also exhorted free blacks to acquire skills by whatever means they could. "We must become valuable to society in other departments of industry than those servile ones from which we are rapidly being excluded," he wrote in 1853. "We must show that we can do as well as be; to this end we must learn trades."

Rather than aiming at the white-dominated trades, however, most skilled blacks did work that whites did not want to do, often involving personal service. The business of catering, for example, was created by black Philadelphia entrepreneurs, who conceived the idea of providing food and hiring out waiters and chefs for special occasions. Barbering, another common black enterprise, offered the advantages of a low start-up cost and steady demand. Former Mississippi slave William Johnson, freed in 1820, earned a modest fortune operating barbershops in Natchez, Mississippi, in the 1830s and 1840s. To the delight of modern-day historians, Johnson was a meticulous recordkeeper. He kept track of receipts, expenditures, and small loans in

more than 2,000 pages of business journals and diaries. These pages also document the details of his business and personal life, from his purchase of a large farm to the political and social doings of Natchez.

Johnson, who had learned to barber from his brother-in-law, started his own barbering business in Port Gibson, Mississippi, in the late 1820s. In 1830, he took his profits of $1,094.50 and moved to the city of Natchez, where in time he accumulated three barbershops, a public bathhouse, investments in local rental properties—and several slaves. Although, even in his time, many wealthy free blacks in the North joined with the abolitionist cause, Johnson was among a handful of slaveholding black southerners.

Inevitably, Johnson's journals depict the racial climate of mid-19th-century Mississippi—an atmosphere that made his business success remarkable. In 1841, he recorded de-

tails of what he called the Inquisition, in which local whites, terrified by the possibility of slave unrest, began to question the right of any free black person to be free, or to live in Mississippi. "Poor Andrew Leeper was, I understand, ordered off to day, and so was Dembo and Maryan Gibson They are as far as I Know inocent and Harmless People And Have never done a Crime," he wrote of some free blacks who were expelled from the state. "Oh what a Country we Live in." Johnson himself was wealthy enough to escape the Inquisition. When he died in 1851, shot by an adversary in a lawsuit, the barber of Natchez left an estate worth about $25,000—a substantial sum at that time.

While Johnson was building up his businesses in Natchez, two free blacks in Philadelphia were setting an even faster pace. Hairdresser Joseph Cassey built a $75,000 estate by turning out wigs and lending money, while sailmaker James Forten made a fortune in the maritime industry, in which blacks were represented at every level (*pages* 90-95). Lumber magnate and former slave Stephen Smith, the business partner of black abolitionist William Whipper, also built up a vast estate in Pennsylvania. In 1849 his assets were valued at more than $100,000. They included 2.25 million board feet of lumber, 22 railway freight cars, and 52 brick houses.

New Orleans, with its somewhat more fluid Latin-influenced racial culture, produced the largest number of wealthy black antebellum entrepreneurs, an assortment of slave-owning traders, planters, and landlords. Not all were men. In the 1840s, New Orleans merchant Cecee McCarty used her 32 slaves to sell imported dry goods throughout Louisiana, accumulating a fortune of $155,000.

As the slavery issue dominated national politics in the 1850s, thousands of free black Americans were dealing in real estate, construction, and mining, and making everything from pickles to fine furniture. New York City tax records before 1855 include 21 black businessmen who made more than $100,000 a year. Despite such exceptions, however, economic opportunities remained risky and rare, even for those who were not chattel slaves. It would take the Civil War to end slavery and to begin to improve economic prospects for blacks in the United States.

The war brought physical freedom for four and a half million slaves, most of whom were forced into economic peonage as sharecroppers. Emancipation also worked other transformations. For many of the black Civil War veterans now pouring into the work force, military life had brought with it the first experience of a regular paycheck—however small—as well as such useful economic skills as reading and writing. Still, the postwar world was hardly a welcoming one. For black workers, it was, for the most part, a time of implacable union hostility. Before the war, no unions had accepted blacks. Now, only a few white unionists sought black cooperation, generally with the goal of stopping blacks from serving as strikebreakers.

Conditions after the war drove some African American workers to form their own unions. In the fall of 1865, white workers in Baltimore, with the support of local police, drove black caulkers and longshoremen away from work along the docks. Isaac Myers, a 30-year-old black dock supervisor, responded by setting up the Colored

"I am always ready for Anything," wrote 19th-century barber William Johnson (*above*), who enjoyed alligator hunting, horse racing, toy boats—and keeping a diary.

The tale of an 1836 fistfight between a Mr. Bledsoe and a Mr. Hewit enlivens a page from Johnson's diaries, which offer a rare glimpse of the business and social life of the Mississippi of his day. A rough sketch illustrates the subsequent chase, in which Bledsoe introduced a pistol into the fray.

Caulkers' Trade Union Society of Baltimore so that blacks could pool their savings to buy their own shipyard and railway. Within a year, stock in the new venture was issued, finding ready buyers in the black community, including Frederick Douglass. That February the proceeds went toward a six-year mortgage on a shipyard and railway. By fall the Chesapeake Marine Railway and Dry Dock Company employed 300 blacks for an average wage of three dollars a day. It would later add white mechanics to its work force as well.

In 1869, Myers spoke by invitation at the annual convention of the historically white National Labor Union. "I speak to-day for the colored men of the whole country," he told the convention, "from the lakes to the Gulf—from the Atlantic to the Pacific—from every hill-top, valley and plain throughout our vast domain, when I tell you that all they ask for themselves is a fair chance; that you and they may make one steady and strong pull until the laboring man of this country shall receive such pay for time made as will secure them a comfortable living for their families, educate their children and leave a dollar for a rainy day and old age." But if black workers continued to be barred from unionized jobs, Myers said, American citizenship for blacks would be "a complete failure." He added, "If citizenship means anything at all, it means the freedom of labor, as broad and as universal as the freedom of the ballot." It was a stirring appeal, interrupted often by applause. But in the end, the convention rejected integration, instead urging blacks to form separate affiliated unions. The black delegates were stunned: They were not looking for "parlor sociabilities," one of them observed, "but for the rights of mankind."

Under Myers's leadership, the Chesapeake company went on to complete the payment on its mortgage in 1871. The Baltimore caulkers' success had already inspired black dockworkers in Mobile, Charleston, and Savannah to unionize as well. Two years after the company paid off its note, however, there was a nationwide financial panic. Revenues dropped, and the shipyard never fully recovered, closing in 1883.

The Chesapeake company had suffered from two key weaknesses—a lack of financial experience by its employee-owners and an equally fatal lack of local black financiers. In other cities, the first black-owned banks were beginning to bridge both gaps. For depositors, these banks took the place of the failed Freedmen's Savings and Trust Company, a bank set up for blacks by the federal government at the end of the Civil War. Freedmen's had been a great success at first. By 1872, more than 70,000 African American depositors had demonstrated their thrift by placing a total of $3.7 million in the bank's 34 branches. Two years later, deposits peaked at $55 million. But the bank, although organized by the federal government, did not have the government's backing. In 1874, Freedmen's collapsed, a victim of the financial panic of 1873, inexperienced management, and a number of irregular loans to white businessmen. Its depositors were left penniless. "Of all disgraceful swindles perpetrated on a struggling people," scholar and activist W. E. B. Du Bois later wrote, "the Freedmen's Bank was among the worst, and the Negro did well not to wait for justice, but went to banking himself as soon as his ignorance and poverty allowed."

In fact, there was nothing mysterious about banking to the black banking pioneers. Since the 1700s, benevolent societies of free blacks had pooled funds for mutual aid. After the Civil War, many of these societies evolved into full-fledged banks. Between 1888 and 1934, more than 130 black-operated banks were organized, often with names reflecting their heritage. In 1903, for example, Maggie Lena Walker led the Independent Order of Saint Luke in forming the Saint Luke Penny Savings Bank of Richmond, becoming the first American woman to found a bank (*pages 96-97*).

Even as these banks took over the financial concerns once handled by the mutual aid societies, new, black-owned insurance companies—including Durham's North Carolina Mutual—began replacing the societies in other ways. Starting with small life insurance policies designed to cover the burial costs once guaranteed by the mutual aid groups, the insurance firms grew alongside the black banks. Although some of these institutions are still in business, many did not last long, encountering the same problems that most black firms endured at the turn of the century. Chief among them: limited capital and the iniquitous segregation laws. Most black businesses were small, owner-operated, single-shop concerns: grocery stores, restaurants, bakeries, funeral parlors, barbershops, and the like. In these small enterprises, however, educator Booker T. Washington saw the beginnings of economic self-determination.

In 1900 Washington founded the National Negro Business League, an association that offered practical advice and support to black businesspersons. The league also kept track of the growth of black business, reporting in 1914 that the number of African American firms had doubled, from 20,000 to 40,000, since the year 1900. During that period, thousands paid the league's two-dollar membership fee and about 1,200 attended its national conventions each year.

The conventions were meant to showcase black achievers, but on at least one occasion a highly successful merchant had trouble getting heard. Sarah Breedlove McWilliams Walker, a wealthy hair-care entrepreneur known professionally as Madame C. J. Walker, had met Booker T. Washington and even visited his Tuskegee Institute. Yet at the 1912 convention she found herself repeatedly ignored by the chair.

Hair-care entrepreneur Madame C. J. Walker poses with Booker T. Washington (*holding hat*) and other black dignitaries at the 1913 dedication of an Indianapolis YMCA. Walker contributed $1,000 to the project, more than any other African American benefactor.

Finally, on the third morning of the gathering, Walker strode to the podium. "Surely you are not going to shut the door in my face," she exclaimed. "I am a woman who came from the cotton fields of the South. I was promoted from there to the washtub," she said ironically. "Then I was promoted to the cook kitchen, and from there I promoted myself into the business of manufacturing hair goods and preparations. I have built my own factory on my own ground." Her speech was unauthorized—apparently, Washington had not considered hair preparations worthy of notice—but, with its dramatic autobiographical style, it was the hit of the meeting. A year later, at the league's insistence, she was the keynote speaker.

The remarks that had caused such a stir only hinted at Walker's extraordinary achievement. Born in Delta, Louisiana, in 1867, she was a wife and mother at 17 and a widow at 20. To provide a better life—including college—for her daughter Lelia, she washed clothes for $1.50 a week for 17 years. Gradually her hair began to thin, and she experimented with various hair-thickening remedies. In 1905 she moved to Denver, where she started selling her hair treatment. A few months later, she married Charles Joseph Walker. Her husband felt that the hair product should only be sold locally. But

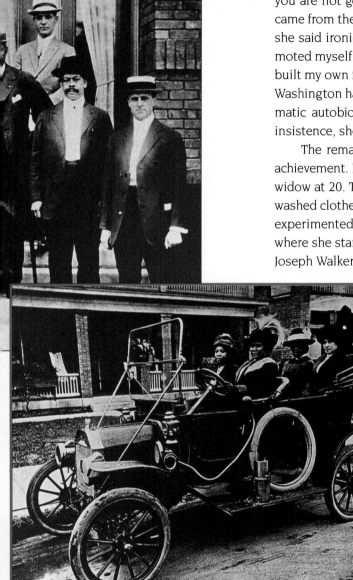

Stylishly attired, Madame Walker takes the wheel of a Model T Ford. Her niece Anjetta Breedlove sits beside her, while her secretary, Lucy Flint, is directly behind the driver's seat. Alice Kelly, the Walker factory forewoman, shares the backseat with Flint.

instead, adding the Parisian-flavored prefix "Madame" to her married name, she went on the road, securing order after order on lengthy sales trips. In 1910 Madame C. J. Walker and her husband moved to Indianapolis, a transportation hub that was also the nation's largest inland manufacturing city. Two years later, they divorced in a dispute over how to manage the company.

Within a decade, Madame Walker's business was making half a million dollars a year in gross revenues, her factory payroll came to $200,000 a year, and she had 2,000 salespersons, known as agents. The job of agent offered black women a rare escape from the drudgery that Walker had once endured. "I have made it possible for many colored women to abandon the washtub for a more pleasant and profitable occupation," Walker proudly said.

Some blacks condemned her for promoting hair straightening, an imitation, they believed, of white standards of beauty. But Walker vehemently denied the charge. "I have always held myself out as a hair culturist," she said. "I grow hair." Certainly, black women welcomed her various products, buying enough to make her the first self-made female millionaire in United States history.

In 1916 Walker moved to Harlem, where she became well known as a philanthropist who supported the civil rights causes of the day, most notably the NAACP antilynching campaign. She also commissioned Villa Lewaro, a Hudson River mansion designed by black architect Vertner Tandy that opened in August 1918 with a gathering of black notables. Madame C. J. Walker died there of hypertension less than a year later, leaving the business to her daughter, who had changed her name to A'Lelia, and thousands of dollars to black schools, civic organizations, and various in-

dividuals. Her last words were said to have been "I must get better to help my race."

Walker's story was extraordinary, and yet in one way it was entirely typical of her era. She was one of more than two and a half million black Americans who left the South between the 1880s and the 1930s in what came to be called the Great Migration. W. E. B. Du Bois, who edited the NAACP publication the *Crisis*, reported that the migrants cited low wages, poor schools, fear of lynching, and bad treatment. For many, southern racism was the primary reason to move. As one Texas man, seeking a position in the North in 1917, wrote, "I am 30 years old and have Good Experence in Freight Handler and Can fill Position from Truck to Agt. would like Chicago or Philadelphia But I dont Care where so long as I Go where a man is a man."

Particular events also swelled the migration. In 1915 and 1916, widespread flooding in the Deep South destroyed much of the cotton crop, driving thousands more north and west. During World War I, labor shortages led to southern blacks being recruited in massive numbers for jobs up north. After the war, restrictions on foreign immigration prolonged the shortage, and recruiters enticed blacks north with free railroad passes. When boll weevils damaged the 1923 cotton crop, still more migrants went north. For those who remained undecided, black newspapers such as the *Chicago Defender* and the *Pittsburgh Courier* kept up a barrage of editorials telling southern readers why and how to leave.

New York, Chicago, Philadelphia, Cleveland, Detroit, and Saint Louis attracted most of the migrants, who found work in industries such as steel, meat packing, and automobile and truck production. During the war years, the new workers faced appalling living conditions, eased somewhat by social organizations such as the National Urban League (*right*) at war's end. As in the past, only a very few unions were open to black workers: The International Longshoremen's Association included blacks, and black miners had helped found the United Mine Workers of America. Black ties to both occupations dated from many decades before the Civil War.

The 1942 painting at left, captioned "In every town Negroes were leaving by the hundreds to go North to enter into Northern industry," is one of 60 in a series by black artist Jacob Lawrence that depict the Great Migration of southern black Americans.

THE URBAN LEAGUE

Though some of the blacks moving north in the early 1900s were professionals and others had jobs waiting, the majority were unskilled rural laborers. Unprepared for city living, they knew only a fierce desire to "work in some place where I can elevate my self & my family," as one man wrote. Upon arrival, the migrants faced a confusing urban landscape, slum housing like the tenement above, and the North's own racial barriers to employment. To help the migrants find their feet, some northern blacks and whites came together in 1911 to form the National League on Urban Conditions Among Negroes—later the National Urban League (NUL)—from three existing social-work organizations. Black sociologist George Edmund Haynes became the league's first executive director. The NUL national office and its local affiliates helped newcomers find housing, warned them of urban dangers, and taught work skills and city behavior, including urban homemaking and sanitation. The league also trained black social workers and published studies to help educate whites about African American issues. Most important, it found the new migrants jobs—which often meant persuading white employers to hire black workers for the first time. Today the NUL offers a greater range of services, but its original self-help motto endures: Not Alms, but Opportunity.

The American Federation of Labor (AFL), founded in 1886, advocated organizing workers "without regard to creed, color, sex, nationality, or politics." But for the most part American unions remained as strictly segregated as any Mississippi Delta town. Samuel Gompers, the labor pioneer who became the first AFL president, encouraged AFL-affiliated unions to bar or segregate blacks, whom he considered not potential allies against the company owners but a threat to white jobs. In 1910, Gompers openly declared that black people could not think like whites and were unfit for the AFL.

Just a year after the Gompers statement, 22-year-old Asa Philip Randolph, the son of a black Florida minister, joined the Great Migration by moving to New York City, swayed, as he later recalled, by "a feeling that there was more freedom here." In the city, Randolph worked at odd jobs and took classes at New York's City College. The jobs showed him how black laborers were abused and despised; the classes taught him public speaking, economics, and socialism. Randolph had found his life's task: to better the conditions and treatment of black workers.

Activism takes time and money. Randolph owed both to his wife Lucille Green, whom he married in 1914. One of the first graduates of Madame C. J. Walker's cosmetology school and a member of Walker's own social circle in Harlem, Green's sizable income allowed Randolph to pursue his interests. Green helped underwrite Randolph's magazine the *Messenger*, a radical publication that opposed American involvement in World War I. The Justice Department called it "the most able and the most dangerous of all the Negro publications."

Buddy, as Randolph called his wife (she had the same nickname for him), also supported her husband as he formed a series of labor and political organizations between 1917 and 1923, all of which were short-lived. For all practical purposes, Randolph seemed to be a failure. Then, in 1925, he was approached by railroad sleeping-car porters working for the Pullman Palace Car Company, which supplied and operated railroad sleeping cars. The porters needed him—an outsider, largely immune from the company's pressure tactics—to organize a union.

Black men had worked as porters since just after the Civil War; a persistent story has it that George Pullman created the job with former slaves in mind. By the 1920s, fifteen thousand held what was still, appallingly, the best job many black college graduates could find, and the Pullman Company was the largest private employer of black workers in the country. The work was tough and paid poorly; newcomers earned just $67 a month and 15-year

veterans received a paltry $94.50. The pay was so low that porters went to sometimes humiliating lengths to earn gratuities. One recalled that "passengers used to have the porters doing the buck and wing, cutting up on the platform, and so forth. The porters would do it for the extra tip." The company paid nothing for the hours porters worked to prepare a train for service or for runs with no passengers. Moreover, each porter had to deduct the cost of his uniform and meals.

The ground seemed fertile for a union organizer, yet Randolph hesitated for two months, during which he wrote articles for the *Messenger* on the problems of the porters. Finally he agreed to take on their cause. For Randolph, a mobile, national work force like the porters offered special advantages. The Pullman porter, he later said, "seems to be made to order to carry the gospel of unionism in the colored world. His home is everywhere."

With the porters behind him, Randolph fought and won representation rights in 1935—although the victory took countless rounds of litigation and strike threats. As part of the struggle, the Brotherhood of Sleeping Car Porters became an AFL affiliate in 1928. It also became a touchstone for black workers, demonstrating their ability to set an economic course without white cooperation. Randolph once wrote that the Brotherhood's strength lay in the fact it was "of Negroes by Negroes for Negroes."

But the segregated status of other American unions barred black workers from full participation in the labor movement. In 1934, Randolph got the AFL to agree to study racial desegregation; in 1935, it voted the idea down. The same year marked the formation of the Congress of Industrial Organizations (CIO), an association built around the already-integrated United Mine Workers. Although courted by the CIO, Randolph kept the Brotherhood in the segregated AFL. "My fight, the fight to organize Negro workers, is in the AFL. I must stay here and carry on that fight," he said.

Segregation was still the norm in American industry a few years later, as businesses readied themselves for the coming war. By 1940 American firms were experiencing a defense-related bonanza, but the nation's five million black workers were effectively shut out. Some defense plants had signs welcoming all applicants "except Germans, Italians and Negroes." Here again, Randolph spoke for black labor, calling

Barred from segregated unions, African American laborers often served as strikebreakers. Above, a line of millinery workers marches into a Chicago packing plant during a 1904 strike.

In the turn-of-the-century scene below, a respectful Pullman porter carries a woman's luggage. Black porters were instructed not to touch female passengers while helping them to board or disembark, unless they were specifically asked for assistance.

for black workers to march on the capital if President Roosevelt did not issue an executive order banning racial discrimination in war industries.

The vision of angry black laborers filling the streets of Washington, D.C., horrified the administration. A delegation that included First Lady Eleanor Roosevelt met with Randolph to put an end to the march. Eleanor Roosevelt warned Randolph there could be violence against the protesters, he later recalled. "I replied there would be no violence unless her husband ordered the police to crack black heads," he recounted. "I told her I was sorry, but the march would not be called off unless the President issued an executive order banning discrimination in the defense industry."

Next came a meeting between black leaders and President Roosevelt, who tried to spend the allotted time on small talk. Randolph politely interrupted, asking him again for the executive order. "If I issue an executive order for you, then there'll be no end to other groups coming in here and asking me to issue executive orders for them, too," Randolph later quoted Roosevelt as saying. "In any event, I couldn't do anything unless you called off this march of yours." But Randolph refused—and Roosevelt agreed to the executive order after all, signing it on June 25, 1941, six days before the black workers were expected to march. Roosevelt also established the Fair Employment Practices Committee (FEPC) to investigate and correct cases of discrimination. In return, Randolph canceled the threatened protest.

Roosevelt's decision, combined with the wartime manpower shortage, had a slow but seemingly irresistible effect. In March 1942, the new FEPC reported that black workers held less than 3 percent of defense jobs. Two years later, that percentage had almost tripled. Meanwhile, the federal government opened its doors as well. By 1944 nearly 300,000 federal government workers, or roughly 12 percent, were black.

Randolph and other black leaders kept up the pressure on the White House in the postwar years, with some results. Between 1946 and 1951, President Harry S Truman convened several panels that called for an end to legalized racial bias. In 1948, he signed an executive order requiring the federal government to begin hiring on a fair employment basis. He also ordered the armed forces to provide equal treatment and opportunities regardless of race, a mandate that led to desegregation of the military.

For black Americans who didn't collect a government paycheck, prospects were mixed at best. Some black Americans did share in America's postwar prosperity, as a trickle moved into professional, managerial, clerical, and sales jobs, expanding the ranks of the black middle class. But the nation's labor unions were still split on the issue of letting black workers into the higher paid, unionized part of the labor force. The gap did not close until 1955, when the AFL merged with the CIO. The resulting desegregated organization chose Asa Philip Randolph as one of its vice presidents.

Black-owned businesses also continued their struggle for survival in the 1940s and 1950s, remaining for the most part small and underfunded. One of the few exceptions—and a remarkable one at that—was the Johnson Publishing Company. Black Americans had been in the publishing industry since the early 19th century. But John H. Johnson's success is the greatest of the publishing sagas. In 1918, the founder of what would become the world's largest black-owned publishing company was born into poverty in Arkansas City, Arkansas, the only son of a sawmill laborer and a do-

Florida-born Asa Philip Randolph, the nation's foremost African American union leader by the time this photograph was taken in 1935, had originally dreamed of becoming an actor when he came to New York City in 1911.

mestic worker. When he was 15, he and his mother moved to Chicago, where he graduated from high school, took courses at the University of Chicago and Northwestern University, and found employment at the black-owned Supreme Liberty Life Insurance Company. At one point the company president asked Johnson to summarize articles from the black press. Johnson soon realized that no single source brought together articles and information of interest to black Americans. He conceived and nurtured the idea of a *Reader's Digest*-style magazine for blacks.

But first he had to get a lender to believe in the idea too. No one did. Every potential investor—black or white—told Johnson that blacks would not be interested in such a magazine. But Johnson stuck by his dream, eventually borrowing $500 by using his mother's furniture as collateral. Supreme Life gave Johnson access to the company's mailing list of 20,000 policyholders, and he used the loan money to send out a description of the planned magazine to every one of them.

The response was, by mail-order standards, phenomenal. By October 1942, three thousand people—15 percent of those who had received the mailing—had sent in two-dollar subscriptions to *Negro Digest, A Magazine of Negro Comment,* eager to believe in Johnson's promise of a journal that recorded black accomplishments. The first issues of the magazine contained published articles selected by Johnson that he obtained permission to reproduce. By mid-1943, Johnson was selling more than 50,000 copies a month. As he later wrote, he had discovered "a black gold mine."

It was only the first in a series of rich strikes. In 1945 Johnson began publishing a second magazine, *Ebony*, which proved to be even more successful than *Negro Digest*. Inspired by the picture magazines of the day, *Ebony* used photographs and original reporting to present, as Johnson put it, "black life and black achievements." *Ebony* and *Negro Digest* were joined six years later by a weekly newsmagazine entitled *Jet*. The publication EM (for "*Ebony* Man") followed in 1985.

Many of the black Americans profiled in Johnson's magazines were part of a growing black middle class. The stepped-up industrial production during and after World War II had triggered yet another migration from the South and helped increase the average black household income from a prewar level of $384 to $1,070 in the mid-1950s. Black wage earners could even support New York City's first black securities brokerage house, Special Markets, run by a black businessman, Philip M. Jenkins. The accouterments of black middle-class life were also present in the South, though only visible through segregation's veil. This was particularly true in Atlanta, Georgia, home to a growing industrial base and several black colleges and universities.

Black economic progress still had far to go, however. In corporate America, tokenism rather than broad inclusion was the hallmark of the period. The AFL-CIO merger may have ended top-level labor endorsement of segregation, but many union locals still excluded black workers. Most of the federal jobs offered to blacks paid less than $5,000 a year in 1962. And the early milestones of the civil rights movement—the school desegregation victory in *Brown v. the Board of Education of Topeka, Kansas,* and

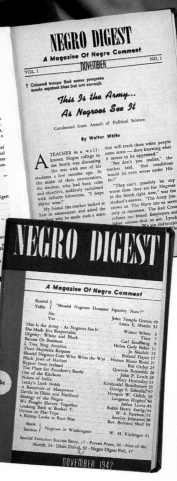

Johnson Publishing patriarch John H. Johnson, shown with his daughter and handpicked successor, Linda, in 1983, built a multimillion-dollar empire starting with his first magazine, *Negro Digest* (*left*), in 1942. In addition to book and magazine publishing, the company is now also involved in cosmetics and television production.

the Montgomery, Alabama, bus boycott that propelled Martin Luther King, Jr., into the nation's consciousness—left the economic status of black Americans essentially unchanged. But as the cause of civil rights gained momentum, its goals broadened. On August 28, 1963, the forces of the movement gathered for a massive March on Washington, led by 74-year-old A. Philip Randolph. Their slogan—suggesting both economic and political goals—was Jobs and Freedom.

Influenced by the march, and shaken by the assassination three months later of President John F. Kennedy, Congress passed the Civil Rights Act of 1964, outlawing most forms of segregation in public facilities, and established the Equal Employment Opportunity Commission to investigate complaints of discrimination in private companies. Many African Americans thought economic as well as social equality was on the horizon. They were wrong. Although some blacks became visible in prominent jobs that had been previously denied to African Americans, black unemployment remained double that of white throughout the 1960s, with many industrial jobs still off-limits. Unemployment was most visible in the stagnant inner cities, where frustration at the lack of change ran high. Beginning in 1964, a devastating series of urban riots sounded a clear alarm. In one five-day outbreak in August 1965 in the Watts section of Los Angeles, 34 people died, 28 of them black. A presidential commission suggested that the cure for urban unrest was the creation of new businesses and jobs.

Partly in response, the federal government turned to the Small Business Administration (SBA)—an agency established in 1953 to help small businesses find the capital they needed. In 1968 the SBA created the 8(a) program, under which minority-owned companies were guaranteed a percentage of government contracts outside the competitive-bidding process. The selected firms also acquired training in how to compete after leaving the program. In the next 24 years, more than 9,400 companies went through 8(a); 57 percent were black owned. President Richard M. Nixon continued the strategy of encouraging black capitalism by creating the Office of Minority Business Enterprise in 1969 to coordinate federal efforts on the issue.

Some individual black achievers were also recruited under public and private initiatives referred to as affirmative action programs, which were meant to foster the hiring of minority workers. In the late 1960s and early 1970s, federal and state courts ruled that municipalities and unions with a record of discriminatory hiring and promotion had to do more than simply abolish those practices. To remedy the effects of past actions, they were ordered to institute preferential hiring procedures—including numerical goals and timetables—for minorities and women. Many private corporations also created their own affirmative action programs. Some of the black employees they hired formed the first wave of black corporate senior executives.

Not all the changes were taking place inside the system. In 1972 civil rights activist Jesse Jackson formed Operation PUSH (an acronym for People United to Save Humanity; "Save" was later changed to "Serve"), an organization that effectively used threats of black consumer boycotts to force American business to open its doors to black hiring. "We've been excluded from participation in the productive economy, but exploited for our consumption of goods and services by the major companies in the nation," Jackson declared. "Now we're saying, 'Cut us in, or we'll cut you out of our

budgets.' " Coca-Cola, Anheuser-Busch Company, Southland Corporation (owner of the 7-Eleven convenience-store franchise), and Burger King were among those that signed agreements with Jackson to hire more minority vendors and executives.

Between 1972 and 1982, the number of African American managers rose 83 percent. Considering how few black managers there had been to start with, however, the actual increase was paltry; the number of black executives at all levels was still only a relatively tiny 445,000. Moreover, in later years many of those executives found themselves hitting a so-called glass ceiling, beyond which they could not be promoted.

Some frustrated black managers reacted by becoming entrepreneurs, often using their experience to supply goods and services to their previous employers. Their firms were part of an explosion of black-owned companies, which by the mid-1980s numbered in the hundreds of thousands. As in the past, many were mom-and-pop affairs without paid employees. And although there were some giant black companies, the vast majority—99.5 percent according to the Census Bureau—earned less than a million dollars a year.

But black businesses of all sizes became numerous enough to spawn a successful African American business magazine, *Black Enterprise*, in 1971. In June 1973, the magazine published the first *Black Enterprise* 100, a list of the nation's 100 largest black-owned industrial and service firms. The first BE 100 companies had total revenues of $473 million. Two decades later, *Black Enterprise* had two lists, one for automobile dealerships and the other for all other industrial and service companies. The combined revenue of the 200 companies was $7.9 billion.

That phenomenal growth reflected the economic expansion of the 1980s—and yet the decade had been an odd one for black businessmen and businesswomen. On the one hand, the black baby boomers born just after World War II included America's largest and best-educated group of black professionals to date, many of whom achieved high-ranking positions previously unimagined. For example, during the 1980s, Harvard Law graduate Kenneth Chenault was made president of the American Express charge-card group, assuming responsibility for the success of one of the major American retail cards. By the end of the decade, the federal Bureau of Labor Statistics reported that 5.1 percent of all corporate managers were black, about three-fifths of them men. These executives had top responsibility, served on corporate boards, and often held advanced degrees. Also during the 1980s, many black firms came of age financially, professionally, and technologically, as the first generation of businesses unaffected by Jim Crow laws was actually helped by the federal government rather than hindered.

But the decade also witnessed a corporate and federal backlash against minority advancement. As African American unemployment remained twice that of whites, the administration of President Ronald Reagan dramatically reduced the budgets for the Minority Business Development Agency, as the Office of Minority Business Enterprise is now called, and for the 8(a) program at the Small Business Administration. Outside the federal government, the idea of affirmative action also came under attack. A series of legal challenges to various racial remedies culminated in a 1989

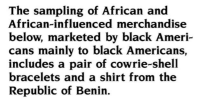

The sampling of African and African-influenced merchandise below, marketed by black Americans mainly to black Americans, includes a pair of cowrie-shell bracelets and a shirt from the Republic of Benin.

Supreme Court decision in *City of Richmond v. J. A. Croson*. The ruling, which was accompanied by a blistering dissent from African American justice Thurgood Marshall, found that set-aside programs based upon an unproven history of bias were unconstitutional. As a result, many state and local affirmative action programs were abolished. By the early 1990s, however, several cities had commissioned studies that legally established that discrimination had occurred in the past. This enabled them to continue set-aside and other programs.

In any event, black businessmen continued to create their own opportunities. In 1991, BET Holdings, the parent company of Black Entertainment Television, became the first black-owned company traded on the New York Stock Exchange. Company founder Robert L. Johnson, a former National Cable Television Association executive, had seen the market for a black-oriented cable network early on. He began Black Entertainment Television with a $15,000 personal loan in 1979. The next year, the BET cable network was launched, filling the hours with black college football games and music videos. The network soon proved popular—and profitable. BET Holdings expanded to include *Emerge* and YSB magazines, but the network itself remained the company flagship. By 1991, when BET Holdings went public, Black Entertainment Television was watched by 31.6 million cable television subscribers and earning $50 million in annual revenues. By far the largest black-owned company of the 1990s, however, was TLC Beatrice International Holdings, a multinational food distributor purchased in a leveraged buyout by Reginald F. Lewis in 1987. The next year, TLC Beatrice became the first company in four years to displace Johnson Publishing from the top of the *Black Enterprise* 100.

The BE 100 does not include insurance firms, but the magazine offers companion lists that do. As the 1990s began, the top black-owned company on the BE insurance chart remained none other than North Carolina Mutual. Like other black insurance firms, the company was hurt by high unemployment among its clients, by aging customers, and by competition from larger firms. But the NCM legacy lives on in Durham, not only in the parent company but at NCM Capital Management Group. Maceo K. Sloan, the NCM Capital president and chief operating officer, is the great-grandnephew of NCM founder Aaron Moore and the son of one of NCM's former chief operating officers. After working at NCM for several years, Sloan helped found NCM Capital Management in 1986, aided by his former NCM boss, Cicero Green.

At first, Sloan encountered considerable sales resistance from some companies, who appeared reluctant to entrust their portfolios to the guidance of black investment analysts. "That is the attitude we were up against," he later recalled. " 'Black folks are OK in their place, and money management is not their place.' " But a steady performance in the market slowly changed that perception; by 1993, NCM Capital Management was investing more than $1.5 billion for more than 50 public and private institutions. For many at NCM Capital, however, Durham and the NCM tradition is not measured only by the bottom line. "In my mind, I was coming back to work for North Carolina Mutual," said research analyst Isaac Green, who took a lower salary to join NCM Capital Management in 1988. "As we used to say, we were coming back to play for the home team."

THE CALL OF THE SEA

It was one of the largest funerals Philadelphia had ever seen. In February 1842, more than 3,000 residents, both black and white, gathered to mark the passing of 76-year-old black sailmaker and abolitionist James Forten. An avid patriot, Forten had served as a teenage gunpowder boy aboard a Revolutionary War privateer; during the War of 1812, he helped organize 2,500 black Philadelphians to defend the city in case of invasion. Later, his attention turned to the abolition of slavery. And all the time, Forten was amassing a fortune of more than $100,000 manufacturing canvas sails. Like thousands of other African Americans, James Forten made his living from the sea.

As Forten would have been among the first to point out, many black Americans had long toiled in the maritime business without getting a cent. Slaves had worked at sea since the 1600s, when New England colonists imported them for service in the region's growing fleets of fishing, whaling, and trading ships. By the 1700s, slaves in the South were harvesting oysters, crabs, and fish from local waterways and operating craft along coastal waterways. Throughout the period before emancipation, enslaved African Americans—including a young Frederick Douglass—were employed onshore to build and repair ships and carry cargo on the docks. Some slaves skilled in the maritime arts were also hired out or sold for work at sea.

Slavery and seafaring were a volatile mix, however. Maritime slaves developed a knowledge of geography, language, customs, and boat handling that equipped them for escape attempts. Over the years, thousands of enslaved watermen, taking advantage of the freedom of movement their jobs afforded, stole boats or stowed away on ships bound for free lands. In the ports, shipmasters anxious for able-bodied crewmen provided one of the few safe havens for runaway slaves.

Not surprisingly, slave owners hated the unsettling influence of free black mariners, who seemed to bring with them a whiff of the liberty of the open sea. In 1822, former sailor Denmark Vesey planned a slave revolt in Charleston, South Carolina, in which thousands of black men and women were to seize and burn the city, then escape by ship to Vesey's homeland in the West Indies. The plot was discovered, however, and Vesey and 34 others were hanged. South Carolina then passed a law requiring that all free black sailors and free black passengers be detained while their vessels were in port. Violators risked being sold into slavery. Five other southern states adopted similar codes. Free black sailors who entered slave ports also faced the danger of illegal enslavement, and in a few instances, captains sold their own crewmen into servitude.

For all its dangers, however,

At age 20 James Forten (*left*) was foreman of a Philadelphia sailmaking concern; at 32, he owned it. His thriving firm employed some 40 workers, both black and white, and earned him a fortune, much of which he devoted to the abolitionist cause.

the sea offered free black Americans economic opportunities lacking onshore. As a body of black sailors informed the Massachusetts legislature in 1788, the maritime industry was one field in which "thay might get a hanceum livehud for themselves and theres." Black men, as a result, were far likelier than their white counterparts to go to sea. Between 1800 and 1820, for example, free blacks made up about 5 percent of the population in and around the major port of Philadelphia—but 17 to 22 percent of Philadelphia's maritime workers. Black mariners were so numerous that in 1839 a "colored sailors" boardinghouse was established in New York City.

By far the greatest number of blacks in the American maritime industry worked in and around the Chesapeake Bay, many on oyster boats. As oyster harvesting spread, black communities centered on the trade sprang up from the Georgia coast to as far north as Staten Island. In the South, both slaves and free blacks also worked as coastal pilots, supplying transportation, communication, and trade.

In the supposedly more enlightened free North, however, blacks could almost never find work as pilots or captains. An escaped slave named George Henry, who had captained a Virginia schooner for years, later wrote: "I found prejudice so great in the North that I was forced to come down from my high position as captain, and take my whitewash brush and wheelbarrow and get my living in that way."

One of the few paths to professional advancement was through the dirty, dangerous business of whaling. Black sailors—including patriot and hero Crispus Attucks—often shipped aboard New England whalers, serving not only as deck hands but in the trusted position of harpooner or as first or second mates. Paul Cuffe (*pages* 94-95) was among a handful of blacks who sailed as whaling captains. In Nantucket alone, whose ships represented 40 percent of the nation's whaling fleet by 1820, about a third of the 1,500 whalemen were black.

Whaling enabled a few extremely profitable black busi-

In an image from 1872, African American men working on a Chesapeake Bay oyster boat pull oysters off the bottom with large iron rakes known as tongs.

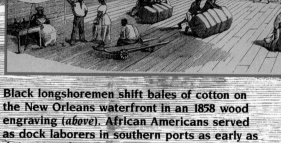

Black longshoremen shift bales of cotton on the New Orleans waterfront in an 1858 wood engraving (*above*). African Americans served as dock laborers in southern ports as early as the 1700s; after the Civil War, some found work in northern harbors as well.

nesses to spring up onshore. In 1848 Lewis Temple, a black American who operated a whale-craft shop in the whaling center of New Bedford, Massachusetts, developed the toggle harpoon—a device that has been called the most important invention in the history of whaling. Older harpoons were arrowhead-shaped and often slipped out of place, allowing the whale to escape. Temple's harpoons came instead with a movable head, or barb. The barb was held parallel to the shaft by a matchstick-size wooden pin; as the whale pulled away, the pin snapped and the barb toggled at a right angle until it anchored firmly.

Another African American operating successfully in New Bedford was John Mashow, who was the town's second-largest builder of whaling ships. Mashow, born in South Carolina in 1805, was the son of a slave woman and a white planter. Upon the death of his owner, and father, in 1815, Mashow was freed. He moved to New Bedford, where he was apprenticed as a shipwright. In 1832, at age 27, Mashow established his own shipyard. Over the years he designed and built about 60 ships of various types, including 14 whalers.

Tragically, Mashow's accomplishments ultimately came to nothing. In the late 1850s, the whaling business was hit by a whale-oil glut, which was followed a few years later by the discovery of oil deposits on land. Mashow lost his business and became a ship's carpenter, dying in obscurity in 1893.

Long before his death, maritime opportunities of all kinds were dwindling for African Americans. As funds shifted from the maritime business to industry onshore, the number of seafaring jobs dropped, and those that came open were often filled by Irish and German immigrants. After the Civil War, as notions of racial segregation became increasingly rigid, crews were often all white (except, perhaps, for a black cook or steward) or, more rarely, all black with white officers. The few exceptions, known as checkerboard ships, generally practiced segregation in living quarters on board. The unionization of white mariners only accelerated these trends.

Still, a limited black American presence aboard ship continued, as is evidenced by the early-20th-century whaling scenes shown here. For some black mariners, the ocean continued to beckon as it always had—and not solely for economic reasons. In 1880 Charles Benson, a trained navigator who served for almost 20 years as a steward, wrote of the emotional and practical reasons for his love affair with the sea. "It is the excitement, danger, and money that a sea life brings, that keeps me at sea," he confided. "Nothing else."

In the early-20th-century photograph above, black crew members mend sails aboard ship—a routine chore on all whaling and trading vessels.

With all sails set, the *Morning Star* (*left*) glides across smooth ocean waters—one of 14 whaling ships credited to black Massachusetts shipbuilder John Mashow (*above*).

Roughly a hundred feet above the deck of their whaling ship, two black lookouts scan the horizon in a photograph taken between 1907 and 1912 (*above*).

The black third mate of the *Daisy* works at the head of a recently killed sperm whale to recover the animal's sper-maceti, a substance used in candles and cosmetics.

Formerly based in New England, Captain William T. Shorey was in San Francisco by the 1890s, the time of the family portrait above. Shorey made 14 voyages from California to the whale grounds off Alaska and Siberia.

93

CAPTAIN, TRADER, WHALER—AND COLONIZER

When Captain Paul Cuffe sailed his schooner *Ranger* into the port of Vienna, Maryland, in the late 1790s, white residents stared in amazement and fear. The confident African American and his all-black crew seemed to them to set a dangerously unsettling example for local slaves—so dangerous, in fact, that some favored jailing Cuffe as soon as he stepped onshore. But the black captain's papers were in order and his calm dignity proved hard to resist. Far from being imprisoned, Cuffe was soon giving tours of the ship. After several days in port, captain and crew set sail for Massachusetts with a hold filled with Maryland corn.

One of the wealthiest black Americans of his day, Paul Cuffe was the son of an enslaved Ashanti tribesman in Massachusetts who was freed by his Quaker master and subsequently married a Wampanoag Indian. The father's name, Kofi, later became the family name Cuffe. Paul shipped out as a teenage hand on a whaler in 1773, a commonplace start to what would be an extraordinary career.

During the Revolutionary War, Cuffe made a small fortune running food and other goods through the British blockade of New England in boats he and his brother David built by hand. In his first known political effort, Paul, David, and a few others also unsuccessfully petitioned the legislature, protesting the fact that Massachusetts taxed black residents but did not grant them political representation.

At war's end in 1783, Cuffe married Alice Pequit, a woman of his mother's Wampanoag people. Working together with his brother-in-law Michael Wainer, Cuffe parlayed his old blockade-running profits into the first in a series of merchant and whaling vessels. Every ship in the Cuffe fleet was manned by black and Native American sailors.

A decade before he and just such a crew horrified the Maryland port of Vienna, Cuffe was snubbed by New Englanders when he and nine black whalemen sailed the 25-ton *Sunfish* to the Grand Banks off Newfoundland. As was the custom, Cuffe intended to hunt together with the four whaling ships he encountered there. Instead, their white captains told him to go home. Nothing daunted, Cuffe waited until whales were sighted, then lowered a lone boat to chase them. The other captains were shamed into joining him, and the *Sunfish* eventually killed six whales—two of them harpooned by Cuffe himself.

Cuffe ran into more racial barriers onshore when he could not get white neighbors near his farm outside Westport, Massachusetts, to agree to build a schoolhouse that his children could attend. In 1797, with his own money, he built one on his own land. "Cuff's School" became the state's first integrated school.

Two years later, Cuffe bought a larger farm and invested in both a gristmill and a windmill. In

1803, he expanded again with his first transatlantic venture, a trading trip to France. Cuffe's ships later sailed to Portugal, Spain, Sweden, Britain—and the African colony of Sierra Leone, established by the British as a haven for former slaves.

Cuffe, who converted to Quakerism in 1808, had long advocated the abolition of slavery, but his constant, wearying encounters with American racism had convinced him that freed blacks would only achieve independence in a land of their own. Sierra Leone seemed a logical site, and he sailed to the colony in 1811 to negotiate the immigration of African Americans there. The next year, war broke out with Britain. Cuffe had to wait until 1815 to return to Sierra Leone with 38 black American settlers.

That voyage was to be the high point of Cuffe's project, however. The tide of black opinion had turned against such repatriation schemes, which were seen as a way of removing free black Americans and thus consolidating the slave status of the rest. Cuffe's health had also begun to fail. In September 1817 he died at the age of 58 and was buried at the Quaker cemetery in Westport.

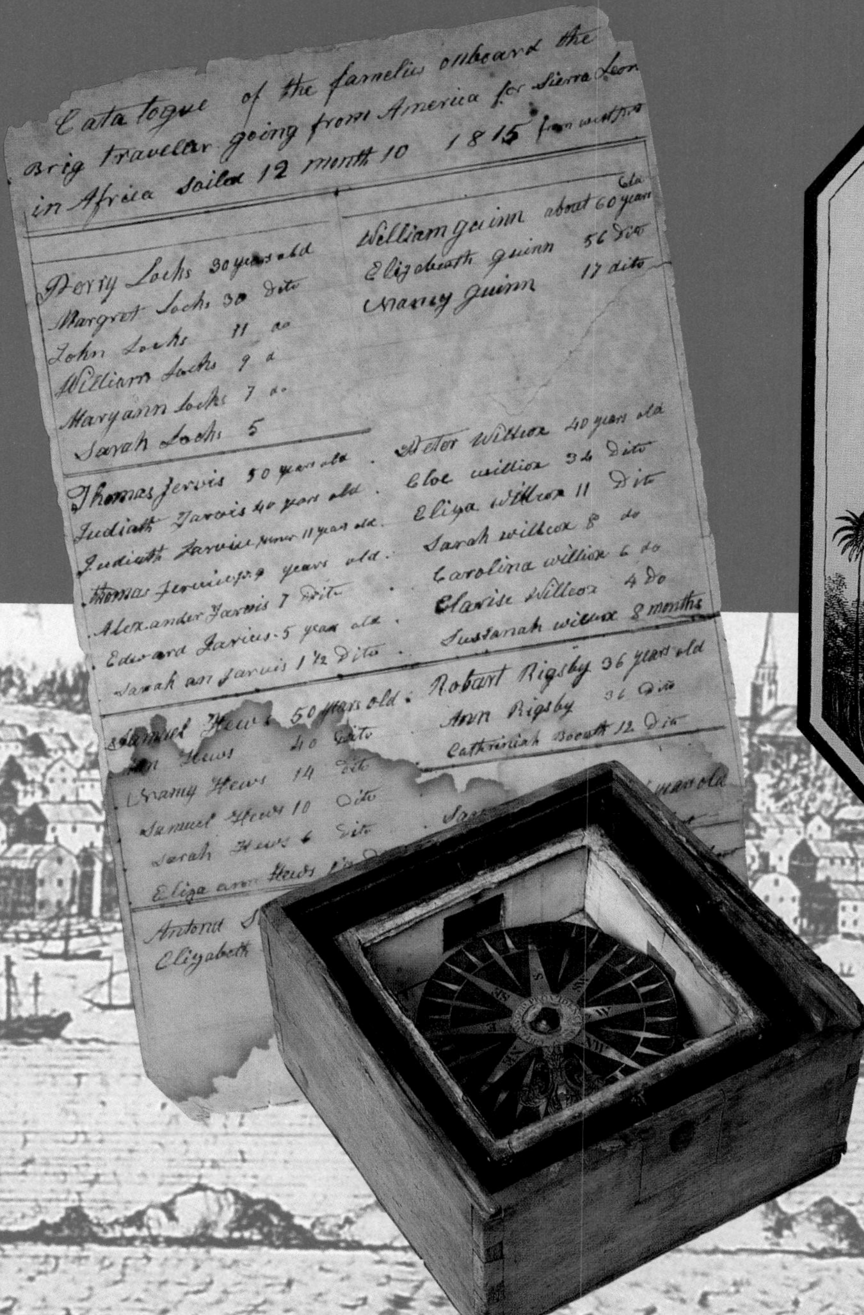
Catalogue of the families onboard the brig traveller going from America for Sierra Leon in Africa sailed 12 month 10 1815 from westport

Perry Locks 30 years old
Margret Locks 30 ditto
John Locks 11 do
William Locks 9 d
Maryann Locks 7 do
Sarah Locks 5

William Guinn about 60 years old
Elizabeath Guinn 56 ditto
Nancy Guinn 17 ditto

Thomas Jervis 50 years old
Judiath Jarvis 40 years old
Judiath Jarvise Junr 11 years old
Thomas Jervis 9 years old
Alexander Jarvis 7 ditto
Edward Jarvis 5 year old
Sarah ann Jarvis 1 1/2 ditto

Peter Willcox 40 years old
Cloe willcox 34 ditto
Eliza willcox 11 ditto
Sarah willcox 8 do
Carolina willcox 6 do
Clarise willcox 4 do
Susanah willcox 8 months

Samuel Hews 50 years old
Hews 40 ditto
Nancy Hews 14 ditto
Samuel Hews 10 ditto
Sarah Hews 6 ditto
Eliza ann Hews

Robart Rigsby 36 years old
Ann Rigsby 36 ditto
Cathrinah Booth 12 ditto

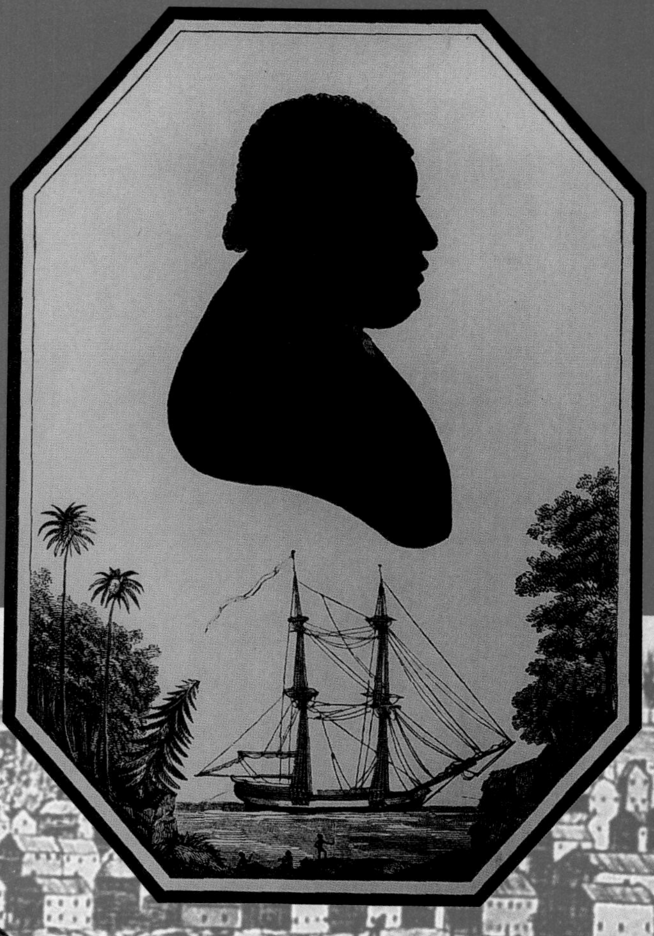

The only known likeness of Paul Cuffe (*above*) incorporates a ship enroute between the palm trees of West Africa and the rugged coast of New England. Cuffe, whose own compass appears at left, repatriated 38 free black Americans to Sierra Leone in 1815. Some of their names, and the cargo that accompanied them, are listed on the water-stained page of his ship's log reproduced at upper left.

TURNING NICKELS INTO DOLLARS

"The Negro is so wedded to those who oppress him," Maggie Lena Walker declared in 1905, "that he carries to their bank every dollar he can get his hands upon and then goes back the next day, borrows and pays the white man to lend him his own money." By then, the black Richmond woman was already doing what she could to change that pattern. Two years earlier, at age 36, she had started the black-owned and -operated Saint Luke Penny Savings Bank, becoming the first American woman to found a bank.

It was a high flight for the daughter of an impoverished laundress. "I was not born with a silver spoon in my mouth," Walker later said, "but instead, with a clothesbasket almost upon my head." She spent much of her childhood carrying laundry to and from her mother's white customers and looking after her younger brother. As a teenager, Maggie Mitchell somehow found time to join the Independent Order of Saint Luke, one of many mutual aid societies that offered African Americans help in coping with sickness, acquiring burial insurance, and other services. She stayed active in the order after starting work as an elementary-school teacher in 1883 at age 16.

She quit that job three years later to marry contractor Armstead Walker, Jr., with whom she had three sons, one of whom died in infancy. The young matron nev-

In one of several publicity photographs taken in 1917, Maggie Lena Walker (*left*) stands at the central teller's window of the Saint Luke Bank and Trust.

Walker, sometimes affectionately called the Saint Luke Grandmother because of her fondness for children, poses at left with black youngsters in Richmond in 1917.

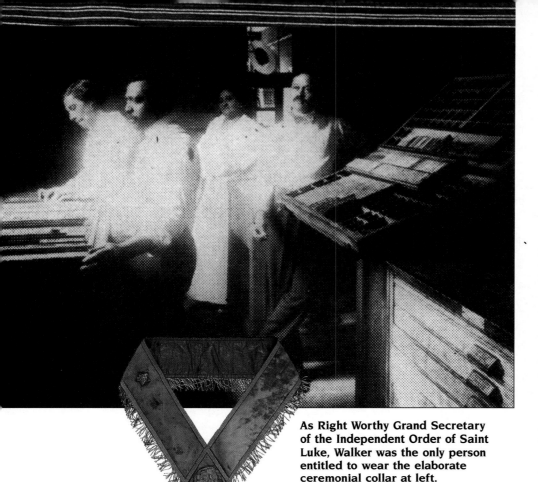

In another 1917 photograph, Walker (*left, center*) presides over the composing room of the Order of Saint Luke. Movable type was set there for the *Saint Luke Herald* weekly newspaper, bank brochures, and business cards.

As Right Worthy Grand Secretary of the Independent Order of Saint Luke, Walker was the only person entitled to wear the elaborate ceremonial collar at left.

er left Saint Luke's, however, rising in the ranks until she was chosen to lead the order in 1899.

By then the organization had fallen on hard times. With just over 1,000 members, it had $31.61 in the treasury and $400 in unpaid bills. Walker immediately launched an energetic membership drive, arguing so powerfully for black self-reliance that some listeners wept. Within two years, "1,400 new soldiers," as she put it, had joined Saint Luke's. That was only the beginning. Over the next 30 years, membership swelled to 100,000 as Walker led the order in establishing a newspaper, a department store, and—most enduringly—a bank.

The colorful pins and ribbons shown here, symbolizing different ranks within the Order of Saint Luke, were worn by members at meetings and other events.

Started with about $9,000 in deposits, the Saint Luke Penny Savings Bank (later the Saint Luke Bank and Trust Company) grew rapidly under Walker, who worked tirelessly giving speeches and writing articles to recruit customers. Within a year, deposits had reached $21,362; by 1919, the sum had risen to $376,288. The bank helped black women and men "take the nickels and turn them into dollars," in Walker's words. It also issued education loans and home mortgages. By 1920, she reported, there were 645 black homes "entirely paid for through our bank's help."

Walker's triumphs, however, were not unmixed with profound griefs. In 1915 her older son accidentally shot and killed her husband and had to stand trial for murder before being cleared. Walker also began to lose the use of her legs, which had never been quite right since she fell and fractured a kneecap in 1907. By 1928 she was confined to a wheelchair. Undaunted, she installed a home elevator and had her desk at the bank cut out to accommodate the wheelchair.

As the Great Depression began, Walker helped arrange mergers between her bank and two other black lending institutions to form the Consolidated Bank and Trust Company. The strategy worked; Consolidated survived the Depression, and it is now the oldest continuously operating African American bank. But Walker did not live to see prosperity return; she died in late 1934. Her funeral, attended by crowds of black and white mourners, was among the largest in Richmond history.

"FIND A NEED AND FILL IT"

As a child in rural Alabama, Arthur George Gaston had the only swing in his neighborhood—and the business savvy to make something of it. Young Art's playmates paid him a pin or a button for one ride on the swing, and before long the budding entrepreneur had a cigar box full of sewing notions. Already, he was following a rule that would one day make him one of the richest black men in America: In his own words, "Find a need and fill it."

Going from pins and buttons to real capital took Gaston several more years. After serving overseas as a sergeant in World War I, he found work at a steel mill outside the big city of Birmingham. "A young man on his way up should keep his eyes open," Gaston later counseled, writing of this period. "He should study the people around him. How do they live? What makes them tick? What do they want?" He added, "Out of

The staff of the Smith & Gaston Funeral Home—purchased by Gaston and his father-in-law A. L. Smith about 1923—lines up beside the home's limousines.

At right, Gaston employees learn secretarial skills in a company class in the late 1930s. Gaston offered instruction in shorthand, typing, and bookkeeping because black men and women could not attend white business schools. The classes proved so popular that he went on to found the Booker T. Washington Business College in 1939.

these questions, out of a real need, came the first substantial Gaston business."

Observing his fellow workers, Gaston found out that the custom of taking up collections to pay for poor people's funerals had become something of a local racket. "Some people were out collecting money for 'dead people' who were very much alive," he later wrote. "I got the idea of starting a burial society and collecting so much money each week from people and guaranteeing them a decent burial." The Booker T. Washington Burial Society, formed in 1923, was an immediate success.

Nine years later, the society became the Booker T. Washington Burial Insurance Company, the cornerstone of a business empire that eventually would be worth tens of millions of dollars. Gaston concentrated on supplying services to African Americans who were shunned or otherwise treated shabbily by white Birmingham businesses. Among other enterprises, Gaston started the Booker T. Washington Business College in 1939, bought New Grace Hill Cemeteries in 1947, and in 1954 established the Gaston Motel (*opposite, below*), which offered its guests the almost-unheard-of lux-

ury of air conditioning. In 1957 he and other investors raised $350,000 to found Citizens Federal Savings and Loan Association, enabling African American families to secure mortgages.

As a leading southern black businessman, Gaston was inevitably drawn into the civil rights movement of the 1950s and 1960s. In 1957, when white bankers in the eastern Alabama city of Tuskegee threatened to foreclose on the home loans of local black citizens staging a boycott to obtain voting rights, Gaston pledged to advance the mortgage money. During nationally publicized protests in Birmingham in 1963, he guaranteed bonds totaling $160,000 to free protesters jailed during the demonstrations. And when the city's white business leaders negotiated an end to segregation, Gaston was instrumental in attaining some black demands.

In 1966, Gaston founded the A. G. Gaston Boys' Club, later expanded to a boys' and girls' club, which still offers educational courses and recreation to 1,200 Birmingham children a year. He also continued to seek out business opportunities, acquiring in 1975 what he called his favorite properties—a gospel-oriented Birmingham radio station and another that plays rhythm-and-blues. In the 1980s, he helped start a construction company.

For Gaston, however, his wealth remained something he had acquired "accidentally," in the course of meeting people's needs. When he was a boy, he said in 1992 (at the age of 99), his grandmother had often reminded him "that God was watching me all the time, so I better be good." The grown man never forgot: "It scared me then and I'm still scared. I knew I'd better do right."

In a 1941 advertisement (*left*) that boasts "100% Negro organization," a smiling model urges customers to try A. G. Gaston's "Brown Belle" soda. Gaston, shown below in the 1960s, later said the soft drink company was the only venture he undertook just for the money— and the only one that failed.

Gaston's motel (*left*), intended as "a fine motel for the Negro citizens of Birmingham," was headquarters for Martin Luther King, Jr., during the 1963 desegregation protests. It was bombed, but not destroyed, soon after King left.

Below, a triumphant Berry Gordy holds aloft the trophy marking his induction into the Rock and Roll Hall of Fame in 1988. Gordy launched Motown Record Corporation in the low-rent Detroit building at right in 1959. Fourteen years later, the company—now known as Motown Industries—was America's largest black-owned business.

BUSINESS MAGIC BEHIND THE MUSIC

If a young featherweight boxer named Berry Gordy, Jr., hadn't stopped to stare at a poster hanging in a Detroit gym one day in 1951, there might never have been a Motown Records. No high-stepping Temptations blowing kisses to screaming ladies in the audience. No teen-queen Supremes singing in look-alike gowns bought on sale at Saks. No number one hits or decades of chart-busting revenues.

As Gordy later told the story, the poster promoted a "Battle of the Bands," with images of prizefighters and musicians—and the contrast between the two groups shocked him. "I looked at this poster and saw those two young fighters who were 23 but looked like 50, all scarred and beat up," Gordy recalled. "Then I saw the musicians who were 50 and they looked 23." At five feet six inches, Gordy already knew he was too small to be a heavyweight, and he began to doubt that the thrill of battling with tough guys would last a lifetime. The poster was the last straw. Gordy quit the fight game, convinced it would never be his road to riches.

Making money, in fact, was something of a family tradition. After moving to Detroit in 1922, Gordy's father sold the mineral rights to his share of the family land in Georgia for $10,000; his brothers had got only

A sampling of classic Motown hits begins at right and continues on the pages that follow.

Motown artists, including the Supremes (*center*) and Stevie Wonder (*far right*) gather around Berry Gordy at the piano in the early days of the company.

$100 for theirs. Berry senior and his wife went on to found several small businesses in Detroit while raising their family; Berry junior, the seventh of eight children, was born in 1929. Now the son wanted to find his own pot of gold. Soon after hanging up his gloves, however, he was drafted into the army, where he served two years. It was 1953 by the time a newly married Berry Gordy, Jr., opened a record shop in Detroit, financed by his army discharge pay and a $700 loan from his father. Following his own tastes, Gordy sold nothing but jazz records, even though the market for them was small. The 3-D Record Mart went bankrupt in 1955, teaching Gordy an important lesson—make sure whatever you produce will sell.

Gordy then went to work on a Ford assembly line, tacking upholstery onto automobiles—64 cars an hour, eight hours a day. It was a grim time for the would-be entrepreneur, and his marriage was a casualty of the stress. But somehow, despite his discouragement, songs danced and strutted their way through Gordy's head, echoing the nonstop beat of the assembly line and its roaring machines. Perhaps this was the real beginning of the Motown sound, the music that would one day make people want to follow the big beat and go dancing in the streets.

Gordy began polishing some of the songs, composing for his friend Jackie Wilson, an ex-boxer who had become a professional singer. Wilson's nearly operatic delivery and a stage act replete with dips and twirls

MONEY—1960   PLEASE MR. POSTMAN—1961   YOU'VE REALLY GOT A HOLD ON ME—1962

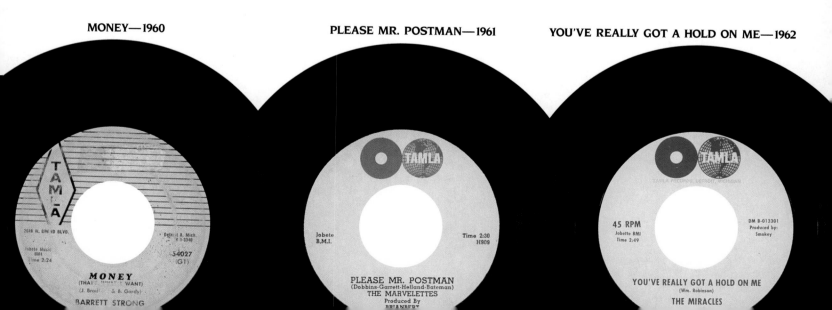

Singer Tammi Terrell (*far left*) confers with arranger Johnny Allen (*center foreground*) and executive Maurice King (*near left*), with grooming consultant Maxine Powell in the background beside a chalked rehearsal list.

whipped audiences into a fever. Gordy and another songwriter, Billy Davis (who wrote under the name Tyran Carlo), wrote Wilson's first hit, "Reet Petite," followed by other chart busters such as "To Be Loved," "I'll Be Satisfied," "That Is Why," and the million-copy-seller "Lonely Teardrops." But Gordy had the business sense to see he would never earn much money writing songs. "You can go broke with hits if someone else is producing the records," he said to an interviewer.

And so, in the late 1950s, Gordy became a producer.

Together with singer Raynoma Liles, who would become his second wife, he formed Rayber Voices, offering to produce records for $100 a song and to provide background and vocal accompaniment for groups that lacked it. (Customers who couldn't afford to pay the full fee up-front could pay in installments.) Rayber Voices had no recording studio of its own, however. Liles later recalled that when a client appeared, they rented time at the home of a Detroit disc jockey who had a small studio set up in his basement.

Although she was married to Berry for only a year and a half, Raynoma added to his early success. Unlike her husband, she had musical training and could write songs out in rough sheet-music form. Another major influence was a 19-year-old tenor named William Robinson, Jr., one of the male vocalists whom Berry recorded. It was Smokey Robinson, as he was generally known, who convinced Gordy to take the logical—but financially daring—step of making and distributing his own records. "Why work for the man?" Robinson asked him. "Why not *you* be the man?"

In January 1959, Gordy followed Robinson's advice. He borrowed $800 from family members and moved into an old house on Detroit's West Grand Boulevard. Cramped and decrepit, it would be the first home of Motown Records, named after carmaking Detroit, the Motor City. Gordy's office was an 8-by-10-foot downstairs bedroom; he lived in a similar room upstairs.

It was Berry junior's big move, and the family was right behind him. The Gordys embraced Motown, shutting down the family's grocery store and print shop so they could concentrate on helping to build

DANCING IN THE
STREET—1964

MY GIRL—1965

REACH OUT I'LL BE THERE—1966

Berry's dream. His father served as constant adviser—and as unpaid maintenance man. Sisters Loucye and Esther set up the company's business offices. (As the years went by, still more family members would come on board, including Gordy's sister Gwendolyn and her husband, singer-producer Harvey Fuqua, as well as another brother-in-law, Marvin Gaye, who came to the company as a pianist and drummer but became one of its singing stars.)

Gordy immediately signed up Smokey Robinson's

Some of the Marvelettes and other Motown artists rehearse under the eagle eye of choreographer Cholly Atkins. Like the music, Motown stage acts were planned to the last detail.

group, the Miracles, but his new company needed a whole stable of performers. Fortunately for Motown, the stages, the talent shows, and even the streets of Detroit were crammed with gifted black youngsters eager for a chance at the big time. It didn't take long to

GET READY—1966   I HEARD IT THROUGH THE GRAPEVINE—1967   TCB—1968

At right, star performer Stevie Wonder, who called Motown headquarters "a music store with all kinds of toys," jams with artist and repertoire director Clarence Paul.

round up the performers who went on to become such superstars as the Temptations and Martha and the Vandellas. Some of those he signed on moved right in to Motown headquarters, an arrangement that made it all the easier for the company to begin shaping its unsophisticated teenagers into top-rank entertainers.

From the very beginning, the company took charge of the performers' grooming, wardrobes, and makeup, and taught them how to move—and dance—onstage. Maxine Powell, proprietor of the Maxine Powell Finishing and Modeling School, eventually came aboard in 1964 to help polish the groups and give them confidence. Powell also chaperoned the "girl groups" and improvised outfits for the Supremes, sometimes picking up dresses on sale that were too big and cutting them down. Motown's own producers and writers wrote many of the songs, adding to the company's tight control over its product.

More than any other record company, Motown tried to make every release a hit (a "hit," in the music industry, is defined as one of the nation's 100 top-selling records in a given week). Gordy held down production to one or two records a week—less than half the output of other labels—and insisted that each satisfy his own high standards, sometimes ordering a dozen or more takes to get just the right polished, professional sound. He also tried out all the songs on listeners around the company. "Would you buy this record for a dollar?" he would ask. "Or would you buy a sandwich?"

The obsession with quality paid off: Motown's first national release, "Money (That's What I Want)" (1960), co-written by Gordy and Janie Bradford and sung by

Barrett Strong, spent 17 weeks on the charts. A year later, "Shop Around," a Smokey Robinson song recorded by Robinson and the Miracles, sold more than a million copies. Ordinarily, that would have earned Motown its first official gold record, but the company limited access to its books so severely that the Recording Industry Association of America was not able to certify Motown's sales and could not award the company any gold or platinum records until Motown permitted access to its records in the late 1970s.

LOVE CHILD—1968

DIANA ROSS PRESENTS
THE JACKSON 5—1969

I'LL BE THERE—1970

Gordy also kept a tight rein on spending. Early salaries were low; publicist Al Abrams, for example, was hired for $25 a week and all the chili he could eat. Motown paid low royalties, and sometimes there was no guaranteed minimum for the artists. In some cases, Gordy even deducted the cost of making the record before paying artists any royalties at all. The dollar squeezing, which remained typical of Motown long after it became a success, was one reason many performers eventually left the label.

In one of Motown's many carefully staged publicity shots, Martha and the Vandellas ride down a Detroit assembly line.

Gordy's tight-fistedness paid off for many years, however, for "Shop Around" was only the beginning of a seemingly endless stream of hits. Later in 1961, the Marvelettes, discovered by Gordy at a high-school talent show, became Motown's first successful female vocal group with "Please Mr. Postman." Nineteen-year-

ABC—1970

JACKSON 5
THIRD ALBUM—1970

WHAT'S GOING ON—1971

old Mary Wells, a solo act, topped the charts three times in 1962 with "The One Who Really Loves You," "You Beat Me to the Punch," and "Two Lovers," all written by Smokey Robinson. Steveland Morris, a blind Detroit youngster who was renamed Little Stevie Wonder by the Motown publicity machine, recorded his first release, "Thank You," that November. He had his first hit song in 1963 at age 13, a harmonica tune called "Fingertips, Part 2." Wonder went on to record a

A marquee ablaze with Motown stars marks the arrival of the first Motor Town Revue at Harlem's Apollo Theater in 1962. The show's 45 performers toured in one bus and five cars.

string of typical Motown hits, including "I Was Made to Love Her" and "For Once in My Life," before moving on to more varied material in the 1970s.

The group most closely identified with Motown's heyday was the Supremes—Diana Ross, Mary Wilson, and Florence Ballard. A neighborhood trio that started off passing the hat at backyard concerts, the Supremes were earning $5,000 a performance by 1966. In 1964, three hits by the Supremes—"Where Did Our Love Go?" "Baby Love," and "Come See about Me"—helped Motown cross over to the lucrative world of mainstream pop music.

Previously, the major white record labels had rejected most music by black artists as unacceptable to white audiences. Songs by black artists were recorded almost exclusively by small independent record companies, freezing African American performers and producers out of the big audiences and the big money. But the songs performed by the Motown artists were so lollipop sweet, so sincere, and yet so danceable, that they—and Motown—slipped right over the color line.

The Motown sound, as it came to be called, was so consistent from record to record that it became one of the few musical styles linked to a company instead of to a particular singer. As Gordy put it, "Rhythm is basic. If you get that, that's what people want." Often the beat came first, then the melody and lyrics. Gordy insisted that the words tell a story, and he urged the songwriters to compress a tale into a couple of verses

The most popular female vocal group of their day, with a string of number one hits to their credit, the Supremes take center stage on an American television show in the mid-1960s.

At right, the Four Tops perform on British television as part of an immensely popular one-hour Motown show.

and a chorus. Present tense was favored, to suggest that the story was unfolding.

Gordy and his songwriters drew on African American traditions, including the music of black church choirs and revival meetings. They preserved the gospel flavor, but stylized and updated it with elements of jazz, pop, and rhythm-and-blues—producing a unique sound that captivated blacks and whites, jazz lovers, and country-and-western fans alike.

By the mid-1960s, that sound was helping Motown Records sell more 45s than any other record company in America. And the company's success began to attract musical acts from elsewhere. In 1965, Gladys Knight and the Pips (the name was later said to stand for "Perfection in Performance"), a group that had recorded with four different companies, signed on with Motown. The group did well in its eight years there but never really became part of the close-knit Motown family. Yet it was Gladys Knight who ushered in a new era at Motown when she discovered five singing brothers from Gary, Indiana. At first, Gordy hesitated, but when Diana Ross took up their cause, the Jackson 5 got a contract. They recorded four number one singles in 1969 and 1970, "I Want You Back," "ABC," "The Love You Save," and "I'll Be There," and then went on to a stack of other hits.

In 1973, the first year that *Black Enterprise* magazine published its list of the largest African American firms, Motown topped the list, staying there until 1984, when it was surpassed by Johnson Publishing. During the 1980s, Motown continued to score hits with Stevie Wonder and Lionel Richie, but the magic was gone. Gordy's attention drifted toward films and television, and many of the company's other headliners left for more money elsewhere. In 1988, Berry Gordy, Jr., finally called it quits. He sold the company he had started on an $800 loan to MCA for $61 million.

LADY SINGS THE BLUES—1972

BEN—1972

TALKING BOOK—1972

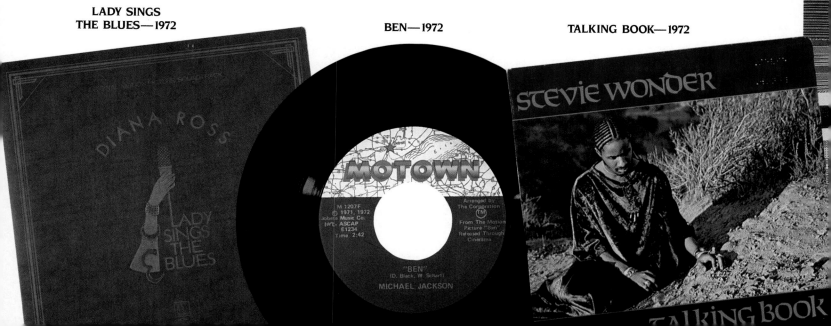

CAPTAINS OF BUSINESS AND INDUSTRY

By the early 1990s, more than 400,000 black-owned firms, each with its own history of entrepreneurial adventure, dotted the American business landscape. Most of them were small operations like those chronicled on pages 116-119. But others were giants, reporting revenues of tens of millions of dollars a year. The leaders shown on these and the following two pages represent only a small sampling of the gutsy and determined entrepreneurs who led those companies to success. Born in different regions of the United States, some to affluence and some in modest circumstances, these diverse African Americans have in common a knack for identifying opportunity—and the know-how to make it pay.

J. Bruce Llewellyn

Growing up in White Plains, New York, during the Great Depression, James Bruce Llewellyn often heard his father say, "You're going to have to work twice as hard to get half as much." Llewellyn's Jamaican immigrant parents also taught him that prejudice could be defeated by education and ambition. The lesson was not lost on Llewellyn, whose business holdings in the bottling, broadcast, and cable TV industries would one day make him one of the most successful black entrepreneurs of his generation.

Llewellyn was 16 and just out of high school when he enlisted in the army in 1944, emerging five years later as a first lieutenant. The young veteran opened a retail liquor store in Harlem while attending the City College of New York, and went on to earn three separate graduate degrees in business, law, and public administration. After a stint at the New York district attorney's office, Llewellyn opened his own small firm in 1962. He left in 1965 to become regional director for the Small Business Administration.

For Llewellyn, the turning point in his business career came in 1969, when he learned through a former law school classmate that Fedco Foods Corporation, a chain of 10 grocery stores in the economically depressed South Bronx, was for sale. Llewellyn mortgaged his house, sold everything he owned, and joined with two partners to purchase Fedco for $3 million. His courage was rewarded: In the next 14 years, the chain grew to 29 stores. It sold in 1984 for $20 million.

A year later, Llewellyn, basketball star Julius Erving, and other investors borrowed $75 million to buy a majority interest in the Philadelphia Coca-Cola Bottling Company, which was then Coca-Cola's 15th largest bottler. Also in 1985, he and some associates borrowed another $65 million to buy a television station in Buffalo, New York, and in 1989 he purchased New York Times Cable in Cherry Hill, New Jersey.

Llewellyn, whose shrewdly timed investments have earned him a fortune, is a staunch believer in the free-market system. "Business is the emancipator of a group of people," he has said, although he recognizes the special problems facing black entrepreneurs. "It's always going to be harder if you're a minority," he said in 1990. "You can't worry about it, though. You have to ask, What can I do for myself? Then go out and do it. That's what my father told me, and that's what I tell my kids."

Joshua I. Smith

On Valentine's Day, 1978, the MAXIMA Corporation, a computer information management company, was started, in the words of owner Joshua I. Smith, "in one room, with $15,000 and a borrowed typewriter." From that humble beginning, the Lanham, Maryland, corporation grew by 1992 into a $50 million business employing 800 people.

A 1963 graduate of Central State University in Ohio, Smith briefly taught biology and mathematics in a Washington, D.C., high school, but was frustrated by the low pay. "I loved the kids, but I didn't like allowing someone else to put a limit on my future," he said later. And so, in 1965 Smith found his way into the nascent field of information management, working his way through a series of positions to

become executive director of the American Society for Information Science in 1973. Throughout this period, he dreamed of founding a business of his own in the field. "I knew there would be a compa-

ny," he later recalled. "I just didn't know what it would do."

Once he founded MAXIMA, it grew so rapidly that by 1986 it was no longer eligible for federal minority set-aside contracts—a potentially disastrous blow. Smith reconfigured his company and acquired several smaller businesses in related lines. The gamble paid off when MAXIMA emerged three years later stronger than ever.

By this time, Smith had also become a popular lecturer, urging minorities to seek economic parity through business development. "Say what you will do loud and clear. Do it better than anybody else," he told one audience. "And then remind people to death about how well you did it."

Herman J. Russell

By the time he was 12, Herman J. Russell was already an experienced tradesman in his father's plastering business in Atlanta. The work habits he learned then would later prove invaluable as he built the same firm into H. J. Russell and Company, the nation's largest black-owned construction firm.

Young Russell also had a sharp eye for business opportunities. At age 16, he bought his first piece of real estate for $125 and a few years later began building a duplex on it with his own hands. The money he made from renting the place helped pay his tuition at Tuskegee Institute in Alabama. Russell graduated in 1953 and returned to Atlanta, taking over the family business four years later when his father died.

Russell quickly expanded be-

yond plastering to all aspects of construction. He began with duplexes and by the early 1970s was building 400- and 500-unit apartment complexes in Atlanta and taking on contracts in other southern states. In 1974 Russell became a subcontractor on the Equitable Life Insurance Building, one of Atlanta's tallest buildings. In the 1980s, he began winning public contracts, including an $18 million parking garage and the $30 million City Hall, both located in Atlanta.

Amid the business building, he found time in 1989 to start a special program at a local elementary school to nurture the entrepreneurial spirit in youngsters. Russell hoped the program would pass on to others his belief in the value of education, determination, and hard work.

Don Barden

One of a number of black entrepreneurs to profit from the cable TV boom of the 1980s and early 1990s was Don Barden, chairman and CEO of Barden Communications, Inc. (BCI). Barden, pictured above with a satellite dish, founded the company in 1981; by 1991 its revenues, in addition to those from his other holdings, were earning him more than $90 million a year.

Such wealth seemed distant indeed in 1963, when Barden, the ninth of 13 children, had to drop out of Central State University in Ohio after only a year because he couldn't afford the tuition. He landed in Lorain, Ohio, where he took on odd jobs before deciding he had had enough of working for other people. "I wanted to control my own destiny," he later recalled. "I said to myself, 'I am going to take risks.'"

Barden quit his job, withdrew $500 from his savings account, and opened a local record store.

Soon he added a nightclub, which brought in acts such as the Four Tops and James Brown.

In 1968, Barden sold both the store and the club and opened a public-relations office. One day, he heard that a group of army recruiters was planning to move out of a nearby building. Told they were looking for more comfortable quarters, he scoured the city and came up with a likely prospect. Barden secured a $25,000 loan to buy the building and lease it to the government. Two years later he sold the property for $50,000.

During the 1970s, Barden formed a real-estate development firm and served two terms on the Lorain City Council. He also hosted a weekly Cleveland TV show—an experience that piqued his interest in the business of television. His initial foray, in 1980, was to purchase two-percent shares in two cable franchises in Ohio for $2,000 each. Two years later, he sold his interest in the franchises for $200,000, having founded BCI in the meantime. In 1983, he got the Detroit cable contract and began securing the capital needed to wire the city. At the same time, he bought two radio stations and started his own record label.

Clearly one of Detroit's movers and shakers, Barden sees his seemingly meteoric rise as a logical step-by-step progression. As he says, "Every position is a springboard for the next."

Reginald F. Lewis

During the prosperous 1980s, Wall Street went wild with an extraordinary number of corporate takeovers and leveraged buyouts. And Reginald F. Lewis (*below*) was in the thick of it. Before dying in 1993 from a cerebral hemorrhage at age 50, Lewis exemplified what *Black Enterprise* magazine called a new kind of black entrepreneur—one who "finds it more lucrative to line up investors and capital in order to acquire existing companies than to build a firm from scratch."

The description is an apt one for the deal that was the capstone of Lewis's career: his 1987 leveraged buyout of Beatrice International Food Companies. The negotiations resulted in TLC Beatrice International Holdings,

the largest company owned by a black American, with revenues of more than $1.5 billion a year.

Lewis, the son of a middle-class Baltimore family, graduated in 1968 from Harvard Law School. He then spent two years in the corporate law department of a prestigious Wall Street firm before hanging out his own shingle in 1970. His fledgling firm specialized in raising venture capital for small and medium-size minority-owned businesses.

By 1983, when he launched his own investment firm, TLC Group, Lewis was well versed in the art of the deal. The first big TLC Group acquisition was McCall's Pattern Company, purchased in 1984 with $1 million of Lewis's own money and a $24 million loan. Three years later Lewis sold McCall's for $63 million, with the purchaser assuming the remaining debt. Already he had his sights on an even bigger prize—the Beatrice International food conglomerate.

To put the financing together, Lewis worked with an old acquaintance—Michael Milken, the influential head of investment house Drexel Burnham Lambert's high-yield junk bond department. Milken's later fall from grace on federal charges of securities violations would mark the end of an era, but in 1987 he was a powerful ally.

Lewis invested some of his own money and took control of Beatrice, immersing himself in the business. He sold off parts of the company and parlayed his stake into a $400 million fortune. Of this he donated $1 million to Howard University in Washington, D.C., and gave $3 million to his old law school—which used the money to build the first Harvard building ever named for an African American.

Dave Bing

Making the leap from professional sports to a business career is a feat most athletes never manage. Dave Bing, a Detroit Pistons guard, NBA All Star, and Basketball Hall of Famer, vowed he would be one of the exceptions.

Bing had been a star player on his high-school team in Washington, D.C., before being recruited by Syracuse University in 1962. By the time he graduated, he was Detroit's top choice in the NBA draft. He went on to win the league title of Rookie of the Year. In all, Bing spent 12 years as a pro. But he was always looking ahead to his life after basketball. "I'd like to say I did that because I was smart enough to realize I had to prepare for a second career," Bing wryly admitted later. "But the truth is, the Pistons weren't paying me enough to feed my family." In his first season with Detroit, the Rookie of the Year was paid just $15,000. By the end of his basketball career, he was making about $250,000.

During the off-seasons, Bing worked for a bank and for the Chrysler Corporation. He also saved his money, accumulating about $150,000 by the time he left the game in 1978. The former athlete worked two years for Paragon Steel in Detroit, learning the ropes. By 1980, he was ready to start his own company.

Using his banking contacts, Bing got financing to set up his first plant, a steel-processing facility that cut, shaped, and bent raw steel into parts used in cars and farm equipment. "My first year I lost $100,000," he later said. "I expected to lose money, but I didn't expect to lose that much." But the second year he won a contract with General Motors' Fisher Body division that put the company on a solid footing. Sales grew to $45 million by the late 1980s. Meanwhile, Bing started Superb Manufacturing, which makes stamped parts for automobiles, and Heritage 21, a construction management firm.

As part of his commitment to Detroit, the former Piston established each of his enterprises within the city limits. "I want to bring people back from the suburbs," he says. "If we turn our backs on the central city, we turn them on our kids. And if we do that, we all lose."

HAUTE COUTURE

In May 1969, a coterie of New York's fashion elite gathered for a highly unusual show staged by Bergdorf Goodman. As in any fashion show, models dressed in the latest styles sashayed down the runway—but the clothes they were wearing were nearly all created by black designers.

"Basic Black," as the show was called, is remembered as a watershed event. A handful of African American fashion designers, including Ann Lowe (*below*), had long since crashed the race barrier. But it was in the 1960s, as the nation became more conscious of racial issues, that a generation of black designers—including Stephen Burrows, who later became the first African American to win the prestigious Coty Award—emerged and thrived, a fact celebrated by the Basic Black show. In the decades that followed, still more African American talents blossomed, three of whom are showcased at right and on pages 114-115.

Ann Lowe

When 16-year-old Ann Lowe's seamstress mother died in 1915, she left behind four unfinished ball gowns commissioned by the wife of the governor of Alabama. Her daughter completed all four. Soon after, Lowe married an older man and at his insistence abandoned her sewing career. But about a year later, a Florida woman offered her the chance to design a wedding gown and trousseau. With her infant son Arthur, Lowe boarded a train to Tampa, effectively ending her marriage.

Rapid success in Tampa enabled Lowe to attend New York City's S. T. Taylor Design School in 1917. Although white students refused to associate with her and she was seated near a washroom, she completed the course at Taylor and returned to Tampa. By 1920 she owned the city's leading dress shop.

New York represented the height of fashion, however, and Lowe journeyed north again in 1928. During the next 20 years, she designed for various salons, earning a quiet reputation in the trade for her "fairy tale" gowns, although the public credit went to the shop owners. Lowe was a

At lower left, Ann Lowe arranges satin roses on a debutante dress she designed in 1964. Lowe's most famous gown (*below*) is the one she created for Jacqueline Bouvier's wedding to John F. Kennedy.

partner in her own shop by 1953, when Jacqueline Bouvier asked her to design the bridal party's gowns for her wedding to Senator John F. Kennedy. Reporters were surprised by this choice of what one of them described as "a modest, Negro seamstress."

Ten days before the wedding, a water-filled pipe in the dress shop ceiling burst, destroying 10 of the 15 gowns, including the wedding dress. Lowe worked around the clock to re-create all 10. The gowns were an artistic triumph, but the duplicated work and materials made them a financial disaster. There was worse to come.

In 1958 Lowe's son, her only financial adviser, died. By August 1962, she owed $12,800 in back taxes, and in September the IRS closed her shop. That same year, after a longstanding glaucoma condition worsened, Lowe had to have her right eye removed.

When she left the hospital, her fortunes improved. An anonymous donor had paid the taxes, and she found work in a boutique. Then a cataract dimmed the vision of her remaining eye. Lowe begged a surgeon to operate, despite the risk of blindness. If she could not design, she said, "I'd rather just fly off the top of the Empire State Building."

The operation succeeded. Slowly rebuilding her customer list, Lowe opened Ann Lowe Originals on Madison Avenue a few years later, working there until her retirement in the 1970s. Despite her many tribulations, Lowe had few regrets about her trailblazing career. "All the pleasure I have had," she once said, "I owe to my sewing."

ing for several sportswear companies. WilliWear took his success to a new level. In 1983, he became the second African American to earn the Coty Award, following pioneer Stephen Burrows. Although he grew to dislike being categorized as a black designer, Smith also felt that being black helped his work. White designers "who have to run to Paris for color and fabric combinations should go to church on Sunday in Harlem," he once said. "It's all right there."

Smith went on to win the Cutty Sark Award for men's sportswear in 1986, but he did not have much time left. On April 17, 1987, Willi Smith died of AIDS at age 39.

Willi Smith
Launched in 1976, twenty-eight-year-old Willi Smith's WilliWear clothing line was an immediate hit. The designer later described his natural-fiber sportswear as "easy, comfortable, and fun." It was also inexpensive. "My mother and grandmother were always ladies of style," recalled Smith, who grew up poor. "They taught me that you didn't have to be rich to look good."

After attending design school, Smith built his reputation work-

Willi Smith, relaxing at left with his dog Rufus in 1986, once said his WilliWear clothes—some of which are modeled at right—were designed not "for the queen" but "for the people who wave at her."

Patrick Kelly

Speaking no French and practically broke, Patrick Kelly arrived in Paris in 1980 on a one-way ticket, determined to break into the fashion business. The glittering capital of international chic was a far cry from the fields of Vicksburg, Mississippi, where he had grown up. But Kelly landed on his feet. To support himself, he found a job sewing costumes for the nightclub Le Palace. He also peddled original designs on the city streets and at a flea market. It was at the market that Kelly saw a roll of cotton-tube jersey that inspired his line of so-called tube dresses—short, tight, simple dresses without even a hem. Kelly later liberally embellished the basic cylinder of his design with bows and buttons.

The ornamentation, which became Kelly's signature, was borrowed from another designer—his Mississippi grandmother. As an active boy in Vicksburg, Kelly had lost a lot of shirt buttons. Unable to match all the missing buttons, his grandmother camouflaged the odd-colored substitutes by sewing decorative buttons on other parts of his shirts.

Kelly left Vicksburg in 1972 to attend Jackson State University. But he grew restless and soon left school and moved to Atlanta, where he restored and sold old gowns as well as his first original designs. He eventually owned two stores and began staging fashion shows. At one, he met model Pat Cleveland, who persuaded him to move to New York City.

Kelly enrolled in the Parsons School of Design, but when he left to look for a design job on Seventh Avenue, no one was interested. Once again, he ran into Cleveland, who advised him this time to go to Paris. That night his one-way ticket to France mysteriously appeared.

Kelly had been in Paris for about five years when he was introduced to the well-known boutique owner Françoise Chassagnac. Chassagnac had never before admitted clothes by an

American designer into her trend-setting shops, but she agreed to sell his. When Kelly walked into her boutique, accompanied by a beautiful African American model, "He was like a thunder of creativity, enthusiasm, and cheerfulness," she said. "I immediately knew I was in the presence of a great designer. It's very rare that I am stunned by a sense of novelty. His approach to fashion was completely new." Kelly's work soon proved popular with buyers—and designers. In 1988, he became the first American voted into the elite French design group known as the Chambre Syndicale.

The dramatic success story came to a sudden end when Kelly died of AIDS on New Year's Day, 1990, at the age of 40. Christian Lacroix, one of France's top designers, once called Patrick Kelly's clothes "Parisian in spirit." But Kelly himself said in 1986, "I design differently because I am Patrick Kelly, and Patrick Kelly is black, is from Mississippi."

Byron Lars

When high-school sophomore Byron Lars could not find the style of baggy pants he wanted, he made his own pattern and asked a friend to teach him to sew. The result was so satisfying that the Oakland, California, teenager gave up his earlier thoughts of becoming an architect and decided to enter the risky world of fashion.

After graduating from high school in 1983, Lars studied at the Brooks Fashion Institute in Long Beach for two years, then attended New York City's Fashion Institute of Technology. In the years that followed, the neophyte designer "worked, slaved, freelanced for anybody," as he later recalled,

and won awards in several international design competitions. By 1990 he was anxious to strike out on his own.

Lars spent weeks on the telephone trying to persuade buyers to look at his designs. He also pounded the pavement. Mary Ann Wheaton of Wheaton International, which launches new fashion businesses, remembers Lars turning up "on a day I didn't want to see one more young designer." But, impressed by the young man and his work, Wheaton broke her own rule of accepting only clients who already had financing. Before finding him a backer, Wheaton

persuaded major New York stores to carry Lars designs, including a line of cotton shirt-dresses in pinstripes that spoofed men's business shirts. The dresses were an instant hit: Bloomingdale's alone sold $20,000 worth in one day. In April 1991, *Women's Wear Daily* dubbed Byron Lars Rookie of the Year, one of a series of accolades that continued in the following seasons.

In a quirky sketch (*below*) by fashion designer Byron Lars (*inset*), pinstriped Wall Street men seem taken aback by the sight of a woman in a Lars shirt-dress.

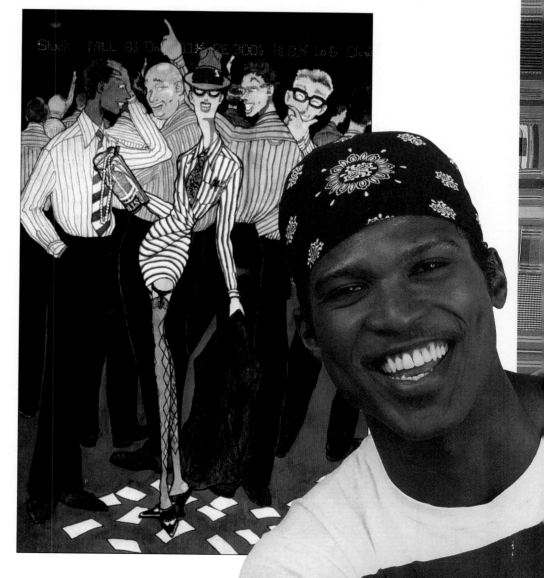

SMALL CAN BE BEAUTIFUL

The big, driving corporations may get the lion's share of kudos for African American enterprise—and they earn their plaudits—but the heart and soul of black business are the thousands upon thousands of small entrepreneurs whose ideas span the rainbow.

The government needs special railroad cars to transport nuclear fuel; a black businessman supplies them. Three brothers lose their jobs in a steel mill; they become successful fur farmers, breeding mink, fox, and fisher. An advertising copywriter cannot find just the right greeting card; she starts her own innovative company. A 16-year-old sees women jostling around the hat table in a five-and-dime store; he goes into the ladies' hat business and does well for nearly half a century.

This is where intelligence and initiative come into play on a nationwide, peoplewide scale—along with courage, common sense, stick-to-it-iveness, and plain old sweat. In the early 1990s, black business sales topped $35 billion annually. Among the successes:

James M. Woods, Sr.

A man is likely to know something about planting seeds and nurturing crops when he grows up on a farm. James M. Woods, the son of a cotton-plantation supervisor in Georgia, remembers helping his dad repair the houses occupied by tenant farmers, and that his mother "made sure the clothes we had were shared with others."

Today, in his late seventies, Woods is one of the Los Angeles area's foremost black businessmen—not the biggest, certainly, but among the best known and most respected. For he has made a life of planting the seeds of free enterprise in his community and nurturing them until they grow into sturdy trees. As Woods has put it, "I've always felt that if we try hard enough, we can do a lot of things. The opportunities in this country are unlimited."

James Woods's career is a paradigm of that patented American philosophy. As a young man at Alabama State College in Montgomery, Woods learned that no taxicabs served the city's black sections. So he started his own cab company, which grew to 20 cars and a service station by the time he graduated in 1940.

By then, the United States was gearing up for World War II. Woods enlisted and earned an unusual dual air force rating—as both a mechanic and a pilot-instructor at Tuskegee Institute, helping train the African American airmen who would win combat laurels in Europe. He himself saw no fighting: "They said that those of us who could teach were more valuable doing that than serving in combat."

The teacher/entrepreneur blossomed further after the war when he and a brother started a home-construction business in Los Angeles. Construction meant mortgages, and that led to Safety Savings and Loan, so blacks could own their homes. Woods had no pretensions as a banker. "You have to be able to find good people," he says, "That's how we did it. We hired people who knew the industry." Woods's Safety S&L not only had a strong multiplier effect on the local economy but also returned to its numerous small investors $325 for every initial $50 share when the company was sold in the early 1970s.

Meanwhile, the catastrophic Watts riots of 1965 had devastated the black neighborhoods of Los Angeles. Together with Aerojet General, the big aerospace firm, Woods helped establish Watts Manufacturing Company to bring some hope to the people of Watts. Setting up shop in an abandoned furniture factory, Watts Manufacturing nailed down an initial $2,500,000 Pentagon contract for tents and wooden loading pallets. Then it started hiring and training the first among thousands of disaffected people who would gain by working there at one time or another.

Woods did something else to heal Watts. In the early 1970s, he cofounded the Kedren Community Health Centers, which serve 280,000 people from two locations in central and south-central Los Angeles. The centers care for both inpatients and outpatients, and offer a mental health and Head Start program. Chairman of the Board Woods oversees a staff of 300 with a $20 million annual budget.

All the while, the companies kept sprouting. In the 1970s, Woods Industries grew into the largest black-owned precision machine shop in California, making parts for aircraft giants Boeing and McDonnell Douglas. Two other Woods companies have

hooked up with Detroit in a $10 million yearly business, making everything from trunk springs to glove boxes and bus seats. Woods is very proud of the fact that Ford Motor Company has given his Automotive Products, Inc. (API) its Q-1 Preferred Quality Award; in practical terms, being Q-1 meant that API survived when Ford lopped off 1,400 suppliers in the early 1990s.

Beyond Ford, beyond business, three American presidents have recognized the caliber of Jim Woods. He was tapped by Lyndon Johnson and, later, Gerald Ford for a variety of special assignments. The high point came in the early 1970s when, as Richard Nixon's ambassador-at-large to Africa, Woods spent six months on the continent, assessing the effectiveness of U.S. aid programs. "I felt connected with it," he remembered later. "Once you get out into the communities in Africa, you find that there's a very warm relationship and kinship, especially when they feel that you're there to help them."

As one observer has said, James Woods is "loved by his community because he has put so much of himself back into the people around him."

Barbara Walden

As a child, Barbara Walden watched her grandmother dab powder scraped from bricks on her cheeks because no stores carried the right rouge for her complexion. When Walden grew up, she, too, was frustrated by cosmetics blended strictly for white skin tones. But now, thanks in good measure to the pioneering company Walden established in 1968, African American women no longer have to scrape bricks for rouge or walk around, she says, "looking as though they've fallen into a flour barrel."

Success did not come easily for this daughter of a well-to-do Camden, New Jersey, businessman. Blessed with beauty,

Walden had Hollywood ambitions as a young woman. She was rebuffed three times before finally cracking the color barrier at New York's Vogue Finishing School, but then found movieland wanting. "I didn't mind playing maids," she recalled, "but the dialogue was ridiculous." What's more, the makeup made her face look purple.

A chemist friend developed a number of cosmetics to enhance her richly colored skin. And when friends begged her to share her treasures, Walden got an idea. She and a partner put up $350 each to start a business. As it turned out, she says, "I started a revolution."

Part of it was good timing. In

the early 1970s, explains Walden, "black women were getting better jobs, had more money to spend, and were interested in their looks." They began to realize their needs. "Black women have undertones of red, orange, yellow, even blue in their skin," says Walden. "Products for white women don't work for us because they highlight pink undertones."

Walden, who had sold a household cleaning product door-to-door in Los Angeles to make ends meet between acting jobs, organized a cadre of neighborhood saleswomen. The sales force proved so successful that she soon established a beauty clinic in the most prominent African American neighborhood in Los Angeles. By the early 1990s, the sixtyish Walden bossed a multimillion-dollar annual operation with a complete line of beauty products sold in leading department stores and beauty clinics around the world.

She firmly believes that if she can do it, so can others. She travels the country urging African American women to become entrepreneurs. And she instills pride by doing glamour makeovers in women's jails, drug and rehabilitation centers, and shelters. "I want black women to believe that everything about them is beautiful," she says. "If you look good, you do good."

Sandra Williams Bate

The year was 1973, and the Arab oil embargo had put a quietus on motor-home sales. Sandra and Bill Bate wanted to sell their recreation vehicle (RV)—a luxurious Laguna 250—but found no takers. Then 20-year-old Sandra had one of those blindingly brilliant flashes: Why not rent it out? She put an advertisement in the Los Angeles papers—and the phone rang off the hook until the whole summer was booked by people who wanted the Laguna just for a week or two.

It was a first in the field. Yet Sandra Bate might have let it pass; husband Bill was doing all right selling insurance. However, her parents had always pushed their children to be, as she puts it, "more than average—to be better than we thought we were." Within a year, Sandra Bate was coordinating the rental of 60 privately owned motor homes and had hired four people to help. Costs were low; rates were reasonable; and at a 40/60 split with owners, the money came rolling in.

Then she made a mistake that almost sank her. Bate decided to acquire a lot and service rentals. That labor-intensive job gobbled up the profits; worse, vandals kept breaking into the vehicles. She went back to being a broker and started refining her idea.

Quality control remained critical, naturally. It was no easy matter to line up reliable independent service centers that would check out motor homes offered for lease, then keep them roadworthy. Bate offered 10 percent of her fee, plus the cost of repairs to be borne by the owners. After considerable trial and error, she assembled a first-rate team.

To broaden her market, she hooked her company up with the airlines and the travel industry. Inclusion in the industry's Consolidated Tour Manual meant that she was listed with 22,000 travel agents in 125 countries.

Today, Bates Motor Home Rental Network is a multimillion-dollar enterprise headquartered in Las Vegas. Its computers hold all the details on 4,000 RVs in a hundred U.S. cities and 18 foreign countries. The rentals start at around $500 a week for a 23-footer and climb to $1,200 for a 32-footer that sleeps six. Bate's customer list includes movie stars and the U.S. Secret Service, but the bulk of her clients are tourists. Europeans in particular enjoy taking along the comforts—and cuisine—of home as they travel around.

Sandra Bate thinks she might build her brainstorm into a $20 million business eventually. "Set your goals," she advises others. "Make the commitments, and stick with them until they become a reality."

THE BLACK CHURCH

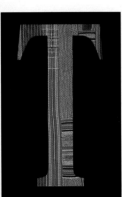

he first Sunday service at the newly expanded Saint George's Methodist Episcopal Church in Philadelphia had begun routinely on a November morning in 1787 with the opening hymn—and the usual attention to segregated seating. White churchgoers had their choice of the pews on the main floor, while the Africans—as both free blacks and slaves were then called—were relegated to spots along the walls, in the back, and in certain sections of the gallery above. When two free black preachers—Richard Allen and Absalom Jones—entered the church that Sunday, they mounted the stairs to the gallery, which had recently been built to accommodate the growing congregation. The strains of the first hymn were just ending as the pair knelt in front of their chairs and bowed their heads.

Suddenly Allen was jarred out of his quietude by the sounds of scuffling and struggle. He looked up to see an angry white trustee roughly pulling Jones from his knees. Trying to maintain the decorum of a house of worship, Jones shook off the churchman's grasp and murmured, "Wait until the prayer is over."

"No, you must get now," barked the trustee, "or I will call for aid and force you away!"

"Wait until the prayer is over, and I will get up and trouble you no more," Jones repeated.

Ignoring him, the trustee called to another, and together they attempted to drag Jones from the gallery. Allen sprang to his feet, realizing in his rage that in the newly expanded church, where the additions had been financed by black parishioners as well as white, none of his race were allowed to sit in that section of the gallery. As the prayer ended, Allen, Jones, and several other blacks rose and swept out the door of Saint George's, vowing never to return. "Our Methodist brothers and sisters in Christ," Allen wryly noted later, "were no more plagued by us in that church."

The defiance of that moment signaled a coming new era. Soon Richard Allen would establish the Bethel African Methodist Episcopal Church in Philadelphia—the first church in the United States entirely organized and directed by African Americans. Bethel, in turn, would be the seed for the first independent black Christian denomination, the African Methodist Episcopal church. Over the next two centuries, the number of major black denominations would grow to seven, attracting almost nine of every 10 churchgoing black Americans. Of the remaining worshipers, some would form smaller denominations and black congregations of white mainstream churches, others would join integrated congregations of these white churches,

and still others would choose to adopt non-Christian faiths altogether.

From slavery times through the 20th century, the collective black church—often called the first African American institution—has served not only the religious and spiritual needs of the community but its practical and emotional ones as well. The church united families after the Civil War and has cared for the hungry, sick, and poor throughout its history. It has also fostered black businesses, financial institutions, schools, and colleges. All the while, the church has affirmed African American identity and served as a focal point of movements for liberation, equality, and justice. Out of this institution have sprung the leaders of a continuing struggle—from Richard Allen to Martin Luther King, Jr., to Jesse Jackson—and a theology of freedom that sustains African Americans to this day.

As with all else in their history in the New World, African Americans did not come by their church easily. Victims of the African slave trade not only lost their families, their homeland, and their freedom, but they also lost the right to their own customs and beliefs. At a time when a continuing relationship with the divine could have provided a profound source of comfort and hope, the slaves were forced to relinquish the rich spiritual traditions of their heritage. Moreover, most were kept from any possible opportunity to fill the void. During the first decades of the ignominious trade, the white church declined to share Christianity with Africans. For one thing, the English colonists perceived a potential moral dilemma in holding Christians—as opposed to so-called pagans—in bondage. For another, slaveholders feared that Africans who learned from the Christian church that all human beings were equal in the eyes of God would demand their freedom.

In 1787, Methodist preachers Richard Allen (*above*) and Absalom Jones opened the Free African Society, a spiritual center for black Philadelphians. From that beginning, Allen went on to establish the first independent black Christian denomination in 1816.

Not surprisingly, then, when missionaries from the Church of England petitioned the colonists in 1701 to allow them to "bring Christ to the Africans" on the plantations, almost all slaveholders resisted—until the Anglican missionaries assured them that Christians made more reliable slaves than pagans. By the 18th century, governments throughout the South, as well as in New York and New Jersey, had passed laws for the benefit of those few colonists who did own Christianized slaves, decreeing that baptism did not alter the condition of a slave "as to his bondage or freedome." Given this measure of protection, many planters were willing to allow the Anglicans access to their slaves. In 1740 in Saint Helena Parish, South Carolina, three brothers—Joseph, Hugh, and Jonathan Bryan— even opened a school and offered religious instruction to the 130 Africans on their plantation.

Around this time, a religious movement called the Great Awakening was spreading like wildfire both throughout Europe and the colonies. Traveling evangelists moved from town to town, preaching a stirring message of the soul's transformation, redemption, and eternal salvation through what was termed a new birth in Jesus Christ. In the South, large numbers of

A KEEPER OF ISLAM

For one in five Africans brought in chains to the New World, converting to Christianity meant abandoning an Islamic past. Omar ibn Said, who is pictured in the daguerreotype above, appears to have been among the few who managed to retain a devotion to Islam, at least in part. Born in about 1770 in what is now Senegal, Omar had been a teacher and a merchant before he was violently captured by slave traders and, in his words, sold "into the hands of the Christians." Taken to Charleston, South Carolina, around 1807, he fled the state some four years later to escape from a cruel master. Eventually he was acquired by a man from North Carolina named James Owen, who expected only light duties from his diminutive but stately slave. When Omar, who, remarkably for that time, lived to see the outbreak of the Civil War (he died in 1864), was given an Arabic Bible he seemed to convert readily to Christianity; however, translations of his extant writings suggest that he remained faithful to his original Islamic beliefs. Evidence to support this conclusion is provided by the biblical prayers he transcribed, which, in every case, are preceded by traditional introductions from the Koran. A copy of the Lord's Prayer written in his hand, for example, begins, "All praises to Allah, who created all to worship Him Who tests their words and deeds."

slaves accompanied their masters to rousing camp meetings and revivals, most hosted by itinerant Baptist missionaries and preachers in the emerging Methodist movement, which had begun in the 1720s in England. In America, the movement's emphasis on emotional responsiveness provided an alternative to austere Puritan churches. Slaves in particular, repressed in so many ways, found a welcome outlet in the movement's joyous message of salvation.

In late summer or early fall, after the backbreaking work of harvesting tobacco and cotton was complete, time could be made for revival meetings. Upon the arrival of an itinerant preacher, white and black alike would gather in a clearing in the woods by the light of flickering torches. After participating with their masters in the regular services, slaves often assembled nearby and immersed themselves in cathartic outpourings of singing, shouting, and testifying about their spiritual experiences. African drums were forbidden, but the slaves punctuated their call-and-response dialogues, which in themselves were an ancient African tradition, with innovative body percussion whose rhythms echoed their ancestry. The clapping of hands and rhythmic striking of other parts of the body with open palms live on as a prominent feature of much of the glorious gospel music that resounds in the black churches of the 20th century (*pages* 156-159).

Along with whites, many blacks wholeheartedly embraced the message of rebirth at these revivals and underwent a profound shift, called conversion, in their approach to life in this world. Tradition required "saved," or converted, individuals to "tell their religion," or relate their conversion experience to everyone who challenged them so that a public appraisal of its authenticity could be made. Those who spoke convincingly were immediately welcomed into Christian fellowship with hearty congratulations and much rejoicing.

Throughout the 18th century, converted slaves tended to try to separate themselves from white churches and form their own Baptist and Methodist congregations. Although the new black churches were monitored by white officials, they provided African Americans with a community focus of their own—a rare opportunity in the South. Baptist churches were more easily established than their Methodist counterparts because each local church was autonomous and not subject to the oversight of an ecclesiastical bureaucracy. Baptist preachers were expected to have first been "called of God," after which they could be called by a particular congregation to be its pastor. Each Baptist congregation cherished its independence, and although many of them formed loosely knit voluntary associations, these associations had no power or jurisdiction over any local church. All power belonged to the congregation.

The first known black church in America, the African Baptist or "Bluestone" Church, sprang from such a climate of autonomy. Established in 1758 on the William Byrd plantation, the church was named for its proximity to the Bluestone River in Mecklenberg, Virginia. Sometime between 1773 and 1775, the Silver Bluff Baptist Church in Silver Bluff, South Carolina, was founded by a slave preacher named George Liele, and around 1788 a slave baptized by Liele founded the First African Baptist Church in Savannah, Georgia. Other independent black Baptist churches sprang up throughout North Carolina, South Carolina, and Virginia, drawing more than 25,000 blacks by the end of the century.

Unlike the Baptists, Methodists had set up a formal structured association, or "connection," among their churches. Each local church functioned under the parent denomination according to a strict governing hierarchy. Within these more rigid confines, Richard Allen led a determined group of black Methodists in Philadelphia in a long struggle to break away from the mother church; in 1794 they finally succeeded in establishing a church of their own.

Born a slave on February 14, 1760, in Philadelphia, Allen grew up on a plantation in Delaware. At the age of 17 he had watched helplessly as his master sold off most of his family to other plantations, and he may well have turned to the consolations of religion at that time to help him cope with his grief. The Delaware farmer who owned Allen's family later experienced a change of heart about the institution of slavery and allowed Allen, then 20, to purchase his freedom. Allen began to preach that same year, choosing the Methodist faith, in large part because it had taken a strong stand against slavery. In 1786, his reputation for eloquence earned him an invitation to preach at Saint George's Methodist Episcopal Church in his birthplace, the City of Brotherly Love. Within a year, Allen's sermons greatly increased the number of Africans worshiping there.

But as the black presence at Saint George's grew, white members and clergy reversed their once-positive racial attitudes. Black members, who had once worshiped from the same pews as everyone else, were now subject to segregation. Allen went to the elder of Saint George's to propose a separate parish where blacks could worship on their own in dignity. When the elder rejected the request—in "very degrading and insulting language," Allen later recounted—Allen, fellow preacher Absalom Jones, and some of their colleagues took matters into their own hands. In May 1787, the Free African Society was born. Although most members of the new group—including Allen and Jones—continued to attend services at Saint George's, the society in many ways filled the role of the church for the black community, holding regular meetings and expecting upright conduct from its members. The society also offered help to the sick and the poor, and to widows and orphans.

When Allen and Jones were accosted for unwittingly sitting in off-limits seats at Saint George's in November of that year, they had had enough, and they left the church for the last time. "We all went out in a body," Allen wrote, and thereafter the group turned to the Free African Society for spiritual uplift. When officials at Saint

Southern revival meetings converted thousands of slaves to Christianity during the 18th and 19th centuries, as is illustrated in this drawing from the *Harper's Weekly* of August 10, 1872. "The speaker," reported a Virginia slave, "talks very slowly, until feeling the spirit, he grows excited, and in a short time, there fall to the ground twenty or thirty men and women under its influence."

The First African Baptist Church of Savannah, Georgia—shown here in a drawing probably done when its first permanent house of worship was built in 1795—was one of the earliest and largest black congregations in the South. Organized in barns and arbors around 1788, the congregation had swelled to 700 members by 1802, at which point local white Baptists grew uneasy about its size and divided it into three churches.

George's continued to oppose a separate black congregation and threatened to excommunicate any who joined such a movement, Allen responded that his people could not remain in a congregation that had treated them "scandalously," declaring, "If you deny us your name"—Methodism—"you cannot seal up the scripture from us, and deny us a place in heaven."

To Allen's dismay, though, the meetings at the Free African Society began increasingly to emphasize silence and meditation rather than the Methodists' more expressive style of worship. When the society eventually voted to establish an Anglican (Episcopal) church and asked Allen to be their pastor, he declined the honor in favor of his friend Jones, confessing, "As for me, I could never be anything but a Methodist." To create a meeting place for black Methodists, Allen and a small group of supporters bought a blacksmith shop and had it moved to a lot owned by Allen on Lombard Street, in the middle of Philadelphia's black community. On July 29, 1794, the converted shop was dedicated and named Bethel, a Hebrew word meaning "the House of the Lord."

Although Allen owned the real estate, under the rules of the Methodist polity Bethel Church belonged to the Philadelphia Conference of the Methodist Episcopal church. To make it clear that the Bethel congregation did not consider itself an African extension of Saint George's, Allen issued on November 3, 1794, a "Declaration of Independence," using for the first time the name African Methodist Episcopal church. For 10 years, Bethel and Saint George's coexisted amicably, but those first years

proved to be the calm before the storm. Beginning in 1805, a series of elders at Saint George's used various tactics to try to take control of Bethel. Their efforts climaxed in 1815 when they claimed rights to the Bethel property and put it up for auction. Allen himself repurchased his own land and the church building for $10,125—an enormous sum at the time—and in a court battle on the last day of the year, a judge released Bethel Church from the grip of the white Philadelphia Conference.

News of the court's decision was cause for rejoicing in Baltimore, where another black Methodist Episcopal church, also named Bethel, had modeled itself on Allen's congregation. On April 9, 1816, the Reverend Daniel Coker, pastor of the Baltimore church, joined Allen and 14 other black church leaders from Delaware, New Jersey, and Pennsylvania for the organizing conference of the new and separate denomination, the African Methodist Episcopal (AME) church. The following day the delegation elected Allen the first bishop of the fledgling denomination.

By then, a second black Methodist denomination had emerged in the North. In 1796, just two years after the dedication of the Bethel Church in Philadelphia, black parishioners at New York City's John Street Methodist Episcopal Church withdrew from the congregation to protest their church's refusal to fully ordain black preachers. Led by a former slave named Peter Williams, they set up a makeshift chapel in a cabinetmaker's shop, where local black preachers conducted services. Four years later they moved into a new building, which they named Zion Church. In 1801 the denomination

In 1793 horses hauled a blacksmith shop away from its location near Philadelphia's imposing Walnut Street Jail to a new address at the corner of Sixth and Lombard streets—an event depicted by a local artist at the time. The shop had been purchased by Richard Allen to be converted to the Bethel African Methodist Episcopal Church, the mother church of the AME denomination. Bethel has been rebuilt three times since its dedication in 1794.

In 1889, when the third Bethel was torn down to erect a bigger church, an artist painted an image of the razed building on a chunk of its own bricks.

was incorporated as the African Methodist Episcopal Church of the City of New York.

Believing in the strength of a unified black community, Richard Allen journeyed to New York in 1820 to discuss bringing the Zion Church into the AME fold. Zion Church declined, however, and the following year held a conference with four other congregations in New York, Connecticut, and Allen's own state of Pennsylvania to organize the African Methodist Episcopal Zion (AMEZ) denomination. Like the AME church, the AMEZ demonstrated a firm commitment to social justice. Many abolitionists, including the great Underground Railroad conductor Harriet Tubman and the preeminent orator Frederick Douglass, belonged to the AMEZ church, and it became the first Methodist denomination—black or white—to give the vote in church matters and clerical ordination to women.

Although he was unsuccessful in New York, Richard Allen's dream of extending the reach of the AME church seemed about to come true in 1820 when Methodist preacher Morris Brown of Charleston, South Carolina, enrolled his congregation. In a city with an unusually high number of free blacks, Brown's South Carolina conference of the AME church soon claimed 2,000 members, including the charismatic preacher Denmark Vesey. Using religious meetings as a cover for recruitment and strategy planning in 1822, Vesey organized an ambitious plot for rebellion that, though a failure, cast new suspicions on black churches as seedbeds of insurrection. When word of the revolt leaked out, Charleston authorities captured and executed Vesey and 30 other insurgents, and burned the local church building to the ground. Brown—who was not a party to the plot—was nevertheless forced to flee for his life.

White slaveholders across the southern states responded to the news of the failed revolt with vigorous efforts to suppress the black church. The AME church was virtually banned from the South, and the black Baptist congregations that had begun to flourish now withered under such severe restrictions that they could no longer be considered free from white supervision. Thus, the first attempts to organize all-black Baptist associations, or conventions, occurred not in the South—where most of the Baptist churches had emerged—but in Ohio, Illinois, Michigan, and Canada during the 1830s and 1840s. Like the northern Methodist churches, these black Baptist associations assumed a strong abolitionist posture, and many of them participated in the Underground Railroad in Ohio and Canada.

As the controversy over slavery gained momentum in the 1830s, wary slaveholders in the South kept a careful watch over the black population. Convinced that religion could be used to control the slaves, they brought blacks into their own churches and set aside segregated pews, sections, and galleries for them. Of course, the Christianity then preached to the slaves was one of black obedience, loyalty to the master, and the moral obligation to work hard day in and day out without complaint. But more than anything else, the slaves yearned for earthly freedom and prayed for deliverance from bondage. This shared thirst drew them together in secret gatherings of prayer and song. "My father would have church in dwelling houses and they had to whisper," said one slave woman named Lucretia Alexander. "That would be when they would want a real meetin' with some real preachin'."

By singing spirituals such as "Steal Away to Jesus," slaves spread the word that a "real meeting" would take place that very night or weekend, if not in one of their cabins, then somewhere at a "brush harbor" in the woods or swamps, away from the big house and the prying eyes of the overseer. Within the boundaries of what has been called the invisible church, African Americans created their own sustaining worldview. "God wants you free," they heard from the black preachers who risked their lives to nurture the faith of their black brothers and sisters. These preachers taught that the law of God was superior to the law of man and that his justice would not be forever delayed. One day would come a reckoning, a "great getting-up morning." God had delivered Israel out of the hands of Pharaoh, and God would deliver the children of Africa, who were as precious to him as any other.

It was only natural that a people in bondage would adopt the Old Testament view of an avenging, liberating God, a God who took care that justice would ultimately prevail. When a white man murdered his wife in the early 1800s, for example, the family's slave Isabella grieved—but was keenly aware of what she called the "special providence of God." Some days before, the murderer himself had brutally flogged Isabella's son, and the mother of the woman who would soon be killed had laughed at Isabella's anguish. "Oh Lord, 'render unto them double' for all this!" the slave had prayed that night. Although she felt no joy over the family's suffering, Isabella—who years later would gain freedom and a new name and become the great evangelist and reformer Sojourner Truth—thought she saw clearly the Lord's hand meting out a stark retribution.

The secret prayer meetings that fostered these convictions were both a profound expression of resistance to slavery and a testament to the courage and faith of the slaves, who persevered no matter what. A bondman named Moses Grandy reported that his fellow slaves were routinely beaten if the master found them singing or praying, and that his brother-in-law was "flogged, and his back pickled" for preaching. But because the slaves "like their own meetings better," as Grandy put it, they found ways to conceal their activities. From Louisiana to Virginia, they slipped under cover of darkness to the brush harbors; or when gathering in their quarters, huddled behind quilts and rags to muffle their voices.

With the defeat of the Confederacy in 1865, newly liberated African Americans everywhere rejoiced in the sense of divine justice that had set them free. "I remember I was sittin' on the fence when the soldiers in them blue uniforms with gold buttons come," recalled former slave Dolly Whiteside. "I didn't know what it was all about but everybody was sayin' 'Thank God.' I thought it was the Judgment Day and I was lookin' for God."

The once-invisible church that was the secret heart of the African American community soon emerged as the center of black life during the wrenching transition from slavery to freedom—and the tasks before it were enormous. Its ministers baptized, counseled, married, and buried thousands of freed men, women, and children. The church-sanctioned marriages of couples who had formerly been slaves, in particular, laid a foundation of security for families who no longer had to fear losing each other on the slave auction block. The early churches also functioned as schools where ex-slaves learned to read and write, as savings institutions and places where

new wage earners could learn how to use and save money, and as burial societies.

Finally free to choose their own way of worship, tens of thousands of blacks abandoned their marginal status in white congregations, later heeding black preachers and evangelists who followed the advance of Union troops with a call for blacks to "be African." Southern black Baptists quickly withdrew from white churches; black Methodists affiliated with the AME and AMEZ churches. In 1867, seeking to stem the exodus, white bishops of the southern branch of the Methodist Episcopal church began to organize meetings for the black membership who had not yet left the church for the northern black denominations. But by 1870, the church and its 70,000 remaining African American parishioners had come to an amicable agreement to part ways. A licensed black Methodist preacher named Isaac Lane, who had ministered to fellow slaves before the war, wrote in his autobiography, "We made it known that we preferred a separate organization of our own, regularly established and organized after our own ideas and notions." And so the black brethren were "set aside" in the Colored Methodist Episcopal Church in America (CME), which would later change its name to the Christian Methodist Episcopal church.

Lane, who became a CME bishop in 1873, believed that the new church's arrangement with the southern Methodists suited the "peculiar conditions" that existed in the postwar South—namely, the unstable racial climate stirred by the war and the abolition of slavery. In exchange for land, buildings, and other assets from the southern Methodists, the CME church agreed to engage in no political activity. "As ministers of the gospel," wrote Lucius H. Holsey, who along with Lane helped establish the church and also became a bishop in 1873, "we make no stump-speeches and fight no battles of the politicians." Having won their independence, the CME membership sought to coexist as peacefully as possible with their former owners; for the greater part of the next century the CME church maintained a uniquely benign relationship with the southern Methodists. Nonetheless, the new denomination did announce a commitment to social justice—a commitment shared with northern churches and expressed in its "Social Creed" as "the liberation of the oppressed from all forms of bondage."

Around this time, black writer William Wells Brown of Boston traveled through the South, attending a number of revival meetings conducted by itinerant preachers. Brown, often called America's first black man of letters, was unimpressed with the emotional style of worship that he witnessed. In *My Southern Home: or, The South and Its People*, he denounced the preachers as "a plague" all over the South. "The only remedy," he

A Reconstruction-era drawing titled *Marriage of a Colored Soldier at Vicksburg by Chaplain Warner of Freedmen's Bureau* shows one of thousands of black couples who sanctified their unions in religious ceremonies after emancipation.

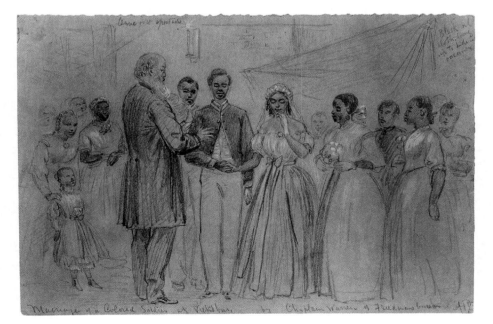

wrote, "lies in an educated ministry." Brown's criticism was characteristic of the era, when such impassioned behavior in rural areas of the South was attributed to ignorance or a lack of sophistication. But even as many black churches, notably those in the cities and northern society, began to adopt a newly restrained form of worship, a significant portion of black Christians were looking for more emotional fulfillment.

In 1867, the National Camp Meeting Association for the Promotion of Holiness, later to be known as the National Holiness Association, headed a reform movement within Methodism that promoted the energetic expression of feeling as evidence of God's grace. Over the next two decades, the association hosted some 70 interracial, interdenominational camp meetings that maintained the enthusiasm of the Great Awakening and emphasized sanctification, or holiness in thought and behavior. In Holiness meetings, fervent praying and singing and demonstrative preaching were expected during ordinary worship, along with dancing and other forms of physical exuberance, shouting, and testifying.

Eventually, during the 1890s, the Holiness movement—which had also attracted Baptists and others—cut its remaining ties with the Methodist church and formed independent sanctified sects. In 1895, for example, black Baptist preacher Charles Harrison Mason, who had been sanctified two years earlier, was dismissed from his church in Arkansas because of his Holiness beliefs. A year later he and Charles P. Jones, another former black Baptist preacher, began to hold Holiness revivals in Mississippi, and in 1897 they set up a congregation in an old cotton-gin house in the town of Lexington, naming the new body the Church of God. Townspeople persecuted its early members because of their radical views, once attacking them with pistols and shotguns. Nevertheless, the church incorporated as an independent denomination called the Church of God in Christ (COGIC); a decade later the church turned Pentecostal after Mason introduced glossolalia, or speaking in tongues, to his congregation (*pages* 152-155). Spreading outward from its southern base to the urban centers of the West and North, the Pentecostal COGIC has become the largest denomination to spring from the Holiness movement. Moreover, it is the only major black denomination that does not trace its roots to a white church.

Meanwhile, the Roman Catholic church—arguably the original white Christian church—attempted to bring more African Americans into its fold. Two orders of black nuns had been founded by the end of the 19th century (*pages* 146-147), and Frederick Douglass noted that the church welcomed "to its altars and communion men of all races and colors." However, African Americans had joined the Catholic church in significant numbers in only a few areas of the country, where the church was already well established, and by 1886 there was only one black priest—Augustus Tolton—who had been ordained in Rome that April. Convinced that Catholicism's lack of appeal to the African American community lay in its unwillingness to ordain black priests— even as it claimed to condemn social segregation—the Josephite order of priests sought to desegregate the American priesthood around 1890 by ordaining black men as Josephites (*pages* 148-149). Also, in January 1889, the First Black Catholic Congress convened in Washington, D.C., to discuss the concerns of black Catholics, especially the matter of priests. Four more national congresses took place through 1894, but de-

One of the best-known evangelists in the Holiness movement and a member of the African Methodist Episcopal church was Amanda Berry Smith. The "singing pilgrim," as newspapers called her, riveted both blacks and whites at revivals in the United States, West Africa, Europe, and India during the last decades of the 1800s. Smith also wrote an autobiography and spent her life savings to open an orphanage and school for black children near Chicago.

spite these efforts, only a handful of black Americans had been ordained by 1900, and racism continued to plague the church well into the 20th century. In contrast, the Baptist church, with its lack of restrictions, drew more than 60 percent of all worshiping African Americans to its doors. After more than three decades of forming alliances among growing numbers of black Baptist congregations, the National Baptist Convention, USA, an independent black denomination, was created in 1895. On September 28 of that year, more than 500 delegates and observers attended a convention in Atlanta to join three small Baptist alliances into one. The NBC established departments to carry on the special interests of each of the original groups, including foreign missions and education, and to handle such domestic concerns as the use of alcohol and tobacco. Soon it added a publications division as well, which produced a wealth of material by the finest black writers of the day. In 1915, in the wake of the nationwide success of these publications, the publishing house broke away from its parent organization and formed a separate denomination with a large constituency of its own. Eventually the new denomination adopted the name National Baptist Convention of America, distinguishing itself from the National Baptist Convention, USA.

About this time, hundreds of thousands of African Americans began migrating north to escape increasingly oppressive conditions in the postwar South. Nearly 1.5 million made the journey between 1910 and 1920, settling largely in all-black enclaves in the big cities. There, black churches and their congregations tended to be much larger and to place as much emphasis on the real-world demands of black survival as on salvation after death. The churches established social service organizations to meet the practical needs of their parishioners and encouraged them to take a greater hand in their own destinies by voting, buying land, and going to school.

One of the most prominent advocates of this self-help doctrine was the powerful and charismatic leader who presided over the Abyssinian Baptist Church in New York City. On the eve of the First World War, the Reverend Adam Clayton Powell, Sr., witnessed a flood of black southerners into the city—100,000 strong. Most of them came to rest in Harlem—an "invasion," wrote Powell in his autobiography, that "scared the white people almost to death. They literally ran in every direction from the most beautiful section of Manhattan." The upheaval was underscored by the arrival in 1914 of Marcus Garvey. The West Indian-born orator and organizer preached an inspirational message of racial pride that promoted such ideas as a black government, a black military, and a black religion with a black God. "Harlem became the symbol of liberty and the Promised Land to Negroes everywhere," according to Powell, who had been campaigning long before Garvey's arrival to move the Abyssinian Church from its location on 40th Street in Manhattan to this rising black urban center, where it could serve the needs of so many.

Winning support and financial backing for the move took years, but finally, on June 17, 1923, the largest black Baptist church in the United States opened at 138th Street between Seventh and Lenox avenues. The new Abyssinian Church was de-

signed to be a community center as well as a place of worship. Its sanctuary seated 2,000, and the center also featured a large lecture room and 14 smaller classrooms, a gymnasium, reading rooms, and facilities for teaching practical skills such as cooking, sewing, and nursing. Under Powell's leadership, the church sponsored housing for the elderly, missions in Africa, endowments for African American colleges, and other similar activities. "Work for others will heal our sorrows and make us forget most of our troubles," he counseled. When the Great Depression devastated the country, Abyssinian assisted those in need with job clinics, employment referrals, an unemployment relief fund, and free food kitchens. Adam Clayton Powell, Jr., who succeeded his father as senior minister, led a campaign to procure jobs for unemployed blacks in businesses patronized by African Americans and was eventually sent to Congress by the Harlem constituency.

Other churches with extensive memberships and broad social-service outreach programs grew up in other major cities, but, because of their very size and scope, they proved less appealing to some of the African Americans who had migrated from the South and were accustomed to more intimate worship practices. In an attempt to preserve the type of worship they were used to, many newcomers opened their own small churches in abandoned stores along commercial blocks of the city—and a thriving urban storefront ministry was born.

During the 1920s, for example, of the 140 churches in Harlem, 86 were housed in

Participants at the First Black Catholic Congress, held in January 1889 to address concerns of the 100,000 Catholic African Americans at the time, assemble for the camera on the front steps of Saint Augustine's Church in Washington, D.C. Concluding the four-day meeting, the black delegates issued a statement requesting from the Catholic church "fellowship in the great and noble work which we have thus inaugurated for the welfare—social, moral, and intellectual—of our entire people."

storefronts. Many of these ministries were Baptist, Holiness, or Pentecostal, and a number were of a sect called Spiritualist. Much of the Spiritualist service resembled the practices of Holiness, Pentecostal, and the more expressive Baptist churches, except that the Spiritualists emphasized public prophecy in "bless services," a feature that replaced the traditional sermon. A prophet—who might have been the church's pastor, a medium from the congregation, or a visiting prophet—would deliver a message of healing or clairvoyance by revealing details of the present, past, and future of selected church members.

The urban experience produced the flowering of a number of different religious groups that sought to define the relationship of black people to the world and to God. Among the most unorthodox was Father Divine's Peace Mission. After the First World War, Father Divine, who was born George Baker, moved to Long Island from the South, where he had been an itinerant preacher. He established the Peace Mission during the Depression to assist the struggling black population. Like other black churches, the Peace Mission sought to provide its followers with food, shelter, clothing, jobs, and medical aid. Father Divine also set up business and agricultural cooperatives, attempted to reform black prison inmates, and in the mid-1930s developed a 14-point Righteous Government Platform covering education, economics, and a number of racial issues.

But the Peace Mission was more than a social movement. It portrayed Father Divine as the incarnation of God, and forbade its members to drink alcohol, smoke, dance, or engage in any form of sex. Throughout the Depression, he presided daily over enormous banquets and fed thousands of hungry people in his "heavens" in New York and Philadelphia. "We feed as many as come," he said. "We serve from early morning to midnight."

Not all in the black community accepted Father Divine. Many considered him a charlatan, and others rejected the message he preached for racial integration, objecting to the fact that a large number of the Peace Mission followers, including Mother Divine, were white. Prominent among Divine's critics was Elijah Muhammad, a self-proclaimed Muslim who in the mid-1930s established a black sect that condemned the merging of black culture with white.

Islam was both an old and a new religion among African Americans. As many as one-fifth of all Africans who were brought across the Atlantic during the slave trade had come from Islamic areas of the continent. However, the religion had not survived among them, because they were thereafter exposed almost exclusively to Christianity. Later Muslim immigrants from Africa, Asia, the Middle East, and the Caribbean gradually reintroduced the traditional worship of Allah to their communities in the New World. In the 1920s, for example, Sheik Daud Faisal from Trinidad opened the Islamic Mission of America in Brooklyn, New York, and its international membership included many African Americans. Meanwhile, in New Jersey, Noble Drew Ali (born Timothy Drew) had established a modified version of Islam called Moorish Science—which, unlike traditional Islam, had as part of its purpose the promotion of black unity. However, Elijah Muhammad is generally credited with reintroducing Islam to the largest number of African Americans, in the form of the Nation of Islam.

Born Elijah Poole in Sandersville, Georgia, in 1897, Elijah Muhammad later moved to Detroit, where he was instructed in the tenets of Islam by Wali Farad Muhammad. Farad Muhammad, as he was known, claimed to have come from the Holy City of Mecca on a mission of redemption and restoration of black people in America. He taught that members of the black African diaspora were all of Muslim heritage and were the original inhabitants of the earth, destined to free themselves from white domination. But in keeping with his mysterious past, he vanished without a trace in 1934, and Elijah Muhammad, who had assumed the title of Messenger, transferred the movement's headquarters to Chicago. There he built up the black separatist Nation of Islam. During the tumultuous racial climate of the 1950s and 1960s, the Nation achieved international prominence through its charismatic spokesman Malcolm X, who urged African Americans to respond to white violence by laying down their lives if need be to protect their human rights.

After Elijah's death in 1975, his son Wallace (Warith) Deen, or W. D., Muhammad assumed leadership of the movement and steered it toward conformity with orthodox Islam. Orthodox Muslims derive guidance from their holy book, the Koran, which commands devotional duties such as fasting, prayer five times a day, charitable giving, a strict code of moral behavior, and a pilgrimage to Mecca if possible. Many members of the Nation of Islam chose not to follow W. D. Muhammad, though, and turned instead to Minister Louis Farrakhan. A recruit and student of Malcolm X and the official spokesman for Elijah Muhammad in 1975, Farrakhan resuscitated the Nation and has attempted to return it to its former power and status in the black community.

Islam is today the fastest-growing religion in the world, and more than 40 percent of the nearly six million Muslims in the United States are black. Since the civil rights era, black mosques have served their communities in the same way as other black churches, developing businesses, farms, schools, and service industries, and owning banks, real estate, and newspapers.

The civil rights movement itself found its earliest direction and grounding in the black church. Churches became the favored meeting places for organizing local movements in the small-town South—and as a result, scores of them were burned or bombed by hooded nightriders in an effort to crush the liberation fervor. Martin Luther King, Jr., pursued a strategy of nonviolent civil disobedience through the church, forming a coalition of Christian ministers who planned some of the movement's major events. The Atlanta-based Southern Christian Leadership Conference, organized by King in 1957, encouraged churches and black ministers to participate in routinely dangerous activism across the South. Other African American ministers, north and south, used their churches more than ever as platforms to address the grievances of black people.

But political activity on the part of the churches was not universally accepted by their members, and disagreement over the issue sparked another schism within the National Baptist Convention, USA, the largest of the black denominations. In 1957

Italian marble and imported stained-glass windows adorn the magnificent sanctuary of Harlem's Abyssinian Baptist Church, photographed soon after its completion in 1923. Adam Clayton Powell, Sr.—shown at left in 1897—became Abyssinian's pastor in 1908 and was the man responsible for building the Harlem church and increasing its membership. By the 1930s the congregation numbered 14,000, making it the largest of any Protestant congregation in the country—black or white.

Dr. Joseph H. Jackson, its president at the time, began to stress the church's spiritual mission and discourage political protest. His conservative stance alienated many Baptist ministers, and at the convention's annual meeting in 1960, held in Philadelphia, several of Jackson's opponents—including Martin Luther King, Jr.—were expelled. At a meeting held in November 1961 at the Zion Baptist Church in Cincinnati, King and representatives from 14 states voted to start a separate convention—the Progressive National Baptist Convention. Unlike the National Baptist Convention under Dr. Jackson's leadership, the Progressive Convention involved itself heavily in the civil rights movement, lent its voice to the stirrings of black power activists, and was one of the earliest groups to publicly oppose the Vietnam War. Half a million Baptists joined King in the new denomination.

In the mid-1960s, when nonviolent civil rights protests evolved into the more militant Black Power movement, the black church, in large part, embraced the change. On the morning of April 26, 1969, at the all-white Riverside Church in New York City, James Forman—the young black activist and former international affairs director of

the civil rights group known as the Student Nonviolent Coordinating Committee—strode to a microphone during the service and demanded to be heard. As the stunned congregation looked on, Forman read aloud from a document titled the Black Manifesto. Among other things, the manifesto called for white-controlled mainstream Protestant and Catholic churches and Jewish synagogues to pay half a billion dollars in reparation for racial injustices inflicted on blacks over the centuries. The manifesto also espoused solidarity between African Americans and African nations and attacked capitalism and imperialism. "We are dedicated to building a socialist society inside the United States," Forman proclaimed, "led by black people . . . concerned about the total humanity of the world."

Perhaps equally surprising to the white community, the National Conference of Black Churchmen (NCBC)—a group of black clergy from mostly white-controlled denominations that had been formed two years earlier—fully supported the manifesto. Inspired by the stand taken by the NCBC, other African American clergy also created caucuses in the National Council of Churches and other religious organizations dominated by whites. In effect, the NCBC acted as the religious counterpart of the secular Black Power movement.

The black consciousness and Black Power movements of the 1960s prompted theologians in divinity schools and seminaries to develop visions of Christianity from a distinctively African American perspective. In 1969, James H. Cone, professor at Union Theological Seminary in New York City, published *Black Theology and Black Power*, followed the next year by *A Black Theology of Liberation*, which linked Jesus' struggle against human oppression with the African American struggle against racism in America. According to Cone, whose groundbreaking work earned him the title "the father of black theology," the black community needs "a theology whose sole purpose is to emancipate the gospel from its 'whiteness.' " In the world-view he described, the community must not accept oppression as God's will but instead must adopt values that "stress the beauty of being black." As Cone put it, "The task of Black Theology is to inform black people that because of God's act in Christ they need not offer anyone an apology for being black. Rather, be glad of it! Shout it! It is the purpose for which we were created."

Although Cone supported the political views preached by Malcolm X during the 1960s, he eventually included in his theology Martin Luther King, Jr.'s concept of a "beloved community" that accepts and even celebrates its individual differences. In 1978, the seven largest black Christian denominations—three Methodist, three Baptist, and one Pentecostal, representing 20 million members in 60,000 churches across the United States—formed a "beloved community" with the organization of the Congress of National Black Churches. In the ongoing black church tradition of responsiveness to all facets of black life, the congress included in its goals the building of social and economic institutions within the African American community. Indeed, many credit unions, small businesses, social outreach programs, and educational scholarships are the result of the efforts of the black church.

The Rainbow Coalition, an organization created by the Reverend Jesse Jackson—who was originally a minister with the National Baptist Convention, USA—also em-

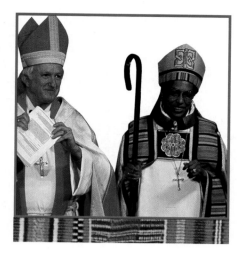

A NEW BREED OF BISHOP

At her consecration in February 1989 as the first woman bishop of the Episcopal church, the Reverend Barbara Clementine Harris wore vestments that included a stole of Ghanaian kente cloth, a proud symbol of her African ancestry (above). An outspoken cleric, she once lambasted her denomination, which is only five percent black, as "a male-dominated racist church." Harris now serves as suffragan, or assistant bishop, of the diocese of Massachusetts, having followed a career path that was unconventional from the start. Ordained as a priest in 1980, she brought 20 years of experience as a public relations executive to her new office. Harris had also registered voters in Mississippi during the 1960s and marched with Martin Luther King, Jr., in Selma. In her view, being elevated to the bishopric has enabled her to fight even more effectively against social injustice. "I want to offer my peculiar gifts as a black woman," she has said, "a sensitivity and an awareness that come out of more than a speaking acquaintance with oppression."

bodies that ecumenical vision, with a membership of African Americans, Hispanics, Asian Americans, Native Americans, and even whites. As an organization for political reform, the coalition has a strong base in the black church. When it presented Jackson as the first black candidate for president in 1984, more than 90 percent of the church's clergy endorsed him. These ministers coordinated at least half of the state campaigns for Jackson's presidency, and millions of African Americans were inspired to vote.

In the last years of the 20th century, even as the reach of the black church has extended farther and farther into the realms of social service, social change, and politics, nurturing the spirit of its people has remained as important as ever. On Sundays at the 7,000-strong Bethel AME Church in Baltimore, a jazz band invigorates members of the congregation between moments of sermon and prayer, while across the country, a huge, vibrant mural of African and African American faces fills the sanctuary of Los Angeles's First AME Church. In South Carolina at the Silver Bluff Baptist Church, now the oldest African American church, still in existence more than 200 years after its founding by a slave preacher, a dozen or so worshipers quietly gather for services on Wednesday evenings. And in Memphis, drums and tambourines electrify the Sunday morning services at the Pentecostal Temple Church of God in Christ as parishioners sing gospel hymns and dance in the aisles.

In its abundant variety, the black church remains the core of the black community. The first African American institution—born centuries ago in southern brush harbors and northern shop buildings—continues to be the place where black America puts its best foot forward, for itself and for its deepest beliefs. The services taking place in every house of worship, from the most intimate country churches to the vast urban sanctuaries, are wellsprings of faith and support that also inspire great joy as African Americans gather to celebrate their part in the divine. As renowned black author James Baldwin wrote, "There is no music like that music, no drama like the drama of saints rejoicing, the sinners moaning, the tambourines racing, and all those voices coming together and crying holy unto the Lord. I have never seen the fire and excitement that sometimes, without warning, fill a church."

A LEGACY IN SONG

"The human spirit in this new world has expressed it-self in vigor and ingenuity rather than in beauty," wrote W. E. B. Du Bois in 1903. "And so by fateful chance the Negro folk song—the rhythmic cry of the slave—stands today not simply as the sole American music but as the most beautiful expression of human experience born this side the seas."

Du Bois was among the first to recognize the artis-tic importance of the African American songs known as spirituals. Spirituals are true folk music, the collec-tive creation of countless unknown bards handed down from generation to generation. They express the deepest yearnings of the slaves—their longing for freedom and their newfound faith in Christianity, with its promise of reward in heaven for the injustices and trials suffered on earth.

Many of the songs contain covert messages or ap-peals to flight, warning of the overseer's approach or urging slaves to "steal away" north on the Under-ground Railroad. Originally intended for group singing with spontaneous harmonization, they were later written down by such renowned composers as Harry T. Burleigh, Hall Johnson, William Dawson, James Weldon Johnson, and R. Nathaniel Dett, who collected hundreds of songs and arranged them for the concert stage. Du Bois's assessment of the music remains as apt today as when he set it down nearly a century ago: "Negro folk song has been, and is, half despised, and above all it has been persistently mis-taken and misunderstood; but notwithstanding, it remains as the singular spiritual expression of the nation and the greatest gift of the Negro people."

One of the most familiar examples of what W. E. B. Du Bois called the sorrow songs, created by American blacks during the era of slavery, is "Nobody Knows de Trouble I See," a mournful anthem that nevertheless confirms the slaves' abiding faith in God's ultimate justice in its final words— "Glory, hallelujah!" The famous "code" song "Steal Away to Jesus," often attributed to Nat Turner, the African American preacher who led a bloody slave insurrection in Virginia in 1831, urged its listeners to "steal away" to a clandestine reli-gious meeting—or to freedom.

NOBODY KNOWS DE TROUBLE I SEE

No-bod-y knows de troub-le I see, No-bod-y knows but Je-sus;

No-bod-y knows de troub-le I see, Glo-ry, hal-le-lu-jah!

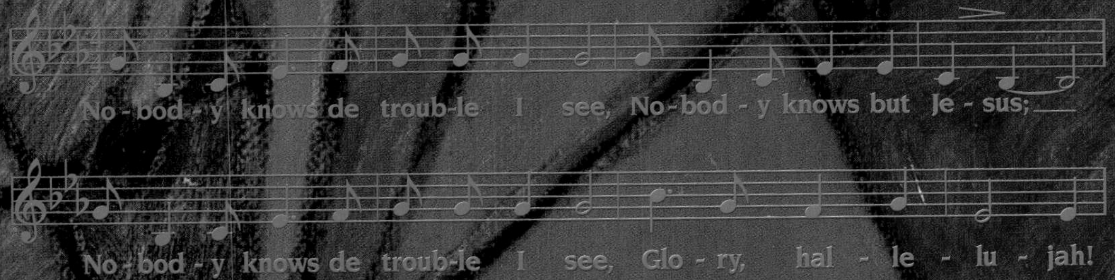

Sometimes I'm up Sometimes I'm down, Oh, yes, Lord;
Sometimes I'm almos' to de groun' Oh, yes, Lord.
Altho' you see me goin' 'long so, Oh, yes, Lord;
I have my trials here below, Oh, yes, Lord.

STEAL AWAY TO JESUS

Steal a-way, steal a-way, steal a-way to Je-sus!

Steal a-way, steal a-way home, I ain't got long to stay here.

My Lord, He calls me, He calls me by the thunder,
The trumpet sounds within-a my soul,
I ain't got long to stay here.
Steal away, steal away, steal away to Jesus!

Slaves held fast to the belief that God somehow would intervene on their behalf, and the spirituals they sang were testament to that faith. "Ev'ry Time I Feel de Spirit" celebrates God's power and affirms that the souls of his people can never be chained. In "Lord, I Want to Be a Christian in-a My Heart," the singer strives to "be like Jesus"—forgiving of those who perpetrate injustice. The idea of spiritual autonomy was often conveyed in songs that promised compensation in heaven for the bondman's wretched mortal existence. Yet the slaves never lost hope of gaining their freedom in this world, and songs such as "Joshua Fit de Battle ob Jerico" and "I Thank God I'm Free at Las' " express their intense yearning for liberation on earth.

I THANK GOD I'M FREE AT LAS'

Free at las' Free at las' I thank God I'm free at las'

Free at las' Free at las' I thank God I'm free at las'

Way down yonder in de graveyard walk,
I thank God I'm free at las'.
Me an' my Jesus gwineter meet an' talk,
I thank God I'm free at las'.

LORD, I WANT TO BE A CHRISTIAN IN-A MY HEART

Lord, I want to be a Chris-tian in - a my heart, in - a my heart,

Lord, I want to be a Chris-tian in - a my heart.

I don't want to be like Judas in-a my heart, in-a my heart
I don't want to be like Judas in-a my heart.
In-a my heart, In-a my heart,
Lord I want to be a Christian in-a my heart.

140

JOSHUA FIT DE BATTLE OB JERICO

Josh-ua fit de bat-tle ob Jer-i - co,_ Jer-i - co,_ Jer-i - co,_

Josh-ua fit de bat-tle ob Jer-i - co,_ An' de walls come tum-blin' down.

You may talk about yo' king ob Gideon,
You may talk about yo' man ob Saul,
Dere's none like good ole Joshua,
At the battle ob Jerico!

EV'RY TIME I FEEL DE SPIRIT

Ev'- ry time I feel de spir - it, move-

- in' in my heart, I will pray: O, ev'ry time I

- feel de spir - it, move - in' in my heart, I will pray.

Upon de mountain my Lord spoke,
Out o' his mouth came fire an' smoke,
An' all aroun' me look so shine,
Ask-a my Lord, if all was mine.

A GALLERY OF ANTEBELLUM PREACHERS

The black preacher in the days of slavery was indeed all things to all people; not only was he a source of spiritual guidance, but he was also a political leader, social reformer, and entrepreneur. In the antebellum South the role was never a comfortable one, for he was obliged to walk a fine line between the slave masters, ever alert to the threat of subversion, and the toiling masses, to whom he brought hope, succor, and, above all, leadership from their own ranks.

Some early African American preachers were educated freemen who traveled a circuit from plantation to plantation. Others were unlettered field exhorters, who made up for their lack of formal training with vivid storytelling that could hold audiences spellbound for hours. Often they were called on to display their skill before white congregations as well, and many became celebrated for the eloquence and power of their oratory.

But educated or not, virtually all black preachers plied their trade at considerable risk. Especially after the 1831 slave uprising in Virginia led by the fiery black preacher Nat Turner, slave owners sought to suppress preaching by blacks. Those who defied the ban were subject to severe penalties that included being sold off, beaten, or even killed.

Yet so strongly did some slaves feel the call to preach—for one, it was "like a fire shut up in my bones"—that even the harshest measures couldn't stop them. Famous sermons often lived on in the memories of audiences for years after they were delivered. At the turn of the century, for example, Ned Walker, a former slave in South Carolina, still recalled how a sermon given some three decades earlier at the funeral of the town blacksmith by a slave named Uncle Pompey had mesmerized blacks and whites alike. During the Civil War, a Union soldier who visited a black camp meeting in Virginia later wrote his wife that "the old black minister began to preach and in 15 minutes he gave us a better sermon than the chaplain this morning did in an hour."

Harry "Black Harry" Hosier (c. 1750-1806)

One of the first black Methodist circuit riders, Harry Hosier carried the faith to the most isolated corners of the South and New England. Unable to read and write, he nevertheless could quote long passages from the Bible from memory. Whites who heard Hosier were awed by his eloquence. The physician and theologian Benjamin Rush considered him "the greatest orator in America."

Indeed, so moving was Hosier's oratory that on one occasion, several people standing outside the church where they could hear but not see him remarked on the brilliance of "the bishop's" sermon. Told it was not the bishop but his servant who was preaching, they could only reply, "If such be the servant, what must the master be?"

Henry Evans (c. 1760-1810)

Born in Virginia of free parents, Henry Evans was on his way to Charleston, South Carolina, to work as a cobbler when he stopped over in Fayetteville, North Carolina, in 1780. There he was so appalled by conditions among the city's slaves that he resolved to stay, and to preach. Evans built a large following that soon attracted the attention of the town officials, who tried to ban his services. Yet it became apparent that his influence was salutary, not only on the slaves who heard him but also on those of their masters and mistresses who accompanied them to services.

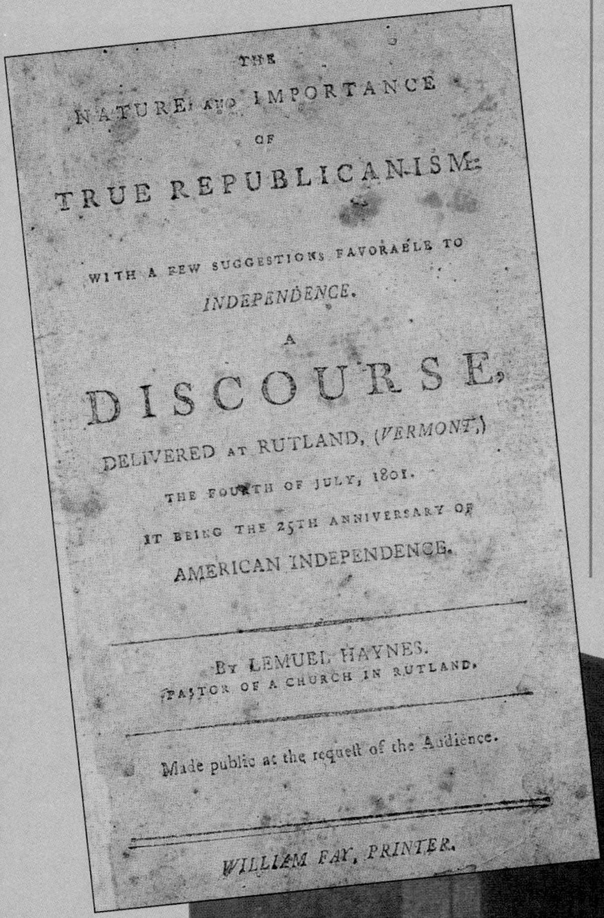

THE

NATURE AND IMPORTANCE

OF

TRUE REPUBLICANISM:

WITH A FEW SUGGESTIONS FAVORABLE TO

INDEPENDENCE.

A

DISCOURSE,

DELIVERED AT RUTLAND, (VERMONT,)

THE FOURTH OF JULY, 1801.

IT BEING THE 25TH ANNIVERSARY OF

AMERICAN INDEPENDENCE.

BY LEMUEL HAYNES.
(PASTOR OF A CHURCH IN RUTLAND.)

Made public at the request of the Audience.

WILLIAM FAY, PRINTER.

Lemuel Haynes (1753–1833)

War hero, biblical scholar, and Federalist, Lemuel Haynes was born in 1753 in West Hartford, Connecticut, to an African father and a white mother, who abandoned him in infancy. Haynes grew up in the home of a local deacon, David Rose, where he learned to read from the Bible and to recite sermons. Upon hearing one of his speeches, Rose asked who had written it. Haynes replied simply, "It's Lemuel's sermon." His career in the pulpit seemed assured. Indeed, in 1785 he was ordained a minister and eventually settled in Rutland, Vermont, where he remained for some 30 years.

On his death in 1833 the New York Colored American, a black newspaper, eulogized him as "the only man of known African descent who has ever succeeded in overpowering the system of American caste." The paper added that this was possible because of "his wisdom and piety, aided also by the more favorable times in which he lived."

A serving tray (below) depicts Lemuel Haynes addressing his all-white congregation from the pulpit of his Rutland, Vermont, church. Haynes also wrote political tracts like the one at left from 1801, in which he attacked both slavery and the French monarchy.

Andrew Cox Marshall
(1775-1856)

Andrew Cox Marshall was born in South Carolina in 1775, the son of an African woman and a white overseer. As an adult he managed to buy his freedom and move to Georgia, where his uncle was pastor of the First African Baptist Church of Savannah, one of the first independent black Baptist churches in the country. Marshall evidently had a natural gift for preaching, for he took over as pastor when his uncle retired. His talent aroused the envy of jealous white churchmen, who tried to seize his church.

Marshall's courage and eloquence became legendary throughout the South. When he died in 1856, his funeral cortege stretched for over a mile, prompting one citizen to remark that "not more than two or three funerals had witnessed so large a collection of people in the course of the present century."

Jarena Lee (1783-?)

One of the few women of her era of any race to attempt what was considered a man's calling, Jarena Lee was born in 1783 in Cape May, New Jersey. As a young woman she had doubts about her salvation and even considered suicide. Then she experienced sanctification—the committing of one's soul to God's divine grace. Believing that she had now been called to preach, she approached Richard Allen, founder of the African Methodist Episcopal church. Though Allen initially discouraged her because of her sex, he later gave his blessing to her traveling ministry. By 1835 she was delivering hundreds of sermons a year, and her missionary work was critical to the rapid growth of the AME church. "Why should it be thought impossible or improper for a woman to preach," she once asked, "seeing the Savior died for the woman as well as the man?"

James W. C. Pennington
(1809-1870)

James W. C. Pennington knew the bitterness of bondage and used his pulpit to preach against it. Born a slave on Maryland's Eastern Shore, he was trained as a blacksmith but ran away at 21 and was taken in by Pennsylvania Quakers, who taught him the rudiments of reading and writing. He continued his education in New York, eventually becoming a schoolteacher and Presbyterian minister. From the 1830s onward he was pastor of churches in New York and Connecticut and a member of the abolitionist movement, traveling widely in Europe to lecture on the evils of slavery. "If the New Testament sanctions slavery," he wrote, "it authorizes the enslavement of whites as well as us." His autobiography, *The Fugitive Blacksmith*, became a bestseller when it was published in London in 1849.

Samuel Ringgold Ward (1817-1878?)

Samuel Ringgold Ward was born in 1817 in Maryland of slave parents. Three years later the family escaped and settled in Greenwich, New Jersey. Ward spent his early career preaching to white congregations in upstate New York and working as an agent of the American Anti-Slavery Society. After the passage of the Fugitive Slave Act in 1850, he traveled throughout the North denouncing the law. In 1851 he fled to Canada after helping a runaway slave in Syracuse, New York, escape from prison. From there he traveled widely, raising money for black refugees in Toronto. After the Civil War he refused to return to the United States. He died in the British colony of Jamaica.

John Jasper (1812-1901)

John Jasper was an imposing figure—tall, good-looking, and impeccably groomed. Born a slave in Virginia in 1812, he began preaching after his owner became so impressed by Jasper's religious ardor that he gave him leave to devote himself to his calling. "Go anywhere you want to, and tell the good news," Jasper's master is said to have told him.

Jasper's ministry was well established in the years before the Civil War. During the war he ministered to hospitalized Confederate soldiers in Petersburg, Virginia, where he was pastor of the Third Baptist Church. After the war he moved to Richmond and established a new church, the Sixth Mount Zion Baptist Church. Jasper's compelling preaching style drew heavily on the rhythmic qualities of African American southern dialect, which he used to great effect in fashioning extemporaneous sermons filled with imagery so vivid that audiences were riveted to their seats.

His most famous sermon, "The Sun Do Move," a refutation of Copernicus's theory of planetary motion based on biblical sources, was so widely admired that he was called upon to deliver it more than 250 times in churches throughout Virginia. Jasper became so well known that the *Richmond Times* carried an obituary on his death, noting that "his implicit trust in the Bible and everything in it was beautiful and impressive."

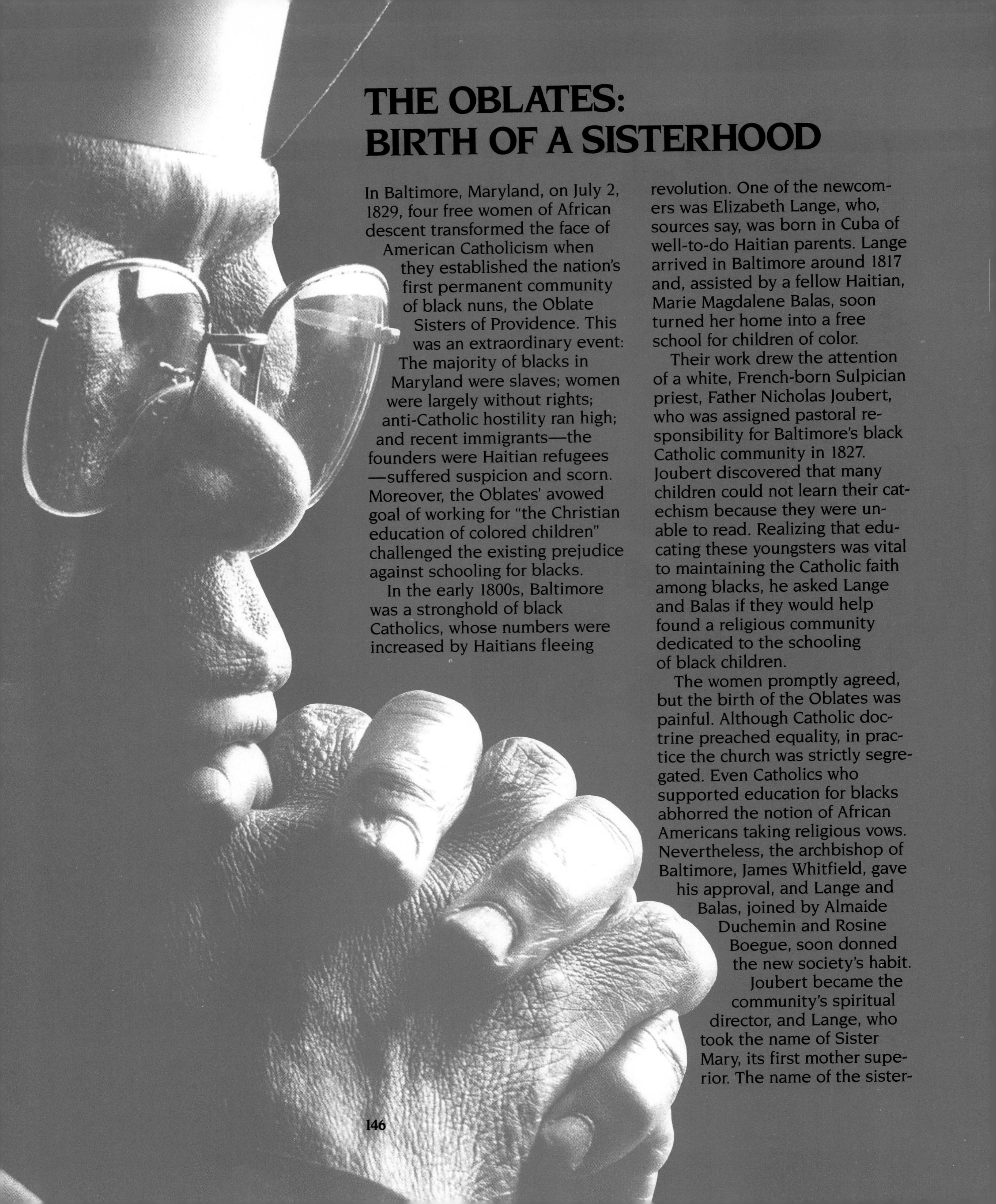

THE OBLATES: BIRTH OF A SISTERHOOD

In Baltimore, Maryland, on July 2, 1829, four free women of African descent transformed the face of American Catholicism when they established the nation's first permanent community of black nuns, the Oblate Sisters of Providence. This was an extraordinary event: The majority of blacks in Maryland were slaves; women were largely without rights; anti-Catholic hostility ran high; and recent immigrants—the founders were Haitian refugees —suffered suspicion and scorn. Moreover, the Oblates' avowed goal of working for "the Christian education of colored children" challenged the existing prejudice against schooling for blacks.

In the early 1800s, Baltimore was a stronghold of black Catholics, whose numbers were increased by Haitians fleeing revolution. One of the newcomers was Elizabeth Lange, who, sources say, was born in Cuba of well-to-do Haitian parents. Lange arrived in Baltimore around 1817 and, assisted by a fellow Haitian, Marie Magdalene Balas, soon turned her home into a free school for children of color.

Their work drew the attention of a white, French-born Sulpician priest, Father Nicholas Joubert, who was assigned pastoral responsibility for Baltimore's black Catholic community in 1827. Joubert discovered that many children could not learn their catechism because they were unable to read. Realizing that educating these youngsters was vital to maintaining the Catholic faith among blacks, he asked Lange and Balas if they would help found a religious community dedicated to the schooling of black children.

The women promptly agreed, but the birth of the Oblates was painful. Although Catholic doctrine preached equality, in practice the church was strictly segregated. Even Catholics who supported education for blacks abhorred the notion of African Americans taking religious vows. Nevertheless, the archbishop of Baltimore, James Whitfield, gave his approval, and Lange and Balas, joined by Almaide Duchemin and Rosine Boegue, soon donned the new society's habit. Joubert became the community's spiritual director, and Lange, who took the name of Sister Mary, its first mother superior. The name of the sister-

During ceremonies in 1979 marking the 150th anniversary of the community's founding, three Oblate Sisters of Providence wear historic habits, from the oldest, shown at right, to the most recent, at far left.

Depicted in early portraits, Father Nicholas Joubert (*far left*) and Elizabeth Lange (*left*) were the principal founders of the Oblate Sisters of Providence.

hood derives from the word *oblation*, or spiritual offering.

New members soon followed, and the community's mission expanded. In 1829 the sisters opened St. Frances Academy, whose chapel served for a quarter of a century as the unofficial parish church of Baltimore's black Catholics.

Joubert died in 1843, and for a time the Oblates foundered without his energetic advocacy. Several members left, enrollment dropped at St. Frances, and the community, always poor, neared destitution. Archbishop of Balti-

more Samuel Eccleston reportedly suggested that the sisterhood be dissolved and its members become domestics.

But in 1847 the community received a new spiritual director, a young Bavarian Redemptorist priest named Thaddeus Anwander, and the decline was halted. Soon the community began growing and extending its mission beyond Baltimore, eventually expanding into another 14 states and the District of Columbia. At its peak in the mid-1960s,

the sisterhood counted more than 300 nuns.

Although membership has since declined, as it has in nearly all American religious communities, the Oblates continue their mission in eight states plus the District of Columbia and Costa Rica. The sisters can point with justifiable pride to another measure of their success: The Oblates' pioneering example encouraged the foundation of two other communities of black nuns, the Sisters of the Holy Family in New Orleans in 1842 and the Handmaids of Mary in Savannah, Georgia, in 1916.

INTEGRATING THE PRIESTHOOD

In the early 1870s, those religious bodies that did not ignore African Americans frequently viewed them as they did Africans: as heathens to be converted to Christianity. That blacks, once converted, should be welcomed as equals by their white brethren was neither expected nor particularly desired.

The four young English priests who arrived in Baltimore just before Christmas in 1871 were missionaries, members of a new religious order, St. Joseph's Society of the Sacred Heart, and their assignment was to minister to the city's black Roman Catholics and to make new converts to Catholicism. In the late 19th century, the Catholic church in America was infested with racism and had yet to ordain its first African American clergyman.

The Josephites, as the order is better known, changed that. From the beginning, the society's goal was the education and ordination of African American priests. At first these priests were intended, in the words of founder Herbert Vaughan, an English priest, to "carry the faith into their own land," meaning Africa. But in the early 1890s the American Josephites became independent of their English founders, and the new superior general, John R. Slattery, became persuaded that black priests were necessary at home because there was "no chance to win the Negroes to the faith without priests of their own."

Under Slattery, the Josephites brought African Americans into their seminaries and, in 1891, Charles Randolph Uncles became the first black to be trained and ordained in this country. Eleven years would pass before the second, John H. Dorsey, was ordained, but the third, John J. Plantevigne, received holy orders only five years later, in 1907.

Uncles spent his priestly life as a seminary professor. Dorsey and Plantevigne took up pastoral work—and shouldered the heavy burden of racism within the church. Dorsey, assigned as assistant pastor to a Pine Bluff, Arkansas, church in 1904, was removed three years later at the insistence of a white bishop who was not a Josephite. For the next 10 years, Dorsey traveled through the South, conducting dozens of successful parish missions—the Catholic equivalent of traveling tent meetings. Finally, no longer able to endure the daily indignities of the Jim Crow system and humiliation by white priests and bishops, he retreated to Baltimore, where he served as pastor of St. Monica's Church until his death in 1926.

John Plantevigne of Louisiana, like Dorsey, was tormented by racial prejudice and hounded by the white Catholic clergy as he traveled through the South conducting missions. Although he was immensely popular and effective, in 1909 Plantevigne was barred from conducting missions in New Orleans by Archbishop James H. Blenk, a turn of events that left him shattered. "To be put off, under any pretense, from working for my own people is the thing that is tearing my very vitals away," he wrote Blenk. He died in Baltimore four years later. By this time Slattery, too, had left

Josephite Father William Norvell teaches a class at St. Augustine's School in New Orleans in the 1960s.

the Josephites and the church, declaring that "the stand of the Catholic church toward the Negro is sheer dishonesty."

Although the Josephites continued their missionary work among black Americans, recruitment of African American seminarians virtually ceased until after World War II, when the doors of the Josephite seminaries were once more flung open and the society reclaimed its tradition of integrating the priesthood. More recently, during a time of general decline in the numbers of Catholic clergy, the number of black priests has increased. By the 1990s the Catholic church in the United States could claim more than a dozen black bishops.

Josephite John Ricard (*below, center*) leaves the Church of Mary Our Queen after his installation as auxiliary bishop of Baltimore.

Josephite Father Charles R. Uncles (*top left*) was the first African American to be trained and ordained into the Catholic priesthood in the United States. He received holy orders in 1891. The second, John H. Dorsey (*above*) was ordained in 1902, and the third, in 1907, was John J. Plantevigne (*left*).

A VOICE FOR AFRICAN PRIDE

Henry McNeal Turner was a force to be reckoned with. A leader in the African Methodist Episcopal (AME) church for 50 years, he was, among many other things, a powerful politician in Georgia, an editor and author of religious publications, and the chancellor of Morris Brown College in Atlanta. As an early proponent of the back-to-Africa movement, Turner was quintessentially a man of his time—the latter half of the 19th century.

But Turner may be best known to later generations as one of the first leaders to encourage American blacks to exult in their African heritage. In the mid-1880s, almost a century before they became catch phrases, Turner taught the principles of black pride and black power.

"Respect black," he counseled people of color, and black will be respected. "A man must believe he is somebody before he is acknowledged as somebody."

In fact, Turner's message became far more insistent as he grew increasingly frustrated by racism in America. African Americans, he taught, must reject any teachings of the white church that imply black inferiority, such as the association of whiteness with purity and holiness. "God is a Negro," he asserted to dramatize his point.

Turner was born of free parents in 1834 in Newberry Court House, South Carolina. His father died while Turner was still a child, and the boy was soon sent to work in the cotton fields.

Throughout his childhood, Turner's mother and grandmother instilled in him a strong sense of pride in his ancestry. They told the boy that he was the grandson

In the early 1890s, at the height of his powers as an eloquent orator and African American leader, Bishop Henry McNeal Turner posed in his episcopal robes.

For refuge from the world's demands, Bishop Turner turned to this home at 30 Yonge Street in Atlanta.

A successful missionary, Bishop Turner (*seated, fifth from left, second row*) presided over the Transvaal Annual Conference of the AME church in Pretoria, South Africa, in 1898.

of an African prince who had been brought to America as a slave in the 1700s. Although the story may have been more inspirational than historical, Turner credited it with awakening his passion for Africa.

He learned to read at the age of 15, and at 19 was licensed to preach in the Methodist Episcopal church, a primarily white denomination. In 1858, after several years as an itinerant preacher in the Deep South, he left the Methodist Episcopal church for the black-controlled African Methodist Episcopal church.

Appointed pastor of Israel Church in Washington, D.C., in 1862, Turner used the pulpit to urge his flock to join the fight against the Confederacy, declaring that "we will show the world by our bravery what the Negro can do." He helped raise the First Regiment of U.S. Colored Troops and was appointed its chaplain by President Abraham Lincoln in 1863.

After the Civil War, Turner moved to Georgia to revitalize the AME church, which had been scorned by the Methodist Epis-

copal church leadership in the South for more than 30 years. The massive missionary effort he launched won thousands of former slaves to the faith, and the new churches became rallying points for political organization and voter registration. Turner soon became one of the most powerful religious and political leaders in Georgia and served in the state legislature from 1868 to 1870. Then Reconstruction collapsed, and Turner left secular politics in the early 1870s.

He was hardly quiet, however. Elected an AME bishop in 1880, Turner turned his attention to what he believed was God's plan for African Americans—to return to the land of their ancestors in order to Christianize it. Turner supported several colonization attempts and himself became a missionary in Africa, making four journeys during the 1890s and helping to establish the AME church in several countries, most successfully in South Africa.

After Turner's death in 1915, W. E. B. Du Bois eulogized him as the last of "the spiritual progeny of African chieftains."

THE BLACK ROOTS OF PENTECOSTALISM

In the spring of 1906, the city of Los Angeles was abuzz with reports of a remarkable religious revival meeting that ran daily—and well into most nights—in a derelict church at 312 Azusa Street. Surrounded by stables and stockyards, the site itself was unremarkable. Rather, the meeting's fame spread because its participants were often so overcome by spiritual ecstasy that they began speaking in tongues.

The phenomenon is described in Acts 2:4, where Jesus' disciples, upon being visited by the Holy Spirit, began speaking in unknown tongues. The event happened to take place on the Jewish feast of Pentecost, 50 days after Passover. Now a Christian holy day, Pentecost is celebrated on the seventh Sunday after Easter, and speaking in tongues has long been considered evidence of infusion of the Holy Spirit.

The Azusa Street Revival was led by a young black minister named William Joseph Seymour, whose boundless energy and conviction launched a new Christian movement, Pentecostalism. Within three

The home of modern Pentecostalism: the empty church building at 312 Azusa Street in Los Angeles in 1906, shortly before it became famous as William Seymour's Azusa Street Mission.

years of its founding, Pentecostalism had become an interracial, international phenomenon. As of this writing it claims more than 50 million adherents worldwide and is the fastest-growing Christian denomination in the African American religious family.

Seymour, born in Louisiana in 1870 to former slaves, was largely self-taught. Around the turn of the century he was ordained a minister of the Holiness church, a denomination that began as a reform movement within Methodism in 1867. The Holiness church taught that two experiences were prerequisites for salvation: to be born again; that is, to experience an intense recommitment to Christ; and sanctification, to be instantaneously and dramatically purged of sin and filled with perfect love by the grace of the Holy Spirit. To this theology Seymour added his own belief that speaking in tongues, or glossolalia, was certain evidence of the divine presence of the Holy Spirit. The idea was destined to transform the lives of millions of people, but at first it only brought him trouble.

In January of 1906 Seymour became pastor of a small black Holiness mission in Los Angeles. He declared during his first sermon that no one who had not spoken in tongues had truly received the Holy Spirit—a blessing that Seymour readily acknowledged he himself had yet to earn. Seymour's new pastorate abruptly ended: Church leaders locked him out of the afternoon service.

But Seymour was determined to spread the word,

Bishop William Joseph Seymour (*seated, second from right*) attracted an interracial audience and led an integrated staff at the Azusa Street Mission. He later married Jennie Evans Moore (*standing, third from left*).

Bishop Charles Harrison Mason, cofounder of the Church of God in Christ, led his denomination into the Pentecostal movement after receiving the baptism of the spirit at the Azusa Street Mission in March of 1907.

and soon he was holding prayer meetings in the home of a sympathetic black couple. By April the preacher had finally experienced the Pentecostal gift for himself, and soon he moved the meetings to Azusa Street. As news of his teaching spread, he drew ever larger crowds, including a large number of white visitors. For the next three years the mission thrived. Skeptics and believers, ministers and missionaries of all races flocked there to witness the new phenomenon. They came from across the nation and around the globe. Many carried the new gospel home. Pentecostalism was born.

Glossolalia began to assume a social, as well as a religious, role in Seymour's plan, since the Holy Spirit recognized no difference between races in bestowing the Pentecostal gift. At the Azusa mission, everyone was welcome, and everyone worshiped as equals. "God makes no difference in nationality," stated the first issue of the mission's periodical. But it was not to be. By 1911, white Pentecostals began to withdraw to form their own separatist denominations, and Seymour's influence diminished.

Pentecostalism has continued to thrive in the African American community, however, thanks in no small part to Charles Harrison Mason, a founder of the Church of God in Christ (COGIC). In 1907 Mason became one of a parade of clergy who attended the Azusa Street Revival. He spent five weeks there, an experience that was like none other in his life. "When I opened my mouth to say Glory," Mason later wrote, "a flame touched my tongue which ran down to me.

My language changed and no word could I speak in my own tongue. Oh! I was filled with the Glory of the Lord. My soul was then satisfied." When Mason returned home to Memphis, he sent the Church of God in Christ firmly down the road of Pentecostalism.

A staunch pacifist who was jailed several times during World War I for his opposition to the war, Mason was also a visionary leader who oversaw COGIC's expansion from its rural beginnings into a predominantly urban church. In the early years, many white ministers sought ordination by Mason. In 1914, however, segregation's influence caused many of them to leave and found the Assemblies of God, now the largest white Pentecostal denomination.

Nevertheless, Mason's efforts caused COGIC to grow rapidly; the membership increased eightfold between 1926 and the mid-1960s. Following his death in 1961 at the age of 95, the church lapsed into several years of turmoil as various factions struggled to name his successor. In 1968, James Oglethorpe Patterson, Sr., Mason's son-in-law, was elected presiding bishop, and COGIC once again resumed its extraordinary growth. Indeed, in 1993, the church was the largest Pentecostal denomination in the world, with more than 6.3 million members.

Thriving in the 1990s, the congregation of the Temple Church of God in Christ in Memphis, the mother church of the rapidly growing Pentecostal denomination, listens to the word of Rev. David Hall, Sr.

Encouraged by fellow worshipers, members of the Temple Church of God in Christ speak in tongues (*top and above*), a sure sign to Pentecostals of baptism in the Holy Spirit.

A saxophonist plays a call to prayer at Memphis's Temple Church of God in Christ. The saxophone, drums, guitar, tambourine, and other instruments supplement the church's choir, organ, and piano during services.

Thomas A. Dorsey (*center, waving*),
generally acknowledged to be
"the father of gospel music,"
boards a train in Chicago in 1939.

A JOYFUL NOISE UNTO THE LORD

"The blues are the songs of despair," the great gospel singer Mahalia Jackson once remarked, but "gospel songs are the songs of hope." Jackson's description was apt, for the body of religious song known as gospel is probably the most joyful of all American musical forms, expressing both the devotional reverence and the exuberance with which African Americans traditionally have celebrated their faith.

The word *gospel* comes from the Greek word for "good news," and the first four books of the New Testament are called the Gospels because they tell the good news about the life and works of Jesus Christ. Gospel songs are thus expressions of profound joy and religious conviction in the face of an often hostile world. In this they resemble traditional spirituals (*pages* 138-141). But unlike the spiritual, gospel music is a fairly

recent creation. Starting in the 1920s, individual artists worked to blend the various strands of African American music into a new religious art that would reflect the rapid changes of American society during the first half of the 20th century.

Foremost among these pioneers was Thomas A. Dorsey, born in Villa Rica, Georgia, in 1899. Young Dorsey showed an early aptitude for the piano, em-

The cover of a record album by the Ward Singers features their hit song, "Surely God Is Able," which sold a million copies in 1950.

SURELY GOD IS ABLE

SAVOY MG 14001

featuring
THE FAMOUS
WARD SINGERS

SURELY GOD IS ABLE
HE KNOWS HOW MUCH
WE CAN BEAR
JESUS — EACH DAY
SINCE I FOUND THE LIGHT
ON MY LORD, WHAT A TIME
HOW MANY TIMES
THIS LITTLE LIGHT OF MINE
I KNOW IT WAS THE LORD
UNTIL I FOUND THE LORD

Mahalia Jackson flashes the winsome smile that endeared her to audiences of the 1930s.

Gospel singer Willie Mae Ford Smith (center) performs in Say Amen, Somebody, a 1982 documentary film on gospel music.

barking on a career as a musician while still in his teens. Yet this son of a Baptist minister turned to the "devil's music," earning his living playing the blues in Atlanta's bars and bordellos.

A few years later Dorsey moved on to the vaudeville circuit, where he adopted the name Georgia Tom and achieved a modest fame as accompanist for blues diva Gertrude "Ma" Rainey. In 1928 Rainey cut a record of Dorsey's salacious tune "It's Tight Like That," which earned for Dorsey his first royalty check of

$2,400.19 and so scandalized composer W. C. Handy that he accused Dorsey of inspiring "a flock of lowdown, dirty blues."

Dorsey might have continued in this vein had he not been prone to periodic depressions, the most serious of which befell him in 1926 and lasted nearly two years. It was while Dorsey was struggling with this illness that a neighbor died suddenly, leaving the composer to contemplate his own mortality and inspiring him to write his first gospel song, "If You See My Sav-

ior, Tell Him that You Saw Me." The song languished for nearly two years. Then, in 1930, composer Lucie Eddie Campbell, singer Willie Mae Ford Smith, and a minister named E. H. Hall introduced Dorsey's work at the National Baptist Convention in Chicago, forcing conservative black church leaders to take notice of the new-style church music Dorsey had created.

His success with the Baptists led Dorsey to devote himself to church music. He began building on the work of such earlier reli-

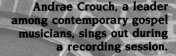

Andrae Crouch, a leader among contemporary gospel musicians, sings out during a recording session.

The legendary Dixie Hummingbirds perform at Greater Saint Stephen's Baptist Church in New Orleans in 1982.

Rev. James Cleveland, who began writing songs at age 16, belts out a solo at the 1974 American Song Festival in Saratoga, New York.

gious songwriters as Charles Price Jones, a minister and founder of the Church of Christ (Holiness), USA, and Charles Albert Tindley, a composer, minister, and music publisher, whose seminal compositions inspired a generation of gospel tunesmiths. Often Dorsey had to struggle to get his music heard over the vociferous objections of skeptical ministers who still identified gospel with its honky-tonk origins. "I got thrown out of some of the best churches," Dorsey once confided to a historian.

Dorsey's music represented a fusion of several traditional genres, notably Protestant church hymns and the spirituals. To these Dorsey added elements of ragtime, jazz, and the blues along with instruments typical of the dance-hall band. The result was an entirely new idiom, characterized as much by its infectious rhythms as by its inspirational fervor. The music was uniquely urban but with strong rural roots, mirroring the experience of the hundreds of thousands of blacks who had recently

abandoned the farms and small towns in the South for a better life in the urban North.

In 1932 Dorsey wrote his most famous song, "Take My Hand, Precious Lord," a moving hymn inspired by the death of his first wife in childbirth and that of their infant son shortly afterward. "Precious Lord" has been translated into more than 50 languages and recorded by singers all over the world. In all, Dorsey wrote more than 1,000 gospel tunes, earning the title "the father of gospel music."

Take 6, a contemporary a cappella gospel group, perform without any instruments other than their own voices.

The Winans, a vocal group of three sisters and four brothers, is backed by a live band at a concert in the 1980s.

Shirley Caesar, who gained fame as a singing evangelist, ministers to her flock at a church in Durham, North Carolina, in 1987.

If Dorsey was gospel music's father, its midwives were Sallie Martin and Mahalia Jackson, whose electrifying performances sealed the new sound in the hearts of Americans of all races. Martin toured extensively with Dorsey during the 1930s, bringing the gospel-music revolution to black churches nationwide.

Jackson met Dorsey in 1928, when the singer was just 17 years old. She possessed a regal bearing, a rich contralto voice, and a personality that audiences found irresistible. Dorsey became her mentor, helping her refine her vocal technique and teaching her his music; he may even have written "Precious Lord" with Jackson partly in mind. Her recording of the song is still regarded as the definitive performance of Dorsey's signature tune.

Contemporary gospel musicians have continued to build upon Dorsey's work, which has also influenced the style of such pop singers as Aretha Franklin, Whitney Houston, and Anita Baker. The jubilation of the Edwin Hawkins Singers' 1968 hit, "Oh Happy Day," attracted an entirely new audience of younger listeners. Singers such as Andrae and Sandra Crouch, the Winans, and the jazz-inspired a cappella ensemble Take 6 have won millions of new fans for the music Dorsey pioneered. By the time of Dorsey's death in 1993, gospel music had spread to virtually every corner of the globe and its creator was widely recognized as one of the great innovators of American music as well as the composer of some of the world's most joyful sounds.

THE FORCE OF NONVIOLENCE

Howard Thurman was a teacher, theologian, mystic, scholar, and pacifist, whose belief in the power of nonviolence helped shape the civil rights struggle of the 1960s.

Judged to be one of the 20th century's greatest preachers, Thurman was the personification of humility, acting never for personal gain but always out of a conviction that he was an instrument of God's word.

"I have always felt that a word was being spoken through me," he once said, adding, with characteristic modesty and humor, "Three-fourths of the time, I didn't get it right."

Most of the time Thurman did get it right, however, making him an intellectual force in African American life for more than half a century, until his death in 1981. In 1935, when Mahatma Gandhi was using the tactics of passive resistance in his fight for Indian independence from the British, Thurman traveled to India to learn firsthand about Gandhi's philosophy of nonviolence as an agent of social change.

Returning home, Thurman passed on Gandhi's wisdom—and his own—to his students at Howard and Boston universities. Among those who listened were James Farmer, founder of the Congress of Racial Equality (CORE), and Martin Luther King, Jr. Howard Thurman was, as one admirer put it, an advocate of "liberation theology" long before the term was invented.

Thurman was born in 1900 and raised by his grandmother, a former slave, in segregated Day-

Boston University students listen raptly as Howard Thurman, professor in the school of theology and dean of the university chapel, teaches a seminar around 1960.

tona, Florida. Public education for Daytona's black children extended only to the seventh grade, but Thurman was an outstanding student, and the school principal volunteered to teach him the eighth-grade material so he could qualify for high school.

Since there was no black high school in Daytona, young Howard's family scraped together enough money to send him to live with cousins and attend high school in Jacksonville.

The journey nearly ended before it began. As he was about to board the train for Jacksonville, the youngster learned that his trunk could not be checked as baggage but must be sent as freight—for an additional charge. The train ticket had left Thurman

On one of his many tours as guest lecturer and professor, Howard Thurman teaches a class at the University of Ibadan, Nigeria, in 1963.

Wearing Indian clothes for a formal occasion, Howard and Sue Bailey Thurman pose during their 1935 Pilgrimage of Friendship.

nearly penniless. Without money to ship his belongings, the boy sat down on the station steps and began to cry. Minutes later, he was saved by an anonymous black man dressed in overalls, who paid the freight charges and walked away.

Many years afterward, when Thurman came to write his autobiography, he dedicated it "to the stranger in the railroad station in Daytona Beach who restored my broken dream sixty-five years ago."

Thurman was valedictorian of his high-school class and won a scholarship to Morehouse College in Atlanta. From there he progressed to Colgate-Rochester Theological Seminary and, after graduation in 1926, became pastor of Mount Zion Baptist Church in Oberlin, Ohio. Within months, Thurman's oratory was locally famous. As blacks and whites drove for miles to hear his powerful sermons, Mount Zion— once an all-black congregation— became interracial.

In Oberlin, Thurman encountered the works of Rufus Jones, a Quaker mystic who taught philosophy. Thurman moved to Haverford, Pennsylvania, to study briefly with Jones at Haverford College, and then, in 1929, began his teaching career at Morehouse and Spelman colleges.

Thurman counted his short time with Rufus Jones as the watershed event of his life, but where Jones had concerned himself with global issues, Thurman eventually came to focus on the central problems of being black in the United States. "How can we immunize ourselves against the destructive aspects of the environment?" he asked. "How can we manage the carking fear of the white man's power and not be defeated by our own rage and hatred?"

The search for answers to these questions motivated the rest of Howard Thurman's life. Activist the Reverend Jesse Jackson has paid tribute to Thurman the nurturer as well as Thurman the scholar and preacher. As Jackson once observed, "He sowed the seeds that bred generations of activists who tore down ancient walls of oppression."

NOURISHING SOUL AND BODY

The growth of urban black populations in the wake of migrations north and west after 1900 spurred a matching growth in city churches and in the services those churches provided. Antioch Baptist Church in Chicago, Bethel African Methodist Episcopal in Baltimore, and Concord Baptist in Brooklyn are a few of the oldest and most famous congregations.

In Oakland, California, Allen Temple Baptist Church has been ministering to its congregation since 1919. For the last 23 years, the Reverend J. Alfred Smith, Sr., has been the church's pastor, offering, as he puts it, "holistic" care to the inner-city community of East Oakland.

Along with his staff, which includes his son and co-pastor, the Reverend J. Alfred Smith, Jr., Dr. Smith serves a congregation of 4,000 people. Allen Temple's ministry includes two Sunday services for adults and one for children, as well as prayer and Bible-study sessions conducted throughout the week.

In collaboration with other religious and local groups, the church also works with a surrounding community of more than 150,000 to provide a number of social-service programs. The church runs a tutoring program for elementary- and secondary-school students, for example, as well as an AIDS ministry and information program, a drug intervention program, and a prison outreach program that helps guide newly released former convicts.

Allen Temple, in partnership with other organizations, also operates a 30-bed shelter for the homeless as well as a highly-rated credit union—a service that is a particular boon to a neighborhood that has few banks.

In addition, the Allen Temple Development Corporation has built two senior-citizen housing complexes containing 126 apartments. As the Reverend J. Alfred Smith, Sr., says when he describes the church's philosophy and wide-ranging ministry, "We are trying to serve the total person."

A public-school teacher during the day and a volunteer tutor at night, Michael Scott helps fifth grader Philip Reaves, one of the children enrolled in Allen Temple's High-Rise Tutorial Program.

Volunteer Ike Dixon, Jr., and Othea Weathers, deaconess of Allen Temple, fill grocery sacks for the church's Brown Bag program, which distributes groceries to 125 seniors every week.

Allen Temple Federal Credit Union's Carol Carter (*right*) assists Sheryl Brown-Alexander and her son, two of the 1,200 members of the credit union.

Esther Green relaxes in her apartment (*top*) at Allen Temple Arms (*above*), a 126-unit complex for senior citizens and handicapped persons that opened in 1981. The church plans a new addition to provide nursing care for residents too frail to live independently.

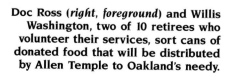

Doc Ross (*right, foreground*) and Willis Washington, two of 10 retirees who volunteer their services, sort cans of donated food that will be distributed by Allen Temple to Oakland's needy.

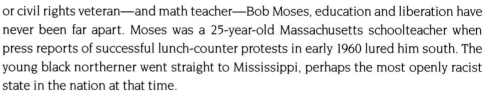

THE EDUCATORS

Johnetta Cole, the first African American woman president of Spelman College in Atlanta, Georgia, hands a diploma to a proud member of the 1991 Spelman graduating class.

or civil rights veteran—and math teacher—Bob Moses, education and liberation have never been far apart. Moses was a 25-year-old Massachusetts schoolteacher when press reports of successful lunch-counter protests in early 1960 lured him south. The young black northerner went straight to Mississippi, perhaps the most openly racist state in the nation at that time.

During the four years of unremitting struggle that followed, Moses and others endured beatings, arrests, harassment, and death threats as they fought beside black Mississippians for that most basic of civil rights, the vote. Often the struggle went hand in hand with an equally radical campaign: teaching reading, writing, and basic citizenship to men and women once condemned to lifelong semiliteracy. Both efforts culminated in the "Freedom Summer" of 1964, when Moses guided hundreds of volunteers who spread across the state to educate and register black voters. Freedom Summer met many of its goals, but at a terrible cost: By September, four volunteers had been killed and 80 beaten, and 67 black churches, homes, and businesses had been destroyed. Moses himself had his head slashed open with a knife as he escorted two black farmers to register to vote.

Almost two decades later, as a Harvard graduate student and father of four, Moses once again found himself plunged into a leadership role. In 1982, his eighth-grade daughter Maisha rebelled at being tutored at home in math to make up for inadequate instruction in class. So her father got permission to become a teaching assistant at the school, helping members of her algebra class in an improvised, grass-roots style reminiscent of Freedom Summer. In his system, everything began with a real-life example. He used the local subway system to teach a number of mathematical concepts, beginning with the notion of negative and positive integers. Central Square station was the zero point, stations to its east represented the positive integers, and those to its west were negative. Trips along the line demonstrated integer subtraction and addition.

Moses soon added weekend tutorials for parents and breakfast workshops for students. Within the year, the school's traditionally low scores on advanced-placement tests were rising. Aided financially by a no-strings-attached "genius grant" from the MacArthur Foundation, Moses cut short his own studies in philosophy to advocate his new way of teaching algebra. He did so with the same commitment he had brought to Mississippi voter registration, conducting teacher training and program support for schools in disadvantaged areas of Milwaukee, Oakland, Los

Angeles, and other cities, reaching and motivating thousands of inner-city children. Nineteen Chicago elementary schools adopted the program in 1990, reporting noticeable improvements in reading, writing, and mathematics within the year.

In 1992 the program went south, training teachers from Louisiana, Kentucky, Arkansas, and Mississippi and reaching an estimated 2,000 children, black and white, in the first year. The inner-city curriculum took some adapting: The subway-line project, for example, became a study of a country bus route and its stops. But the message of hope was the same. Howard Sanders, superintendent of schools in Hollandale, Mississippi, told the *New York Times Magazine* that he and Hollandale's business leaders believed that the Algebra Project could renew the town's economy. A white teacher from the depressed coal town of Williamsburg, Kentucky, told the magazine that she hoped a better-educated labor pool might attract business there as well.

As for Moses, the southern initiative of the Algebra Project brought his old concerns for education and empowerment full circle. "Math has been politicized, particularly algebra, in our culture and school system," he has said. "They've used algebra as a subject to sort students." By teaching algebra skills to minority and disadvantaged youths, traditionally expected to do poorly at math, the Algebra Project reverses that screening process, using algebra, as Moses puts it, "to pump students into a broad mathematical pipeline." During a visit to Mississippi in 1993, Moses made note of some other changes. "It's interesting to work with teachers who 30 years ago you couldn't talk to," he said. "It's taken a quarter of a century to move through this, but it may be that the times are ready."

The story of Bob Moses and the Algebra Project is unusual, but it is also part of a larger, centuries-old movement dating back to slavery days. Highly dedicated African American educators have long worked together to instruct their students in the face of mob violence, abysmal funding, poverty, or wearying prejudice. These black men and women have aimed to educate to liberate, striving for economic and social uplift at the most basic level, one small child—or one college student—at a time. The obstacles have varied from century to century and from decade to decade, but the stakes remain terribly high. Since the time when African American slaves faced cruel punishment for learning to read and write, few black Americans have doubted that knowledge, in one form or another, is power.

Most of the captive Africans who lived and died as American slaves came to North America well educated in African culture. In the 17th century, secret societies in the village kingdoms of West Africa trained young men and women for their adult roles and the requirements of village life. At a given age, the youths left their childhood vil-

In the early 1990s, three decades after his daring civil rights efforts to register black Mississippi voters, Bob Moses discusses a math exercise (*above*) with a new generation of Mississippi youngsters as part of his nationwide Algebra Project. At right, another Algebra Project class in Indianola, Mississippi, studies the concept of equivalence by making measurements of everyday objects.

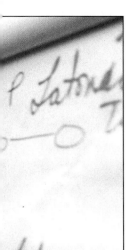

lages, where they may have learned their first lessons in crafts and perhaps Arabic writing, to submit to training in remote, isolated areas. Ahead lay lessons of responsibility—and the immutable secrets of their ancestors. Both in the hideaway classes and in the village, students mastered intricate lessons to become metalworkers, weavers, boat makers, hunters, religious leaders, and oral historians. In fact, secret societies were only one facet of the African educational system. During the years when the transatlantic slave trade was just beginning, large-scale centers of African academic excellence flourished in the city of Timbuktu and in what would become Guinea and Ghana. Very few of Africa's professional scholars, however, fell into the hands of the Atlantic slave traders.

Upon arrival in the Americas, many African adults became skilled craftspeople in their new environments. Some, in fact, were prized by slave owners specifically for the skills they brought from Africa. Yet other aspects of their African learning could not be passed on to their children. As time went on, their ancestral past began slipping away, to linger only in a dim cultural memory. At the same time, law and custom barred them from most education in the slaveholder's culture.

In 1740, the colony of South Carolina enacted the first compulsory ignorance laws in North America, forbidding the teaching of blacks, whether free or enslaved. Similar laws were soon adopted in other colonies, although rules governing the education of free blacks changed from place to place over time. Occasionally a slave might be given some form of technical education, but only as "a collateral means by which he was rendered a more efficient machine," as Hosea Easton of Boston, a black minister, commented bitterly in 1830.

Literacy for enslaved African Americans was clearly viewed as a potential weapon against the slave system. Educated slaves were thought not only more likely to rebel but also to pose a greater threat if they did. "Any slave caught writing suffered the penalty of having his forefinger cut from his right hand," one former slave remembered later. "Yet there were some who could read and write."

Indeed, thousands of enslaved blacks defied the laws against literacy. Thomas H. Jones, a slave in mid-19th-century North Carolina, learned to read at great risk, while hiding in the back of his master's store. "It seemed to me that if I could learn to read and write, this learning might, nay, I really thought it would point out to me the way to freedom, influence and real secure happiness," Jones later recalled. One morning, his master appeared unexpectedly when Jones was reading a book. With only a second to react, Jones threw it behind some barrels in the store. His master saw him throw something, but not what the object was, and ordered Jones to retrieve it. "I knew if my book was discovered that all was lost," Jones wrote, so he refused to obey. "I felt prepared for any hazard or suffering rather than give up my book and my hopes of improvement." To guard his secret, Jones endured three brutal whippings.

For free blacks—roughly 10 percent of the American black population before the war—formal education was somewhat more available, although still a rarity. Schools for blacks operated, sometimes in secret, in Charleston, New Orleans, Savannah, and other southern cities. In the North, prejudice against the education of black students often ran high, yet a scattering of schools for blacks not only survived but flourished. In New York City, the African Free School, founded by white abolitionists in 1787 and eventually run by black instructors, grew to include at least seven separate schools, providing lessons in reading, writing, spelling, composition, grammar, and mathematics to hundreds of young pupils. Older girls were taught sewing, knitting, and other topics, while studies for senior boys included astronomy, navigation, and geography—training that many later put to use as sailors.

To demonstrate black intellect and educability to a still-skeptical white public, the schools held well-publicized annual exhibitions that included readings from the Bible, recitations, public addresses by students as young as seven, and demonstration classes in subjects such as mathematics. The African Free Schools' extraordinary roll of graduates included scholar Alexander Crummell, an early black American Episcopal priest; James McCune Smith, one of the first black American physicians; Ira Aldridge, a Shakespearean actor whose portrayal of Othello was greeted with glowing reviews in Europe for nearly two decades; clergyman and abolitionist Samuel Ringgold Ward; and fiery antislavery orator Henry Highland Garnet.

Other schools admitted students of both races, but that policy could be dangerous—as Garnet and two of his classmates found out in 1835 when they became the first black students to enroll at the Noyes Academy in Canaan, New Hampshire. As Garnet and his friends watched warily from a boardinghouse, angry local farmers, using teams of oxen, dragged the school building into a swamp. A rider on horseback shot at the young black students and was met with a return blast from Garnet's shotgun. When Garnet and his companions finally left Canaan, a mob gathered at the edge of town and fired a cannon at their wagon.

Not surprisingly, given such a climate, very few black Americans had access to higher education before the Civil War. By the time the war broke out in 1861, there were only 28 known black college graduates in the United States; others—perhaps a few hundred—attended college briefly but did not graduate. Only two American colleges consistently admitted African Americans before the war. One was Oberlin College, a predominantly white institution in an abolitionist Ohio town, which began admitting black students in 1835. The other was Wilberforce University, named for British abolitionist William Wilberforce. Founded in 1856 by the Cincinnati Conference of the Methodist Episcopal church, the school was meant to educate escaped

Wilberforce University, pictured here in 1856, the year it was founded to provide higher education to free blacks, made history again three years later when it hired Sarah Early, the first African American woman professor.

One of the few colleges to regularly admit black students before the Civil War, Ohio's Oberlin College continued to educate blacks after the war. The class of 1884, pictured here, included future educator-activists Anna Julia Cooper (*red circle, top*) and Mary Church Terrell (*red circle, bottom*).

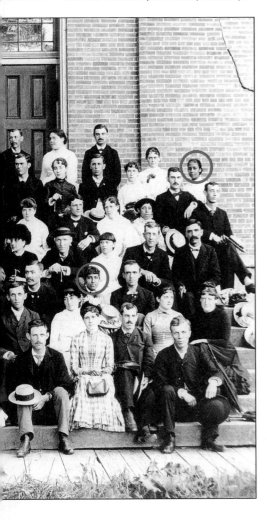

slaves and freedmen. In 1863, during the Civil War, Wilberforce was purchased by the African Methodist Episcopal church; AME Bishop Daniel L. Payne became the institution's president—and the nation's first black college president.

Despite such gleams of triumph, the educational status of African Americans before the war, both the free and the enslaved, was grim indeed. Literacy remained a rarity, denied to an estimated 90 to 95 percent of all African Americans. Only the military, social, and economic cataclysm of civil war could change that.

During the war, more than 180,000 black American volunteers fought on the Union side, committed to ending the hated institution of slavery. One of the few to serve above the rank of sergeant was physician Martin Delany (*pages* 184-185), who traveled a typically obstacle strewn road to professional standing. Delany had been educated in Pittsburgh, where he had attended night school. Despite his schooling, his experience as an assistant to Pittsburgh doctors, and recommendations that characterized him as "an upright and intelligent man" with "considerable intellectual power," he was rejected out of hand by medical schools in both Pennsylvania and New York. Finally, he was admitted to Harvard Medical School—his last hope—in 1850.

The victory did not last. When Delany first entered one of the medical school's lecture halls, elbows nudged and necks craned. Less than a month later, many of his fellow students signed petitions protesting his presence. The two other black students enrolled at the medical school apparently provoked less anger from whites since they planned to practice in Africa. The medical faculty gave in to the white protesters' wishes. Delany and the other black students were allowed to finish the semester, but they and all other African Americans were barred from further study at the school. Before he left Harvard, as he later wrote, Delany made good use of his time in the dissecting room, where he found there were no anatomical differences between whites and blacks—the size of their brains, the configuration of their bones, even the structure of their skin, were identical.

In those less regulated days, the lack of a medical school diploma was no reason not to practice medicine. Delany soon opened a medical practice in Pittsburgh, where he helped stamp out a cholera epidemic. An editor, author, and abolitionist, he went on to serve as a Union army doctor with the rank of major.

As the war raged, thousands of slaves in occupied parts of the South found themselves abruptly liberated. In November 1861, with Union soldiers fast approaching, white planters fled the South Carolina sea islands, freeing about 10,000 enslaved men, women, and children. Their legal status and that of other former slaves was not settled until the next July, when all slaves liberated from rebel territory were declared free. As a practical matter, those on the sea islands remained there for the duration of the war under Union supervision. Informally promised their own land, the adults continued to work the fields; the children went to schools organized by northern philanthropic groups. This arrangement, known as the Port Royal Experiment after Port Royal, one of the sea islands, was often presented as a gigantic social experiment, one that would prove decisively whether former slaves, as a group, could be educated.

Most of the teachers at Port Royal were white; trained black teachers were still

relatively rare, and some northern agencies did not welcome them. Perhaps the best known of the black teachers was 25-year-old Charlotte Forten, an experienced teacher and granddaughter of Philadelphia abolitionist James Forten (*pages* 90-91). Sailing to take up her post in October 1862, Forten came within sight of the blockaded Confederate harbor of Charleston—a frightening reminder that the Union coastal enclave was deep in enemy territory. Forten would spend the next 18 months instructing formerly enslaved children in reading, writing, spelling, and history. She also taught them abolitionist songs and told them the story of Haiti's black liberator, Toussaint L'Ouverture. At night, she informally tutored adults.

In the spring of 1864, Forten wrote a two-part series about the Port Royal Experiment for the *Atlantic Monthly*, articles that helped establish the success of the "experiment," and the fact of the intellectual capacity of former slaves, in the public eye. By then, however, Forten had returned north because of failing health and the death of her father. She later took up a postwar job as liaison between a northern philanthropic bureau and its teachers in the South. As for the Port Royal Experiment, it ended with mixed results: success for the black students and schools, but economic failure when the land promised to the ex-slaves was instead returned to its former owners.

Even as Forten and other northern volunteers were teaching in the sea islands, local schools for ex-slaves were springing up in other occupied areas, often organized by local black churches or black leaders. By the time the war ended in April 1865, many of the four and a half million former slaves were pursuing their education throughout the South. "The whole colored population, of all sexes and ages, is repeating from morning to night, a-b, ab; e-b, eb; i-b, ib; c-a-t, cat; d-o-g, dog; c-u-p, cup," wrote one reporter in Charlottesville, Virginia, in October of that year. "If we pass a blacksmith's shop, we hear a-b, ab; if we peep into a shoemaker's shop, it is a-b, ab; if we pass by a negro cabin in the suburbs of the town, we hear the sound, a-b, ab."

Nor was the hunger for education limited to the ABCs. Former slave Francis Grimké, who had served in the war as valet to a Confederate army officer, moved quickly through primary education at Charleston's Morris Street School and then enrolled at Pennsylvania's newly renamed Lincoln University, formerly a training school for black ministers, where he earned a bachelor's and a master's degree. In 1874 Grimké began working for a law degree at another new institution, Howard University, founded seven years earlier in Washington, D.C. But he cut short his legal studies to attend Princeton Theological Seminary, graduating in 1878. The same year, Grimké married Charlotte Forten. The center of an eager intellectual circle wherever they traveled, the gently raised northerner and the former southern slave worked together to serve the church and fight against racial discrimination until Charlotte's death in 1914 at the age of 76.

Howard and Lincoln, the schools Francis Grimké attended before entering the seminary, were part of a spate of new black educational institutions founded or created from preexisting academies in the years and decades after the Civil War, an era in

Charlotte Forten (*above*), who spent a year as the first African American teacher at Epes Grammar School in Salem, Massachusetts, went on to teach freed slaves in the South Carolina sea islands during the Civil War.

American history marked by the founding of many new schools for all races. During this period, black community leaders, churches, philanthropists, and government agencies founded dozens of the institutions now known as the historically black colleges and universities (HBCUs). In the very early days, the schools were staffed largely by white instructors, but they trained a generation of black teachers, professors, and college presidents, as well as leaders in politics, religion, and business.

Many of the HBCUs began as primary or vocational schools, then evolved over the decades into junior colleges, colleges, and universities, often changing their names in the process. Nashville's Fisk University—later to graduate such luminaries as historian John Hope Franklin—began six months after the war as a primary school housed in an old Union army barracks, where eager pupils ranging in age from seven to 70 learned to read and write. Similarly, the Augusta Institute, founded in 1867 in the basement of the Springfield Baptist Church in Augusta, Georgia, at first offered future black ministers instruction at what would now be considered the elementary and high-school levels. The institute later moved to Atlanta, becoming in turn the Atlanta Baptist Seminary and then Atlanta Baptist College. In 1906 John Hope, the school's first black president, converted it to a liberal arts college and renamed it Morehouse College in honor of Henry Lyman Morehouse, secretary of the American Baptist Home Mission Society and a key figure in the school's early history.

At Hampton Normal and Agricultural Institute, one of several colleges that were founded in the 19th century by the federal Freedmen's Bureau, early students pursued a practical curriculum that included studying the physics of a cheese press (*bottom*) and constructing a staircase (*below*).

Even as they served a practical purpose, the black schools were an inspiring symbol of emancipation's new possibilities. In one of many emotionally weighted gestures, African American residents of Nashville sold old slave leg irons to finance the purchase of books at Fisk University. Talladega College in Alabama was started in a pre-Civil War school building for whites; among its first graduates was a former slave who had helped build the school when it was intended for the sons of slaveholders.

Still more black institutions benefited from the federal government's Morrill Act. Originally passed in 1862, the act directed states to allocate federal funds to establish industrial and agricultural schools, either by founding new schools or by expanding existing institutions. A renewal of the act in 1890 extended its provisions to black schools. A total of 17 black land-grant colleges emerged, principally in the South, including Mississippi's Alcorn University, Alabama's Tuskegee Institute, Florida's State Normal College for Colored Students—now Florida Agricultural and Mechanical University—and North Carolina Agricultural and Mechanical College for the Colored Race, since renamed North Carolina Agricultural and Technical State University.

African Americans took pride in the growing roster of black colleges, but for most the daily struggle for economic survival still made any education past the primary level a distant dream. Establishing even a basic educational system took time because of the sheer size of the South and of its black population; school founders also faced violence from the Ku Klux Klan and other white terrorist groups, who burned black schools and threatened or even lynched black teachers. By 1870, despite the efforts of the Freedmen's Bureau, local black leaders, and private philanthropic groups, only one in 10 black children was attending school.

Black southerners and some liberal whites turned to the notion of public education—a novel idea for the South, where government-funded schooling had never caught on. During the brief period before federal troops withdrew in 1877, racially mixed southern state legislatures voted for public schools across the South. Most blacks hoped for integrated schools, but that idea proved so inflammatory that racial segregation was the norm from the beginning.

In the resulting dual school systems—later emulated in the North as blacks migrated there in large numbers—black teachers were paid less than their white counterparts, and black students struggled with poor or nonexistent supplies, short school years (four months in South Carolina, for example, where white schools operated for six months), and in some cases a lack of secondary schools altogether.

Other sources of money became essential. Black parents raised what they could, but much of the support came from several philanthropic funds, most of them endowed by wealthy white northerners. For good or ill, the funds' trustees exercised considerable power over black school policy. The George Peabody Fund, for example, established in 1867 with an endowment of a million dollars, was vital in the early training of black teachers, besides making direct contributions to both black and

At the height of his national influence, black educator Booker T. Washington stands beside President Theodore Roosevelt on a flag-bedecked reviewing stand at Alabama's Tuskegee Institute on October 24, 1905 (right).

About 19 years old when this photograph of his Hampton Institute graduating class was taken in 1875, a playful Booker T. Washington (front row, second from left) reclines with a finger pointed at the camera. Washington later based his own work as principal of the Tuskegee Institute on his experiences at Hampton.

white schools. Yet it also lobbied in favor of school segregation and formed a policy of contributing two-thirds as much to a black school as it would to a white one, on the apparent theory that blacks were cheaper to educate.

Similarly, the John Slater Fund, established in 1882, pushed to extend rural black schools to grades above the primary level and trained many black teachers. Then, after a period of support for liberal arts studies, its trustees declared themselves firmly in favor of vocational and industrial training as more appropriate, cutting back their support for traditional academic subjects. Many HBCUs dependent on the Slater Fund had to shut down certain programs, although they survived as institutions. By contrast, schools that favored the vocational model thrived, including Virginia's Hampton Normal and Agricultural Institute and Alabama's Tuskegee Institute. In some years, Hampton and Tuskegee received more than half of the Slater money.

Hampton was founded by the Freedmen's Bureau in 1868 to train black teachers and leaders in practical skills. One of its graduates, former slave Booker T. Washington, went on to devote his life to building up the Tuskegee Institute along predominantly vocational lines similar to those of his own Hampton training. When Washington arrived to take over Tuskegee in 1881, there was no land for the planned school, no buildings, and only $2,000 for salaries. On behalf of the school, Washington borrowed money and purchased an abandoned plantation, whereupon students built a kiln and made bricks to build the school from the ground up. Even as Tuskegee became an international model of black education, its students continued to construct additional college buildings as needed as well as raise much of their own food.

Viewed as the most influential black leader of his day by whites and by most blacks, Washington would eventually be criticized by W. E. B. Du Bois and other black scholars, who felt black students should be treated as the equals of their white counterparts and have the same opportunities for academic excellence in all fields, not just in industrial and vocational arts. The black educators on both sides of this debate—covered in greater depth on pages 182-183—shared an abiding commitment to black education, but from profoundly different perspectives.

In his day, however, Washington's view largely prevailed, and his openly accommodationist stance brought him immense power and prestige. In Washington he dined at the White House with President Theodore Roosevelt, on a journey to England he sipped tea with Queen Victoria, and when at home he was regularly visited by Africans, West Indians, Asians, and European missionaries. Harvard and Dartmouth gave him honorary degrees, and industrialist Andrew Carnegie invited him to his Scottish castle.

173

Far from being a passive recipient of white largess, Washington helped to direct or influence the policies of several philanthropic funds. The Anna T. Jeanes Foundation, established by a Philadelphia Quaker in 1905, stipulated that Washington, together with the principal of Hampton, should approve all monies distributed by the fund to rural black schools. When Chicago businessman Julius Rosenwald, head of Sears, Roebuck, decided to contribute heavily to black southern education, his meeting with Washington at Tuskegee in 1911 shaped Rosenwald's vision of how to help. At about the same time, Washington served as a key adviser in the establishment of the Phelps-Stokes Fund.

Through visits and speeches, Washington also lent his enormous prestige to a number of other black schools, including Florida's Daytona Normal and Industrial School for Girls. The Daytona school, which was later renamed Bethune College and merged with another school in 1923 to become Bethune-Cookman College, was the vision of a single black educator, a remarkable woman who would later become one of the most influential black New Dealers (*pages 222-223*). But when Mary McLeod Bethune first dedicated herself to educating others, she was an impoverished unknown. Born in Mayesville, South Carolina, in 1875, the 15th child of former slaves, Mary McLeod dated her interest in teaching to the first time she held a book in her hands as a child. As she later told the story, the white daughter of one of her mother's employers snatched the book away, explaining that since Negroes could not read, the book was no business of hers. To McLeod, reading came to symbolize the economic distinction between blacks and whites. After attending the Scotia Seminary (now Barber-Scotia College) in Concord, North Carolina, and Moody Bible Institute in Chicago, McLeod found employment as an instructor at a private black academy, the Haines Institute in Augusta, Georgia. The lifework of black teacher Lucy Laney, Haines was the pride of Augusta's black community, a thriving institution despite fire, flood, financial difficulties, and restive white neighbors. After a year at Haines, Mary McLeod left to teach in Sumter, South Carolina, where she married Albertus Bethune in 1897. The couple had a son, Albert, the following year. In 1899 the young family moved to Palatka, Florida, where Mary McLeod Bethune taught at the Palatka Mission School.

While there, she began to plan her own school in nearby Daytona Beach, where she hoped to teach the daughters of black workers laying railroad tracks. In 1904 the idea became a reality, largely as a result of Bethune's driving personality. Offered the chance to rent a ramshackle Daytona Beach building, she somehow persuaded the owner to take $1.50—her entire resources—and wait for the balance later. Black neighbors eager for the school helped Bethune repair and clean the building, which she furnished with discarded barrels, boards, and boxes. Three years later, she moved her school to a permanent campus—on a site known as Hell's Hole, an inexpensive property that was the former city dump. There the institute's first structure, the four-story, white-framed Faith Hall, was erected. In 1910 the school added a farm. Bethune often joined her faculty and students in the fields, where they raised sugarcane, melons, and pumpkins.

Lucy Laney (*above*) braved local hostility to found the Haines Institute in Augusta, Georgia, in 1883 with five black pupils; by 1884 she had about 230. An inspiration to Mary McLeod Bethune, Laney emphasized the liberal arts at a time when industrial education for blacks was in vogue.

Like many black educators before and since, Bethune had to spend much of her time raising funds. "One of my important jobs was to be a good beggar," she later wrote. "I rang doorbells and tackled cold prospects without a lead. I wrote articles for whoever would print them, distributed leaflets, rode interminable miles of dusty roads on my old bicycle, invaded churches, clubs, lodges, chambers of commerce." She also won over major contributors such as James Gamble of Procter and Gamble.

While pupils fortunate enough to attend such institutions acquired the skills and knowledge for later success, the plight of the black public schools of the South—still the only educational opportunity for the vast majority of black American children—worsened decade after decade. In 1916, fewer than 20,000 black students were enrolled in black public high schools in the South, primarily because there were only 67 such institutions in the entire region. During the same period, most black pupils were able to attend only the first eight grades. In the 1930s, black college professor Horace Mann Bond published two classic books on the status of black education, coming back again and again to the disparate funding for black and white schools.

While Bond credited individual black institutions, black and white educators, and the philanthropic funds for their efforts, he meticulously detailed the lack of real educational opportunity for most American blacks, a deficiency for which the segregated school systems were clearly to blame. Racism was so deeply entrenched, however, that Bond could only suggest—as an ideal scenario—the gradual increase of black teachers' salaries over a 20-year period, to eventually equal white salaries. He did not even put forward the idea of desegregation, although he clearly favored it; mixed-race schools, he wrote resignedly in *The Education of the Negro in the American Social Order*, "were opposed to the logic of history and the reality of human nature and racial prejudices." A generation later, with school desegregation well under way and his own son Julian Bond one of the leaders of a nationwide civil rights movement, Horace Mann Bond marveled at the changes history had wrought.

In 1936, not long after Bond's book was published, Martin Luther King, Sr., helped lead a fight by the black community in Atlanta, Georgia, to do what Bond had thought impractical: Equalize black and white teachers' salaries. Although the impetus came from the teachers, King, whose son would become the best-known leader of the civil rights movement, became the public spokesman. "Leadership in this fight was going to have to come from outside the teaching profession," King wrote in his 1980 autobiography, *Daddy King*. "Too much pressure could be applied to the teachers themselves, all of whom held their jobs without any real security. As a minister with a growing church family, I simply wasn't in the same position."

Soon after King took up the fight, white ministers began urging him to drop it. He also received hate letters and death threats. But in 1947—eleven years after the first

Seven 1914 graduates of the Daytona Normal and Industrial School for Girls pose beside a chalked slogan, "We have crossed the Bay—the Ocean is before us." Founded by Mary McLeod Bethune, the school, later renamed Bethune College, merged to become Bethune-Cookman.

organizing meeting—the cause was won. Two black teachers whose legal costs were paid by King's church were victorious in a case testing whether differential pay based on race was constitutional.

By the mid-1940s, in fact, the first hints of racial change seemed to be in the air. In 1944, the Carnegie Foundation published a massive work, *An American Dilemma*, that examined the corrosive effects of American racial discrimination in a new way. Previously, the Carnegie Foundation, like the other philanthropic funds, had contented itself with supplying money to black colleges. In about 1935, its trustees had begun to wonder if that was really enough. They commissioned an "outsider"—Swedish sociologist Gunnar Myrdal—to lead a comprehensive study of American race relations.

Myrdal immediately hired a large interracial research team that included Ralph Bunche, a Howard University professor. Bunche, who would later become a United Nations ambassador, wrote thousands of pages of notes on such topics as the political status of the black, which Myrdal found useful despite Bunche's emphasis on economic class rather than race. Myrdal also consulted with a host of prominent black Americans, from NAACP president Walter White and activist W. E. B. Du Bois to author Alain Locke. The resulting report, released at the height of World War II, had a powerful impact. As the title suggested, it concluded that for white Americans, race posed a profound dilemma. The American ideals of fairness and equality—for which

With all public schools in Prince Edward County, Virginia, closed to avoid desegregation, four young black residents make do with an outdoor tutoring session (*below*) in 1962. The schools stayed shut for five years, from 1959 to 1964, during which time some children received no teaching at all.

Guarded by a heavy police escort against stone-throwing attacks, buses filled with black students roll cautiously into South Boston on September 16, 1974, the third day of court-ordered busing. Violent racial clashes continued in the predominantly Irish American district for more than two years.

Americans of all races were then fighting and dying—were fundamentally at odds with the reality of American racial segregation and discrimination.

A decade after the book's publication, the work of the black and white scholars of the Carnegie team was still so well respected that the United States Supreme Court cited *An American Dilemma* in its groundbreaking opinion in the case of *Brown v. the Board of Education of Topeka, Kansas.* That unanimous 1954 decision ruled all school segregation unconstitutional—a turnaround that came as a thunderclap for many observers. W. E. B. Du Bois wrote, "I have seen the Impossible happen. It did happen on May 17, 1954."

The *Brown* decision did not come out of nowhere, and it was far from the end of the story. The decision was the climax of a long series of NAACP court victories, many won by chief counsel Thurgood Marshall, that had slowly laid the legal groundwork for school desegregation. In some schools it had an immediate and powerful effect. By 1958, desegregation was under way in a number of southern school districts with both white and black pupils. Black children in Wilmington, Delaware; Baltimore, Maryland; and Washington, D.C., sat in classrooms beside white children, as did African American students in certain counties in Missouri, Arkansas, and West Virginia. In Louisville, Kentucky, the school system became a national model of smooth desegregation.

But most southern jurisdictions strenuously resisted desegregation, encouraged by a Supreme Court ruling—a year after the *Brown* decision—that the transition need only take place "with all deliberate speed." States and counties passed more than 145 laws designed to hold off desegregation altogether; the Georgia legislature, for example, decided to withhold state funds from any school that enrolled students of both races. Prince Edward County, Virginia, closed all of its public schools from 1959 to 1964—when it was forced to reopen the school system by order of the Supreme Court.

And yet the clock could not be turned back. From the late 1950s to the mid-1960s, one previously white school after another grudgingly admitted its first black students—from the nine black teenagers in 1957 who endured harassment and threats to attend Central High School in Little Rock, Arkansas, to air force veteran James Meredith, who in 1962 became the first black student to enroll at the University of Mississippi. School segregation based on race received its final blow in 1969, when an exasperated Supreme Court overturned its "all deliberate speed" ruling and ordered full desegregation immediately. A few years later, federal courts began ruling that school segregation based on residential patterns should also be remedied, sometimes by busing groups of students to other schools. In some cases, buses filled with black children became magnets for mob violence, especially in South Boston, where white residents stoned buses carrying black students in 1974.

Even within seemingly integrated public schools, subtle mechanisms often continued to divide the races. Standardized tests, for example, are thought by many educators to be culturally biased in favor of the white middle class, yet grouping by ability, or tracking, was often based on such tests, or on sometimes-faulty teacher expectations. In addition, so-called white flight became a pattern in urban centers as white students left for suburban or private schools.

African American educators had weathered worse challenges in centuries past, however, and they were not about to give up. In November 1970, black school superintendents from across the nation gathered for the first meeting of the National Alliance of Black School Educators (NABSE). Joined by other black school administrators and by education students, NABSE has since worked on the special issues of school systems with high percentages of minority students, especially African American students. Meanwhile, in schools and classrooms across the country, black instructors gave unstintingly of themselves, innovating, inspiring, counseling—teaching. Perhaps the best publicized of this rugged corps of educationists was Marva Collins (*page* 199), a veteran Chicago public-school teacher who left the system in 1975 to found her own private academy for young black students.

Meanwhile, some African American teachers began exploring and promoting another strategy: substituting an Afrocentric point of view for the mainstream, or Eurocentric, vision that has long shaped public school presentations of history, the arts, the history of science, and other topics. This approach is not a new one, as Afrocentrists are the first to point out. In 1933, the great black historian Carter G. Woodson (*page* 186), wrote that " 'educated Negroes' have the attitude of contempt toward their own people because in their own as well as in their mixed schools Negroes are taught to admire the Hebrew, the Greek, the Latin and the Teuton and to despise the African." To rectify the situation, Woodson wrote, "we should not underrate the achievements of Mesopotamia, Greece, and Rome; but we should give equally as much attention to the internal African kingdoms, the Songhay empire, and Ethiopia, which through Egypt decidedly influenced the civilization of the Mediterranean world."

For many years, few public school systems followed Woodson's advice very far.

THE UNCF

During World War II, private black colleges and universities were fighting their own battle for survival on the home front. Reporting on a decade-old decline in philanthropic donations, Frederick Patterson, president of Tuskegee, summarized the crisis in the Pittsburgh Courier in January 1943. He also proposed a solution: that the schools "pool their small monies and make a united appeal to the national conscience." The appeal became the United Negro College Fund (UNCF), founded in April 1944. Not only did the UNCF immediately attract hefty donations from industrialists, but it also won the backing of Franklin Roosevelt, the first in an unbroken line of U.S. presidents to support it. Within a year it raised $765,000, three times what its members would likely have collected on their own. Later campaigns reached the tens of millions. A decade later, the UNCF weathered something of a crisis when the Supreme Court's Brown v. Board of Education of Topeka, Kansas, *decision overturned segregated public school education. The ruling did not affect private black colleges and universities; most, in any case, had charters that welcomed all races. But for some people it raised questions about the future of black institutions of higher learning. UNCF supporters argued that desegregation would take years and that, moreover, the black schools offered African American students a uniquely supportive environment. In the decades that followed, the latter argument prevailed. Ever more successful in its fund-raising efforts, the UNCF was clearly here to stay.*

Except for a few classes during Black History Month, African American students found themselves cast in the role of spectator, absorbing a stream of information that included little mention of black achievers or even of the continent of Africa. But the ideas of Afrocentricity gained new currency in the 1980s. In 1980, Molefi Asante, chairman of Temple University's Department of African-American Studies, published a book, entitled simply *Afrocentricity*, espousing an approach that, in his words, gave African American students "ownership of knowledge rather than seeing blacks as marginal to Europeans."

Depending on the teacher and the school which implement it, Afrocentricity can come in many varieties. But its main thrust is to view all of learning through an African or African American prism, providing a continuum of black culture, history, and achievement against which students can be conscious of their own identity. As one advocate has suggested, an Afrocentric way to view the Civil War "might start with Frederick Douglass or my great-grandmother as the focus."

In 1989 the public school system of Atlanta, Georgia, where most students are black, began testing a curriculum based on infusion, a strategy that adds elements of Afrocentricity to the curriculum. Afrocentric classes and materials have also been used in schools in Philadelphia; New York; Indianapolis; Cleveland; New Orleans; Oakland, California; and Portland, Oregon, among other cities. Multiculturalism, a related approach, includes the contributions of blacks, whites, Latinos, Asians, and Native Americans. Some would argue that this approach also benefits from Afrocentricity. As Robert L. Harris, Jr., president of the Association for the Study of Afro-American Life and History, puts it, multiculturalism "cannot be achieved without a perspective that centers the various cultures within their own history."

Whether or not they incorporated the tenets of Afrocentricity—and most were influenced to some degree by the idea—black educators in the 1980s and 1990s carried on the age-old fight to keep the torch of knowledge and self-respect alight—despite the odds, despite the lack of funds, despite the drugs, violence, and despair of inner-city poverty that increased the odds against many of the children they instructed. One such fighter is John P. Haydel, Jr., a Louisianan who in 1984 became principal of John C. Fremont High School in south-central Los Angeles, where about three-quarters of the students are black and most of the rest are Latino. When he arrived, the school was a shambles. The ceiling tiles on all three floors of the classroom building had been knocked out, water pipes and electric wires were exposed, and every surface was covered with graffiti. Fremont also had a history of low test scores, poor relationships between its faculty and the school administration, and little support from the local community or former students.

Pulling together available funds, Haydel immediately set a new tone by changing the look of the school, with new lights and ceilings and a fresh coat of bright paint inside and out. He let it be known that discipline was now the order of the day. Convinced that students involved in school activities were more likely to excel academically, he resurrected defunct school clubs and organizations and hired former athletes to rejuvenate school teams. He also inducted successful Fremont alumni, including judges, doctors, lawyers, business executives, and others, into a new Hall of Fame for

those who "found a path or made one," who "dared to be different" and to dream.

Fremont was selected for a Pacific Bell program under which 30 company employees who lived or worked in the community volunteered their time in various classrooms. Haydel also worked with United States Labor Secretary Lynn Martin, Mayor Tom Bradley, and local business leaders to form a training program that provides jobs at retail companies for students in their junior and senior years. The teenagers work for pay and go to school, earning scholarships to community colleges. After attending community college, they get jobs.

With the support of the community, the school turned around. By the early 1990s, some 75 percent of each graduating class were entering four-year colleges or two-year community colleges. Fremont was also selected as a model school for the school district's math, science, and engineering enhancement programs. "There is really no magic to what we've done," Haydel has said. "These are good kids who want to learn and we're giving them the opportunity."

Fremont students who go on to four-year schools have their choice of predominantly white colleges and universities or the HBCUs, most of which remain in operation despite the desegregation of previously white institutions. Even before the *Brown* decision, some black students outside the South had been attending predominantly white colleges in small numbers. For a decade or so after the decision, those numbers rose only slowly as HBCUs, championed by the United Negro College Fund (*page 178*), continued to attract the great majority of black undergraduates. By the end of the 1960s, however, the gradual impact of the civil rights movement had transformed policies at predominantly white colleges and universities. In 1968, almost half of all American colleges and universities were actively recruiting or providing special services for minority and disadvantaged students. This trend, accompanied by the founding of many new community colleges, led to a dramatic surge in black enrollments at predominantly white colleges. Enrollments at HBCUs dwindled, and a number of small colleges closed. As the 1970s began, only about half of all black college students attended HBCUs.

Although individual reactions differ, many African American students at HBCUs seem to thrive on the sense of tradition and pride, while blacks in predominantly white educational settings often report a sense of isolation or alienation. In some regions, HBCUs remain the choice of the majority of black college students. In Mississippi, more than 70 percent of African Americans enrolled in higher education attend HBCUs. However, for many HBCUs, funding remains a life-or-death matter, a constant and seri-

One of the many black public school principals who made a difference in the 1980s and early 1990s, John P. Haydel, Jr., of Fremont High School in Los Angeles joins Black Student Union members for a group portrait in 1992.

ous worry. Publicly funded HBCUs, including the old land-grant colleges, face another threat from state governments attempting to consolidate them with predominantly white schools.

Among the greatest resources of any HBCU are its faculty members, many of them known not only for their scholarly achievements but also for their commitment and dedication to teaching. At Clark Atlanta University in Georgia, the chairman of the mathematics department is Abdulalim A. Shabazz, who has been phenomenally successful in producing black doctorates in mathematics. In 1986 Shabazz came back to Clark College, as it was then known, after a 23-year absence. During his earlier tenure, from 1957 to 1963, Shabazz had encouraged his students not only to major in mathematics but also to pursue doctorates in the field. About a third of his math majors did, and many went on to become mathematics professors and advise the next generation of black doctoral candidates. By the early 1990s, almost half of the 200 professional black mathematicians in the United States could be traced back, directly or indirectly, to Shabazz.

As chairman of the Clark Atlanta University mathematics department, Abdulalim Shabazz (*above*) says anyone can excel in higher mathematics, given the chance. "I assume that if the students are in my class, they're here to learn," he said in a 1992 interview. "I emphasize hard work. It's hard work that separates so-called geniuses from the also-rans."

Born Lonnie Cross in Bessemer, Alabama, in 1927, Shabazz graduated in 1949 from Lincoln University, then earned a master's degree in 1951 at Massachusetts Institute of Technology and a doctorate at Cornell University in 1955. He taught at Tuskegee for a year before going to Clark College, where he soon developed a reputation for teaching mathematics to students of all ability levels. "If you're not brain-damaged, you can learn math," he has said cheerfully.

During his time at Clark, Cross became a member of the Nation of Islam and changed his last name to Shabazz (he changed his first name to Abdulalim some years later). Malcolm X was among the influential figures he invited to speak to his classes. Shabazz and his students also joined in the sit-in movement of the day, protesting at public libraries where they weren't allowed to sit by reading books they weren't allowed to check out because of Jim Crow laws. "Yes, I taught people to think and reason," he says. "But my students were thinking people. They could put one and one together and get two." Accused of sparking student protests, Dr. Shabazz left the university in 1963. For the next several years he served as an official of the Nation of Islam, later traveling to Saudi Arabia, where he taught math and studied Arabic before his return to Atlanta. In 1992 the American Association for the Advancement of Science, the world's premier scientific organization, awarded him its Mentor Award for his accomplishments. Shabazz, however, insists there is no secret to his teaching success—except, perhaps, for his supreme confidence in his students' abilities. "There's no magic potion or hocus-pocus," he told one interviewer in 1993. "It's simply believing everyone can learn if they put forth the effort."

TWO EDUCATORS IN A CLASSIC DEBATE

When he published a small collection of essays entitled *The Souls of Black Folk* in 1903, thirty-five-year-old historian William Edward Burghardt Du Bois was already the most famous black intellectual in America, with a doctorate from Harvard University and several articles and texts to his credit. But in this book, especially, it was his heart as well as his insightful mind that spoke, in powerful, emotive prose that surveyed the grim American racial scene of the day. One chapter in particular hit readers with the force of a thunderclap. In it, Du Bois singled out a black leader who he believed had stimulated and virtually condoned black disenfranchisement and repression: Booker Taliaferro Washington, principal of Alabama's Tuskegee Institute.

Washington, with his philosophy of black political invisibility, had come to the fore as a black spokesman in 1895 after the death of longtime activist Frederick Douglass. In a stance celebrated especially by whites, Washington called for African Americans to leave the political arena and concentrate on educat-

Booker T. Washington

ing themselves for individual economic uplift. To do so, he argued, black Americans should devote themselves mainly to vocational studies rather than to higher education. "One man may go into a community prepared to supply the people there with an analysis of Greek sentences. The community may not at that time be prepared for, or feel the need of, Greek analysis, but it may feel its need of bricks and houses and wagons," he wrote in *Up from Slavery*—an autobiography published in 1900 which, like Du Bois's book, is still in print. "If the man can supply the need for those, then, it will lead eventually to a demand for the first product, and with the demand will come the ability to appreciate it and to profit by it." Focused on the practical aspects of the transition from slavery and from the rural poverty that had followed it, Washington also wrote that "one of the saddest things" he had seen in his travels was "a young man who had attended some high school, sitting down in a one-room cabin," with "filth all around him, and weeds in the garden, engaged in studying a French grammar."

Washington's emphasis on practical education was very influential. And yet, Du Bois argued, blacks had gained little from years of following Washington's lead. "Mr. Washington distinctly asked that black people give up, at least for the present, three things,—First, political power, Second, insistence on civil rights, and Third, higher education of Negro youth,—and concentrate all their energies on industrial education, the accumulation of wealth, and the conciliation of the South," Du Bois wrote. The results of this strategy, he argued, were just as easy to list: disenfranchisement, second-class citizenship, and dwindling financial support for black liberal arts colleges. These developments, he acknowledged, "are not, to be sure, direct results of Mr. Washington's teachings; but his propaganda has, without a shadow of doubt, helped their speedier accomplishment."

African American newspaper editor William Monroe Trotter, a friend of Du Bois's, shared many of these views. In 1903, the same year Du Bois published his book, Trotter and others began challenging Washington at public meetings, culminating in a raucous free-for-all at a packed meeting in Boston at which Washington was to give an address. Several of those present were arrested, including Trotter, who received a 30-day jail sentence.

From the events of 1903 has emanated an often-exaggerated notion of the debate between Booker T. Washington and W. E. B. Du Bois. The disagreements between these two figures have been oversimplified to present Washington as the naive advocate of black racial deference and manual labor and Du Bois as the intellectual champion of immediate integration of all blacks into America's political and economic life. As in many a grand debate, the truth is more complex. And, as at any time in black America's history, having advocates working on different aspects of an issue, from different perspectives, had its benefits. Both men were well aware of the oppressive social realities of their day. Both men saw black leadership for the time being as the prerogatives of a small cadre of gifted individuals, with Du Bois promoting a so-called Talented Tenth (a phrase he repudiated in later life) and Washington describing "the most respectable men" as having a moral duty to guide the masses. Their responses on the educational front differed mainly in emphasis.

Washington did stress industrial education and the dignity of work, but he sent his own children to Massachusetts preparatory schools and—as Du Bois pointed out—hired Fisk and Atlanta liberal arts graduates as faculty members at Tuskegee. In a famous exhortation, Washington urged black Americans to "cast down your bucket where you are" by earning a living wherever they happened to be and by "making friends in every manly way of the people of all races by whom we are surrounded." But the list of occupations that he set forth as examples of this approach included commerce and the professions, as well as agriculture and domestic service. Similarly, Du Bois was not opposed to industrial education; indeed, he stressed that African American survival "lies in the closer knitting of the Negro to the great industrial possibilities of the South." He felt, however, that trade schools were not enough. "The foundations of knowledge in this race, as in others, must be sunk deep in the college and university if we would build a solid, permanent structure," Du Bois argued. In facing "problems of work and wages, of families and homes, of morals and the true valuing of the things of life," he added, "can there be any possible solution other than by study and thought and an appeal to the rich experience of the past?"

The divergent strategies advocated by Washington and Du Bois were perhaps as much as anything a reflection of differences in background and personality. The aloof, scholarly Du Bois grew up in predominantly white Great Barrington, Massachusetts, and only became fully aware of the larger black communi-

W. E. B. Du Bois

ty during his college years at Fisk. By contrast, Washington was born in what is now West Virginia to a slave mother. Formally trained only up to the high-school level at Hampton, he made the South the instrument of what he called "my larger education." Du Bois was most at home among his books; Washington among people he wished to persuade.

Nor was the debate between the two men always so heated. In fact, Du Bois had come close to accepting a teaching appointment at Tuskegee in the late 1890s. When Washington died in 1915 at age 59—having worked himself to death for the educational ideals he held dear—Du Bois wrote a typically balanced epitaph for his old rival. Booker T. Washington, wrote Du Bois, was "the greatest Negro leader since Frederick Douglass, and the most distinguished man, white or black, who has come out of the South since the Civil War." And yet, "in stern justice, we must lay on the soul of this man, a heavy responsibility for the consummation of Negro disenfranchisement, the decline of the Negro college and the firmer establishment of color caste." Washington's death, of course, meant that Du Bois had the last word.

PIONEERS OF BLACK HISTORY

"I shan't be surprised if you laugh in your sleeve at an old man, nigh four score, projecting new work," wrote 78-year-old black clergyman Alexander Crummell in 1897 in a letter to a friend. "I can't help it. Work is life." Crummell was referring to the project that absorbed the

William Cooper Nell

last months of his long and productive career: the founding of the American Negro Academy, a national association of black scholars. He believed that research by members of the group into black life and history would serve as an inspiring example, an intellectual antidote to the rampant racism of the times.

A year later, Crummell was dead—but his academy was a reality. Unlike nearly a dozen black history groups launched at about this time in cities such as Philadelphia, New York, and Chicago, the academy attracted members from across the nation, as well as from the West Indies and Africa. Among its 99 distin-

guished members were historian William Edward Burghardt Du Bois, the first African American to receive a doctorate from Harvard University; AMEZ Bishop Alexander Walters; future college president John Hope; the West African aristocrat J. E. Casely Hayford; and renowned painter Henry Ossawa Tanner. During its 31-year history, the academy published more than two dozen scholarly papers. Perhaps equally important, it served as an inspiration for African Americans enlisting in the battle to redefine the past, illuminate the present, and introduce African American history as a recognized topic of professional scholarship.

The establishment of the American Negro Academy marked the beginning of a collaborative era in black history research. For the most part, earlier investigators into the African American past had to work by themselves. In 1851, for example, William Cooper Nell, a black abolitionist who helped lead the battle to desegregate Boston's schools, had pioneered the writing

of black military history with a pamphlet entitled *Services of Colored Americans in the Wars of 1776 and 1812*. He wrote a book-length treatment of the same topic, *The Colored Patriots of the American Revolution*, in 1855. Nell, who hoped to bridge a widening chasm between the races, believed white

Martin Robinson Delany

readers would be most readily moved by learning about African American contributions to the whole society's defense.

Physician Martin Delany, who would himself later serve as a Union army officer (*left*), expressed similar goals in a preface to his book *The Condition, Elevation, Emigration and Destiny of the Colored People of the United States, Politically Considered*, a more general account of African American history published in 1852. "One part of the American people, though living in or near proximity and together, are quite unacquainted with the other," Delany wrote. "One of the great objects of the author, is to make each acquainted. Except that the character of an individual is known, there can be no just appreciation of his worth; and as with individuals, so it is with classes."

And yet derogatory images of African Americans endured, outlasting slavery to "justify" a new round of repression and violence against blacks in the last quarter of the 19th century. To combat the antiblack pseudohistories of his day, attorney George Washington Williams spent six years preparing his *History of the Negro Race from 1619 to 1880*, a meticulously researched 1,100-page text published in 1882. "Not as the blind panegyrist of my race, nor as the partisan apologist, but from a love of the 'truth of history,' have I striven to record the truth, the whole truth, and nothing but the truth," Williams wrote. "I have avoided comment so far as it was consistent with a clear exposition of the

truth. My whole aim has been to write a thoroughly trustworthy history; and what I have written, if it have no other merit, is reliable." He achieved that purpose so thoroughly that the book remained the basic account of the African American experience for more than six decades.

In 1887 Williams published *History of the Negro Troops in the War of the Rebellion*. He then set off for

George Washington Williams

Africa, financed by commissions from *McClure's* magazine and from an American railroad magnate. Upon his return, Williams was considered an authority on conditions in Africa. In that capacity, he became the first black historian to confer with a U.S. president and the first to testify before the Senate Committee on Foreign Relations. Williams also represented the United States at the Antislavery Conference of European Powers, a gathering that led

to the Brussels Act of 1890 outlawing "the African slave trade on land and sea."

With the founding of the American Negro Academy later in the same decade, the era of isolated, individual historians like Williams began to give way to an emerging community of black history scholars. It was also during this period that W. E. B. Du Bois began publishing the Atlanta University studies, accounts of annual conferences that studied the African American experience using sociological tools. The series continued into the next century, analyzing everything from the black church to black landholders in Georgia and the practical record of black economic self-determination. Each volume represented a scholarly achievement all the more remarkable because it came at a time when all African Americans were increasingly under siege.

Turn-of-the-century America was an extremely dangerous place for black people. Lynchings were still reported regularly in the South, and white polemicists continued to turn out such books as Charles Carroll's *The Negro a Beast*, published in 1900. Urban riots directed against blacks broke out in Atlanta in 1906 and in Springfield, Illinois, in 1908. (The latter led to the formation of the NAACP, whose first black staff member was none other than Du Bois.) In 1913, the federal government moved to exclude blacks from civil service. Two years later, much of America marveled at the dazzling technical innova-

"If a race has no history, if it has no worth-while tradition, it becomes a negligible factor in the thought of the world, and it stands in danger of being exterminated," wrote Carter G. Woodson in 1926 in a call for the first national observance of Negro History Week. "The achievements of the Negro properly set forth will crown him as a factor in early human progress and a maker of modern civilization." Even as Woodson wrote those words in his Washington, D.C., office, the Ku Klux Klan was organizing a march of 10,000 people down Pennsylvania Avenue. Racial violence had become a common urban occurrence, and racial repression had gone national. But Woodson was never given to despair. He himself had already overcome truly horrendous odds to become a professional scholar.

Born to former slaves in Buckingham County, Virginia, he had spent much of his youth as a coal miner, having little formal education before age 20, when he enrolled in high school. He graduated a year and a half later. For the next 16 years he supported himself—usually by teaching—while earning several degrees, finishing in 1912 with a doctorate in history from Harvard.

It was not until 1915, however, that Woodson found his calling as head of the Association for the Study of Negro Life and History, which he cofounded. He also served as founding editor of its authoritative *Journal of Negro History*, launched in 1916. After two brief stints as a college professor at Howard and West Virginia State College, Woodson left the formal classroom for good in 1922, taking the world for his school.

CARTER G. WOODSON

During the 1920s, the association he cofounded nurtured the first full wave of trained black historians. He himself published five books in that decade. With his promotion of Negro History Week—a period in February chosen to include the birthdays of Frederick Douglass and Abraham Lincoln—Woodson also brought information about black history to a larger audience. (Decades later, the observance expanded to Black History Month.)

Revenue from philanthropic foundations began to dry up by the 1930s, however. In part this was because Woodson refused to merge his association with a black college or any other body. Money was also shifting away from black historical research and toward sociological studies of the present.

Yet Woodson and the association still had an enormous influence, accelerating the rise of black history as an academic discipline while reaching out to laymen through the *Negro History Bulletin*, founded in 1937. In the two decades before his death in 1950, Woodson's fervent desire to share his findings also led him to journey to land-grant colleges and public schools and speak at student assemblies. In effect, Woodson became the African American equivalent of the African *griot*, the oral historian who preserves the community's past.

tions of *Birth of a Nation*, a racist motion-picture epic that featured the exploits of the Ku Klux Klan.

But against this grim background a new and influential black historian emerged. Carter Godwin Woodson (*opposite*), the son of former slaves, was a high-school teacher when he helped to found the Association for the Study of Negro Life and History in 1915. The group—and its pub-

Alexander Crummell

lication, the *Journal of Negro History*—would become his life's work.

Under Woodson, the association nurtured an impressive array of black historians, among them Charles Wesley, who studied the abolitionist era and the evolution of black labor. "Ours then is the first step," Wesley later wrote. "To write, to publish, to read and to believe in ourselves and our capacities. To this first task, may we devote ourselves confident of success, for pride in self has been the touchstone of destiny for nations and races in all the past."

Woodson had established black history once and for all as a legitimate and necessary topic of study. Still, from an academic

perspective, the field was in its infancy. In 1940, only 14 African Americans held doctorates in any field of history. Not until after World War II, when social scientists focused more attention on previously marginalized groups, did support for research into black history began to build. For the first time, American social and historical studies were infused with a nonracial, universalistic ethos.

The new approach had its effect on the work of postwar black historians. Rayford Logan, one of Woodson's many protégés, took a broad international perspective in his books *Diplomatic Relations of the United States with Haiti* and *The Betrayal of the Negro*. Similarly, John Hope Franklin's *From Slavery to Freedom*, published in 1947, treated the black experience as integral to the American experience, part of the warp and woof of the tapestry of American history. A concise but comprehensive survey of black history, Franklin's book became an instant classic, finally displacing Williams's 65-year-old *History of the Negro Race* as the standard basic reference. Franklin explained his lifelong dedication to objectivity in historical work in a 1963 essay: "In the face of forces that deny him membership in the mainstream of American scholarship and suggest that he is unable to perform creditably, the task of

John Hope Franklin

remaining calm and objective is indeed a formidable one," he wrote of the dilemma confronting every black scholar. But by "maintaining the highest standards of scholarship," the black historian "sets an example that many of his contemporaries who claim to be arbiters in the field do not themselves follow."

Meanwhile, both black history and black historians have be-

come essential parts of the study of American history. Moreover, the black experience has come to serve for some as a kind of historical laser—a topic that cuts deeply and cleanly through the veils that all Americans tend to draw over the nation's unfinished agendas, to reveal the richly detailed story of a struggle that continues today.

CENTRAL TENNESSEE COLLEGE.
MEHARRY MEDICAL, DENTAL & PHARMACEUT'C'L FACULTY AND GRADUATES. 1898.

NASHVILLE, TENNESSEE

CALVERT BROS & TAYLOR PHOT.

TOWARD A MODEL FOR THE COUNTRY

In the first decades after the Civil War, there were those—deeply concerned blacks as well as unreconstructed whites—who believed that African Americans were doomed, if not to slavery, then to extinction.

Flocking to the cities in search of opportunity, freed slaves found only desperate poverty, terrible disease, and early death. Nashville, Tennessee, provided a grim

example: With only two black physicians to care for its huge black community, the city in 1876 suffered the highest urban death rate in the country—and the fifth highest in the world. Noting the squalid living conditions, the rampaging cholera, smallpox, and diphtheria, the *Daily American* reported, "From three to ten live crowded up together until disease seizes them and they die."

Yet 1876 was also a year of hope, for it marked the establishment of the first medical school in the United States devoted to the training of black physicians— as a tiny department of Central Tennessee College, founded a decade earlier by the Freedmen's Aid Society of the Methodist Episcopal church. At the start, the school had white leadership: Dr. George W. Hubbard, a recent

The class of 1898 shows two women among its 38 graduates. Dean George Hubbard (*far left, center*) led an increasingly black faculty.

graduate of Vanderbilt University who had committed himself to medical training for African Americans ever since observing how a young black woman cared for a sick friend. He was joined by Samuel Meharry, an Irish-born businessman. Fifty years before, Meharry had pledged to assist African Americans after a black family in Kentucky offered their help when his wagon broke down. Meharry supplied the wherewithal to start the college and gave it his name. In time, he and his family would donate half their fortune to the cause of African American medical education.

Eleven young men started out in Meharry Medical College's first class. Only one made it through the two-year course to graduation; some dropped out, others succumbed to the very diseases they hoped to fight. Three more

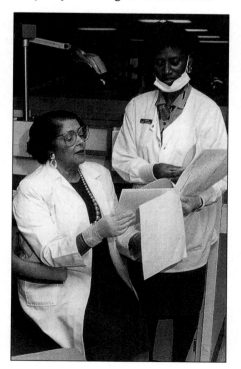

Associate Professor Wilda Seibert (*seated*) discusses procedures with a student at Meharry Medical College's School of Dentistry.

men earned medical degrees in the next class, and one of them, John S. Bass, spoke for everyone at Meharry when he said, "I know there is a class of people who say that we gradually will die out. But we will prove them false." Dr. Bass himself saved scores of blacks when a yellow fever epidemic ravaged Chattanooga in 1878.

In 1880, with funds from the Meharry family and the Freedmen's Aid Society, the college moved into its own building. Meharry expanded into dentistry and pharmacy, and by 1900 had established Mercy Hospital (later renamed George W. Hubbard Hospital) to care for Nashville's black community. Physicians packed into the operating amphitheater to observe such eminent specialists as Daniel Hale Williams, the African American doctor who had pioneered open-heart surgery in the early 1890s.

Meharry became independent in 1915, but its first years of autonomy were troubled by poor management and a chronic lack of funds. For a time, the American Medical Association withdrew the school's coveted A rating. Yet Meharry regained its excellence, and in the early 1930s built a new campus in the very heart of Nashville's black community.

In good times and bad, the school has never flagged in its dedication to high-quality medical education for African Americans. And along with other institutions, it is bringing down those brutal mortality rates: In the last century, life expectancy for black Americans has risen from 32 years in 1900 to 70 years in 1990.

In 1992 Dr. David Satcher, the

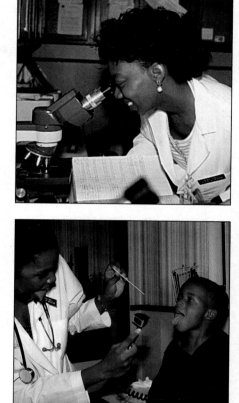

An undergraduate at Meharry (*top*) studies cultures under a laboratory microscope at Hubbard Hospital, while another medical student prepares to examine the throat of a young outpatient.

eighth president of Meharry, proudly noted that in its 116 years of operation, the college had produced no less than 40 percent of the nation's African American physicians and dentists—11,500 graduates in all. And he took the occasion to announce a signal triumph: The city of Nashville had agreed to make Meharry Medical College and Hubbard Hospital the town's primary public health providers. "It will lead not only to the end of segregated health care," said Dr. Satcher, "but to a very positive community health care system that can serve as a model for the country."

PHI BETA KAPPA KEYS FOR MOREHOUSE

There never was any question of identity in the mind of Benjamin E. Mays. Even as a child in the turn-of-the-century South, he could not believe "that my people were inferior, that God had sent them into the world to hew wood, scatter guano, draw water, pick cotton, pull fodder, and plow with a mule." On the contrary: The Scriptures told him "that God created of one blood all races of men to dwell on the face of the earth." That faith in his own fundamental worth and that of black people would lead Mays to become one of the great African American educators of his age.

Born on August 1, 1894, in Epworth, South Carolina, the eighth child of freed slaves turned sharecroppers, Mays was quickly perceived to have a brilliant mind and a natural flair for leadership. But the young man was 17 years old before he was able to enjoy a full year's schooling, and 21 by the time he graduated from high school. Until then, his family needed him too badly in the fields.

Ambitious and determined, Mays applied for admission to a number of prestigious northern colleges, but blacks in those days were routinely rejected on racial grounds. Eventually, he was accepted by Bates College in Lewiston, Maine. He had just $90 in his pocket when he arrived in the fall of 1917, and made his way by waiting table, stoking furnaces, cleaning toilets, and changing sheets as a railroad Pullman porter.

When he graduated in 1920, it was as captain of the debating team and with honors in his studies—yet without the Phi Beta Kappa key for distinguished scholarship that he thought he deserved. Bates's Phi Beta Kappa chapter eventually rectified the oversight 15 years later. But it was, so to speak, academic. For by then Mays had earned his master's and doctorate in religion from the University of Chicago—and was well along on an amazing double-barreled career as both teacher and preacher in the black vanguard.

The two went hand in hand, he believed. His childhood faith in equality under God, combined with a gift for oratory, led him to the pulpit of Atlanta's Shiloh

Atlanta Board of Education president Benjamin Mays (*far right*) leads a January 15, 1976, birthday observance at the tomb of his former pupil Martin Luther King, Jr. Martin Luther King, Sr., bows his head at left. King's daughter Bernice and widow Coretta Scott King are at right.

The Benjamin Elijah Mays Award

This award, established in 1982 and first awarded to Dr. Benjamin Elijah Mays of the class of 1920, is conferred upon the Bates alumna or alumnus who has performed distinguished service to the larger community and been deemed a Bates graduate of outstanding accomplishment.

Awarded in 1982 to Dr. Benjamin Elijah Mays for his tireless work toward the betterment of the human condition. As a student, a teacher, a college president, a minister, mentor to Martin Luther King, and as president of the Atlanta School Board, he has instructed us in sensitivity, responsibility, and diligence, and inspired us by his example.

Thomas Hedley Reynolds
President
Bates College

Richard H. Pierce, '57
President
Alumni Association

Among the many honors—including more than 45 honorary degrees—bestowed on Benjamin E. Mays during a long and illustrious career was this 1982 award named after him by his alma mater, Maine's Bates College.

Baptist Church soon after college in 1922. At the same time, he was revolutionizing the curriculum at nearby Morehouse College by introducing young African Americans to higher mathematics—"making history," as he later recalled with pleasure, "by teaching the first course in calculus ever given there."

So it went for the next several decades, Mays leading the way across the twin bridges of religion and learning. In the mid-1920s, he was teaching English at South Carolina State College, his high-school alma mater. In the early 1930s, he was directing a massive study of nearly 800 urban and rural black churches that he turned into a seminal book, *The Negro's Church*. The president of Howard University asked him in 1934: Would he be dean of its School of Religion? And for the next six years he helped that institution to a higher level of excellence—organizing, defining, clarifying, conciliating, and in all ways preparing blacks for future fulfillment.

In 1940 it was time to return to Morehouse, now as its president. The small liberal arts men's college counted but 426 undergraduates; when he retired almost 30 years later, it had grown to 962 students and carried a weight far beyond mere numbers. With a healthy endowment, modern facilities, and an excellent curriculum and faculty, Morehouse had become known as the black Oxford of the South. And it was a matter of considerable relish to Mays that Morehouse had been welcomed into the august fraternity of Phi Beta Kappa.

Among Mays's graduates were scores upon scores of African American leaders in every field of endeavor, including Nobel laureate Dr. Martin Luther King, Jr., civil rights activist Julian Bond, and renowned theologian Howard Thurman. Mays noted with pride that a larger number of Morehouse alumni had gone on to earn their PhDs "than from any other college of comparable size in the United States, irrespective of race."

Nothing aggravated him more than the notion, held by some integrationists, that black colleges basically were "interim institutions that would go out of existence when white colleges became liberal enough to accept Negroes without discriminating against them." Such a thing would itself amount to the worst kind of discrimination. "National, racial, and ethnic identity is inherent to life," he held passionately. "White colleges are designed primarily to meet the needs of white America. The black colleges have a double role," a responsibility only they were likely to redeem. Where else would a young African American learn about Paul Dunbar and Langston Hughes as well as Shakespeare and Tennyson, about John Hope Franklin and Charles Wesley as well as Arthur Schlesinger and Arnold Toynbee, about the problems of black small businessmen as well as the complex economics of capitalism?

Benjamin E. Mays was still pursuing his philosophy when he died in 1984 at the age of 89. By then, he had just retired from a dozen years at another job: as the first black president of the Atlanta Board of Education.

Phi Beta Sigma

Alpha Kappa Alpha

Zeta Phi Beta

Kappa Alpha Psi

BONDS TO LAST A LIFETIME

It was the autumn of 1905 in the rural college town of Ithaca, New York. Isolated in the midst of Cornell University's largely white student body, nine black undergraduates decided to form a society for fellowship and mutual support. That year, their small organization served as a convivial study group, with a recorded tendency to "general good times, which lasted until the small morning hours." But for some of those present, it was not enough. The next fall, several of the remaining members called for a deeper commitment.

On October 23, 1906, the informal circle of friends adopted the name Alpha Phi Alpha. A week later they gathered in a rented Masonic hall to toast one another with Alpha Phi Alpha punch, enjoy a "Brotherhood Smoke," and enroll several nervous initiates who "were led trembling into our midst," as one of those present later recalled. It was not until early December, however, that the men decided to call their organization a fraternity.

Soon a second chapter of Alpha Phi Alpha sprang up at Howard University in Washington, D.C. In the next several years, five other African American Greek-letter organizations were founded at Howard: The Alpha Kappa Alpha Sorority came into being in 1908, followed by the Omega Psi Phi Fraternity in 1911, the Delta Sigma Theta Sorority in 1913, the Phi Beta Sigma Fraternity in 1914, and the Zeta Phi Beta Sorority in 1920. Meanwhile, in 1911, black students at Indiana University had formed the Kappa Alpha Psi Fraternity. Sigma Gamma Rho Sorority, established in 1922 at Indi-

ana's Butler University, is the youngest of the eight major Greek-letter organizations, which are represented by their seals at left and on page 195.

From the beginning, these eight groups—now united in the National Pan-Hellenic Council—have mixed fraternal bonding with community activism. In 1922, for example, Kappa Alpha Psi Fraternity began the Guide Right program, aimed at mentoring young black men in career development and other issues. Members of the Delta Sigma Theta Sorority worked against Jim Crow laws and volunteered in soup kitchens and hospitals in the 1920s and 1930s, and Alpha Kappa Alpha founded a mobile health clinic in Mississippi in 1935 and a civil rights lobby in 1938. The 1930s also saw Alpha Phi Alpha launch a voting drive.

Today the national sororities

An Alpha Kappa Alpha member leads a group exercise session at an AKA arts camp held in Chattanooga, Tennessee, in August 1991. Like other black Greek-letter organizations, Alpha Kappa Alpha stresses community service; AKA's other projects include a jobs center in Cleveland and support for village development in Africa.

At left, Phi Beta Sigma members join hands in a gesture of brotherhood as they sing the fraternity hymn at the group's 1990 Blue and White Ball in Syracuse, New York.

and fraternities operate senior-citizen housing, sponsor development projects in Africa, tutor inner-city youth, and support programs aimed at the troubling problems of unemployment, teen pregnancy, drug abuse, and the spread of AIDS and other diseases. They also raise considerable sums for such organizations as the NAACP and the Urban League. Former NAACP executive director Benjamin Hooks, himself an Omega, once commented that "the active financial, moral, and physical support of black fraternal organizations" had been vital to voting-rights drives, the push for a Martin Luther King, Jr., national holiday, and to fund-raising for the NAACP, the United Negro College Fund, and other national black groups.

A Kappa Alpha Psi alumni member tutors northern Virginia schoolchildren in 1990 as part of his chapter's Mentor Program.

Since their inception, the black fraternities and sororities have formed networks of mutual aid and information as well. Members offer one another practical career and job-hunting advice and assistance in every aspect of professional life. Congressman John Lewis of Georgia, for example, has been aided in his congressional campaigns by many of his fellow Sigma members—Republicans and Democrats alike.

Over time, the popularity of the black Greek-letter organizations has waxed and waned, reaching a low in the 1960s. But the organizations' renewed commitment to social activism in the 1980s helped bring them to new heights. By the early 1990s, about 200,000 black undergraduates—some 20 percent of all black college students—belonged to one of the eight Greek-letter organizations. Another 400,000 or so men and women actively par-

ΔΣΘ

Delta Sigma Theta

ΩΨΦ

Omega Psi Phi

ΣΓΡ

Sigma Gamma Rho

ΑΦΑ

Alpha Phi Alpha

ticipated in the alumni chapters, which can pledge adult members long after graduation.

Fraternities and sororities are also a key source of black leadership in all aspects of society. The list of prominent Delta Sigma Theta members, for example, ranges from opera star Leontyne Price, poet Nikki Giovanni, and singer Roberta Flack to former congresswomen Barbara Jordan and Shirley Chisholm. Each of the other fraternities and sororities includes many equally well known black achievers. In fact, some three-quarters of the black Americans noted in *Who's Who* list an affiliation with a Greek-letter organization.

The ties that bind each group of men and women in lifelong fellowship vary from organization to organization, but most feature se-

"Go to High School, Go to College," a slogan Alpha Phi Alpha originated in 1929, decorates a float carrying Alpha members in the 1992 Circle City Classic Parade in Indianapolis, Indiana.

cret initiation ceremonies, including a secret rite known as crossing the sands; colors; songs; and special performing acts called step dances. Like many other aspects of African American culture, "stepping" has some distinctly African elements, from the call-and-response audience participation to the body percussion of hands and feet. Stepping may have begun as fraternity high jinks, says author Maurice Henderson, "but it is subconsciously rooted in the African tradition of celebrating culture and heritage."

195

"LET US THINK BIG"

"The schoolteacher today has to be mother, father, counselor, everything. The majority of children have nobody to sit down with them and teach them the little things that are right from the things that are wrong. Sometimes I have to stop the class, close the book and say, 'Let's talk.' Because their parents just don't have the time." That was Ruby Middleton Forsythe speaking a few years ago, and while what she said may not be universally true, she certainly has a point. In this hurly-burly, got-to-keep-up world of working mothers and two-job fathers, a child's schoolteachers increasingly are called upon to lay the foundations for their charges to build upon. Fortunate indeed are the African American youngsters who get to know dedicated educators like Ruby Forsythe and her colleagues portrayed below:

Ruby Middleton Forsythe

She was 22, the bride of an Episcopal minister, when she started teaching with her husband on Pawleys Island, South Carolina. It was 1927, and before she died in 1992 at the grand old age of 87, "Miss Ruby," as everyone called her, had devoted 65 years to the fresh young minds in her care.

Technically, the Holy Cross Faith Memorial School was private, an arm of the Episcopal church. But it drew no lines in educating the island's African American children. The church gave a little money, the parents paid what they could, friends made donations, and the Forsythes made up the rest. In the little schoolhouse, Miss Ruby taught preschool through grade four; her husband, William, took the older children up to grade eight. When he died in 1974, she carried on with the younger ones, living upstairs in the two-story building and teaching 50 or so children in the big room below.

Miss Ruby was a fervent believer in basic virtues: love, honesty, discipline,

along with the three Rs. She never wanted to hear, "I can't," and instead urged, "Let us think big, even though we may miss our aim." No one would dream of disobeying her, and she saw her pupils become doctors, lawyers, ministers, engineers, and small-business owners. "I even had a girl graduate from the Air Force Academy," she once said proudly. That may have been why she never retired. She thought about it at times but always concluded, "I've got a lot of work to do."

Enjoying her golden years, Ruby Forsythe takes a break during school recess on Pawleys Island, South Carolina.

Corla Wilson-Hawkins

On winter mornings, Corla Wilson-Hawkins arrives early at the inner-city Chicago school where she teaches sixth grade and fixes hot cereal for her 30 students. If a child lacks warm clothing, she provides it. Knowing all about pinchpenny budgets, she supplies extra books and learning aids. In a year, she may spend half her salary on her pupils.

But "Mama Hawk" is a lot more than kindhearted. At 44, she is a 20-year veteran of the school system, with a PhD in education, an armful of prizes—including the

coveted Essence Award—and a fierce determination not to waste young African American minds.

Her great innovation is called Recovering the Gifted Child. Many underprivileged inner-city youngsters show great potential at the start but then develop learning problems and drop out. In Mama Hawk's classroom, the desks are pushed together into "departments"—doing geometric "math art" or writing about heroes. Right away, lost kids feel as if they are a part of something; the spark of motivation is struck.

Some children have never seen Lake Michigan; the Traveling Geography Program corrects that. The Buddy Program pairs 12-year-olds with preschoolers: Responsibility dawns. Job-For-A-Day takes pupils into offices to sample real-life working environments.

The youngsters start talking about their futures. "Don't let your address be your destination," Mama Hawk tells them. On the achievement tests now, her fledglings score highest in her school district.

George McKenna III

At a 1983 White House conference on school violence, some people were advocating a hard line: Expel the miscreants, end the chaos. Then, a black principal spoke out. "A law enforcement agenda, kicking kids out, is not an education agenda," said Los Angeles's George McKenna. "I came here to support kids and schools."

When he took over L.A.'s Washington High in 1979, it was a combat zone. The largely black school was the turf of two gangs: the Crips and the Bloods. Classes were held behind locked doors; truancy averaged 25 percent.

"We have to rescue these kids," said McKenna. "Otherwise they become predators and prey." He changed the name to George Washington Preparatory High to signal a college-oriented thrust for his 2,400 students. Then, he announced that "the school, not the gang, would be family."

Buttons proclaimed "We Are Family," and people started helping people. Student volunteers—700 of them—tutored delinquent classmates, offered advice on jobs, made wake-up calls to truants, saying, "We love you."

McKenna recruited parents to volunteer as campus monitors. Teachers were expected to tutor on weekends and to telephone the parents of every student who missed a class. Moreover, teachers were expected to help students express themselves well and present a neat appearance.

McKenna's campaign inspired a 1986 TV documentary called "The George McKenna Story." His efforts cut Washington Prep's dropout rate to 14 percent and resulted in perhaps 45 percent entering college. Even those who might not graduate would still be a world away from the gangs.

A leadership group at L.A.'s once-embattled Washington High stands with George McKenna, their much-admired principal.

Edouard E. Plummer

In 1964, New York City math teacher Edouard Plummer had a brainstorm: to establish a scholarship program for disadvantaged blacks at some of the country's top prep schools. "After seeing so many bright children go down the drain, with no one doing anything special for them," said Plummer, "here was an opportunity to help the bright students in the inner-city community of Harlem."

Plummer contacted Groton, Hotchkiss, Choate, Andover, Exeter, Rosemary Hall; they were excited by the prospects. He then recruited a number of kindred teachers at his Wadleigh Intermediate School—grades six through eight—and launched the Wadleigh Scholarship Program. Prom-

ising youngsters were invited to stay after school for rigorous tutoring; they had to meet tough educational standards and prepare for a new social environment. Plummer taught them letter writing, interview techniques, etiquette, and good grooming.

By 1993, Wadleigh Scholarships had placed 306 inner-city pupils in no fewer than 82 preparatory schools—and then seen 210 of them go on to graduate from such colleges as Harvard, Yale, Dartmouth, Columbia, Brown, MIT, and Sarah Lawrence. What a beautiful brainstorm.

Princess Whitfield

Princess Whitfield is the principal of Lemon G. Hine Junior High in Washington, D.C. When she arrived a decade ago, the largely African American school on Capitol Hill was known as "terrible Hine" for the bad attitude of students, parents, and teachers alike, and for its run-down facilities.

Whitfield set out in dynamic fashion to remedy all that. "It was hard to gain the trust of the kids," she says. But she got it, and went on from there to motivate everyone from the government to her teaching staff.

She has recruited no less important an agency than the U.S. Department of Transportation to help out at the school; nearly 400 DOT employees work with Hine pupils tutoring, raising funds, and sponsoring field trips. Community businesspeople chip in their help as well, tutoring youngsters and inspiring them to academic excellence. Washington Redskins football players act as substitute older brothers for many of the teenage boys in need of someone to look up to. And then, for teachers, Whitfield has revamped the curriculum to bring in more creative techniques in English, science, and math.

Terrible Hine is now "the thrill on Capitol Hill." And in 1992, Whitfield was selected over 450 nominees to receive the *Reader's Digest* American Hero in Education Award. Princess Whitfield spent the $5,000 prize on her school.

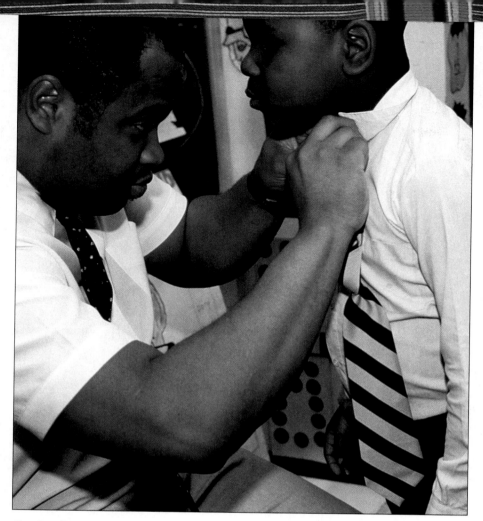

Marva Collins

Quite a few people regard Marva Collins as a "miracle worker" and "superteacher," even a "national treasure." She might smile at all the encomiums and honors flowing her way, but she does not deny her success.

Collins left the Chicago school system in 1975 to found her own school because she believed that children live up to what is asked of them—and that most educators ask far too little.

Some three-year-olds at Collins's Westside Preparatory School can read. The 11-year-olds tackle Tolstoy and Shakespeare. At all levels, her 200 students—with a waiting list of 800—do exceptionally well on scholastic achievement tests. When asked how she gets pupils to extend themselves so, she says it never occurs to her that they cannot.

Collins starts out with a simple promise to every child: "I will not let you fail." From then on, it is a matter of total involvement, creating an atmosphere of discipline and love, instilling confidence, pride, and self-esteem, teaching not just the subjects at hand but morals, values, the old-fashioned work ethic. "This is what works for America, what has always worked for America," she insists.

Carter Bayton

It may not be fashionable to put boys and girls in separate classes, especially in first grade. But at Baltimore's Robert W. Coleman Elementary there was nothing else to do. These 17 boys had been so disruptive during their kindergarten year that they were about to be dismissed as "throwaway kids"—at six years of age.

Enter unflappable, greathearted Carter Bayton. He sat his charges in a semicircle and said, "Boys, I know you didn't learn anything last year. But you can learn, and I promise you will learn."

Bayton emphasized loving discipline, praise, and a sense of belonging. He built self-esteem by never scolding a child for being slow, and the boys learned to help, not hoot at, others. When spirits flagged, Bayton led them in the cheer: "One, two, three—HARD WORK." And he was there with hugs whenever needed. "I was lucky," says Bayton. "I had a strong and loving father. That's what I had to be for these boys."

At the end of the school year, Bayton set up a math contest with the class his boys had been unfit to join. His lads whomped their rivals by a score of 10 to 4.

Upset by a lesson, a youngster gets comfort and advice from Marva Collins during a demonstration in Ponca City, Oklahoma.

A HAVEN FOR LEARNERS

The geometric architecture of the Marcus Garvey School stands like a bright green beacon amid the decay of south-central Los Angeles. Inside the building, the smell of lunch wafts through the halls, and in a second-floor classroom, two five-year-olds are at the blackboard, intent on multiple-column addition.

Across the playground in a low building, three-year-olds are doing multiplication tables and counting to 10 in English, Swahili, and Spanish. A class of four- and five-year-olds runs through the planets in the solar system, confidently names their congresswoman, then briefly explains how a bill becomes law.

Welcome to the Marcus Garvey Elementary and Junior High School, where small miracles occur every day.

Garvey's founder, Dr. Aynim Palmer, is a teacher and administrator who began the school in 1975 because he felt that African American children were lost in the public school system. In many ways, he says, Garvey is modeled after the school he grew up in, a one-room, strictly-for-blacks schoolhouse in Fort Worth, Texas. "I was very fortunate to have gone to one of the old-type segregated schools," grins Palmer. "My teachers saw me as an extension of themselves, and they probably would have committed mass suicide had I graduated from school not being able to read and write."

The current norm, he fears, is to pass students on to the next grade whether or not they can make it. Naturally, such youngsters feel frustrated and alienated. "Not good enough," thought Palmer. So when he left California State—a casualty of the disbanding of the African studies program—he realized it was time to start educating young black minds his way: with TLC and a focus on their heritage.

Taking $20,000 of his savings, Palmer bought a building, recruited a few like-minded teachers, and named his school after Marcus Garvey, the great nationalist. The school began with five children and counted 70 by the end of the first year. A few fund-raisers later, Palmer built the present building, which today holds 450 youngsters from kindergarten through ninth grade. The waiting list is a long one, and plans are under way for a high school.

"Our kids hear terrible things about themselves," Palmer muses. "They hear they are incapable of learning—or of learning certain things. Here, we show them that there is no work they cannot do. And the Afrocentricity of this school makes them much more receptive to learning."

Garvey students start each day reciting affirmations of themselves and their ancestry. In small classes of no more than 30 students, they learn that many of the subjects they seek to master have African roots. "History has always been the European's story. We teach our story here," Palmer says. "Even our second

Instructor Brenda Spencer joins in as a high-flying youngster plays jump rope after lunch at Los Angeles's Marcus Garvey School.

graders know there's no such thing as Greek philosophy—the Greeks got their philosophical education from exposure to Egyptians, who are Africans. And we let them know that Africans had a mathematical heritage—their ancestors created math."

Garvey students thrive on a regimen that has them doing elementary algebra by the end of the third grade; fifth graders work up to calculus and trigonometry. Most pupils read several grade levels above average.

Although some Garvey students come from affluent families, the norm is distinctly modest. Parents willingly make the sacrifice because they agree that their children have been overlooked—or purposely ignored—by Los Angeles's overburdened, chaotic public school system.

The school has its critics, of course. Some worry that its Afrocentric approach will make transition to the "real world" a problem later on. A few years ago, however, a group of Garvey third graders took standardized tests in a contest with sixth graders from a prestigious magnet school for gifted children. The Garvey kids came out on top.

Palmer's eyes twinkle with delight. "I rest my case," he says.

People, places, and moments in black history cover the wall of a classroom where students work on essays with instructor Andre Whitmore (top). A student reads a biographical paper to his class; on the blackboard is an outline for the assignment.

WINNING POLITICAL EQUALITY

Chicagoan Carol Moseley-Braun, shown at the 1992 Democratic national convention, furthered African American political progress later that year by becoming the first black woman United States senator.

he place was the tiny Delta town of Mayersville, Mississippi; the time, 1964. "I drove out of my house," recalls Unita Blackwell, "and was arrested every day straight for thirty days." Her crime: trying to register to vote. In the oppressive Jim Crow society Blackwell had known since the day she was born in 1933, she had already beaten the odds once by wresting an eighth-grade education out of a woefully inadequate school system. Now, at 31, she was trying to beat the odds again.

That first day when Blackwell and three companions approached the Issaquena County Courthouse in Mayersville, they had to break out of a circle of pickup trucks driven round and round by armed white men who taunted and threatened them. When they finally got to the voting registrar's office, the registrar required them to interpret a complex portion of the state constitution—one tactic of the many used to deny blacks the vote in the nine decades since the collapse of post-Civil War Reconstruction. To no one's surprise, the registrar found their answers unsatisfactory.

All over Mississippi and other parts of the South that 1964 "Freedom Summer" of the civil rights movement, Ku Klux Klansmen, members of White Citizens' Councils, and random mobs were going to extremes to deny blacks the right to vote. But that did not stop Unita Blackwell. Voting was the path to political power, and Blackwell—and her white enemies—knew that if the black people who made up most of Mayersville's population were ever going to rise up out of the mire of poverty and injustice that had held them down for so long, it would be by means of political power.

Blackwell also knew—like other voter registration activists, black and white— that she would have to lay her life on the line to support her conviction. "I never slept through the night," she said, "because that's when the Klan came to us. We'd take turns watching, walking. . . . You couldn't trust nobody, because the police were the Klans. The police were burning the cross in my yard."

With only a relative handful of Mississippi's eligible blacks registered, it was clear that yet another all-white Mississippi delegation would go off to the 1964 Democratic national convention. But this time Blackwell, Fannie Lou Hamer, and other civil rights campaigners refused to accept the inevitable. They put together an alternate delegation of 64 blacks and four whites, calling it the Mississippi Freedom Democratic party (MFDP). Although the MFDP was denied seating at the convention in Atlantic City and the all-white delegation was left intact, the newcomers made such an impressive stand for electoral fairness that both major parties decided never again to seat a racially discriminatory delegation.

Twelve years after that momentous summer, Unita Blackwell reaped the sweetest fruit of her struggle. She became mayor of Mayersville, the first black woman mayor in Mississippi's history. And her victory was more than a personal one: Through her efforts the little town had been officially incorporated, bringing running water and a sewer service to the residents. And, in what was surely a fitting irony, the voting registrar who had once turned Blackwell away was now one of her employees.

Blackwell went on to other accomplishments and rewards. In 1984 she addressed the Democratic national convention, savoring the turnabout from the convention's refusal to seat her delegation 20 years earlier. In 1990 she was elected president of the National Conference of Black Mayors. And in 1992 she was named a MacArthur Foundation Fellow, receiving a grant of $350,000 to use as she pleased.

In her long, difficult ascent to triumph, Unita Blackwell has personified the struggle that black people have undergone throughout most of American history to combat racial discrimination in the political arena. Yet in winning her right to vote—indeed, in taking public office—she did no more than regain rights that some black Americans had enjoyed more than 300 years earlier.

In the 17th century, the legal position of blacks in the American colonies was unsettled. Many were slaves, but a small number were free, and although slavery began increasingly to be the norm for newly arriving blacks after about 1640, during most of the rest of that century, free black men—even in the foremost slaveholding colony, Virginia—were able to buy property, to vote, and to hold minor public office. A former indentured servant named Mathias De Sousa, for example, was elected to office during this period. De Sousa was one of three blacks in a party of about 200 Roman Catholic settlers sent to the New World by Lord Baltimore in 1634 to find refuge from religious persecution. After gaining his freedom, De Sousa set up a prosperous business trading with the local Indian tribes. In 1641 he was chosen by an overwhelmingly white electorate to represent them in the Maryland colonial general assembly—becoming almost certainly the first black elected official in American history.

But De Sousa's experience proved depressingly unreliable as an indicator of things to come. For as black slavery spread and became commonplace, white colonists increasingly came to view race as the main differentiator between free men and slaves, between full-fledged citizens and those of lesser standing. With each passing year, free blacks found themselves more and more in a no man's land of shrinking rights and multiplying liabilities.

Starting in the 1690s, Virginia adopted a number of restrictive laws against free blacks. First, intermarriage with whites was prohibited. Then it became more difficult for a slaveowner to grant slaves their freedom. Finally, in 1723 Virginia passed an act—soon taken up in the other southern colonies—that put an end to the political life of free black men in the South by wresting from them their right to vote. Over the next century, as many of the northern colonies, and, later, states, followed suit, black Americans entered into a long struggle to regain the political rights denied them.

Left for the time being without a place in normal political life, black people endeavored to influence the political process by using the only means left—the right of

Seated here with neighborhood children, Mayor Unita Blackwell of Mayersville, Mississippi, has followed a time-honored tradition of African American political life—getting involved with foreign affairs. She has visited China many times and speaks authoritatively on U.S.-Chinese relations.

petition. They petitioned for relief from wrongful enslavement, discriminatory poll taxes, and other injustices. And as free blacks were increasingly oppressed by the laws of the 18th and early 19th centuries, their petitions began to ask for permission to return to Africa.

Hardly any issue concerning free African Americans in the 19th century was as tangled as that of whether they should depart the United States. There were two entirely divergent—indeed, antagonistic—movements aimed at the end result of re-settling free African Americans in their ancestral homeland or elsewhere. One, the colonization movement, was an initiative of white people; its mirror image, the emigration movement, was fostered and controlled by African Americans.

The American Colonization Society (ACS) was founded in 1816 to promote the migration of free black people to Africa. Territory for colonization was acquired on the west coast of Africa and named Liberia, meaning "land of liberty." The ACS's basic premise, though couched in benevolent terms, was that black people were inferior to whites, were not competent to make their way in a white world, and were unwelcome in white society. From the start, the society received a hostile reception from most free blacks, who for good reason saw the scheme as nothing more than a way to rid the United States of its free black population.

Nevertheless, small numbers of free blacks fell in with colonization. To them, life among white people was so miserable and dangerous that any alternative would have been better. One who thought so was a Virginia Baptist minister named Lott Cary. When friends asked why he would give up his relatively comfortable situation to face an unknowable future in Africa, he gave a simple answer: "I wish to go to a country where I shall be estimated by my merits, not by my complexion." The black-led emigration movement, for its part, was motivated by many of the same reasons cited by Lott Cary and the other black customers of the ACS. Some black leaders had written off America and wanted to take their destiny into their own hands by organizing parties of emigrants to Africa—as well as to Haiti, Central America, and Canada.

Not surprisingly, many blacks objected to both colonization and emigration. In January 1817, three thousand African American residents of Philadelphia gathered at the Bethel African Methodist Episcopal (AME) Church to denounce the ACS. Their chief argument was as simple as Lott Cary's. Regardless of how Africans came to be in this land, said James Forten, the owner of a Philadelphia shipyard, "we their descend-ants feel ourselves entitled to participate in the blessings of her luxuriant soil, which their blood and sweat manured." The group also believed that by leaving, free blacks would be abandoning their captive brothers and sisters to slavery forever. In any case, free blacks were far from eager to venture to an unknown land in Africa.

The debate over blacks leaving the country, under whatever auspices, became the focal point of a new phenomenon that was to be the mainstay of African American political life right through the Civil War—the National Negro Convention movement.

The 1817 Philadelphia meeting had done more than condemn colonization. It also in-troduced free blacks to the experience of uniting for concerted action on vital issues. There was no immediate move to expand the Philadelphia undertaking to a national

event, however, even though free African Americans were experiencing both increasing threats to their physical safety and legal attacks on their few remaining civil rights and liberties. What got the black convention movement going was another major crisis. This time the trouble erupted in Cincinnati, in 1829.

Located just across the Ohio River from the slave state of Kentucky, Cincinnati was a natural gateway to freedom for escaped slaves, and many settled there. Ohio had long had a racist law on the books that—though never enforced—required all black residents to register with authorities and post a bond in the prohibitive amount of $500. By 1829, Cincinnati's white population had grown restive over the number of African Americans in the city, and a local chapter of the ACS was promoting black "removal." In July, city officials suddenly proclaimed that all blacks had to register and put up the money within 30 days.

The city's shocked and frightened black population held a mass meeting, at which the majority decided that their only recourse was to emigrate to Canada. They received a 30-day extension of the deadline to prepare for the move, but while they were packing up, a white mob went on a three-day orgy of rioting in the black quarter. In the end, about a thousand black Cincinnatians emigrated to a site near London, Ontario.

Free African Americans everywhere were outraged by the events in Cincinnati. One, a 29-year-old Baltimore resident named Hezekiah Grice, hit upon the bold idea of calling a national convention of free black men to consider whether African Americans should embrace mass emigration or remain in the land of their birth to fight for their constitutional rights. He gained the support of Philadelphia's AME bishop Richard Allen, and a call went out for delegates to attend a convention in that city on September 20, 1830.

About 40 men showed up, representing eight states. They spent two days discussing the key issue. At adjournment they resolved in support of emigration to Canada, condemned the still-active American Colonization Society, and, most significantly, set a date for the next convention—June of the following year. Thus was born the National Negro Convention movement, by which black Americans, in effect making bricks without straw, created a political life for themselves despite all the efforts of whites to deny it to them.

In the movement's first phase, the decade of the 1830s, conventions were held annually for five consecutive years. Self-selected natural leaders came forward to serve as delegates—men such as James Forten, Bishop Allen, and wealthy landowner and lumber merchant William Whipper—for the first time giving free blacks a leadership cadre of national stature. Forten and Whipper covered the expenses of the first round of conventions out of their own pockets.

This report on the first National Negro Convention was issued by an organization founded at the convention, the American Society of Free Persons of Colour. The cover reveals that the society, responding to the pressing needs of the country's embattled black population, supported both emigration to Canada and the continued struggle for freedom and equality in the United States.

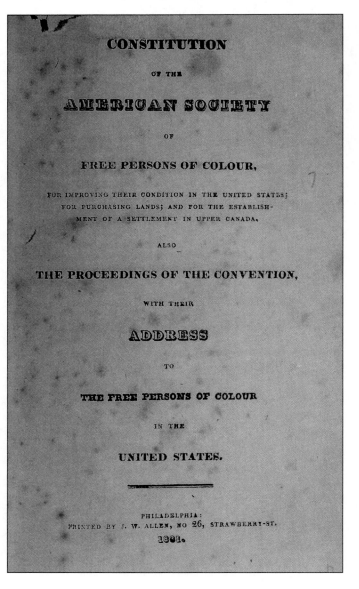

CONSTITUTION

OF THE

AMERICAN SOCIETY

OF

FREE PERSONS OF COLOUR,

FOR IMPROVING THEIR CONDITION IN THE UNITED STATES;
FOR PURCHASING LANDS; AND FOR THE ESTABLISH-
MENT OF A SETTLEMENT IN UPPER CANADA.

ALSO

THE PROCEEDINGS OF THE CONVENTION,

WITH THEIR

ADDRESS

TO

THE FREE PERSONS OF COLOUR

IN THE

UNITED STATES.

PHILADELPHIA:
PRINTED BY J. W. ALLEN, NO 26, STRAWBERRY-ST.
1831.

At most of the conventions of that decade, the delegates agreed with the original 1830 conferees in condemning the American Colonization Society. However, they reversed the other key decision of the earlier group by opposing emigration as well, holding that it constituted a surrender to racists of the rights and privileges due black Americans in their native land. A new generation of black leaders emerged at the conventions of the 1840s, men impatient with the scant results of earlier efforts at "moral suasion" and less committed to working with white sympathizers than earlier delegates had been. Frederick Douglass, Henry Highland Garnet, and other strong new voices led a call for all-black conventions. They were not, however, seeking a divorce from white society. Their somewhat wishful argument was that by taking affairs into their own hands they would demonstrate to white America that they were well qualified for full citizenship and the right to vote.

A fundamental flaw in this argument was that free blacks, even had they all been able to vote, were too few to exert power in the national political arena. Thus, while the national conventions crystallized the issues facing blacks, turned out two generations of African American leaders, and regularly inventoried conditions in black America, the resolutions they produced seldom led to concrete effects in the world at large. More fruitful were associated state and local conventions, where delegates could directly target legislatures or local governments on vital local issues.

An increasingly militant attitude was a feature of almost all conventions after 1840. But rising militancy could not settle the continuing debate between those who favored emigration and those who preferred to struggle for full citizenship. In the face of worsening antiblack political and legal developments, such as the passage of the Fugitive Slave Act in 1850, Frederick Douglass continued to urge increased efforts to gain equal rights, while Martin Delany, a rising young African American of broad accomplishment, advocated that black people stop waiting for white America to repent of its racism and find freedom in a land of their own.

At the 1853 meeting held in Rochester, New York, called the Colored National Convention, even Douglass's vision of a society of free and equal beings took on a different cast. Instead of aiming for a united society of Americans, the delegates proposed a separate black society—led by blacks, based on black institutions, educated in black schools, and informed by black newspapers—existing alongside white society and enjoying the same rights and privileges. Thus was born an idea that would be resurrected and argued over again and again as future generations of African Americans grappled with the seemingly insoluble problem of what to do about America's white people.

No matter how novel or compelling the ideas proposed, however, black communities generally had too few resources and too few liberties to follow through effectively on convention initiatives. Time and again, attempts to organize action councils, establish black schools and other institutions, and support the development of new black newspapers proved abortive.

The last gathering, the National Convention of Colored Men, was held in Syracuse, New York, in 1864, to deal with new issues such as emancipation. The delegates, perhaps overwhelmed by the historic changes they were witnessing, issued a grand-

sounding but passive manifesto. "We believe," read the convention's communiqué, "that the generosity and sense of honor inherent in the great heart of this nation will ultimately concede us our just claims, accord us our rights, and grant us our full measure of citizenship under the broad shield of the Constitution." At first, the confidence expressed by the 1864 delegates was rewarded, at least legally. In the five years immediately after the war, the nation ratified the Thirteenth, Fourteenth, and Fifteenth Amendments to the Constitution, which abolished slavery, extended citizenship to African Americans, and gave them the right to vote. Events were to show, however, that even nine years of Reconstruction could not ensure the permanent establishment of a new era of equality and security for African Americans.

During Reconstruction, the presence of a military government in the South made it possible for freeborn black men and former slaves to participate in political life for the first time. Not only could they vote, but they could also run for office, win elections, and go off to the county seat, state capital, or even to Washington, D.C., to serve their constituencies. And African Americans began to receive nonelective government jobs as well. One of the most notable appointments was that of Ebenezer Don Carlos Bassett to be the nation's first black diplomat; in 1869, he was named minister resident and consul general to Haiti.

In Reconstruction's heyday, 14 African Americans were sent to the House of Representatives from the South. And two more, Hiram R. Revels and Blanche K. Bruce, went to the U.S. Senate—both from Mississippi. Revels, in a supreme irony, became the nation's first African American senator when he was chosen in 1870 to complete the final year of the unexpired term of Jefferson Davis, the former president of the Confederacy. Bruce, the first African American elected to the Senate for a full six-year term, was born a slave in 1841. He escaped during the war and returned to the South in the Reconstruction period, where he caught the eye of white Republican politicians while making a speech in Mississippi in 1869. Soon thereafter, he was appointed voting registrar in Tallahatchie County. Bruce rose rapidly, and in 1875 he defeated two white candidates for election to the Senate. His tenure, however, was undistinguished—no surprise, given that the Reconstruction government that had sent him to Washington collapsed and was replaced by a white supremacist regime two years into his term, leaving him virtually severed from his constituency.

One more African American, P. B. S. Pinchback of Louisiana, was elected to the Senate but was denied his seat. By a vote of 32 to 29, the Senate refused to admit him, possibly because of his long history of outspokenness on civil rights and equal treatment for blacks. To this injustice, Pinchback remarked, "If I cannot enter the Senate except with bated breath and on bended knees, I prefer not to enter at all."

Pinchback's rejection foreshadowed bigger troubles. The nation was growing weary of the effort and cost of propping up Reconstruction governments with military force against the violent resistance of the southern white population. As federal troops were withdrawn from one state after another in the early 1870s, the old white aristocracy, using a combination of terrorism and chicanery, regained control of the political machinery. Finally, in 1876, when Republican presidential candidate Ruther-

ford B. Hayes made a deal with southern Democrats to pull out the last occupation troops in exchange for enough southern electoral votes to put him in the White House, Reconstruction was dead. White supremacy reigned once again throughout the South. Thus was the way paved for the creation of a racial caste system that would last for nearly a century. The hopes and aspirations of former slaves faded quickly in the face of a systematic disenfranchisement that virtually eliminated blacks from southern public life.

But even as conditions went from bad to worse in the late 19th century, most blacks could not imagine any political connection except to the party of Lincoln. In spite of Hayes's sellout, the Republican party, according to Frederick Douglass, was the ship, and all else was the sea. Nevertheless, some blacks were so aggrieved by the Republican betrayal that they actually switched to the Democrats. Unfortunately, this attempt to find a new political home was doomed, for the Democratic party was dominated in Congress by a large contingent of racist white Dixie senators and representatives. By the early 1890s, almost all would-be black Democrats were back in the Republican fold.

As it happened, the returnees found little comfort there either, for their political agenda was at cross purposes with that of the handful of southern white Republicans who controlled the local party machinery. Desperate to throw off the stigma of being the "Yankee party" or the "Nigger party," these Republicans spurned the cause of civil rights for blacks and formed a faction called the Lily Whites. Forced into an opposing faction, African Americans were called Black and Tan Republicans.

At this low point in African American life, it seemed to many that the only way for blacks to improve their situation was to pull themselves up by their own bootstraps. One who tried was journalist T. Thomas Fortune, who made the first attempt to establish a permanent nationwide political organization for blacks. Fortune had left his native Florida in 1879 at age 23 to test his mettle in New York City. Though he had little formal education, he was a voracious reader, and, having developed a distinctive writing style, he managed to find work at the *New York Globe*. He then started his own newspaper, the *New York Freeman*, in 1884. In 1887, Fortune issued a call for the creation of a National Afro-American League, with the express purpose of combating disenfranchisement, lynching, and other injustices. The league formally came into being at a meeting in Chicago in 1890, but when it was unable to raise funds through local chapters, it withered away. African American women, meanwhile, organized the National Association of Colored Women in 1896. This politically active self-help group threw the limelight on a cadre of talented black women, such as educator and social activist Mary Church Terrell, journalist Ida B. Wells, and others who would have a positive impact on the progress of black America.

Taking their own divergent path in the 1880s was a small circle of black leaders whose answer for the woes of the time was a return to the old idea of emigration. Martin Delany, by then in his seventies but still engaged in the struggle, was joined by AME bishop Henry McNeal Turner in forswearing any future for blacks in America. Delany was one of the most gifted men in African American history. As journalist, physician, author, abolitionist, agent of the Underground Railroad, justice of the

T. Thomas Fortune, the leading African American journalist of the late 19th century, was an ardent militant on racial matters. Nevertheless, he became friends with accommodationist Booker T. Washington and was eventually scorned by other black political activists for seeming to give in to Washington's influence.

peace, or army officer, he excelled at everything he attempted. And he took special pride in his African ancestry. "I thank God for making me a man," Frederick Douglass once remarked, "but Delany thanks him for making him a *black* man."

Bishop Turner was as passionate as Delany in his advocacy of a return to Africa, and like Delany, he was a spellbinding rhetorician and a man who did not shy away from speaking out on matters concerning the well-being of black people. Despite the best efforts of Delany and Bishop Turner, however, emigration as a meaningful alternative for African Americans failed once again to gain wide support, defeated by the harsh reality of pulling up stakes in one's native land and moving to an unknown and intimidating place with an uncertain future.

Taking a different tack on the problem of black-white relations was Booker T. Washington, a former slave who in 1881 established Tuskegee Institute, a bellwether of black education in the South and the base upon which he slowly built a reputation as a leader. Washington won nationwide notice with a speech he made in Atlanta in 1895 at a commercial exposition, in which he exhorted black Americans to forget about civil and political rights agitation—to become apolitical—and apply themselves instead to economic betterment through vocational training. With prosperity and stability, he said, would come respect and cooperation from white America and full citizenship. The Atlanta Compromise speech, as it was called, helped to make

Washington the most powerful black spokesman in America, and the one most favored by white leaders. Not all African Americans agreed with Washington's vision, however. Historian and sociologist W. E. B. Du Bois led a countermovement that demanded immediate civil and political equality for blacks and advocated access to liberal or professional education for every African American with the necessary talent.

As Washington and Du Bois carried on their debate, time was running out on the last African American congressional survivor of Reconstruction politics, North Carolina representative George H. White. A unique instance of black-white cooperation in North Carolina had enabled White to win two consecutive terms in the House, starting in 1897. But at the turn of the century, the state's old racist interests finally recaptured political power, and in the increasingly hostile atmosphere White decided not to run again. In January

Four past presidents of the National Association of Colored Women (*left to right*), Mary McLeod Bethune, Mary Church Terrell, Mary Waring, and Elizabeth C. Brooks, gather for a group picture around 1945. Terrell, founder of the organization, campaigned for women's and black causes for more than 50 years, picketing outside segregated Washington, D.C., eating establishments in her eighties.

1901, with his final term drawing to a close, White delivered a poignant but defiant last speech to the House: "This, Mr. Chairman, is perhaps the Negroes' temporary farewell to the American Congress; but let me say, Phoenix-like he will rise up some day and come again. These parting words are in behalf of an outraged, heartbroken, bruised and bleeding, but God-fearing people, faithful, industrious, loyal, rising people—full of potential force."

Congressman White's farewell may have signaled completion of a process of freezing southern blacks out of politics, but black intellectuals like Du Bois continued to wrestle with their people's problems as well as to look beyond the American scene to the issue of African affairs. The world's first Pan-African Conference was held in London in 1900, with Americans such as Du Bois playing important roles. Twenty-eight delegates attended, mostly from the United States and the West Indies. The conferees drew up a petition to Queen Victoria asking that she heed a plea from the world's colored peoples to stop the advance of British imperial hegemony. Of course, most Britons of that era, the queen included, would not have dreamed of restraining the empire's growth.

Du Bois spent considerable energy on the Pan-African cause over the next two decades, but the vexing matter of Booker T. Washington's enormous influence over the lives of African Americans was never far from his mind. In 1905 Du Bois met with William Monroe Trotter, editor of the *Boston Guardian*, Ida B. Wells, and other like-minded black leaders at Niagara Falls to form an activist group to promote alternatives to Washington's accommodationist preachings. The Niagara Movement, as it came to be called, lasted just five years, but its demands for restoration of the vote to southern blacks, an end to racial discrimination in education and public life, and recognition of human rights for all Americans were taken up in 1909 by a new group, the National Association for the Advancement of Colored People (NAACP). Most of the NAACP's founding leadership were prominent whites. Whatever reservations black leaders may have had about its racial makeup, however, the organization came into being none too soon to fight for African Americans' rights during the next major upheaval in black America—the Great Migration.

Buffeted by the everyday indignities of Jim Crow, by lynchings and beatings, and by the economic hopelessness of sharecropping, blacks fled the South in waves from post-Reconstruction times to the Depression of the 1930s. These migrating millions were motivated by more than what they wanted to leave behind; they were also drawn by the promise of jobs and a decent life in the bustling North. On arrival in New York or Chicago or Detroit, however, the migrants quickly learned that the North was no promised land. In addition to being shunted to ghettos with run-down housing and filthy living conditions, they encountered racism almost as bad as anything down South. Even access to the vote did not lead directly to political gains for African Americans. Black voters were just another ethnic minority among a surge of new immigrants from central and eastern Europe.

The problems of migrating black folk, finding themselves at a loss in the fast-moving, inhospitable, alien-seeming cities of the North, led, in 1911, to the founding

of another African American self-help organization, the National Urban League (*page 83*). For all the help they offered, however, the NAACP and the Urban League were not in a position to fill a void many black Americans felt—the absence of a sense of national identity and racial pride. For many, Marcus Garvey's Universal Negro Improvement Association (UNIA), with its espousal of black nationalism, self-help, and a spiritual, if not physical, return to Africa, was emotionally satisfying. Within five years after its creation in Jamaica in 1914, the Garvey movement boasted several hundred thousand members—mostly in the United States. UNIA's adherents were energized by the organization's establishment of black-run businesses, including a newspaper, and by Garvey's fearless demands that Africa be liberated and returned to its natural heirs, the world's black people. The movement lost momentum and slowly petered out, however, after Garvey was jailed in 1922 on what appeared to be a trumped-up mail-fraud charge.

W. E. B. Du Bois, who scorned Garvey and deplored his highly publicized programs and pronouncements, focused instead on trying to gain some say for African Americans in foreign policy affecting Africa and the world's black people. In 1919 he organized another Pan-African meeting, to be held in Paris to coincide with the Paris Peace Conference called at the end of World War I. The three-day Pan-African Congress attracted 57 delegates from 15 countries, including 16 from the United States. The delegates adopted resolutions calling for self-determination for African lands—the same rights the victorious Western powers at the Peace Conference were endorsing for former subject peoples of eastern Europe. As Du Bois had planned, the Pan-African resolutions were submitted to the Peace Conference, but, to no one's surprise, they had virtually no effect except to publicize the case against imperialism and announce to the world that black people had a vested interest in the proceedings of the conference.

While Du Bois focused on the international picture during and after World War I, politically minded African Americans were beginning to make more concrete gains at the local level. In 1915, a Chicago Republican named Oscar DePriest signaled the resurrection of black political life by winning election to the Chicago City Council. Thirteen years later, in 1928, he would crown his career by becoming the first African American elected to Congress in the 20th century and the first ever from the North. DePriest's rise would not have been possible without the growth in black voting power attributable to the migration of blacks from the South. Though DePriest established a mixed record in Congress and was defeated for a fourth term in 1934 by black Democrat Arthur Mitchell, esteem for him never diminished among the masses of black Chicagoans who had been proud simply to have an African American as an important national figure.

The year in which DePriest entered Congress for the first time was also the year black voters in many cities began to rethink their almost automatic support for Republican candidates. A sizable number of black voters in 1928 supported Democrat Alfred E. Smith in his losing run for president. Four years later, with Herbert Hoover in the White House, the disaffection of blacks from the Republican ranks was virtually total. Not only had Hoover embraced the reactionary Lily White Republicans in the

Oscar DePriest, the first African American congressman of the 20th century, points to one of the many racial barriers he encountered when he took office in 1929. One practical interpretation of this sign on the door of the House of Representatives dining room—backed up by a written rule to that effect—was "for whites only."

South, but he had appointed very few African Americans to government jobs and refused to use government to relieve the plight of those made jobless by the Depression. The last straw had been his nomination of a reactionary judge, John Parker, to the Supreme Court.

Not all those who defected went over to the Democrats, however. Given that the Democrats were scarcely less racist than the Republicans in the 1930s, the entire field of civil and political rights agitation for black people was wide open for any group that cared to take it up. The Communist Party of the U.S.A. did not hesitate. As black unemployment rose during the Depression, white Communists and their black comrades tried hard to win over the masses in urban American ghettos. The party staged marches, organized boycotts of businesses that did not employ blacks, and rushed to assist those evicted from their homes. On a national scale, the Communists made history by running a black man, James Ford, as their party's candidate for vice president in 1932, and again in 1936 and 1940. Ford had attended Fisk University, where he was a good student, a track star, and a campus leader. After a hitch in the army, he took a job at the Chicago Post Office. During this period, he joined the Communist party, where he advanced rapidly, traveling extensively to organize black workers in Africa and the Caribbean.

But the party suffered the fatal flaw of being controlled from Moscow. Party recruiters, hostage to Soviet policy directives, could not justify Moscow's abrupt policy shifts, such as Stalin's signing of a nonagression pact with Hitler in August 1939. The obvious cynicism of the American Communists in the light of such actions showed most African Americans that any civil rights agitation by the party was merely a stratagem in a bigger game that held no benefit for black people.

Where the Communists failed to attract a considerable following among black Americans, Democratic president Franklin D. Roosevelt, who entered the White House in 1933, flourished. His New Deal programs to fight the Depression and the presence in his administration of a group of African American government officials who conferred weekly on black affairs—dubbed the black cabinet by the press—won lasting favor for him among African Americans. Most members of this revolving group were not politicians but intellectuals and administrators. Educator, veteran government official, and political activist Mary McLeod Bethune (*pages* 222-223), who directed the Office of Negro Affairs in the National Youth Adminstration, played the largest role in creating the black cabinet and was probably its most visible and influential member. Other notables were Robert Weaver, who later became an actual cabinet secretary in the Johnson administration; and Robert L. Vann, the editor of the *Pittsburgh Courier,* who became special assistant to the attorney general.

Most African Americans taking government posts during the 1930s and 1940s gravitated toward jobs in the domestic sector. But one aspiring young black man set

a course for himself that would give him a major role in conducting U.S. foreign policy. Ralph Bunche was an exceptional student who earned a bachelor's degree from UCLA and a master's and a PhD from Harvard. After a stint on the Howard University faculty, he was recruited in 1944 to work for the U.S. State Department, becoming the first black acting chief of the Division of Dependent Area Affairs. At the close of World War II Bunche was a pivotal member of a team of U.S. diplomats assembled to help establish the United Nations. In 1949, he succeeded in negotiating a cease-fire in the war between the new state of Israel and its Arab neighbors, for which monumental achievement he was awarded the Nobel Peace Prize. Until his death in 1971 at the age of 67, Bunche was under-secretary-general of the United Nations.

Ralph Bunche's work was, in effect, a prelude to a resurgence of black America's longstanding interest in Africa and in U.S. policy toward that continent. One focus of this new interest was, of course, the liberation of Africa from colonial domination. The other was the recalcitrant problem of apartheid in South Africa.

As the decade of the 1960s began, the struggle for independence in colonial Africa dovetailed with the struggle for full citizenship for African Americans, and both achieved remarkable success. When John F. Kennedy brought the Democrats back into the White House in 1961, African Americans were appointed to an unprecedented number of high government offices. During Kennedy's administration, unrest in the black inner cities, combined with demonstrations, sit-ins, and lobbying by such civil rights groups as the NAACP, the Student Nonviolent Coordinating Committee, the Congress on Racial Equality, and the Southern Christian Leadership Conference helped push the nation and Congress toward acceptance of changes that would bring about full political equality for African Americans.

After Kennedy's assassination, the new president, Lyndon B. Johnson, took advantage of a nationwide emotional tidal wave of resolve to carry on the late president's program, pushing through the momentous Civil Rights Act of 1964 and the Voting Rights Act of 1965, which put an end to Jim Crow at the ballot box. An example of the law's dramatic effect could be seen in Alabama, where black voter registration rose over the next several years from 2.3 percent of those eligible to 67 percent.

The resulting electoral gains first came in the North. Liberal Republican Edward Brooke was elected senator from Massachusetts in 1966, the first black since Blanche K. Bruce, 90 years earlier. Then, in 1967, Carl Stokes became mayor of Cleveland, a city with a 34 percent black population. Stokes not only had to gain the votes of a significant minority of white Democrats, he also had to convince the city's black population that he was a serious candidate who actually could win. To illustrate how unheard of it was at the time for a black person to aspire to city hall, Stokes later told a story about riding with his wife in the back of a convertible during a campaign motorcade. A young black child came right up to the car and asked if he was Carl Stokes. When he answered yes, the boy gave a leap of amazed joy and ran down the street hollering "He's colored! He's colored! He's colored!"

By 1969, African American membership in the House of Representatives stood at nine. That year, Congressman Charles Diggs, Jr., led a move to organize all nine into a group that could speak with a unified voice; they called it the Democratic Select Com-

Black vice-presidential candidate James W. Ford of the Communist party makes a radio broadcast in 1936 with his running mate, Earl Browder. Ford was drawn to the Communists because of their militant advocacy of the civil rights of blacks at a time when both major parties were blatantly racist.

Ralph Bunche, a cigarette characteristically dangling from his lips, confers with commanders of United Nations peacekeeping forces in Palestine in 1948. Bunche joined the United Nations staff in 1946 after several years in the U.S. State Department.

mittee. Two years later, that group, now grown to 13, became the Congressional Black Caucus (CBC). The CBC has since moved from strength to strength as its size and political clout have increased. It was instrumental, for example, in overcoming congressional opposition to economic sanctions against South Africa's racist regime, a vital tool in pressuring that country to reform.

At the initiative of the Democratic Select Committee, a Joint Center for Political Studies was established in 1970 to collect data on black political developments around the country. By the mid-1970s, the Joint Center was able to announce that more than 200 African Americans sat in state legislatures, and that, overall, 3,503 African Americans held office out of some half million total elected officials in the nation. Thus, for every 100,000 blacks in the country there were 16 black officeholders—still disproportionately low, but a vast improvement over what had been.

Having demonstrated their newfound political strength in local and state elections, black voters now felt ready to weigh in on the national scene. In the 1976 presidential election African Americans provided the margin of votes to propel Jimmy Carter into the White House. And Carter's subsequent distribution of appointments to blacks exceeded anything seen until then. Congressman Andrew Young, for example, became U.S. ambassador to the United Nations, Patricia Harris joined the cabinet as secretary of housing and urban development, and Eleanor Holmes Norton was appointed chair of the Equal Employment Opportunity Commission.

These high-profile appointments had little impact on the problems of the black poor, however. The nation's black youth suffered record high unemployment, urban housing was deteriorating, and in 1975 the Supreme Court ruled in the Bakke case that the plaintiff's being refused admission to the University of California at Davis was an instance of "reverse discrimination." All were sharp reminders that black political power still fell far short of bringing about major improvements in the lives of most African Americans.

Just as the political strides made by African Americans in the 1960s and 1970s seemed to yield mixed results, so too the efforts of the new nations of Africa. Although they freed themselves from European rule, the nascent countries have had to struggle against the harmful effects of Cold War politics, civil war, and, most tragically, famine caused by an enduring drought in great regions of the continent. In the Republic of South Africa, the issue was not famine but the brutal segregationist system called apartheid, which was more entrenched than ever. The struggle to end apartheid required African

Americans to demonstrate new levels of political sophistication and gain unprecedented influence in American foreign policymaking and in international affairs. A new organization, TransAfrica (*pages* 232-235), led the way, combining careful lobbying in Congress and the executive branch with astute public relations and mobilization of broad support in the black community. In the 1990s, TransAfrica's work was crowned with the official renunciation of apartheid by South Africa's white government.

After the nation experienced almost 20 years of steady, if incomplete, progress in civil rights and economic opportunity for African Americans under either a liberal Democratic White House or a liberal Democratic Congress, mainstream American political sentiment veered rightward in the late 1970s. The chief beneficiary of the shift was Republican Ronald Reagan, who swept into the Oval Office in 1981 like a man with a mission—a mission to undermine most of the civil rights gains made since the Johnson administration.

Reagan proclaimed that balancing the budget and economic austerity were his prime goals. Most black Americans understood that it would be they, as opposed to,

Shirley Chisholm of New York, elected to the U.S. House of Representatives in 1968, blazed a trail for the 12 other African American women who have sat in the House since her history-making tenure as the first black woman in Congress.

The Reverend Jesse Jackson electrifies the 1988 Democratic national convention with his rhetorical fireworks. The vote-pulling power Jackson showed in his run for the nomination that year elevated the notion of a black presidential campaign from a political stratagem to a serious proposition.

say, the Defense establishment, who would be called upon to exercise austerity. Then he added insult to injury when he came out in favor of federal tax exemptions for racially segregated private schools. But Reagan went a step too far when he tried to remove Carter appointee Mary Frances Berry from her post as head of the U.S. Civil Rights Commission in 1982. Having grown up in poverty and having dealt with racism all her life, Berry rated her firing as a minor blow. Her doctorate in history, her expertise in U.S. Constitutional history, and her law degree ensured that she could take her pick of high-paying jobs in the private sector. But she saw winning the commission job back as a matter of principle, and she fought hard. She sued the president, and won full vindication by being reinstated the following year.

By far the most prominent African American front-line campaigner for civil rights and economic justice in recent times has been the Reverend Jesse Jackson. Jackson, who had been an aide to Martin Luther King, Jr., was already a widely known figure when he addressed the 1988 Democratic convention. His rousing speech was the culmination of an equally rousing campaign for the Democratic presidential nomination, the first serious bid ever by an African American.

At a time when liberalism has given ground to conservative stirrings among mainstream white American voters, a school of conservative thought has also emerged in the black community. Conservatives such as Thomas Sowell, Anne Wortham, Shelby Steele, Alan Keyes, and, most prominently, Clarence Thomas may be few in number, but they have attracted considerable notice. Black conservatives oppose affirmative action as morally corrupting and believe that the poor and dispossessed should be responsible for changing their condition and must not be induced into passivity by government social programs.

Riding a wave of conservative sentiment was Clarence Thomas, who was nominated in 1991 by Republican president George Bush to take the Supreme Court seat vacated by retiring justice Thurgood Marshall, the first African American member of the Court. During nationally televised Senate confirmation hearings on Thomas, black Oklahoma University law professor Anita Hill, who had once worked for Thomas on the U.S. Equal Employment Opportunity Commission, charged him with sexual harrassment. The television spectacle of Thomas under public attack and his use of the phrase "high-tech lynching" to describe the proceedings may have gained him support among African Americans. Despite his conservative leanings, the majority of black people polled afterward backed Thomas's confirmation.

In the middle ground between black conservatives and liberals are the practitioners of what pundits call the new black politics—candidates whose backgrounds confound stereotypes and who have built up broad coalitions of supporters. One who fits the description is Virginia governor Douglas Wilder. The grandson of slaves, Wilder became the first black governor in U.S. history when he won election in 1989 as chief executive of the state that was once the heart of the Confederacy. If the success of politicians like Wilder portends an end to racial politics and the start of a new age when candidates are judged not by their color but on the merits of their platforms, then America will have indeed come a long way from those terrible days in colonial Virginia when access to political life slipped inexorably from the hands of blacks.

PARTICIPATING IN THEIR OWN GOVERNANCE

The years of Reconstruction in the South after the Civil War marked the first time in American history that blacks participated widely in their own governance. During the decade ending in 1877, more than 2,000 African Americans held public office in southern states, some of them elected by the newly enfranchised freedmen, others appointed by the victorious Republican party. They ranged from United States senators to county sheriffs, and in numbers from one lonely soul in Missouri to 310 officeholders in South Carolina.

They did not have an easy time. Pressure from white supremacists often was fierce. And contemporary chroniclers tended to view black officials as either accomplices or dupes of venal northern carpetbaggers and southern scalawags—ciphers, who in the words of one historian, "left no mark on the legislation of their time." That attitude took generations to change, for as W. E. B. Du Bois put it, "There was one thing that the white South feared more than Negro dishonesty, and that was Negro honesty, knowledge and efficiency."

Mifflin Gibbs (1823-1915)
The Philadelphia-born son of a Methodist minister, Gibbs earned the distinction of becoming the nation's first black municipal judge when the voters of Little Rock, Arkansas, put him in office in 1873. He served only one term, but remained a power on behalf of African Americans in city and state politics for the rest of his days.

As an ardent and adventurous teenager, Gibbs guided runaway slaves on the Underground Railroad, then followed the gold rush west to California and British Columbia. He may not have struck it exceedingly rich—except in experience. He learned press relations by founding the *Mirror of the Times*, California's first black newspaper, and he cut his political teeth in British Columbia, where he twice won election to the Victoria City Council.

That involvement led him to get a law degree from Oberlin College in 1870, and settle in Arkansas, where he perceived opportunity. A legal victory against a discriminatory saloon owner endeared him both to the black community and to the Reconstructionist Republican party.

Judge Gibbs, as he was known after his term on the bench, had a reputation for fair-mindedness as well as commitment. And though he became a chief lieutenant in Republican politics, even the opposition applauded when he was named U.S. consul to Madagascar in 1897. Wrote the Democratic *Arkansas Tribune*, "Judge Gibbs is one of the best educated colored men in the South. He commands the respect of all who know him."

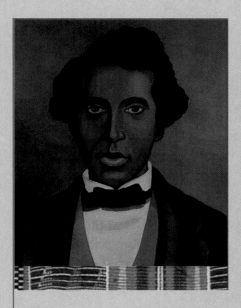

Tunis G. Campbell (1812-1891)
Everything about Tunis Campbell was sure to make white southerners see red. Born free in New Jersey and highly educated, he was astute, magnetic, ambitious, and totally focused on black interests.

Arriving in Georgia's McIntosh County in 1866, Campbell organized one of the few seats of real African American power in that bitterly unreconstructed state. A son sat with him in the legislature; an adopted son was clerk of the county superior court; he himself served as voter registrar and as justice of the peace.

Every action was designed to benefit African Americans, even if it meant skirting the law on occasion. When white Democrats regained control of Georgia in 1872, they ousted Campbell from the legislature and appointed a board of commissioners to replace the county's elected government. Four years later, Campbell himself was jailed and served 11 months on a chain gang for improper arrest of a white man. He left Georgia in 1882 and lived out his days doing church work in Boston.

Oscar Dunn (c. 1820-1871)
Had he not died mysteriously in November 1871, Oscar Dunn would almost certainly have been Louisiana's first black governor and, most probably, its first black U.S. senator.

Nothing is known of his antecedents—he might have been a slave boy who emancipated himself by running away—or of his education. Yet he was well spoken, well read, and of sufficient military skill to serve as a captain in the Union army. But it was as a politician that Dunn truly excelled.

His aim was to conciliate, not confront. As a New Orleans City Councilman in 1866, he insisted on equal public education, but did not press for the mixed schools that would inflame whites. Later, as Louisiana's lieutenant governor, he presided over the state senate with such rectitude that the New Orleans *Bee* wrote, "His character is as spotless as his face is black."

The same could not be said of the governor. Dunn justly accused his white colleague of plotting to exclude blacks from power. He fought back by winning control of the Republican state convention in 1871, and was a shoo-in for governor when he was seized by a violent illness. In 48 hours, he was dead—most likely of poison.

Abraham Galloway (1837-1870)
The son of a white planter and a slave, Galloway nonetheless was raised a slave and grew up to be one of North Carolina's radical black Reconstructionists.

At the 1868 state constitutional convention, Galloway argued hard for heavy taxes on the estates of former slave owners. "I want to see the man who owns one or two thousand acres of land, taxed a dollar on the acre," he cried. And if they could not pay, "then we negroes shall become land holders."

A year later, Senator Galloway demanded a 10-hour working day, all-black juries for blacks on trial, and suffrage for women. His every initiative was blocked. When he died of jaundice in 1870, some 6,000 grieving African Americans made his funeral the greatest in North Carolina history.

Daniel Norton (1840-1918)
Scarcely 10 years old when he ran away to freedom, Norton returned to Virginia's lower Peninsula from New York City in 1864 as a physician intending not only to treat African Americans but to uphold their rights as well. One of the first things he learned was that Civil War or no, the rules remained stacked against blacks.

The immediate issue was the Freedmen's Court, a three-man panel charged with adjudicating the many and severe disputes between the races. But when the freedmen elected Dr. Norton judge, as they were entitled to, the vote was nullified. The black advocate, they were told, would have to be white—because the other two jurists could not be expected to sit with a black man.

Daniel Norton never made it to the Freedmen's bench. Instead, he built a powerful political machine to look after African American interests in general elections. He himself served 12 years in the Virginia senate and 40 years as a York County justice of the peace.

David Augustus Straker (1842-1908)
In his native Barbados, Straker was assured of a rewarding life as a barrister under the British Crown. But he left his comfortable West Indian isle in 1868 to become a champion of black people in the United States.

Earning a law degree from Howard, Straker practiced first in South Carolina, where he was well regarded. But his great triumph came in Detroit in 1890. There, he argued *Ferguson v. Geis*, a case involving discrimination against a black physician in a restaurant. Straker invoked not only Michigan statutes but also the Thirteenth, Fourteenth, and Fifteenth Amendments. He won unanimously before the state supreme court, thereby laying the foundation for the 20th century's rejection of the "separate but equal" doctrine.

Thomas Walker (1850-1935)
Just 21 and with only the experience of servitude when he entered Alabama politics, Walker soon emerged as a tough-minded legislator and, in time, as an eminent lawyer, business-man, and philanthropist.

Not all of this happened in the heart of Dixie. As a legislator, Walker ended discrimination on Alabama railroads, but his idea of legal and educational equality roused such fury that he fled the state.

He found a natural home in Washington, D.C. Earning his law degree from Howard University, Walker had a long career as a renowned attorney and real estate investor, sources of wealth that enabled him to support generously Howard, Tuskegee Institute, and the NAACP.

Jonathan Jasper Wright (1840-1887)
"If the blacks of the South are denied the elective franchise, the war has failed to accomplish anything except a gigantic national debt, for black men to help pay." So said Wright in 1865 as a Pennsylvanian sent to help freedmen in South Carolina. Fate would see Wright himself become an example both of the strides blacks could make under Reconstruction—and of the era's political savagery.

Earning a law degree, Wright settled in South Carolina, where at age 30 he became the first African American ever to sit on a state supreme court.

He was there for seven years, earning wide esteem. His downfall came when the court had to decide a cloudy fight for governor. For reasons that are unclear, Wright sided with the white Democrats, giving them the victory. The action finished him with Republicans and he resigned into obscurity.

A HEART BEATING TO AFRICAN DRUMS

In the early 1940s, an unknowing—and obviously unthinking—White House guard managed to address the most influential black woman in America as "Auntie." Mary McLeod Bethune fixed the young man with a quizzical look, then smiled. "And which one of my brother's children are you?" she inquired, benignly.

A woman of unshakable dignity, Bethune had a way of gloving her admonitions in velvet. Yet the steel within was such that she won renown for not just one but three distinguished careers—as a dedicated educator, as the architect of a powerful African American women's movement, and as one of the foremost "black brain trusters" in the New Deal of President Franklin Delano Roosevelt. "Most people think I am a dreamer," Bethune once said. And she added, "Through dreams many things have come true."

Her parents were former slaves who gave their daughter an abiding interest in education by choosing her as the only one of their 17 children to go to school—on the understanding that she would, in turn, instruct her siblings. The girl honored that promise, and then as a young woman moved from South Carolina to Daytona, Florida, where she founded her own school for black children. She taught the children basic academics and religion along with the vocational skills that would get them work. To keep going, she drilled her youngsters in spirituals, then took them to entertain at hotels—after which she passed the hat.

Daytona's black community—along with some wealthy whites—responded so enthusiastically that by 1922, Bethune's school counted 300 pupils and a staff of 25. After World War I it expanded to include high school and eventually offered nurse's training at a small hospital. In time, it would become Bethune-Cookman College, the proud possessor of an A accreditation, and send graduates out into the world with bachelor's degrees. All this from Mary Bethune's dreams.

Meanwhile, she was pursuing a fresh vision: how to give black women a significant voice in public affairs. A brilliant, even spellbinding speaker, she had long been associated with women's groups in Florida and in 1924 stepped onto a larger stage as president of the 10,000-member National Association of Colored Women (NACW). Under her leadership, the NACW fought for fed-

Mary Bethune (*fifth from right*) presides over a National Council of Negro Women meeting in the 1940s. In World War II, the NCNW worked hard to secure black representation, including officers, in the Women's Army Corps.

eral antilynching legislation and job training for rural women; the status of black women everywhere was her urgent concern.

Yet the NACW was self-limiting as the lone black chapter among 38 in the National Council of Women—"insufficient representation," wrote Bethune, "to work out the many problems which face us as a group." Her answer was an independent National Council of Negro Women (NCNW), which she founded in 1935 and which she served as president for 14 years. By the time she resigned, the NCNW had 800,000 members in 22 affiliated women's organizations. And White House visits to discuss such matters as black female representation in social welfare agencies were an annual event. Another dream realized.

By then, Mary Bethune was no stranger to 1600 Pennsylvania Avenue. Some years before, she had met and become friends with Eleanor Roosevelt. Bethune brought a new dimension to Mrs. Roosevelt's already acute sensitivities. In 1936, the Roosevelts brought Bethune to Washington as chief of the Office of Negro Affairs of the National Youth Administration (NYA). The NYA's charter during the Great Depression was to train and find work for

millions of youths aged 16 to 24.

Mary Bethune's job made her one of the top 20 women in the New Deal, and she swiftly mastered Washington politics. "Mrs. Bethune has gathered everything and everybody under her very ample wing," wrote a newsman shortly after her arrival. Within a year, programs were up and running in 25 southern colleges; six of the schools offered aviation

courses, thus paving the way for World War II's famed Tuskegee Airmen. By 1941, almost 64,000 black students were in NYA vocational programs throughout the United States. And Mary Bethune's fervent belief in higher education had also put 4,118 students through college at NYA expense. "The drums of Africa beat in my heart," she said. "I cannot rest while there is a single Negro boy or girl lacking a chance to prove their worth."

More than that, Bethune made sure that Washington acknowledged an overall black political presence that had been unknown since the demise of Reconstruction. Early on, she herself organized 30 colleagues into FDR's "black cabinet"—brain trusters who made their united voices heard on major issues.

And on some smaller ones, too. An ugly situation developed in Detroit in 1942 when influential whites attempted to usurp a housing project that had been built with federal funds for blacks. Bethune took the matter straight to Eleanor Roosevelt—and the issue was swiftly resolved.

Bethune continued in government until the end of the war. She then retired to spend her golden years traveling, lecturing, and writing about pride and love of oneself as an African American. "Look at me," she would say. "I am black. I am beautiful."

THE BLACK KING OF CAPITOL HILL

Adam Clayton Powell, Jr., once described himself as "the first bad nigger in Congress." What the remark conveyed was his unwillingness to tolerate time-honored racist attitudes and restrictions—in the House of Representatives or anywhere else.

Powell came to politics via the pulpit. Powell senior was pastor of Harlem's Abyssinian Baptist Church, and son joined father after graduating from Colgate University in 1930.

Those were the days of the Great Depression, and African Americans were in desperate straits. Seeing the hungry faces in church, Powell understood his mission: to be champion of the underdog. He and his father organized a church relief effort that fed and clothed 1,000 people a day. He put together a bus boycott until the all-white city bus system hired 210 black drivers and mechanics. He extended the jobs campaign to white-owned businesses in Harlem, then citywide.

By then, Powell had taken over at the church, and when he decided in 1941 to become New York's first black city councilman, he was swept into office by the ready-made power base of his 14,000-member congregation. Three years later he won election to the House of Representatives.

When Powell hit Washington, with its entrenched plantation mentality, he lit it up like a sky-rocket. After racist Mississippi representative John Rankin refused to sit next to him, Powell demanded that Rankin be investi-

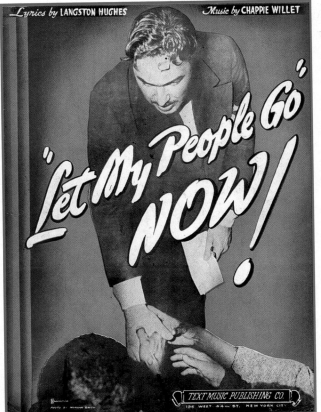

This sheet-music cover was used as a poster in Adam Clayton Powell, Jr.'s 1944 congressional campaign.

gated as a Fascist. When the Daughters of the American Revolution barred Hazel Scott, Powell's jazz pianist wife, from performing at Constitution Hall, he took the issue straight to President Harry Truman.

Powell personally integrated the congressional gymnasium and ordered his African American staff members to haunt the House cafeteria whether they were hun-

The congressman and his wife, jazz pianist Hazel Scott, hold Adam Clayton Powell III aloft—a happy image shattered by divorce in 1960, after 15 years of marriage.

gry or not. Thanks to him, black reporters were accredited to the House press gallery, black faces appeared among the midshipmen at the Naval Academy, and black officials served on the U.S. delegation to the United Nations.

Powell came out swinging in the legislative arena as well. From his seat on the House Education and Labor Committee, he sent up bills to make lynching a federal crime, ban poll taxes, and outlaw race, religion, and gender biases in job hiring.

After the Supreme Court outlawed public school segregation in 1954, Powell tried to tack antidiscrimination riders onto virtually every appropriations measure before the House. The "Powell Amendment" annoyed many House members, but his tactics were no more than other skilled parliamentarians in the House employed to get what they wanted. Millions of blacks across the country followed his career and applauded his success-

es in confounding racist and reactionary congressmen.

By 1961, Powell was chairman of his committee and pushed through legislation on minimum wages, school construction, aid to the elderly, and expanded economic opportunity. But he never swayed from his flamboyant style, which could be courtly or confrontational as needed. Along the way he made staunch friends and unforgiving enemies; the enemies waited for their day.

In an age when most congressmen were discreet about their financial and romantic peccadilloes, Powell did everything out in the open. He was not careful with money, which got him into trouble

with the Internal Revenue Service. He made junkets on public funds. Extramarital affairs added to the aura of scandal gathering around him. Colleagues criticized him for increasing absenteeism.

When Powell added support for the growing Black Power movement to his provocative relations in the House, he made himself vulnerable. He also was caught on the wrong side when young liberal congressmen wanted to break up the seniority system that had given racist southerners so much

power but had also given Powell his all-important chairmanship.

In January 1967, the House, charging him with misuse of public funds and other sins, voted to strip him of his seat and his position as committee chairman. Powell sued on the grounds that the move was unconstitutional. The case went to the Supreme Court, which not only vindicated him but found that the House action was rooted in racial prejudice.

Meanwhile, Harlem voters reelected him in a special ballot later in 1967 and again the following year. He reentered the House in January 1969, but without his seniority, which cost him his legislative clout. With voter support dwindling, he was not nominated for reelection in 1970.

Yet for most of his 25-year run, Adam Clayton Powell, Jr., made enormous contributions to the well-being of black Americans and Americans in general. By the end of that run, the House had 13 black members and, thanks to him, would never be the same.

Black solidarity is the number one issue for Congressman Powell at a 1963 Harlem rally. The united front was making itself felt, for the next year would see passage of the landmark Civil Rights Act of 1964.

A VISION OF BLACK NATIONALISM

On March 10, 1972, Richard Hatcher, the African American mayor of Gary, Indiana, rose to address the first black national political convention to be held in the United States in the 20th century. With 12,000 people packing the huge high-school gymnasium in Hatcher's city, this was one of the largest assemblages of black Americans in history.

The mayor's speech was searing. "We are through believing," Hatcher declared. "We are through hoping. We are through trusting in the two major white American political parties. Hereafter, we shall rely on the power of our own black unity."

The initiative had come from Michigan representative Charles Diggs, Jr., head of the Congressional Black Caucus. Mayor Hatcher, one of the first blacks to head a sizable American city, was a cosponsor. Famed poet and activist Imamu Amiri Baraka—formerly known as LeRoi Jones—completed the convening trio.

Their immediate target was the November presidential election. The convention was to develop a black political agenda for the country's 14.2 million African Americans of voting age. Beyond that, the convention leaders meant to establish a permanent body, the National Black Assembly, that would give voice to black Americans on a daily basis.

There was a third important goal. As in any community, African American political persuasions ranged across every shade of the spectrum. With the rise of the civil rights movement and the emergence of Black Power and Black Nationalism, it seemed vital to provide a forum to deal with the differences.

State delegations included virtually every black elected official in the country—3,009 all told. But these officials, most of them affiliated with a major party, did not dominate the proceedings. Rather, as historian Manning Marable observed: "The political tone of Black Nationalism filled the hall. . . . The collective vision of the convention represented a desire to seize electoral control of America's cities, to move the black masses from the politics of desegregation to real empowerment, ultimately to create their own black political party." Indeed, during one moment of Black Power intensity, moderates such as Jesse Jackson, Dorothy Height, and Coretta Scott King were heard to join in shouting

Mayor Richard Hatcher of Gary, Indiana, addresses the 1972 black national political convention. At his side are the Reverend Jesse Jackson (*right*) and poet-activist Imamu Amiri Baraka.

the Nationalists' slogan: "Nationtime! Nationtime! Nationtime!"

The agenda the convention adopted ran to 55 pages, with more than 70 articles. The delegates rejected federal court-ordered busing to enforce desegregation, preferring instead to focus on celebrating their blackness. They demanded congressional representation strictly in proportion to the black population. They also demanded home rule for Washington, D.C., with its heavily black neighborhoods. In addition, the convention endorsed free national health insurance and day-care centers, a guaranteed annual income, in-

creased spending to combat drugs and organized crime, and more federal grants to cities without matching requirements.

Activists made further demands: freedom for "political prisoners"; economic "reparations" in cash and real estate, the amounts to be determined by black commissions; support for Palestinian self-determination; and the formation of a black separatist Republic of New Africa to be carved out of southern states. To fund the programs on the agenda, the convention postulated a 50 percent cut in military and space spending, along with a 90 percent estate and gift tax

aimed at the country's wealthy.

Radical? Indeed. Yet to many black Americans, the agenda of Gary represented not just a high point for Black Nationalism, but also, after centuries of struggle, a great, culminating cry for liberation that all blacks could join in.

As time passed, however, many groups—among them, the Congressional Black Caucus—backed away from the passions of Gary to search for their own best solutions. The Black Nationalists themselves were riven by dispute, and by 1976, only 1,000 people turned out for a convention in Cincinnati. The vision, while not dead, had faded.

Holding their identifying placards aloft, convention delegates and other participants assemble in the gym at Gary's West Side High School. At the height of the proceedings, more than 12,000 African Americans were on hand.

COLEMAN YOUNG
Detroit, Michigan

SHARIFA WILSON
East Palo Alto, California

A DIVERSE ARRAY OF CITY LEADERS

When attorney Carl Stokes became mayor of Cleveland, Ohio, in 1967, he ushered in a quiet revolution. Aided by greater black political activism and by voting-rights legislation, African American candidates began running for mayor in a number of towns and cities—and many of them won. By the early 1990s, roughly 340 black mayors, about a fifth of them women, held office. A sampling of these diverse leaders appears here and on pages 230-231.

Coleman Young

Detroit's five-term mayor discovered his knack for politics in the 1940s as a postal-union organizer.

He rose quickly to become chairman of the National Negro Labor Council, an organization he helped to found. That position made him vulnerable to anti-Communist hysteria, however, and in 1952 Young was called before the House Un-American Activities Committee. Smeared with the "radical" label, he spent several years scraping by in odd jobs.

In 1964, he made a political comeback, winning election to the state legislature. Nine years later—just as foreign competition and an oil shortage plunged Detroit's main industry, carmaking, into a free fall—he was elected mayor. Young did what he could

to relieve the effects of the city's economic decline, working closely with major employers and helping to secure federal assistance for the Chrysler Corporation in 1979. His hiring of African American and female police officers reduced community tensions and helped cut crime. Young also pushed hard for urban renewal. In June 1993, at the age of 75, Young announced his retirement after 20 years as mayor. "I'd like to be remembered as a good mayor who gave all he had," he said.

Sharifa Wilson

A native New Yorker, Sharifa Wilson moved to California in the

DAVID DINKINS
New York, New York

CARRIE SAXON PERRY
Hartford, Connecticut

1980s—drawn there, she later said, by the "fresh air and trees." She found both in East Palo Alto, but she also discovered a lack of child services, massive unemployment, and violent crime. Seeking to change things, Wilson won a seat on the city council in 1990 and was appointed mayor by the council two years later.

Despite a limited budget to work with, Wilson fought crime by joining forces with two nearby cities to form a cooperative law-enforcement team. She raised money to rejuvenate the city's parks, and she never stopped drawing attention to her community's needs. "People will tell you, I'm very direct," she said in 1993. For example, in speaking to the leaders of more affluent cities

nearby, "I say to them, 'There's doors that I can't get in. You can, but they won't even let me inside. But once you get in there, talk about East Palo Alto.' "

Carrie Saxon Perry
New England's first black woman mayor, Carrie Saxon Perry is known for her stylish hats—she owns at least two dozen—and, more seriously, for her advocacy of Hartford's poor and unemployed. Since becoming mayor in 1987, Perry has pressed for job training, youth outreach, and remedial education. Still, she notes that progress is slow. "Accept the fact that it doesn't happen overnight," she has said, "and that you're doing it probably for another generation."

David Dinkins
When a black New York teenager died at the hands of a group of white teenagers in Brooklyn's Bensonhurst section in 1989, racial tensions in New York City reached the crisis stage. Voters turned to a mayoral candidate who promised to bring the city back together—Manhattan borough president David Dinkins.

Born in 1927 to a working-class family in Trenton, New Jersey, Dinkins had already had a long career in city politics, beginning with his election as assemblyman in 1965. He had been known for some time as an advocate for children and the homeless.

Dinkins's election did not bring about a racial utopia, but his quiet style had a generally calming

RICHARD ARRINGTON, JR.
Birmingham, Alabama

THOMAS BRADLEY
Los Angeles, California

effect. In July 1992, Dinkins put his city on display as an unabashedly positive setting for the Democratic national convention.

Richard Arrington, Jr.

For many, it was a symbol of the South's political transformation when in 1979 Councilman Richard Arrington, Jr., was elected mayor of Birmingham, Alabama. Just 16 years earlier, white police and firemen had turned fire hoses and attack dogs on civil rights demonstrators. Now a black educator with a doctorate in zoology was running City Hall.

Born in Sumter County, Alabama, in 1934, Arrington moved to Birmingham with his family as a child. During the city's civil rights struggles, he was attending graduate school in Oklahoma, but in the early 1970s he was drawn into city politics, building a solid reputation by exposing police brutality. Arrington decided to run for mayor after a white Birmingham policeman shot and killed a young black woman. Once in office, however, his biggest long-term challenge was to guide the city's economic transformation away from making steel. By the mid-1980s, with Arrington still mayor, communications companies in high-rise towers had taken the place of aging steel mills.

Thomas Bradley

Born in rural Texas in 1917, Tom Bradley went to Los Angeles on a University of California athletic scholarship. He later left UCLA to join the Los Angeles Police Department, where he served 21 years, becoming the first black police lieutenant. He was elected a city councilman in 1963 and in 1973 became mayor. "At that moment," he later said, "Los Angeles proved some people wrong: the people who said a black man couldn't go to college—couldn't rise through the ranks of the police force—couldn't attain the highest public offices."

For the next 20 years, Bradley kept Los Angeles a world-class city, with transportation projects that included expanding Los Angeles International Airport, improving the harbor, and developing a 150-mile rapid-transit system. He also won Los Angeles the right to host the 1984 Sum-

SHARON PRATT KELLY
Washington, D.C.

mer Olympics, bringing in an estimated $3.3 billion to the local
economy. But Bradley's fight
against crime and inner-city
poverty was less successful. His
final term in office was marred by
an outbreak of deadly rioting after a state trial in which a jury
found four Los Angeles police-
men not guilty of beating black
motorist Rodney King, despite a
videotape of the incident.

Sharon Pratt Kelly
The first female mayor of Washington, D.C., Sharon Pratt Kelly
came into office in 1990 on a reform platform, promising to
shrink the city bureaucracy,
streamline the delivery of services, and lower the city's soaring
crime rate. Cleaning up the city

government wouldn't require a
broom, the former electric company executive liked to say; it
needed a shovel.

As mayor, Kelly secured more
federal funding, reorganized the
city government to cut several
hundred jobs, and tried to stem
the rising tide of violence. But
making good on some of her
campaign promises proved difficult—in part, Kelly believed, because of the federal government's
unique role in making city policy.
Within three years of her election,
she was in the forefront of the
fight to "Free D.C." by making it
the nation's 51st state.

Freeman R. Bosley, Jr.
In April 1993, Freeman R. Bosley,
Jr., won a landslide victory to be-

come the first African American
mayor of St. Louis, Missouri. In a
city about half white and half
black, Bosley stressed the need
for racial harmony throughout his
campaign. "Just as it takes the
black and white keys of a piano to
play 'The Star-Spangled Banner,' "
he told his supporters on election
night, "it takes blacks and whites
and people of all races to make
this city great."

Breaking barriers was nothing
new for the 38-year-old politician:
In 1982, he won election as the
city's first black circuit clerk. Now
Bosley saw his victory as setting
"a new direction" for the city. It
also fulfilled a family dream.
Bosley's father, a St. Louis alder-
man, had run unsuccessfully for
mayor eight years earlier.

Robinson (*seated*) discusses strategy with his boss, Michigan representative Charles Diggs, Jr. As chair of the Africa subcommittee of the House Foreign Affairs Committee, Diggs called the 1976 meeting of black leaders that led to the creation of TransAfrica.

The vanguard gathers in autumn 1977 to celebrate the founding of TransAfrica. In the left foreground, NAACP executive director Benjamin Hooks chats with NAACP chair Margaret Bush Wilson. Urban League executive director Vernon Jordan is at rear right center; Richard Hatcher, mayor of Gary, Indiana, stands third from right.

Walter Fauntroy, Washington, D.C., political leader and representative to Congress, is led away by police after a sit-in at the South African embassy on November 21, 1984. Next day, Fauntroy, Randall Robinson, and others organized the Free South Africa movement, whose demonstrations led to economic sanctions against the apartheid state and to the release of political prisoner Nelson Mandela.

A BLACK FOREIGN AFFAIRS INSTITUTE

"If we love ourselves, we love Africa and the Caribbean. We are indissolubly joined." That is Randall Robinson speaking. He is founder and executive director of TransAfrica, and in the past 15 years, he has absolutely made his point. From nothing but an urgent moral conviction, TransAfrica has burgeoned into an organization of 40,000 dedicated U.S. members, with enough determination and clout to alter the course of governments.

TransAfrica's agenda is quite simple: to give African Americans a powerful voice in U.S. policy toward areas of their vital concern. It is about time.

All through the Cold War years, the State Department and other agencies focused so closely on communism that equally important issues of democracy and development, hunger and disease in Africa and the Caribbean were submerged. African Americans began to do something about it in September 1976. That month, the Congressional Black Caucus called a meeting of 130 leaders to protest the benign U.S. attitude toward minority white rule in what was then Rhodesia—and their own lack of say in the matter. The next year, TransAfrica was founded in Washington, D.C., with a few thousand dollars in the kitty, a two-room apartment for a headquarters, and a dynamic director in 36-year-old Randall Robinson.

"Polished brass," is what one magazine admiringly

233

called the Virginia-born, Harvard-educated lawyer. At law school, Robinson had been at the forefront of a massive sit-in to demand that Harvard establish a full-fledged department of Afro-American studies. He went on to become an adroit political operative as administrative assistant to Michigan congressman Charles Diggs, Jr. It took a while to get TransAfrica organized and establish credibility. But then in 1984, Robinson put together one of the most effective political protests in recent memory.

He began with a sit-in at the South African embassy in Washington, D.C., vowing not to leave until black leader Nelson Mandela was freed from prison and apartheid was ended once and for all. The cops arrested the protesters—thereby igniting a yearlong Free South Africa campaign in Washington and 26 other American cities. More than 5,000 people, including 23 U.S. congressmen, were arrested in Washington alone for demonstrating before the South African embassy.

At the conclusion, every American understood the issues, and Congress passed into law—over President Ronald Reagan's veto—a stiff set of sanctions that cost South Africa on the order of $50 billion in the next five years. By no coincidence, South Africa's white minority government decided to free Nelson Mandela in February 1990. And as Mandela commenced negotiations with white politicians, the beginning of the end for apartheid was at hand.

TransAfrica and Robinson have not eased the pressure. In October 1991, at Mandela's invitation, 33 prominent Democracy Now delegates toured South African townships to learn for themselves what apartheid had wrought on black South Africans. Famed musician Quincy Jones was on the verge of tears after visiting a squatter camp. "I've never seen anything like that," he said. "I thought slums in places like Tupelo, Mississippi, were as bad as it gets. You have to cling to your sanity."

Angola, Zaire, Liberia, Kenya, Ethiopia, and Somalia all are on TransAfrica's agenda as nations America must pay attention to. And not simply for humanitarian reasons. Robinson points out that a viable Africa with 677 million consumers would do wonders for the U.S. trade balance.

The Caribbean as well demands more consideration. "Most Americans see it as a string of beach resorts," says Robinson. "They don't really see governments and economies." Haiti, in particular, needs help. Here, the issue is a repressive regime that throttles development. Robinson applauds a U.S. decision to apply sanctions but is appalled by a parallel policy of forcibly returning Haitian refugees to certain imprisonment and likely death. Where is the justice, he asks, when no fewer than one million Asians have been admitted to the United States in the past 18 years?

TransAfrica's education and publishing arm, TransAfrica Forum, has been working hard since 1981 to elevate the nation's consciousness. Forum holds foreign policy seminars, helps blacks prepare for Foreign Service exams, evaluates the spending of U.S. aid, and publishes both a quarterly newsletter and a heavyweight journal of opinion. It also holds a stunningly successful annual fund-raising gala that gives people and corporations a chance to put their money where their hearts and minds are. The funds have been growing apace.

The first cramped rooms have given way to a $3.5 million mansion on Washington's Embassy Row. The budget has grown from zero to $800,000 annually, the early volunteers to a staff of 15 professionals, the first few reference books to a splendid 6,000-volume library dedicated to the late great tennis star and black activist Arthur R. Ashe, Jr.

TransAfrica is coming into its own as an institution, a top think tank. When he reflects on what has been achieved, Director Robinson likes to quote his friend Ashe: "Arthur said that this is the foreign policy home for African Americans. Arthur was right."

Nelson Mandela, South African patriot and chief of the African National Congress (ANC), joins wife Winnie in a victory salute after his release from prison in February 1990. A power in her own right, Winnie Mandela was instrumental in keeping the ANC going during her husband's 27-year detention.

ACKNOWLEDGMENTS

Voices of Triumph has been made possible by the generous support of Time Warner Inc.

The editors thank the following for their valuable assistance in the preparation of this volume: Lois Alexander, Harlem Fashion Institute, New York City; Don Anderson, Senior Adviser to the Chairman and CEO, Time Warner Inc., New York City; Lisa Anderson, Black Entertainment Television, Rosslyn, Virginia; Linda Bailey, Photo Curator, Cincinnati Historical Society, Cincinnati, Ohio; Alfred Baltimore, Roster Clerk, Joint Center for Political and Economic Studies, Washington, D.C.; Jeffrey Banks, Fashion Consultant, New York City; Dr. Thomas Battle, Director, Janet Sims-Wood, Joellen El Bashir, Moorland-Spingarn Research Center, Howard University, Washington, D.C.; Cyndi Bemel, Glendale, California; David Bing, Sue Ann Ray, Superb Manufacturing, Detroit, Michigan; Staff of Birmingham Civil Rights Institute, Birmingham, Alabama; Dereca Blackmon, Detroit, Michigan; Mayor Unita Blackwell, Mayersville, Mississippi; Colonel Guion Bluford, NASA, Houston, Texas; Colonel Charles Bolden, NASA, Houston, Texas; Reginald K. Brack, Jr., Chairman and CEO, Time Inc., New York City; Cheryl M. Brown, Office Analyst, North Carolina Mutual Life Insurance Company, Durham, North Carolina; Marie Brown, President, Kubari K. Jordon, Marie Brown Associates, New York City; Randall K. Burquett, Director, W. E. B. Du Bois Research Center, Harvard University, Cambridge, Massachusetts; Andre Carrington, Vice President, Maxima Corp., Landover, Maryland; Dr. George Carruthers, Department of the Navy, Washington, D.C.; Françoise Chassagnac, Paris, France; Dr. Johnnetta B. Cole, President, Spelman College, Atlanta, Georgia; Congressional Black Caucus, Washington, D.C.; Dr. Patricia Cowings, NASA, Moffett Field, California; Pat Cruz, Deputy Director, Studio Museum of Harlem, New York City; Dr. Christine Darden, NASA Langley Research Center, Hampton, Virginia; Carol Dupius, Fashion/Agent PR, Wheaton International, New York City; Toni Fay, Vice President, Community Relations, Time Warner Inc., New York City; Melia Fort, Vice President, Citizens Federal Savings Bank, Birmingham, Alabama; Sister Mary Reginald Gerdes, Baltimore, Maryland; Wilma Gibbs, Madame C. J. Walker Collection, Indiana Historical Society, Indianapolis, Indiana; Dr. Meredith Gourdine, President, Energy Innovations, Inc., Houston, Texas; Vernard Gray, Miya Gallery, The Stables Art Center, Washington, D.C.; Rev. David A. Hall, Sr., Frances K. Flagg, Temple Church of God in Christ, Memphis, Tennessee; Pamela Hamilton, Associate Executive Director, Harlem Hospital Center, New York City; John Haydel, Principal, Fremont High School, Los Angeles, California; Dr. Asa Hilliard, Callaway Chair, Department of Educational Policy Studies, Georgia State University, Atlanta, Georgia; Father Peter Hogan, Archivist, The Josephites, Baltimore, Maryland; Harry James, Historian, First African Baptist Church, Savannah, Georgia; Juanita James, Senior Vice President, Book-of-the-Month Club, New York City; Dr. Franklyn G. Jenifer, President, Howard University, Washington, D.C.; Dr. Anthony Johnson, AT&T Bell Laboratories, Holmdel, New Jersey; Katherine Johnson, Hampton, Virginia; Faustine Jones-Wilson, Silver Spring, Maryland; Barbara Lamb, Harvey Library, Peabody Collection, Hampton University, Hampton, Virginia; Dr. Raphael Lee, University of Chicago, Chicago, Illinois; Gerald Levin, Chairman and CEO, Time Warner Inc., New York City; Dolores Littles, Falls Church, Virgina; Don Logan, President and COO, Time Inc., New York City; Judy Lund, Curator, New Bedford Whaling Museum, New Bedford, Massachusetts; Fritz Malval, Archives, Hampton University, Hampton, Virginia; Dr. Caesar McDowell, Chairman of the Board, The Algebra Project, Inc., Cambridge, Massachussetts; Kevin McGruder, Archivist, Abyssinian Baptist Church, New York City; Rev. Vashti McKenzie, Payne Memorial AME Church, Baltimore, Maryland; Acel Moore, Associate Publisher, *Philadelphia Inquirer*, Philadelphia, Pennsylvania; Raoul Mowatt, Mountain View, California; Colleen Murphy, Director of Corporate Communications, Time Inc., New York City; Donna Mussenden-Van Der Zee, New York City; Mwiza Munthali, Information Specialist, TransAfrica, Washington, D.C.; National Rainbow Coalition, Inc., Washington, D.C.; Press Department, NBC Nightly News, New York City; Beverly Nelson, Special Projects Consultant, Chevy Chase, Maryland; Angela Palmer, Barden Companies, Detroit, Michigan; Dr. Anyim Palmer, Marcus Garvey School, Los Angeles, California; Dr. Henry Ponder, President, Fisk University, Nashville, Tennessee; Dr. Herman Reece, Southern Educational Foundation, Atlanta, Georgia; Pat Roberson-Saunders, Associate Professor, Howard University School of Business, Washington, D.C.; Randall Robinson, Executive Director, TransAfrica, Washington, D.C.; Dr. Griffin Rodgers, National Institutes of Health Laboratory of Chemical Biology, Bethesda, Maryland; Patrick Roger, Vasselin, Paris; Joyce Rosenblum, United Nations Photo Library, New York City; Herman J. Russell, Jackie Parker, H. J. Russell and Company, Atlanta, Georgia; Jorge Saunders, Harlem Fashion Institute, New York City; Schomburg Center for Research in Black Culture, New York City; Bill Schurk, Bowling Green State University, Bowling Green, Ohio; Hyman Schwartzberg, Curator, Richmond National Battlefield Park and Maggie Lena Walker National Historic Site, Richmond, Virginia; David Seavy, Riverside Church Archives, New York City; Dr. Abdulalim A. Shabazz, Chairman, Department of Mathematics, Clark Atlanta University, Atlanta, Georgia; Dr. Robert E. Shurney, Huntsville, Alabama; Lisa Simms, Press Secretary, National Rainbow Coalition, Inc., Washington, D.C.; Rev. J. Alfred Smith, Jr., Allen Temple Baptist Church, Oakland, California; Jon Spencer, Durham, North Carolina; Dr. Michael Spencer, Materials Science Research Center for Excellence, Washington, D.C.; Celia Suggs, Park Ranger, Maggie Lena Walker National Historic Site, Richmond, Virginia; Gladys Twyman, Coordinator, Social Science, The Atlanta Public Schools, Atlanta, Georgia; Dr. Warren Washington, Director, Climate and Global Dynamics Division, National Center for Atmospheric Research, Boulder, Colorado; Alyssa F. White, Blackberry, Alexandria, Virginia; E. Dianne White, Blackberry, Washington, D.C.; Dr. Charles Whitten, Wayne State University, School of Medicine, Detroit, Michigan; Donzella Willford, Archives, Hampton University, Hampton, Virginia; Bob Williams, NASA, Houston, Texas; O. S. Williams, Jamaica, New York; Terrie Williams, President, Jim Murray, Jae Ja Simmons, Karen Taylor, The Terrie Williams Agency, New York City; Mayor Sharifa Wilson, East Palo Alto, California; Frank Wood, The Picture Bank, Alexandria, Virginia; Denise Wright, National Urban League, Inc., New York City.

PICTURE CREDITS

The sources for the illustrations in this volume are listed below. Credits from left to right are separated by semicolons; credits from top to bottom are separated by dashes.
Kente cloth borders, courtesy the British Museum, London. **Cover, 2, 3:** Princess Asie Ocansey and Dayo B. Babalola, ABC International, New York, photo by Fil Hunter. **8, 9:** Courtesy Dr. Henry Louis Gates, Jr.; courtesy Maya Angelou; Austin Hansen, New York; courtesy Johns Hopkins Hospital, Baltimore, Md.; courtesy United Negro College Fund, New York— © Scurlock Studio, Washington, D.C.; courtesy Ruth Love Enterprises, Ltd., San Francisco, Calif.; Toni Parks; © Steve Goodman 1993. **10:** Elizabeth Hamlin— Rob Crandall. **11:** Tommy Lee—Bud Smith—Martin Simon/Saba, New York. **12, 13:** Background, artwork by Alexander Bostic. Courtesy of the Petrie Museum, University College, London. **14-23:** Artwork by Alexander Bostic. **24, 25:** Elizabeth Hamlin. **26:** Robert S. Miner, Jr., PhD. **27:** Maryland Historical Society, Baltimore, Md. **28, 29:** Moorland-Spingarn Collection, Neg. #360, Founders Library, Howard University, Washington, D.C. **30:** Moorland-Spingarn Collection, Neg. #2012, Founders Library, Howard University, Washington, D.C. **31:** From the collections of the Henry Ford Museum and Greenfield Village, Dearborn, Mich. **32:** First Church of Christ in Lynn, Mass.—U.S. Department of Commerce, Patent and Trademark Office, Washington, D.C. **33:** Louis Latimor Collection, Queens Borough Public Library, Long Island Division, New York. **34, 35:** Howard Agriesti, courtesy African American Museum, Cleveland, Ohio. **36, 37:** Bettmann Archive, New York. **38, 39:** Moorland-Spingarn Collection, Neg. #3938, Founders Library, Howard University, Washington, D.C.—courtesy New York Medical College, Valhalla, N.Y. **41:** © Scurlock Studio, Washington, D.C. **42:** Photo by Jean Libby. **43:** AT&T Archives, Murray Hill, N.J. **44:** Medical College of Pennsylvania, Philadelphia, Penna. **45:** Moorland-Spingarn Collection, Neg. #3631, Founders Library, Howard University, Washington, D.C. **46:** Archives and Special Collections on Women in Medicine, Medical College of Pennsylvania, Philadelphia, Penna., courtesy of Hampton University Archives, Hampton, Va. **47:** Black American West Museum and Heritage Center, Denver, Colo. **48-51:**

National Archive Trust, East Point, Ga. **52, 53:** *Baltimore Sun*, Baltimore, Md.; Alan Mason Chesney Medical Archives of the Johns Hopkins Medical Institutions, Baltimore, Md.; Dr. Joseph Beard and Mrs. Clara Thomas, University of Pennsylvania Press, Afro-American Newspapers, Philadelphia, Penna. **54, 55:** Background, Uniphoto, Inc., Washington, D.C. U.S. Air Force—NASA (2). **56, 57:** Background, Uniphoto, Inc., Washington, D.C. Lyndon B. Johnson Space Center, Houston, Tex. (3). **58, 59:** Background, Uniphoto, Inc., Washington, D.C. NASA, Lyndon B. Johnson Space Center, Houston, Tex.; Department of the Air Force, Brooks Air Force Base, Edward H. White II Museum, Tex.—Katherine Johnson. **60, 61:** Background, Uniphoto, Inc., Washington, D.C. NASA, Lyndon B. Johnson Space Center, Houston, Tex. (2); O. S. Williams; Naval Research Laboratory— NASA, Ames Research Center, Moffett Field, Calif. **62, 63:** Dr. Charles F. Whitten, MD (2)—Willard Volz/*Washington Times*, Washington, D.C. **64, 65:** William Branson/NIH, Bethesda, Md.—Dr. Charles F. Whitten, MD (2). **66, 67:** Background, NASA, Lyndon B. Johnson Space Center, Houston, Tex. Dr. Warren Washington; Tom Battge, and Gary Strand (3). **68, 69:** Courtesy of Johns Hopkins Children's Center, Baltimore, Md. **70:** Courtesy University of Chicago Hospitals, Chicago, Ill. **71:** NASA-Langley Research Center, Hampton, Va. (2)—Katherine Lambert. **72:** Drew Donovan Photography, Houston, Tex. **73:** Dr. Anthony Johnson. **74, 75:** Rob Crandall. **76, 77:** North Carolina Mutual Life Insurance Company, Durham, N.C. **78:** From *The Barber of Natchez* by Edwin Adam Davis and William Ransom Hogan, Louisiana State University Press, Baton Rouge, 1973. **79:** William T. Johnson and Family Memorial Papers, Louisiana and Lower Mississippi Valley Collectives, Louisiana State University Libraries, LSU, Baton Rouge, La. **80, 81:** The Walker Collection of A'Lelia Perry Bundles. **82:** Phillips Collection, Washington, D.C. **83:** Bettmann Archive, New York. **84:** Chicago Historical Society, DN-954, Chicago, Ill.—Oregon Historical Society, #ORHI 24858, Portland, Oreg. **85:** Courtesy Time Magazines Picture Collection, New York. **86, 87:** Alen MacWeeney—Larry Sherer, courtesy Moorland-Spingarn Collection, Founders Library, Howard Univer-

sity, Washington, D.C. **88, 89:** Renée Comet, courtesy Blackberry and Miya Gallery. **90, 91:** Background, The Picture Bank, Alexandria, Va. Historical Society of Pennsylvania, Philadelphia, Penna.; The Picture Bank, Alexandria, Va.; Calvert Marine Museum, Solomons, Md. **92, 93:** New Bedford Whaling Museum, New Bedford, Mass., except top left, courtesy of the Kendall Whaling Museum, Sharon, Mass., and lower right, San Francisco Maritime National Historic Park, Victoria G. Francis Collection, San Francisco, Calif. **94, 95:** Background, from the Collection of the Newport Historical Society (91.35.1), Newport, R.I. Used with permission of the Board of Trustees of the New Bedford Free Public Library, New Bedford, Mass.—New Bedford Whaling Museum, New Bedford, Mass. (2). **96, 97:** Katherine Wetzel, courtesy National Park Service, Maggie L. Walker National Historic Site, Richmond, Va. **98, 99:** Courtesy of Dr. A. G. Gaston—Sam J. Irvin, courtesy Birmingham Civil Rights Institute, Birmingham, Ala.; courtesy Dr. A. G. Gaston; photo by Jaxon/J. Cunniff & Associates—Sam J. Irvin, courtesy Birmingham Civil Rights Institute, Birmingham, Ala. **100, 101:** Gary Gershoff/Retna, New York; Karl Wellman; Frank Dandridge—from the Music Library and Sound Recording Archives, Bowling Green State University, Bowling Green, Ohio, courtesy Motown Record Company, L.P. **102, 103:** Frank Dandridge (2)— from the Music Library and Sound Recording Archives, Bowling Green State University, Bowling Green, Ohio (6), courtesy Motown Record Company, L.P.; album artwork, "TCB," used by permission of Motown Record Company, L.P. and The Supremes, Four Tops, and Temptations. **104, 105:** Pierre Bass; Chris Clark Troyman—from the Music Library and Sound Recordings Archives, Bowling Green State University, Bowling Green, Ohio (6), album artwork, *Diana Ross Presents The Jackson 5, ABC, Jackson 5, Third Album*, used by permission of Motown Record Company, L.P. and The Jackson 5. **106:** Michael Ochs Archives, Venice, Calif.— Frank Dandridge. **107:** Relay Photos Ltd., London—from the Music Library and Sound Recording Archives, Bowling Green State University, Bowling Green, Ohio (3), courtesy Motown Record Company, L.P., album artwork, *Diana Ross, Lady Sings the Blues* and *Talking Book*, Stevie

BIBLIOGRAPHY

A PROUD HERITAGE OF LEADERSHIP

BOOKS

Afre, S. A. *Ashanti Region of Ghana.* Boston: G. K. Hall, 1975.

Aldred, Cyril. *Egypt.* New York: McGraw-Hill, 1965.

Anti, A. A. *Akwamu, Denkyira, Akuapem, and Ashanti in the lives of Osei Tutu and Okomfo Anokye.* Accra: Ghana Publishing, 1971.

Asimov, Isaac. *Asimov's Biographical Encyclopedia of Science and Technology.* New York: Doubleday, 1982.

Barrows, David Prescott. *Berbers and Blacks.* New York: Century, 1927.

Bowditch, T. E. *Mission from Cape Coast Castle to Ashantee.* London: Cass, 1966 (reprint of 1819 edition).

Boxer, C. R. *Salvador de Sa and the Struggle for Brazil and Angola 1602-1686.* London: Athlone Press (University of London), 1952.

Budge, E. A. Wallis (ed.). *The Kebra Negast.* London: Oxford University Press, 1932.

Buxton, David. *The Abyssinians.* New York: Thames and Hudson, 1970.

Daaku, K. Yeboa. *Osei Tutu of Asante.* London: Heineman Educational Books, 1976.

Dubois, Felix. *Timbuctoo the Mysterious.* New York: Negro Universities Press, 1969.

Dupuis, Joseph. *Journal of a Residence in Ashantee.* London: Frank Cass, 1966.

Edwards, I. E. S. *The Pyramids of Egypt.* Middlesex, U.K.: Viking-Penguin Books, 1985.

El Mahdy, Christine (ed.). *Mummies, Myth, and Magic in Ancient Egypt.* New York: Thames and Hudson, 1989.

Ephson, Issac S. *Gallery of Gold Coast Celebrities, 1632-1958* (3 vols.). Accra, Ghana: Ilen Publications, 1969.

Fage, J. D. *A History of Africa.* New York: Alfred A. Knopf, 1978.

Flynn, J. K. *Asante and Its Neighbours 1700-1807.* Evanston, Ill.: Northwestern University Press, 1971.

Fraser, Antonia. *The Warrior Queens.* New York: Alfred A. Knopf, 1989.

Gaubert, Henri. *Solomon the Magnificent.* New York: Hastings House, 1970.

Hamlyn, Paul. *Egyptian Mythology.* London: Paul Hamlyn, 1965.

Harris, Joseph E. *Pillars in Ethiopian History* (Vol. 1). Washington, D.C.: Howard University Press, 1974.

Hart, George. *Pharaohs and Pyramids.* London: Herbert Press, 1991.

Hobson, Christine. *The World of the Pharaohs.* New York: Thames and Hudson, 1987.

Holy Bible (Revised Standard). Cleveland and New York: World, 1962.

Horizon History of Africa. New York: American Heritage Publishing, 1971.

Jackson, Guida M. *Women Who Ruled.* Santa Barbara, Calif.: ABC-CLIO, 1990.

Jackson, James Grey. *An Account of Timbuctoo and Housa.* London: Frank Cass, 1967.

Jackson, John G. *Introduction to African Civilizations.* Secaucus, N.J.: Citadel Press, 1970.

Jenkins, Nancy. *The Boat beneath the Pyramid.* New York: Holt, Rinehart and Winston, 1980.

Kaplan, Irving (ed.). *Angola.* Washington, D.C.: American University, 1979.

Kobishchanov, Yuri M., and Joseph W. Michels (eds.). *Axum.* University Park and London: Pennsylvania State University Press, n.d.

Lauer, Jean-Philippe. *Saqqara.* New York: Charles Scribner's Sons, 1976.

Lord, Edith. *Cultural Patterns of Ethiopia* (Vol. 1 of African Culture and History series). Washington, D.C.: Acropolis Books, 1970.

Miner, Horace. *The Primitive City of Timbuctoo.* Princeton, N.J.: Princeton University Press, 1953.

Rattray, R. S. *Ashanti.* Oxford: Oxford University Press, 1923.

Rogers, J. A. *World's Great Men of Color* (Vol. 1). New York: Macmillan, 1972.

Saad, Elias N. *Social History of Timbuktu.* Cambridge: Cambridge University Press, 1983.

Strouhal, Eugen. *Life of the Ancient Egyptians.* Norman: University of Oklahoma Press, 1992.

Van Sertima, Ivan (ed.). *Black Women in Antiquity.* New Brunswick and London: Transaction Books, 1990.

Ward, William Ernest. *A Short History of the Gold Coast.* London: Green Publishers, 1954.

Wright, G. Ernest (ed.). *The Bible and the Ancient Near East.* London: Routledge & Kegan Paul, 1961.

PERIODICALS

Anokye, J. K. "Nnuroso—The Unknown Shrine of Okomfo Anokye." *Ghanaian,* March 1962.

Chilton, Karen. "Makeda—The Queen of Sheba." *Class,* May 1993.

"Okomfo Anokye's Sword." *West African Review,* July 1951.

Van Sertima, Ivan. "Great Black Leaders, Ancient and Modern." *Journal of African Civilizations,* 1988.

1
FRONTIERS OF SCIENCE

BOOKS

Albers, Donald J., and G. L. Alexanderson (eds.). *Mathematical People.* Chicago: Contemporary Books, 1985.

Aptheker, Bettina. *Woman's Legacy.* Amherst: University of Massachusetts Press, 1982.

Bedini, Silvio A. *The Life of Benjamin Banneker.* New York: Charles Scribner's Sons, 1972.

Buckler, Helen. *Daniel Hale Williams.* New York: Pitman Publishers, 1989.

Carson, Ben, with Cecil Murphey. *Gifted Hands.* Grand Rapids: Zondervan, 1990.

Carwell, Hattie. *Blacks in Science.* Hicksville, N.Y.: Exposition Press, 1977.

Cassutt, Michael. *Who's Who in Space.* Boston: G. K. Hall, 1987.

Conley, Kevin. *Benjamin Banneker.* New York: Chelsea House Publishers, 1989.

Goldsmith, Donald. *The Astronomers.* New York: St. Martins Press, 1991.

Haber, Louis. *Black Pioneers of Science and Invention.* San Diego: Harcourt Brace Jovanovich, 1970.

Haskins, Jim, and Kathleen Benson. *Space Challenger.* Minneapolis: Carolrhoda Books, 1984.

Hayden, Robert C. *Eight Black American Inventors.* Reading, Mass.: Addison, Wesley, 1972.

Hine, Darlene Clark. "Co-Laborers in the Work of the Lord: Nineteenth-Century Black Women Physicians." In *Send Us a Lady Physician.* New York: W. W. Norton, 1985.

Hine, Darlene Clark (ed.). *Black Women in America: An Historical Encyclopedia* (Vol. 2). Brooklyn, N.Y.: Carlson Publishing, 1993.

James, Portia P. *The Real McCoy.* Washington, D.C.: Smithsonian Institution, 1989.

Jones, James H. *Bad Blood.* New York: Free Press, 1981.

Julian, Percy. "On Being Scientists, Humanists, and Negro." In *Many Shades of Black,* edited by Stanton L. Wormley and Lewis H. Fenderson. New York: William Morrow, 1969.

Lerner, Gerda. *Black Women in White America.* New York: Vintage Books, 1972.

Logan, Rayford W., and Michael R. Winston (eds.). *Dictionary of American Negro Biography.* New York: W. W. Norton, 1982.

Low, W. Augustus, and Virgil A. Clift (eds.). *Encyclopedia of Black America.* New York: Da Capo Press, 1981.

McMurry, Linda O. *George Washington Carver: Scientist and Symbol.* New York: Oxford University Press, 1981.

Manning, Kenneth R. *Black Apollo of Science: The Life of Ernest Everett Just.* New York: Oxford University Press, 1983.

Morais, Herbert M. *The History of the Negro in Medicine* (Vol. 10 of *International Library of Negro Life and History*). New York: Publishers Company, 1970.

Myrdal, Gunnar. *An American Dilemma: The Negro Problem and Modern Democracy.* New York: Harper & Row, 1962.

Naden, Corinne. *Ronald McNair.* New York: Chelsea House Publishers, 1991.

Pearson, Willie, and H. Kenneth

Bechtel. *Blacks, Science, and American Education.* New Brunswick, N.J.: Rutgers University Press, 1989.

Sammons, Vivian Ovelton. *Blacks in Science and Medicine.* New York: Hemisphere Publishing, 1990.

Smith, Jessie Carney (ed.). *Notable Black American Women.* Detroit: Gale Research, 1992.

Thomas, Vivien T. *Pioneering Research in Surgical Shock and Cardiovascular Surgery: Vivien Thomas and his work with Alfred Blalock.* Philadelphia: University of Pennsylvania Press, 1985.

Van Sertima, Ivan (ed.). *Blacks in Science: Ancient and Modern.* New Brunswick, N.J.: Transaction Books, 1983.

Whitten, Charles F. "Sickle Cell Anemia and African Americans." In *Health Issues in the Black Community.* San Francisco: Jossey-Bass Publishers, 1992.

Whitten, Charles F., and Eleanor N. Nishiura. "Sickle Cell Anemia." In *Issues in the Care of Children with Chronic Illness.* San Francisco: Jossey-Bass Publishers, 1985.

Williams, Jack. *USA Today: The Weather Book.* New York: Vintage Books, 1992.

Wynes, Charles E. *Charles Richard Drew.* Urbana: University of Illinois Press, 1988.

PERIODICALS

Alexander, Leslie L. "Early Medical Heroes: Susan Smith McKinney Steward, M.D., 1847-1918." *The Crisis,* January 1980.

"Black History Month Honors Prominent Black Flight Surgeon." *Discovery,* February 9, 1979.

Borman, Stu. "Black Chemist Percy Julian Commemorated on Postage Stamp." *Chemical and Engineering News,* February 1, 1993.

Brown, Sarah Winfred. "Colored Woman Physicians." *Southern Workman,* December 19, 1923.

Burns, Khephra. "Benjamin Peery, Star Doctor." *Essence,* May 1991.

Burton, William. "Shocking News." *Medicine on the Midway,* Fall 1992.

Cave, Vernal G. "Proper Uses and Abuses of the Health Care Delivery System for Minorities with Special Reference to the Tuskegee Syphilis Study." *Journal of the National Medical Association,* January 1975.

Cheers, D. Michael. "Requiem for a Hero: Touching the Face of God." *Ebony,* May 1986.

Chissell, Crystal R. "Research Profile: Gary Harris and Mike Spencer." *US Black Engineer,* 1986.

Clorens, David. "A Farewell to an Astronaut." *Ebony,* February 1968.

Cobb, W. Montague: "Charles Richard Drew, M.D., 1904-1950." *Journal of the National Medical Association,* July 1950.

"Louis Tompkins Wright, 1891-1952." *Journal of the National Medical Association,* March 1953.

"Percy Lavon Julian, Ph.D., Sc.D., LL.D., L.H.D., 1899-" *Journal of the National Medical Association,* March 1971.

Cooper, Victoria. "The Baby Doctor." *Rocky Mountain News,* February 20, 1991.

Cowan, Angela Yvonne. "Shirley Jackson Honored by Rutgers." *Bell Lab News,* March 19, 1991.

Davis, Ophelia. "Engineer's Life, Career Hitched to the Stars." *Richmond-Times Dispatch,* May 1, 1988.

DeGroot, Morris H. "A Conversation with David Blackwell." *Statistical Science,* 1986.

Douglas, John. "Breakthrough in Electrical Trauma Burn Treatment." *EPRI Journal,* September 1992.

"Drug is Promising in Sickle Cell Test." *New York Times,* April 12, 1990.

Easton, John. "When Lightning Strikes." *University of Chicago Magazine,* December 1991.

Ezzell, C. "Awakened Gene Aids Inherited Anemias." *Science News,* January 23, 1993.

Field, Alan M. "Father of Invention." *Houston Metropolitan,* February 1991.

Frank, Jon. "Woman in Vanguard of Fast-Flight Study." *Virginian-Pilot,* January 7, 1991.

Gallegos, Magdalena. "Doctor Justina Ford, A Medical Legacy Continues." *Urban Spectrum,* September 1988.

Gladwell, Malcolm. "Cancer Drug Offers Hope on Sickle Cell." *Washington Post,* April 13, 1990.

Harris, Mark. "Forty Years of Justina Ford." *Negro Digest,* March 1950.

Haynes, Karima A. "Coming In from Outer Space." *Ebony,* December 1992.

Johnson, Cage S. "Sickle Cell Anemia." *Journal of the American Medical Association,* October 11, 1985.

Kramer, Linda. "The Physician Who Healed Himself First." *People,* Fall 1991.

Leary, Warren E. "A Determined Breaker of Boundaries." *New York Times,* September 13, 1992.

McCabe, Katie. "Like Something the Lord Made." *Washingtonian*, August 1989.

McKinney, Gwen. "Reaching beyond the Outer Limits." *Black Enterprise*, August 1986.

"Making Friends in Africa." *Black Careers*, July-August 1980.

Marshall, Marilyn. "Close-Up: A New Star in the Galaxy." *Ebony*, December 1992.

Neill, Michael. "He Used to Soar with Eagles, but Now Sculptor Ed Dwight Has Landed on His Feet." *People*, May 25, 1987.

Neufeld, Matt. "Jacobi Award to Go to Dr. Scott, a Pioneer in Sickle-Cell Research." *Washington Times*, April 12, 1985.

Nowak, Rachel. "Benjamin Carson: 'I expected to be successful. But I didn't expect all of the other things.' " *Johns Hopkins Magazine*, April 1990.

"Our First Negro Astronaut." *Sepia*, September 1967.

Phillips, Christopher. "Ben Carson: Man of Miracles." *Reader's Digest* (reprinted from the April 1990 issue).

Pierce, Ponchitta. "Science Pacemaker." *Ebony*, April 1967.

Pochedly, Carl. "Dr. Roland B. Scott, Crusader for Sickle Cell Disease and Children." *American Journal of Pediatric Hematology and Oncology*, Fall 1985.

Roberts, Chris. "Mr. Washington Goes to Washington." *Daily Camera*, February 11, 1993.

Robinson, Louie. "First Negro Astronaut Candidate." *Ebony*, July 1963.

"Roland B. Scott, M.D.: A Portrait of Dedication." *Perspectives* (Howard University Medical School publication), Winter 1985-86.

Sanders, Charles L. "The Troubles of Astronaut Edward Dwight." *Ebony*, June 1965.

Saunders, Ellen. "Global Warming Expert Hopes to Encourage Others." *Oregon Stater*, December 1990.

Savitt, Todd L., and Morton F. Goldberg. "Herrick's 1910 Case Report of Sickle Cell Anemia: The Rest of the Story." *Journal of the American Medical Association*, January 13, 1989.

Scanlon, Bill. "Scientist Encourages Young Blacks." *Sunday Camera*, December 27, 1987.

Scott, Gilbert L. "Dr. Mae Carol Jemison, First Black Female Astronaut." *Class*, February 1993.

Scott, Roland B. "Advances in the Treatment of Sickle Cell Disease in Chil-

dren." *American Journal of Diseases of Children*, December 1985.

Seraile, William. "Susan McKinney Steward: New York State's First African-American Woman Physician." *Afro-Americans in New York Life and History*, July 1985.

Shari, Mayer (ed.). "Hopkins 'Headache Man' Honored." *Under the Dome*, March 1971.

"Space Doctor for the Astronauts." *Ebony*, April 1962.

"Space Trio: New Faces among Shuttle Crew." *Ebony*, March 1979.

"Superstars of Science." *Ebony*, June 1991.

"Tests Offer First Hope for Treating Sickle Cell Disease." *New York Times*, January 14, 1993.

"Waking Up Genes." *Time*, January 25, 1993.

Wall, Melissa. "Engineer Pioneer." *Daily Press*, July 22, 1977.

OTHER SOURCES

"Bone Marrow Donor Seeks Minorities." *Sickle Cell News* (published by the National Association for Sickle Cell Disease), Winter 1993.

Carruthers, George. Interview by David DeVorkin, August 18, 1992.

"Celebrating the 20th Anniversary of the Sickle Cell Detection and Information Program, Inc.: 1971-1991." Brochure published by the Sickle Cell Detection and Information Program, Detroit, 1991.

"The Deadly Deception." Transcript, NOVA television program, January 26, 1993.

"Drug Combination Appears Promising for Sickle Cell Disease." News release of the National Institute of Diabetes and Digestive and Kidney Disease, Johns Hopkins Children's Center, Baltimore, January 13, 1993.

"First Boswell Award Goes to NASCD Pioneer." *Sickle Cell News* (published by the National Association for Sickle Cell Disease), Winter 1993.

Hendry, Barbara A. "Cuyler-Brownsville: Retrospect of a Savannah Neighborhood." *Insight* (newsletter of the Coastal Heritage Society), Spring 1993.

"Industrial Chemical Can Reverse Electrical Injuries." News release of the University of Chicago Medical Center, May 14, 1992.

National Aeronautics and Space Administration: Guion Bluford, bio-

graphical data. Houston, Tex.: NASA, December 1992.

Guion Bluford, news release. Houston, Tex.: NASA, June 15, 1993.

Charles Bolden, biographical data. Houston, Tex.: NASA, January 1993.

Frederick Gregory, biographical data. Houston, Tex.: NASA, January 1993.

"Space Shuttle Mission STS-55." Press kit. Houston, Tex.: NASA, February 1993.

National Association for Sickle Cell Disease. Annual Report, 1991.

"Rebecca Lee, M.D." Article published in a Sun Petroleum Company pamphlet (from the files of the Black Women Physicians Project at the Archives and Special Collections on Women and Medicine in Philadelphia), 1980.

Taylor, Teresa. Article on Rebecca Cole (from the files of the Black Women Physicians Project at the Archives and Special Collections on Women and Medicine in Philadelphia), August 31, 1992.

"The Tuskegee Study." Report of the Alabama Committee of the U.S. Commission on Civil Rights, March 1973.

"The Tuskegee Study." Transcript, ABC News Primetime Live, February 6, 1992.

"Warren Washington Elected AMS President for 1994." *Staff Notes* (published by the National Center for Atmospheric Research, Boulder, Colorado), January 1993.

Whitten, Charles F.: Keynote address delivered at the dedication of the Marian Anderson Sickle Cell Anemia Care and Research Center at St. Christopher's Hospital for Children, Philadelphia, January 20, 1991.

"A Primer On Sickle Cell Conditions in Children for Physicians." *Pediatric Basics*, n.d.

2
THE POWER OF ENTERPRISE

BOOKS

Adams, Russell L. *Great Negroes: Past and Present*. Chicago: Afro-Am Publishing, 1969.

Anderson, Jean Bradley. *Durham County*. Durham: Duke University Press, 1990.

Anderson, Jervis. *A. Philip Randolph*. Berkeley: University of California Press, 1986.

Aptheker, Herbert (ed.): *A Documentary History of the Negro People in the United States:*
From Colonial Times through the Civil War (Vol. 1). New York: Citadel Press, 1979.
From the Reconstruction Era to 1910 (Vol. 2). New York: Citadel Press, 1951.
A Documentary History of the Negro People in the United States, 1910-1932. New York: Citadel Press, 1973.
A Documentary History of the Negro People in the United States, 1933-1945. New York: Citadel Press, 1974.

Bailey, Ronald W. (ed.). *Black Business Enterprise: Historical and Contemporary Perspectives.* New York: Basic Books, 1971.

Benjamin, Peter. *The Story of Motown.* New York: Grove Press, 1979.

Berry, Mary Frances, and John W. Blassingame. *Long Memory.* New York: Oxford University Press, 1982.

Bigelow, Barbara Carlisle (ed.). *Contemporary Black Biography* (Vol. 3). Detroit: Gale Research, 1990.

Billingsley, Andres. *Climbing Jacob's Ladder.* New York: Simon & Schuster, 1992.

Blassingame, John W. *Black New Orleans, 1860-1880.* Chicago: University of Chicago Press, 1973.

Bundles, A'Lelia Perry. *Madam C. J. Walker.* New York: Chelsea House Publishers, 1991.

Butler, John Sibley. *Entrepreneurship and Self-Help among Black Americans.* Albany: State University of New York Press, 1991.

Cohn, Michael, and Michael K. H. Platzer. *Black Men of the Sea.* New York: Dodd, Mead, 1978.

Crew, Spencer R. *Field to Factory.* Washington, D.C.: Smithsonian Institution, 1987.

Curry, Leonard P. *The Free Black in Urban America 1800-1850.* Chicago: University of Chicago Press, 1981.

Davis, Edwin Adams, and William Ranson Hogan. *The Barber of Natchez.* Baton Rouge: Louisiana State University Press, 1973.

Du Bois, W. E. B. (ed.): *The Negro in Business.* New York: AMS Press, 1971 (reprint of 1899 edition).
The Philadelphia Negro: A Social Study. Philadelphia: University of Pennsylvania, 1899.

Ebony Success Library, The (Vols. 1 and 2). Chicago: Johnson Publishing Company, 1973.

Foner, Philip Sheldon. *Organized Labor and the Black Worker, 1619-1973.* New York: Praeger Publishers, 1974.

Foner, Philip Sheldon, and Ronald L. Lewis (eds.): *The Black Worker to 1869* (Vol. 1 of *The Black Worker: A Documentary History from Colonial Times to the Present*). Philadelphia: Temple University Press, 1978.
Black Workers. Philadelphia: Temple University Press, 1989.

Franklin, John Hope, and Alfred A. Moss, Jr. *From Slavery to Freedom* (6th ed.). New York: McGraw-Hill, 1988.

Franklin, John Hope, and August Meier (eds.). *Black Leaders of the Twentieth Century.* Urbana: University of Illinois Press, 1982.

Gaston, A. G. *Green Power.* Birmingham: Southern University Press. 1986.

Green, Lorenzo Johnston. *The Negro in Colonial New England.* New York: Atheneum, 1968.

Green, Shelley, and Paul Pryde. *Black Entrepreneurship in America.* New Brunswick, N.J.: Transaction Publishers, 1990.

Harris, Abram L. *The Negro as Capitalist.* New York: Negro Universities Press, 1969.

Harris, William Hamilton. *Keeping the Faith.* Urbana: University of Illinois Press, 1977.

Hine, Darlene Clark. *Black Women in America: An Historical Encyclopedia* (Vol. 1). Brooklyn, N.Y.: Carlson Publishing, 1993.

Hogan, William Ransom, and Edwin Adams Davis (eds.). *William Johnson's Natchez: The Ante-Bellum Diary of a Free Negro* (Vols. 1 and 2). Port Washington, N.Y.: Kennikat Press, 1968.

Johnson, John H., and Lerone Bennett, Jr. *Succeeding against the Odds.* New York: Warner, 1989.

Jones, Edward H. *Blacks in Business.* New York: Grosset & Dunlap, 1971.

Kennedy, William J., Jr. *The North Carolina Mutual Story.* Durham: North Carolina Mutual Life Insurance Company, 1970.

Kinzer, Robert H., and Edward Sagarin. *The Negro in American Business.* New York: Greenberg, 1950.

Kunjufu, Jawanza. *Black Economics.* Chicago: African American Images, 1991.

Litwack, Leon F. *North of Slavery.* Chicago: University of Chicago Press, 1961.

Logan, Rayford W., and Michael R. Winston (eds.). *Dictionary of American Negro Biography.* New York: W. W. Norton, 1982.

Low, W. Augustus, and Virgil A. Clift (eds.). *Encyclopedia of Black America.* New York: Da Capo Press, 1981.

McKissack, Patricia, and Fredrick McKissack. *A Long Hard Journey.* New York: Walker, 1989.

Meier, August. *Negro Thought in America, 1880-1915.* Ann Arbor: University of Michigan Press, 1980.

Newton, James E., and Ronald L. Lewis. *The Other Slaves.* Boston: G. K. Hall, 1978.

Pierce, Joseph Alphonso. *Negro Business and Business Education.* New York: Harper & Brothers, 1947.

Ploski, Harry A., and James Williams (eds.). *The Negro Almanac* (5th ed.). Detroit: Gale Research, 1989.

Quarles, Benjamin. *The Negro in the Making of America, 1900-1986* (3d ed.). New York: Collier Books, 1987.

Rubin, Lester, William S. Swift, and Herbert R. Northrup. *Negro Employment in the Maritime Industries.* Philadelphia: Industrial Research Unit, Wharton School, University of Pennsylvania, 1974.

Schweninger, Loren. *Black Property Owners in the South, 1790-1915.* Urbana: University of Illinois Press, 1990.

Shook, Robert L., and Ramon Greenwood. *The Name of the Game Is Life.* Chicago: Contemporary Books, 1992.

Starobin, Robert S. *Industrial Slavery in the Old South.* London: Oxford University Press, 1970.

Tidwell, Billy J. *The State of Black America 1992.* New York: National Urban League, 1992.

Washington, Booker T. *The Negro in Business.* Chicago: Afro-AM Press, 1969 (reprint of 1907 edition).

Weiss, Nancy J. *The National Urban League, 1910-1940.* New York: Oxford University Press, 1974.

PERIODICALS

"... And the Migrants Kept Coming." *Fortune,* November 1941.

Bailey, David. "The Color of Money." *Business North Carolina,* December 1991.

Blount, Carolyne S. "Joshua I. Smith-Maximizing Information for Effective Decision-Making." *about ... time,* August 1990.

Bolster, W. Jeffrey. " 'To Feel like a Man': Black Seamen in the Northern

States, 1800-1860." *Journal of American History*, March 1990.

Branch, Shelly. "America's Most Powerful Black Executives." *Black Enterprise*, February 1993.

Bray, Hiawatha. "Wired for Success." *Black Enterprise*, June 1992.

Brown, Roxanne. "Blacks with Unusual Businesses." *Ebony*, December 1998.

Bundles, A'Lelia: America's First Self-Made Woman Millionaire." *Radcliffe Quarterly*, December 1987.

"Lost Women: Madam C. J. Walker-Cosmetics Tycoon." *Ms.*, July 1983.

Campbell, Bebe Moore. "Pretty Profits." *Topline*, Summer 1989.

Creque-Harris, Leah. "Bates-Rent-A-MotorHome, Inc." *Minorities and Women in Business*, March/April 1987.

Devroy, Ann, and Sharon LaFraniere. "U.S. Moves to End Hiring Preferences: Affirmative Action Policies Targeted." *Washington Post*, November 21, 1991.

Dingle, Derek T.: "B.E. Entrepreneur of the Decade: Doing Business John Johnson's Way." *Black Enterprise*, June 1987.

"Wealth-Whatever Happened to Black Capitalism?" *Black Enterprise*, August 1990.

Edmond, Alfred, Jr. "Reginal Lewis Cuts and Big Deal." *Black Enterprise*, November 1987.

"Focus-Madam C. J. Walker." *Indiana Junior Historian*, February 1992.

Henderson, Tom. "Dave Bing's Best Turnaround." *Corporate Detroit Magazine*, October 1991.

Hoffer, William. "Black Entrepreneurship in America." *Nation's Business*, June 1987.

Hymowitz, Carol. "Taking a Chance: Many Blacks Jump Off the Corporate Ladder to Be Entrepreneurs." *Wall Street Journal*, August 2, 1984.

Jackson, Harold. "True Grit." *Black Entrepreneur*, June 1992.

"Jesse Jackson's 13 New Targets." *Business Week*, October 7, 1972.

"Johnson Publishing Co. Celebrates Its Golden Anniversary: 50 Years of JPC." *Ebony*, November 1992.

Jones, Edward W. "Black Managers: The Dream Deferred." *Harvard Business Review*, May/June 1986.

Kotkin, Joel. "The Reluctant Entrepreneurs." *Inc.*, September 1986.

LaCayo, Richard. "Between Two Worlds." *Time*, March 13, 1989.

Langley, Harold D. "The Negro in the Navy and Merchant Service, 1789-1860." *Journal of Negro History*, October 1967.

Latham, Charles, Jr. "Madame C. J. Walker & Company." *Traces*, Summer 1989.

Lees, Hannah. "The Not Buying Power of Philadelphia's Negroes." *Reporter*, May 11, 1961.

Leinster, Colin. "Black Executives: How They're Doing." *Fortune*, January 18, 1988.

"Lots More Negroes Are Needed in War Plants." *Life*, June 15, 1942.

McCall, Nathan. "How Herman Russell Built His Business . . . Brick by Brick." *Black Enterprise*, June 1987.

Macnow, Glen. "Business Is the Emancipator." *Nation's Business*, September 1990.

"The Nation's Largest Black Businesses: The B.E. 100s." *Black Enterprise*, June 1993.

"The Negro's War." *Fortune*, June 1942.

O'Hare, William, and Robert Suggs. "Embattled Black Businesses." *American Demographics*, April 1, 1986.

Pomfret, John D. "Negroes Building Boycott Network." *New York Times*, November 25, 1962.

Rice, Mitchell F. "Government Set-Asides, Minority Business Enterprises, and the Supreme Court." *Public Administration Review*, March/April 1991.

"The Rise of Negroes in Industry: Problems . . . and Progress." *Newsweek*, September 12, 1955.

Scott, Matthew S., and Terry Williams. "Black Businesses Woo Hungry Investors." *Black Enterprise*, May 1992.

"Selective Patronage." *New Republic*, July 9, 1962.

Shapiro, Leonard. "Jean Fugett: From TE to CEO." *Washington Post*, June 30, 1993.

Shaw, Russell. "Herman J. Russell: Chairman, H. J. Russell & Co." *Sky*, August 1990.

Simmons, Charles Willis. "Maggie Lena Walker and the Consolidated Bank and Trust Company." *Negro History Bulletin*, February/March 1975.

Taylor, Angela. "Cosmetics for Black Women: The Timing Was Right." *New York Times*, July 8, 1978.

Telander, Rich. "Life Lesson from a Man of Steel." *Sports Illustrated*, August 19, 1991.

Thompson, Kevin D. "Special Report: Is the 8(a) Process Worth All the Trouble?" *Black Enterprise*, August 1992.

"20 Years of Black Business Leadership—Overview: A Tale of Two Decades." *Black Enterprise*, June 1992.

"The U.S. Negro, 1953." *Time*, May 11, 1953.

Waldsmith, Lynn. "The Enigma of Don Barden." *Corporate Detroit Magazine*, February 1992.

Walker, Juliet E. K. "Racism, Slavery, and Free Enterprise: Black Entrepreneurship in the United States before the Civil War." *Business History Review*, Autumn 1986.

Wilson, Clint, II. "The Heritage of America's Largest Black Business." *Sepia*, July 1983.

OTHER SOURCES

Suggs, Celia Jackson. "Maggie Lena Walker." Unpublished paper, n.d.

U.S. Department of Commerce. "1987 Economic Censuses, Survey of Minority-Owned Business Enterprises—Black." Washington, D.C.: U.S. Government Printing Office, July 1990.

3
THE BLACK CHURCH

BOOKS

Allen, Richard (Black Americans of Achievement series). New York: Chelsea House Publishers, 1991.

Anderson, Robert Mapes. *Vision of the Disinherited*. New York: Oxford University Press, 1979.

Anderson, William K. *Methodism*. Cincinnati: Methodist Publishing House, 1947.

Andrews, William L. *Sisters of the Spirit*. Bloomington: Indiana University Press, 1986.

Angell, Stephen Ward. *Bishop Henry McNeal Turner and African-American Religion in the South*. Knoxville: University of Tennessee Press, 1992.

Austin, Allan D. *African Muslims in Antebellum America: A Sourcebook*. New York: Garland Publishing, 1984.

Baer, Hans A., and Merrill Singer. *African-American Religion in the Twentieth Century: Varieties of Protest and Accommodation*. Knoxville: University of Tennessee Press, 1992.

Bailey, Kenneth K. "Protestantism and Afro-Americans in the Old South: Another Look." In *Religion and Slavery*, edited by Paul Finkelman. New York: Garland Publishing, 1989.

Bartleman, Frank. *Azusa Street*. Plain-

field, N.J.: Logos International, 1980.
Bennett, G. Willis. *Effective Urban Church Ministry.* Nashville: Broadman Press, 1983.
Blassingame, John W. *The Slave Community.* New York: Oxford University Press, 1979.
Boles, John B. (ed.). *Masters and Slaves in the House of the Lord.* Lexington: University Press of Kentucky, 1988.
Boyd, Ruby Chappelle (comp.). *On This Rock . . .* Philadelphia: Princeton Press, 1982.
Brawley, Benjamin. *Negro Builders and Heroes.* Chapel Hill: University of North Carolina Press, 1937.
Broughton, Viv. *Black Gospel.* Poole, U.K.: Blandford Press, 1985.
Burgess, Stanley M., and Gary B. McGee (eds.). *Dictionary of Pentecostal and Charismatic Movements.* n.p., n.d.
Burkett, Randall K., and Richard Newman (eds.). *Black Apostles.* Boston: G. K. Hall, 1978.
Campbell, Edward D. C., Jr., and Kym S. Rice (eds.). *Before Freedom Came.* Charlottesville and Richmond: University Press of Virginia, 1991.
Cone, James H.: *The Spirituals and the Blues.* Maryknoll, N.Y.: Orbis Books, 1972. "Black Theology and Black Power." New York: Seabury Press, 1969.
Cooley, Timothy Mather. *Sketches of the Life and Character of the Reverend Lemuel Haynes.* New York: Negro Universities Press, 1969.
Davis, Cyprian. *The History of Black Catholics in the United States.* New York: Crossroad Publishing, 1990.
Dictionary of American Biography. New York: Charles Scribner's Sons, 1936.
Dictionary of North Carolina Biography. Chapel Hill: University of North Carolina Press, 1986.
Du Bois, W. E. B. *The Souls of Black Folk.* New York: New American Library, 1982.
Ferguson, Leland. *Uncommon Ground.* Washington and London: Smithsonian Institution, 1992.
Foley, Albert S. *God's Men of Color.* New York: Arno Press and *New York Times*, 1969.
George, Carol V. R. *Segregated Sabbaths.* New York: Oxford University Press, 1973.
Harris, Michael W. *The Rise of Gospel Blues.* New York: Oxford University Press, 1992.
Hatcher, William E. *John Jasper.* New

York: Negro Universities Press, 1969.
Hill, Samuel S. (ed.). *Encyclopedia of Religion in the South.* Mercer University Press, 1984.
Johnson, James Weldon, and J. Rosamond Johnson. *The Books of American Negro Spirituals.* New York: Da Capo Press, n.d. (reprint of 1926 edition).
Kaplan, Sidney. *The Black Presence in the Era of the American Revolution, 1770-1800.* New York: New York Graphic Society, 1973.
Lincoln, C. Eric: *The Black Church since Frazier.* New York: Schocken Books, 1974. *The Black Muslims in America.* Canada: Beacon Press, 1961.
Lincoln, C. Eric (ed.). *The Black Experience in Religion.* Garden City, N.Y.: Anchor Books, 1974.
Lincoln, C. Eric, and Lawrence H. Mamiya. *The Black Church in the African American Experience.* Durham: Duke University Press, 1990.
Litwack, Leon F., and August Meier (eds.). *Black Leaders of the Nineteenth Century.* Urbana: University of Illinois Press, 1988.
Logan, Rayford W., and Michael R. Winston (eds.). *Dictionary of American Negro Biography.* New York: W. W. Norton, 1982.
Mitchell, Henry H.: *Black Belief.* New York: Harper & Row, 1975. *Black Preaching.* Nashville: Abingdon Press, 1990.
Moore, Rev. M. H. *Sketches of the Pioneers of Methodism in North Carolina and Virginia.* Nashville: Southern Methodist Publishing House, 1884.
Oates, John. *The Story of Fayetteville and the Upper Cape Fear.* Charlotte, N.C.: Dowd Press, 1950.
Ochs, Stephen J. *Desegregating the Altar.* Baton Rouge: Louisiana State University Press, 1990.
Pennington, James W. C. *The Fugitive Blacksmith.* Westport, Conn.: Negro Universities Press, 1971.
Porter, Dorothy. *Early Negro Writing 1760-1837.* Boston: Deacon Press, 1971.
Powell, A. Clayton, Sr. *Against the Tide: An Autobiography.* New York: Richard R. Smith, 1938.
Raboteau, Albert J. *Slave Religion.* Oxford: Oxford University Press, 1978.
Reagon, Bernice Johnson (ed.). *We'll Understand It Better By and By.* Washington, D.C.: Smithsonian Institution, 1992.

Schwerin, Jules. *Got to Tell It.* New York: Oxford University Press, 1992.
Sernett, Milton C. (ed.). *Afro-American Religious History.* Durham, N.C.: Duke University Press, 1985.
Sherwood, Grace H. *The Oblates' Hundred and One Years.* New York: Macmillan, 1931.
Simmons, William J. *Men of Mark.* Chicago: Johnson Publishing Company, 1970.
Smith, Edward D. *Climbing Jacob's Ladder.* Washington, D.C.: Smithsonian Institution, 1988.
Smith, Julia Floyd. *Slavery and Rich Culture in Low Country Georgia 1750-1860.* Knoxville: University of Tennessee Press, 1985.
Smith, Warren Thomas. *Harry Hosier, Circuit Rider.* Nashville: Upper Room, 1981.
Sobel, Mechal. *Trabelin' On.* Westport, Conn.: Greenwood Press, 1979.
Spencer, Jon M.: *Black Hymnody.* Knoxville: University of Tennessee Press, 1992. *Protest and Praise.* Minneapolis: Fortress Press, 1990.
Thurman, Howard. *Deep River.* New York: Harper and Brothers, 1955.
Ward, Samuel Ringgold. *Autobiography of a Fugitive Negro.* New York: Arno Press and *New York Times*, 1968.
Washington, Booker T. *The Story of the Negro.* Gloucester, Mass.: Peter Smith, 1969.
Woodson, Carter G., and Charles H. Wesley. *The Negro in Our History.* Associated Publishers, 1972.
Wright, Richard. *The Bishops of the African Methodist Episcopal Church.* Nashville: AME Sunday School Union, 1963.
Young, Henry J. *Major Black Religious Leaders: 1755-1940.* Nashville: Abingdon, 1977.

PERIODICALS
"America's First Black Catholic Archbishop." *Josephite Harvest,* Summer 1988.
"Early Advocate for Black Priests." *Josephite Harvest,* Winter 1987-1988.
"The 100th Ordination Anniversary of Father Ralph Charles Uncles." *Josephite Harvest,* Winter 1991.
"Josephite History: Origins of the American Josephites." *Josephite Harvest,* Autumn 1992.

Lee, Elliott D. "Churches Building Heaven on Earth." *Black Enterprise*, August 1981.

Lincoln, C. Eric. "Black Religion in North Carolina: From Colonial Times to 1900." Raleigh: North Carolina Museum of History, 1978.

Pace, Eric. "Thomas A. Dorsey Is Dead at 93; Known as Father of Gospel Music." *New York Times*, January 25, 1993.

Reagon, Bernice Johnson. "The Precious Legacy of Thomas Dorsey." *Washington Post*, January 31, 1993.

"St. Joseph's Seminary—100 Years." *Josephite Harvest*, Spring 1989.

OTHER SOURCES

Nelson, Douglas J. "For Such a Time as This: The Story of Bishop William J. Seymour and the Azusa Street Revival." Unpublished dissertation, 1981.

"Welcome to Allen Temple Baptist Church." Brochure from Allen Temple Baptist Church, Oakland, Calif., n.d.

4
THE EDUCATORS

BOOKS

Allen, Robert L. *Black Awakening in Capitalist America*. Trenton: Africa World Press, 1990.

Anderson, James D. *The Education of Blacks in the South, 1860-1935*. Chapel Hill: University of North Carolina Press, 1988.

Aptheker, Herbert (ed.). *The Education of Black People: Ten Critiques, 1906-1960, by W. E. B. Du Bois*. Amherst: University of Massachusetts Press, 1973.

Asante, Molefi Kete. *Afrocentricity*. Trenton: Africa World Press, 1988.

Ballard, Allen B. *The Education of Black Folk*. New York: Harper & Row, 1973.

Barksdale, Richard, and Kenneth Kinnamon. *Black Writers of America*. New York: Macmillan, 1972.

Black Resource Guide, The (10th ed.). Washington, D.C.: R. Benjamin and Jacqueline L. Johnson, n.d.

Bond, Horace Mann: *The Education of the Negro in the American Social Order*. New York: Octagon Books, 1966.

Negro Education in Alabama. Washington, D.C.: Associated Publishers, 1939.

Brelin, Christa, and William C. Matney, Jr. (eds.). *Who's Who among Black Americans*. Detroit: Gale Research, 1992.

Bullock, Henry Allen. *A History of Negro Education in the South: From 1619 to the Present*. New York: Praeger, 1970.

Butchart, Ronald E. *Northern Schools, Southern Blacks, and Reconstruction*. Westport, Conn.: Greenwood Press, 1980.

Cantor, George. *Historic Landmarks of Black America*. Detroit: Gale Research, 1991.

Collins, Marva. *Ordinary Children, Extraordinary Teachers*. Norfolk, Va.: Hampton Roads Publishing Company, 1992.

Collins, Marva, and Civia Tamarkin. *Marva Collins' Way*. New York: Jeremy P. Tarcher/Perigee Books, 1990.

Crump, William L. *The Story of Kappa Alpha Psi*. Philadelphia: Kappa Alpha Psi Fraternity, 1991.

Du Bois, W. E. B. *The Souls of Black Folk*. New York: Penguin Books, 1989.

Du Bois, W. E. B., and Booker T. Washington. *The Negro in the South*. New York: Carol Publishing Group, 1970.

Franklin, John Hope, and Alfred A. Moss, Jr. *From Slavery to Freedom* (6th ed.). New York: McGraw-Hill, 1988.

Goggin, Jacqueline. *Carter G. Woodson: A Life in Black History*. Baton Rouge: Louisiana State University Press, 1993.

Gossett, Thomas F. *Race: The History of an Idea in America*. New York: Schocken Books, 1965.

Hilliard, Asa G., III (ed.). *Testing African American Students*. Morristown, N.J.: Aaron Press, 1991.

Hilliard, Asa G., III, Lucretia Payton-Stewart, and Larry Obadele Williams (eds.). *Infusion of African and African American Content in the School Curriculum*. Morristown, N.J.: Aaron Press, 1990.

Hodge-Wright, Toni. *The Handbook of Historically Black Colleges & Universities*. Seattle: Jireh & Associates, 1992.

Irvine, Jacqueline Jordan. *Black Students and School Failure*. New York: Greenwood Press, 1990.

King, Martin Luther, Sr. *Daddy King*. New York: William Morrow, 1980.

Lanker, Brian. *I Dream A World: Portraits of Black Women Who Changed America*. New York: Stewart, Tabori & Chang, 1989.

Logan, Rayford W., and Michael R. Winston (eds.). *Dictionary of American Negro Biography*. New York: W. W. Norton, 1982.

Low, W. Augustus, and Virgil A. Clift (eds.). *Encyclopedia of Black America*. New York: Da Capo Press, 1981.

Mabee, Carleton. *Black Education in New York State: From Colonial to Modern Times*. New York: Syracuse University Press, 1979.

Mathews, Basil. *Booker T. Washington: Educator and Interracial Interpreter*. College Park, Md.: McGrath Publishing, 1969.

Mays, Benjamin E. *Born to Rebel: An Autobiography*. Athens: University of Georgia Press, 1971.

Meier, August, and Elliott M. Rudwick. *Black History and the Historical Profession, 1915-1980*. Urbana: University of Illinois, 1986.

Miers, Suzanne, and Richard Roberts (eds.). *The End of Slavery in Africa*. Madison: University of Wisconsin Press, 1988.

Moon, Henry Lee. *The Emerging Thought of W. E. B. Du Bois: Essays and Editorials from The Crisis with an Introduction, Commentaries, and a Personal Memoir*. New York: Simon & Schuster, 1972.

Moses, Wilson Jeremiah. *Alexander Crummell: A Study of Civilization and Discontent*. Oxford: Oxford University Press, 1989.

Moss, Alfred A., Jr. *The American Negro Academy: Voice of the Talented Tenth*. Baton Rouge: Louisiana State University Press, 1981.

Myrdal, Gunnar. *An American Dilemma*. New York: Harper & Row, 1962.

Nell, William C. *The Colored Patriots of the American Revolution*. New York: Arno Press and New York Times, 1968.

Peare, Catherine Owens. *Mary McLeod Bethune*. New York: Vanguard Press, 1951.

Ploski, Harry A., and James Williams (eds.). *The Negro Almanac* (5th ed.). Detroit: Gale Research, 1989.

Rigsby, Gregory U. *Alexander Crummell: Pioneer in Nineteenth-Century Pan-African Thought*. New York: Greenwood Press, 1987.

Scott, Emmett J., and Lyman Beecher Stowe. *Booker T. Washington: Builder of a Civilization*. New York: Doubleday, Page, 1916.

Smith, Jessie Carney (ed.). *Notable Black American Women*. Detroit: Gale Research, 1992.

Southern, David W. *Gunnar Myrdal and Black-White Relations: The Use and Abuse of An American Dilemma, 1944-1969*. Baton Rouge: Louisiana State University, n.d.

Sowell, Thomas. *Black Education: Myths and Tragedies*. New York: David McKay Company, 1970.

Sterling, Dorothy. *The Making of an Afro-American: Martin Robinson Delany 1812-1885.* New York: Doubleday, 1971.

Sterne, Emma Gelders. *Mary McLeod Bethune.* New York: Alfred A. Knopf, 1957.

Stevenson, Brenda (ed.). *The Journals of Charlotte Forten Grimké.* Oxford: Oxford University Press, 1988.

Summerville, James. *Educating Black Doctors: A History of Meharry Medical College.* Tuscaloosa: University of Alabama Press, n.d.

Washington, Booker T. *Up From Slavery: An Autobiography.* New York: Doubleday, 1949.

Weinberg, Meyer. *A Chance to Learn: The History of Race and Education in the United States.* London: Cambridge University Press, 1977.

White, John. *Black Leadership in America: From Booker T. Washington to Jesse Jackson.* New York: Longman, 1985.

Willie, Charles V., and Ronald R. Edmonds. *Black Colleges in America: Challenge, Development, Survival.* New York: Teachers College Press, 1978.

Wilson, Charles Reagan, and William Ferris (eds.). *Encyclopedia of Southern Culture.* Chapel Hill: University of North Carolina Press, 1989.

Woodson, Carter G.: *The Education of the Negro Prior to 1861.* Salem, N.H.: Ayer Company Publishers, 1991.
The Mis-Education of the Negro. Washington, D.C.: Associated Publishers, 1933.

PERIODICALS
"African Dreams." *Newsweek,* September 23, 1991.
"Afrocentrism and the All-Black School." *Black Bottomline,* February 1992.
"Afrocentrism in a Multicultural Democracy." *American Visions,* August 1991.
"Alpha Kappa Alpha Sorority." *Ebony,* October 1988.
"Alpha Phi Alpha Fraternity." *Ebony,* November 1989.
Buder, Leonard. "Harlem Teacher Spurs Students to Win Grants by Prep Schools." *New York Times,* May 29, 1965.
Butler, Sidney. "The Solid Foundation of Fremont High." *Herald-Dispatch,* April 22, 1993.
Carlisle, Sharon. "Seniors Say Goodbye to Mrs. Ruby." *Sun News,* June 1, 1989.
Coleman, Larry D. "Local, National Leaders Explore Alternatives to Educat-

ing Black Youth." *Kansas City Globe,* July 1983.
"Commission Honors Five District Women." *Washington Post,* March 26, 1993.
"Delta Sigma Theta." *Ebony,* February 1990.
Du Bois, David G. "Understanding the Legacy of W. E. B. Du Bois." *Emerge,* October 1993.
Dumbell, Jim. "1-Room School a Reminder of Bygone Days." *Charlotte Observer,* October 12, 1985.
"Education Is the Fundamental Ingredient in the Prescription for Saving Our Children." *Ebony,* August 1988.
Freeman, Marilyn, and Tina Witcher. "Stepping into Black Power." *Rolling Stone,* March 24, 1988.
Gaiter, Dorothy J. "Harlem Marks 20th Year of Prep-School Program." *New York Times,* July 8, 1984.
George, Lynell. "Set This Tangle Straight." *LA Weekly,* July 26-September 12, 1991.
"George McKenna Made a Bad L.A. School Good and Proud by Proving It's Not Just the Principal That Counts." *People,* June 17, 1985.
Haydel, John P. "Team Work and Dedication Are Key Ingredients for a Successful Semester." *Pathfinder,* March 1992.
Hutson, Darralyn. "Sororities and Fraternities: In Step with Giving." *Upscale,* April/May 1992.
"Kappa Alpha Psi." *Ebony,* May 1990.
Kirp, David L. "Education: The Movie." *Mother Jones,* January 1989.
"Leadership Makes the Difference." *Black Voice News,* May 14, 1992.
"Maryland: Bayton's Boys Do the Right Thing." *Life,* September 1991.
"Mrs. Ruby's One-Room School Is Still Going Strong." *Parade,* January 25, 1987.
Nelson, Jill. "Stepping Lively." *Washington Post,* May 29, 1990.
"Newsweek Hero Teaches Students in 1-Room Schoolhouse on Pawleys." *News & Courier/Evening Post* (Charleston), August 2, 1987.
"Omega Psi Phi." *Ebony,* September 1993.
"Our Brothers' Keepers." *Urban Profile,* November 1991.
"Phi Beta Sigma." *Ebony,* March 1992.
"Ponca City: A Light in Oklahoma." *Daily Oklahoman,* August 1, 1991.

"Report Card on Marva Collins." *Newsweek,* June 27, 1983.
"Sigma Gamma Rho." *Ebony,* February 1991.
"The Sixth Essence Awards." *Essence,* May 1993.
Star, Jack. "Above All, a Scholar." *Change,* February 1977.
"Tracking A Pioneer." *U.S. News & World Report,* September 17, 1990.
Watkins, James D. "Why Jonathan Can Read." *Baltimore Times,* November 25-December 1, 1991.
Wibecan, Ken. "Marcus Garvey School, Where Great Things Are Happening." *Long Beach Press Telegram,* May 5, 1986.
Williams, Edward G. "Scholarship Program Blooms in Harlem." *Christian Science Monitor,* April 12, 1972.
"Zeta Phi Beta." *Ebony,* May 1991.

OTHER SOURCES
"A Conversation between James Comer and Ronald Edmonds: Fundamentals of Effective School Improvement." National Center for Effective Schools Research and Development, 1989.
Fordyce, Hugh R., and Alan H. Kirschner. "1992 Statistical Report." New York: United Negro College Fund, 1993.

5
WINNING POLITICAL EQUALITY

BOOKS
Altman, Susan. *Extraordinary Black Americans from Colonial to Contemporary Times.* Chicago: Childrens' Press, 1989.
Aptheker, Herbert (ed.): *A Documentary History of the Negro People in the United States:*
From Colonial Times through the Civil War (Vol. 1). New York: Citadel Press, 1979.
From the Reconstruction Era to 1910 (Vol. 2). Citadel Press, 1951.
Bailey, Richard. *Neither Carpetbaggers nor Scalawags: Black Officeholders during the Reconstruction of Alabama, 1867-1878.* Montgomery: Richard Bailey Publishers, 1991.
Barker, Lucius J. *Our Time Has Come: A Delegate's Diary of Jesse Jackson's 1984 Presidential Campaign.* Urbana: University of Illinois Press, 1988.
Barker, Lucius J., and Jesse J. McCorry, Jr. *Black Americans and the Political*

System (2d ed.). Boston: Little, Brown, 1980.

Bell, Howard Holman (ed.). *Minutes of the Proceedings of the National Negro Conventions, 1830-1864.* New York: Arno Press and *New York Times,* 1969.

Berry, Mary Frances, and John W. Blassingame. *Long Memory.* New York: Oxford University Press, 1982.

Biographical Directory of the African Congress 1774-1961. Washington, D.C.: U.S. Government Printing Office, 1961.

Blair, Thomas L. *Retreat to the Ghetto: The End of a Dream?* New York: Hill and Wang, 1977.

Bowen, J. W. E. (ed.). *Addresses and Proceedings of the Congress on Africa.* Miami: Mnemosyne Publishing, 1969.

Brelin, Christa, and William C. Matney, Jr. (eds). *Who's Who among Black Americans.* Detroit: Gale Research, 1992.

Carson, Clayborne, et al. (eds.). *The Eyes on the Prize: Civil Rights Reader—Documents, Speeches, and Firsthand Accounts from the Black Freedom Struggle, 1954-1990.* New York: Penguin Books, 1991.

Chisholm, Shirley. *The Good Fight.* New York: Harper & Row, 1973.

Christopher, Maurine. *America's Black Congressmen.* New York: Thomas Y. Crowell, 1971.

Clay, William L. *Just Permanent Interests: Black Americans in Congress, 1870-1991.* New York: Amistad Press, 1992.

Clemente, Frank, and Frank Watkins (eds.). *Keep Hope Alive: Jesse Jackson's 1988 Presidential Campaign.* Boston: South End Press, 1989.

Cronon, E. David. *Black Moses: The Story of Marcus Garvey and the Universal Negro Improvement Association.* Madison: University of Wisconsin Press, 1969.

Drago, Edmund L. *Black Politicians and Reconstruction in Georgia: A Splendid Failure.* Athens: University of Georgia Press, 1992.

Duberman, Martin Bauml. *Paul Robeson.* New York: Alfred A. Knopf, 1988.

Du Bois, W. E. B. *Black Reconstruction in America.* New York: Atheneum, 1992.

Duncan, Russell. *Freedom's Shore: Tunis Campbell and the Georgia Freedmen.* Athens: University of Georgia Press, 1986.

Edmonds, Helen G. *The Negro and Fusion Politics in North Carolina, 1894-1901.* New York: Russell & Russell, 1951.

Engs, Robert Francis. *Freedom's First Generation: Black Hampton, Virginia, 1861-1890.* Philadelphia: University of Pennsylvania Press, 1979.

Evans, W. McKee. *Ballots and Fence Rails: Reconstruction on the Lower Cape Fear.* New York: W. W. Norton, 1967.

Ferris, William H. *The African Abroad, or His Evolution in Western Civilization* (Vol. 2). New Haven, Conn.: Tuttle, Morehouse & Taylor Press, 1913.

Foner, Eric. *Freedom's Lawmakers: A Directory of Black Officeholders during Reconstruction.* New York: Oxford University Press, 1993.

Foner, Philip S.: *History of Black Americans: From the Compromise of 1850 to the End of the Civil War.* Westport, Conn.: Greenwood Press, 1983.

History of Black Americans: From the Emergence of the Cotton Kingdom to the Eve of the Compromise of 1850. Westport, Conn.: Greenwood Press, 1983.

Foner, Philip S., and George E. Walker (eds.). *Proceedings of the Black State Conventions, 1840-1865* (Vol. 1). Philadelphia: Temple University Press, 1979.

Franklin, Jimmie Lewis. *Back to Birmingham: Richard Arrington, Jr., and His Times.* Tuscaloosa: University of Alabama Press, 1989.

Franklin, John Hope. *Reconstruction after the Civil War.* Chicago: University of Chicago Press, 1961.

Franklin, John Hope, and Alfred A. Moss, Jr. *From Slavery to Freedom* (6th ed.). New York: McGraw-Hill, 1988.

Franklin, John Hope, and August Meier (eds.). *Black Leaders of the Twentieth Century.* Urbana: University of Illinois Press, 1982.

Garrow, David J. *Bearing the Cross: Martin Luther King, Jr., and the Southern Christian Leadership Conference.* Brooklyn, N.Y.: Carlson Publishing, 1989.

Gatewood, Willard B. *Aristocrats of Color: The Black Elite, 1880-1920.* Bloomington: Indiana University Press, 1990.

Gibbs, Mifflin Wistar. *Shadow and Light: An Autobiography.* New York: Arno Press and *New York Times,* 1968.

Giddings, Paula. *When and Where I Enter: The Impact of Black Women on Race and Sex in America.* New York: William Morrow, 1984.

Gilliam, Reginald Earl, Jr. *Black Political Development.* Port Washington, N.Y.: Dunellen Publishing, 1975.

Gomes, Ralph C., and Linda Faye Williams (eds.). *From Exclusion to Inclusion.* New York: Greenwood Press, 1991.

Gosnell, Harold F. *Negro Politicians: The Rise of Negro Politics in Chicago.* Chicago: University of Chicago Press, 1935.

Grant, Joanne (ed.). *Black Protest: History, Documents, and Analyses—1619 to the Present.* New York: Fawcett Premier, 1968.

Graves, John William. *Town and Country: Race Relations in an Urban-Rural Context, Arkansas, 1865-1905.* Fayetteville: University of Arkansas Press, 1990.

Hampton, Henry, Steve Fayer, and Sarah Flynn. *Voices of Freedom: An Oral History of the Civil Rights Movement from the 1950s through the 1980s.* New York: Bantam Books, 1990.

Harley, Sharon, Stephen Middleton, and Charlotte M. Stokes (comps.). *African American Experience: A History.* New Jersey: Globe Book Company, 1992.

Haygood, Wil. *King of the Cats: The Life and Times of Adam Clayton Powell, Jr.* Boston: Houghton Mifflin, 1993.

Higginbotham, A. Leon, Jr. *In the Matter of Color: Race and the American Legal Process, the Colonial Period.* Oxford: Oxford University Press, 1978.

Hill, Adelaide Cromwell, and Martin Kilson (eds.). *Apropos of Africa: Afro-American Leaders and the Romance of Africa.* New York: Doubleday, 1971.

Holt, Rackham. *Mary McLeod Bethune: A Biography.* Garden City, N.Y.: Doubleday, 1964.

Hooks, Bell. *Ain't I A Woman: Black Women and Feminism.* Boston: South End Press, 1981.

Hornsby, Alton, Jr. *Milestones in 20th Century African-American History.* Detroit: Visible Ink Press, 1993.

Huggins, Nathan I., Martin Kilson, and Daniel M. Fox (eds.): *Key Issues in the Afro-American Experience* (Vol. 1: To 1877). New York: Harcourt Brace Jovanovich, 1971.

Key Issues in the Afro-American Experience (Vol. 2: Since 1865). New York: Harcourt Brace Jovanovich, 1971.

Hughes, Langston, Milton Meltzer, and C. Eric Lincoln. *A Pictorial History of Blackamericans.* New York: Crown Publishers, 1973.

Hunton, Dorothy. *The Unsung Valiant: Alphaeus Hunton.* Richmond Hill, N.Y.:

Dorothy K. Hunton, 1986.

Hutton, Frankie. *The Early Black Press in America, 1827 to 1860.* Westport, Conn.: Greenwood Press, 1993.

Jackson, Luther Porter. *Negro Office-Holders in Virginia, 1865-1895.* Norfolk, Va.: Guide Quality Press, 1946.

Jacobs, Andy. *The Powell Affair.* Indianapolis: Bobbs-Merrill, 1973.

Jordan, Winthrop D. *White over Black.* New York: W. W. Norton, 1968.

Lamson, Peggy. *The Glorious Failure.* New York: W. W. Norton, 1973.

Langston, John Mercer: *Freedom and Citizenship.* Miami: Mnemosyne Publishing, 1969 (reprint of 1883 edition).

From the Virginia Plantation to the National Capitol, or The First and Only Negro Representative in Congress from the Old Dominion. Hartford, Conn.: American Publishing Company, 1894.

Lawson, Steven F. *Running for Freedom: Civil Rights and Black Politics in America since 1941.* Philadelphia: Temple University Press, 1991.

Litwack, Leon, and August Meier (eds.). *Black Leaders of the Nineteenth Century.* Urbana: University of Illinois Press, 1988.

Logan, Rayford W. and Michael R. Winston (eds.). *Dictionary of American Negro Biography.* New York: W. W. Norton, 1982.

Love, Janice. *The U.S. Anti-Apartheid Movement: Local Activism in Global Politics.* New York: Praeger, 1985.

Low, W. Augustus, and Virgil A. Clift (eds.) *Encyclopedia of Black America.* New York: Da Capo Press, 1981.

Lowe, Richard. *Republicans and Reconstruction in Virginia, 1856-70.* Charlottesville: University Press of Virginia, 1991.

Marable, Manning. *Race, Reform, and Rebellion.* Jackson: University Press of Mississippi, n.d.

Martin, Tony. *The Pan-African Connection: From Slavery to Garvey and Beyond.* Dover, Mass.: Majority Press, 1983.

Mathurin, Owen Charles. *Henry Sylvester Williams and the Origins of the Pan-African Movement, 1869-1911.* Westport, Conn.: Greenwood Press, 1976.

Morrison, Toni (ed.). *Race-ing Justice, En-Gendering Power: Essays on Anita Hill, Clarence Thomas, and the Construction of Social Reality.* New York: Pantheon Books, 1992.

Naison, Mark. *Communists in Harlem during the Depression.* Chicago: University of Illinois Press, 1983.

Nelson, William E., Jr., and Philip J. Meranto. *Electing Black Mayors: Political Action in the Black Community.* Columbus: Ohio State University Press, 1977.

Ottley, Roi. *New World A-Coming.* New York: Arno Press and New York Times, 1968.

Parsons, Talcott, and Kenneth B. Clark (eds.). *The Negro American.* Boston: Beacon Press, 1966.

Payne, J. Gregory, and Scott C. Ratzan. *Tom Bradley: The Impossible Dream.* Santa Monica, Calif.: Roundtable Publishing, 1986.

Persons, Georgia A. (ed.). *Dilemmas of Black Politics: Issues of Leadership and Strategy.* New York: Harper Collins, 1993.

Phelps, Timothy M., and Helen Winternitz. *Capitol Games: Clarence Thomas, Anita Hill, and the Story of a Supreme Court Nomination.* New York: Hyperion, 1992.

Ploski, Harry A., and James Williams (eds.). *The Negro Almanac* (5th ed.). Detroit: Gale Research, 1989.

Powell, Adam Clayton, Jr. *Adam by Adam.* New York: Dial Press, 1971.

Preston, Michael B., Lenneal Henderson, Jr., and Paul L. Puryear (eds.). *The New Black Politics: The Search for Political Power* (2d ed.). New York: Longman, 1987.

Quarles, Benjamin. *The Negro in the Making of America* (3d ed.). New York: Collier Books, 1987.

Rabinowitz, Howard N. (ed.). *Southern Black Leaders of the Reconstruction Era.* Urbana: University of Illinois Press, 1982.

Redkey, Edwin S. *Black Exodus: Black Nationalist and Back-to-Africa Movements, 1890-1910.* New Haven, Conn.: Yale University Press, 1969.

Reynolds, Barbara A. *Jesse Jackson: The Man, the Movement, the Myth.* Chicago: Nelson-Hall, 1975.

Rich, Wilbur C. *Coleman Young and Detroit Politics: From Social Activist to Power Broker.* Detroit: Wayne State University Press, 1989.

Rigenhagen, Rhonda. *A History of East Palo Alto.* Palo Alto, Calif.: Romic Chemical Corporation, 1993.

Rivlin, Benjamin (ed.). *Ralph Bunche: The Man and His Times.* New York: Holmes & Meier, 1990.

Rogers, J. A. *World's Great Men of Color* (Vol. 2). New York: Macmillan, 1946.

Salley, Columbus. *The Black 100: A Ranking of the Most Influential African-Americans, Past and Present.* Secaucus, N.J.: Carol Publishing, 1993.

Simmons, William J. *Men of Mark: Eminent, Progressive and Rising.* New York: Arno Press and New York Times, 1887.

Sindler, Allan P. *Bakke, Defunis, and Minority Admissions: The Quest for Equal Opportunity.* New York: Longman, 1978.

Sitkoff, Harvard: *The Depression Decade.* (Vol. 1 of *A New Deal for Blacks: The Emergence of Civil Rights as a National Issue*). New York: Oxford University Press, 1978.

The Struggle for Black Equality, 1954-1980. New York: Hill and Wang, 1981.

Skinner, Elliott P. *African Americans and U.S. Policy Toward Africa 1850-1924.* Washington, D.C.: Howard University Press, 1992.

Smith, Jessie Carney (ed.). *Notable Black American Women.* Detroit: Gale Research, 1992.

Smith, Samuel Denny. *The Negro in Congress 1870-1901.* Port Washington, N.Y.: Kennikat Press, 1940.

Still, William. *The Underground Railroad.* New York: Arno Press and New York Times, 1968.

Sufferings of the Rev. Tunis G. Campbell and His Family in Georgia. Washington, D.C.: Enterprise Publishing Company, 1877.

Swain, Carol M. *Black Faces, Black Interests: The Representation of African Americans in Congress.* Cambridge, Mass.: Harvard University Press, 1993.

Tate, Katherine. *From Protest to Politics: The New Black Voters in American Elections.* Cambridge, Mass.: Harvard University Press, 1993.

Taylor, Alrutheus Ambush. *The Negro in South Carolina during the Reconstruction.* New York: AMS Press, 1971 (reprint of the 1924 edition).

Tidwell, Billy J. *The State of Black America 1992.* New York: National Urban League, 1992.

Ullman, Victor. *Martin R. Delany: The Beginnings of Black Nationalism.* Boston: Beacon Press, 1971.

Weiss, Nancy J. *Farewell to the Party of Lincoln: Black Politics in the Age of FDR.* Princeton, N.J.: Princeton University Press, 1983.

Wilkinson, J. Harvie, III. *From Brown to Bakke: The Supreme Court and School Integration: 1954-1978.* New York: Oxford University Press, 1979.

Wolseley, Roland E. *The Black Press, U.S.A.* (2d ed.). Ames: Iowa State University Press, 1990.

PERIODICALS

Barone, Michael: "Detroit's Biggest Survivor." *U.S. News & World Report*, September 25, 1989.

"The Year of Black Power?" *U.S. News & World Report*, March 29, 1993.

Bennet, James. "Bloat People." *Washington Monthly*, September 1991.

Boyarsky, Bill. "Bradley Tops Yorty by Wide Margin." *Los Angeles Times*, May 30, 1973.

Britt, Donna: "Journal of a Mission against Apartheid." *Washington Post*, August 11, 1985.

"Robinson, A Voice for Africa: The Lobbyist and His Power of Persuasion." *Washington Post*, March 13, 1990.

Cannon, Lou. "From Skyscrapers to Seaport, Bradley Brought Growth to L.A." *Washington Post*, July 1, 1993.

Clifford, Frank. "Bradley Won't Run for 6th Term." *Los Angeles Times*, September 25, 1992.

Cummins, Ken. "Prattfall." *New Republic*, February 8, 1993.

Curry, George. "N.Y. Racial Violence Shatters New Mayor's 'Gorgeous Mosaic.'" *Chicago Tribune*, May 15, 1990.

Davis, Ben, Jr. "James W. Ford: 'Frederick Douglass of 1936.'" *Daily Worker*, September 21, 1938.

"D.C. Mayor's Radical Plan Gives Needles to Drug Users, Condoms to Students and Prisoners." *Jet*, June 1, 1992.

"Detroit Mayor Calls It Quits after 20 Years." *News & Observer*, June 23, 1993.

Dickerson, A. J. "Once Industrial Mecca, Detroit Fights Back against Crime and Decay." *Los Angeles Times*, October 28, 1990.

Dinkins, David N. "Foot Soldiers on the March to Freedom." *Focus*, January 1990.

"The Dinkins Ship." *Economist*, November 2, 1991.

"Elections—1979." *Focus*, November 1979.

Getlin, Josh. "Dinkins Descending." *Los Angeles Times*, October 28, 1990.

Haynes, Karima, and Lisa C. Jones. "Black Landslide to Capitol Hill." *Ebony*, January 1993.

Henderson, Nell. "Deep Budget Cuts or No, Kelly Sure to Feel Sting." *Washington Post*, January 31, 1993.

Hinds, de Courcy Michael. "Mayor of Capitol Finds Welcome Wearing Thin." *New York Times*, April 15, 1992.

Jaffe, Harry, and Tom Sherwood. "Trust Me." *Washingtonian*, May 1991.

Kilson, Martin. "The Anatomy of Black Conservatism." *Transition* (Issue 59). New York: Oxford University Press, 1993.

"Live and Let Die." *Economist*, November 2, 1991.

McConnell, Scott. "The Making of the Mayor 1989." *Commentary*, February 1990.

McCoy, Frank. "TransAfrica Explores New Challenges." *Black Enterprise*, August 1992.

Madden, Richard L. "Hartford's New Mayor Says Her First Goal Is to Reduce Street Crime." *New York Times*, November 5, 1987.

Marshall, Marilyn. "Carrie Saxon Perry: More than a Pretty Hat." *Ebony*, April 1988.

Marshall, Steve. "St. Louis Elects 1st Black Mayor." *USA Today*, April 7, 1993.

"May the Force Be with You." *Time*, September 24, 1990.

Moss, Desda. "MacArthur Surprise." *U.S.A. Today*, June 16, 1992.

"Nation's Homicide Capitol: City of Fear, Courage, Hope." *San Jose Mercury News*, January 31, 1993.

Nelson, Jill. "Carol Moseley-Braun: Power beneath Her Wings." *Essence*, October 1992.

"New England Gets First Black Woman Mayor." *Daily Challenge*, November 5, 1987.

"New Face." *Economist*, September 15, 1990.

Pazniokas, Mark, and Bill Keveney. "Carrie Saxon Perry Sworn In as Mayor." *Hartford Courant*, December 2, 1987.

"People to Watch." *U.S. News & World Report*, December 31, 1990.

Perl, Peter. "The Mayor's Mystique." *Washington Post Magazine*, January 31, 1993.

Perry, Carrie Saxon. "Don't Penalize the Poor for Bank Failures." *New York Times*, November 30, 1991.

Purdum, Todd S. "Challenging Giuliani, Dinkins Spells Out His Politics of Race." *New York Times*, October 15, 1993.

Randolph, Laura B. "Mayor Sharon Pratt Kelly On: Her Marriage . . . Her Mission, and . . . Her Mid-Life Formation." *Ebony*, February 1992.

Raspberry, William. "TransAfrica Comes into Its Own." *Washington Post*, May 14, 1993.

Roberts, Steven V. "Victory Over Yorty Sees Further Gains." *New York Times*, May 31, 1973.

Robinson, Randall. "We Lost—And de Klerk Won." *Newsweek*, July 29, 1991.

"The Scarred Soul of the Motor City." *U.S. News & World Report*, January 8, 1990.

Shinkle, Florence. "Family and Community Molded the New Mayor." *St. Louis Post-Dispatch*, April 7, 1993.

Smothers, Ronald. "Charge against Mayor Strikes Chord in Birmingham." *New York Times*, January 20, 1992.

Specter, Michael. "Tale of Two Mayors." *Washington Post*, November 21, 1990.

Stewart, Sally Ann. "Bradley: The Olympics 'Had to Be' the Highlight." *USA Today*, July 1, 1993.

Stuart, Reginald. "The New Black Poser of Coleman Young." *New York Times Magazine*, September 6, 1979.

Terry, Gayle Pollard. "Randall Robinson: Keeping Africa on the Foreign-Policy Front Burner." *Los Angeles Times*, May 30, 1993.

Trippett, Frank. "Broken Mosaic." *Time*, May 28, 1990.

Walsh, Edward. "Detroit Mayor Bars New Race." *Washington Post*, June 23, 1993.

Washington, Patricia. "Bosley: You Got the Right One Baby!" *St. Louis American*, April 8-14, 1993.

OTHER SOURCES

"Congressional Black Caucus, 103rd Congress, 1993-1994." Washington, D.C.: Congressional Black Caucus, n.d.

"Emily's List." Washington, D.C.: A Political Network for Democratic Women, February 1993.

"The National Black Political Agenda: National Black Political Convention, Gary, Indiana, 1972." Washington, D.C.: National Black Political Convention, Inc., 1972.

"One Man, One Vote: The History of the African-American Vote in the United States." Cleveland: League of Women Voters of Cleveland Educational Fund in cooperation with Cleveland State University, n.d.

Tom Dent Oral History Collection. Interview with staff. New Orleans: Amistad Research Center, Tulane University, August 19, 1978.

INDEX

T

Take 6: **159**
Talladega College: 171
Tandy, Vertner: 81
Temple, Lewis: 92
Temple Church of God in Christ: **154, 155**
Temple University: 179
Temptations: 100, 104
Terrell, Mary Church: **169**, 209, **210**
Terrell, Tammi: **102**
Texas Tech University School of Medicine: 58
Third Baptist Church (Petersburg, Virginia): 145
Thomas, Clarence: 217
Thomas, Vivien: **52-53**
Thurman, Howard: **160, 161**, 191
Thurman, Sue Balley: **161**
Timbuktu: 20, 167
Tindley, Charles Albert: 158
TLC Beatrice International Holdings: 76, 89, 110, 111
TransAfrica: 216, 232-235
Trotter, William Monroe: 182, 211
Truman, Harry S: 85, 224
Truth, Sojourner: 128
Tubman, Harriet: 127
Turner, Henry McNeal: **150-151**, 209, 210
Turner, Henry Ossawa: 184
Turner, Nat: 138, 142
Tuskegee Airmen: 116, 223
Tuskegee Institute: 34, 46, 109, 116, 171, **173**, 178, 181, 183, 221; Agricultural Experimental Station, 35; and syphilis research, 49-51

U

Uncles, Charles Randolph: 148, **149**
Underground Railroad: 209, 218
Unions: and black workers, 78-79, 82-84, 85, 86
United Aircraft Corporation: 59
United Mine Workers of America: 82, 84
United Nations: 214
United Negro College Fund (UNCF): 178, 180
United Shoe Machinery Corporation: 33
United States Civil Rights Commission: 217
United States Colored Troops: 151
United States Government: under Carter, 215; desegregation, 85, 86; during Depression, 212-213; exclusion of blacks from civil service, 185; under Reagan, 216-217
United States Minority Business Development Agency: 88
United States Office of Minority Business Enterprise: 87, 88
United States Public Health Service (PHS): syphilis research, **40-51**
United States Small Business Association: 8(a) program, 87, 88
United States Supreme Court: affirmative action decision, 89; *Bakke* decision, 215; *Brown* decision, 89, 177, 178; school desegregation decision, 225; segregation ruling of 1896, 75; and speed of desegregation, 177; and C. Thomas, 217
Universal Negro Improvement Association (UNIA): 212
Universities and Colleges, black: 41; and science, 43
University of California at Berkeley: 41
University of California at Los Angeles (UCLA): 214
University of Chicago: 37, 86, 190; College of Dental Surgery, 62; Medical Center, 70
University of Michigan: 41; Medical School, 68
University of Mississippi: 177
Up from Slavery (Washington): 182

V

Vanderbilt University: 52, **53**, 189
Vann, Robert L.: 213
Vaughan, Herbert: 148
Vesey, Denmark: 90, 127
Virginia: early restrictions on Blacks, 204; Freedmen's Court, 220; and school desegregation, **176**, 177

Virginia State College: 71
Vonderlehr, Raymond: 50
Voting: registration, 203, 214; right removed, 204
Voting Rights Act (1965): 214

W

Wade, Benjamin: 44
Wadleigh Scholarship Program: 198
Wainer, Michael: 94
Walker, Armstead, Jr.: 96, 97
Walker, Charles Joseph: 81
Walker, Lelia (A'Lelia): 81
Walker, Maggie Lena: 80, **96-97**
Walker, Ned: 142
Walker, Sarah Breedlove McWilliams "Madame C. J.": **80-81**, 82
Walker, Thomas: **221**
Walters, Alexander: 184
Wampanoag: 94
Ward, Samuel Ringgold: **145**, 168
Waring, Mary: **210**
Washington, Booker T.: 34-35, 49, 75, **80-81, 172-173**, 174, **182**, 209, 210, 211; Atlanta Compromise speech, 210; and businesses, 80; educational philosophy, 173, 182-183; and H. Johnson, 46; and philanthropic funds, 174
Washington, Warren: **66**, 67
Washington, Willis: **163**
Washington University (St. Louis): 43
Watts Manufacturing Company: 116
Watts riot: 87, 116
Wayne State University: 65
Weathers, Othea: **162**
Weaver, Robert: 213
Wells, Ida B.: 209, 211
Wells, Mary: 106
Wesley, Charles: 187
West Virginia State College: 59, 186
Whaling: 91, **92-93**, 94
Wheaton, Mary Ann: 115
Wheaton International: 115
Whipper, William: 78, 206
White, George H.: 210-211
White, Walter: 176
White Citizens' Council: 203
Whiteside, Dolly: 128
Whitfield, James: 146

Whitfield, Princess: **198**
Whitmore, Andre: **201**
Whitten, Charles: **64**, 65
Wilberforce, William: 168
Wilberforce University: 46, **168-169**
Wilder, Douglas: 217
Williams, Daniel Hale: **28-29**, 30-31, 189
Williams, George Washington: **185**
Williams, James H.: **24-25**, 42-43
Williams, O. S. "Ozzie": **60**
Williams, Peter: 126
WilliWear: 113
Wilson-Hawkins, Corla "Mama Hawk": 196, **197**
Wilson, Jackie: 101-102
Wilson, Margaret Bush: **232-233**
Wilson, Mary: **106**
Wilson, Sharifa: **228**, 229
Winans: **159**
Wisconsin: Appleton, 26
Woman's Medical College of Pennsylvania: 45, 46, 47
Women's Wear Daily: 115
Wonder, Stevie: **101, 106**, 107
Woods, Granville T.: 32
Woods, James M., Sr.: 116, **117**
Woods Industries: 116
Woodson, Carter G.: 178, **186**, 187
World War II: and desegregation of defense industry, 85; and migration, 86
Wortham, Anne: 217
Wright, Jane: 38, **39**
Wright, Jonathan Jasper: **221**
Wright, Louis: 37-38

Y

Yale University: 68; Medical School, 38
Young, Andrew: 215
Young, Coleman: **228**
YSB: 89

Z

Zeta Phi Beta: **192**
Zion Baptist Church (Cincinnati): 135
Zion Church (New York City): 126, 127

O-7835-2255-X

T 8963